DATE DUE

AC 18 02			

DEMCO 38-296

THE LIFE AND BALLETS OF LEV IVANOV

Choreographer of *The Nutcracker* and *Swan Lake*

The Life and Ballets of
LEV IVANOV

Choreographer of
The Nutcracker and *Swan Lake*

ROLAND JOHN WILEY

CLARENDON PRESS · OXFORD

1997

at Clarendon Street, Oxford OX2 6DP

New York

Bangkok Bombay

Dar es Salaam Delhi

Istanbul Karachi
Kuala Lumpur Madras Madrid Melbourne
Mexico City Nairobi Paris Singapore
Taipei Tokyo Toronto
and associated companies in
Berlin Ibadan

Oxford is a trade mark of Oxford University Press

Published in the United States
by Oxford University Press Inc., New York

British Library Cataloguing in Publication Data
Data available

Library of Congress Cataloging in Publication Data
Wiley, Roland John.
The life and ballets of Lev Ivanov: choreographer of The
nutcracker and Swan lake / Roland John Wiley.
p.   cm.
Includes bibliographical references (p.) and index.
1. Ivanov, Lev, 1834–1901. 2. Choreographers—Russia—Biography
I. Title.
GV1875.I88W55 1997   792.8′028′092—dc20 [B] 96-24978
ISBN 0-19-816567-6

1 3 5 7 9 10 8 6 4 2

Typeset by Best-set Typesetter Ltd., Hong Kong
Printed in Great Britain
on acid-free paper by
Bookcraft Ltd
Midsomer Norton, Avon

FOR
MARY CLARKE

Preface

In life and art, Lev Ivanovich Ivanov was an enigma. No artist ever made a stronger claim to posterity's respect for creating half a masterpiece: *Swan Lake*, with Ivanov's memorable images of the swan queen Odette and her companions, stands at the centre of any canon of classical ballet. Perhaps only *The Nutcracker*, another work which Ivanov created half of, outstrips it in popularity, having become a seasonal ritual in England and America.

Yet few artists of such capacity have remained so obscure, an obscurity which deepens the enigma. No egotist, he, in contrast to the stereotype of the great choreographer. Beloved of colleagues and esteemed in balletic St Petersburg for his modesty, Ivanov was a constant and reassuring presence in the Petersburg ballet during turbulent times, without becoming a celebrity. Rarely during his lifetime did the press refer to him with more than a passing compliment. Nowhere in over 5,000 surviving letters did Tchaikovsky, his collaborator on *The Nutcracker*, mention his name. Nor did master choreographer Marius Petipa, who worked with Ivanov for more than fifty years, pay him the least heed in written accounts. Important dancers referred to him but occasionally in reminiscences, while Ivanov's own memoirs are laconic and naïve. He wrote mostly of his early years and virtually nothing of his compositions; *Swan Lake* and *The Nutcracker* are not even mentioned. As for Ivanov's choreography, which appears to have been improvised, no cache of technical documents, such as Petipa left, has been publicly identified. That one ever existed is in doubt.

Ivanov's obscurity would be difficult to illumine were modesty its only cause. He was prey to circumstance, spending most of his near-anonymous dancing career in an age of star choreographers and ballerinas. As that career waned Ivanov, long elegible for a pension, might well have dropped from view had circumstance, now defined by Petipa's illness, not charted a new course for him as 'second balletmaster', his official title. Still subordinate to ballerinas and other choreographers, Ivanov now was more a public

figure than before, and we can glimpse him through his public record. That
is what the present study seeks to do: to review his life, describe his works,
and sample their reception. I will include, fully aware of their incomplete-
ness, lists of works which Ivanov composed and performed. In sum, this is
an appreciation, a first book about Ivanov.

Politics were also a circumstance to which Ivanov was prey. In his life he
suffered for being Russian in an art dominated by foreigners. For most of
the time since his death in 1901, the documents of Ivanov's life have been
available principally to Soviet scholars. With the dissolution of the Soviet
Union, time may have rendered moot any judgements and polemics about
its scholarship, and yet some reprise of Soviet doctrine helps explain the
problems of writing about Ivanov.

That reprise must begin with the observation that imperial-period
specialists, apart from passing reference, did not write about Ivanov. Their
neglect is subject to a range of explanations, which Soviet writers reduced
to a single cause: Ivanov was a victim of rank, calculated prejudice from his
administrative seniors. The late Yury Iosifovich Slonimsky, dean of Soviet
ballet historians before his death in 1978, took this stance in his book,
Masters of the Ballet.[1] One needs read no further than the first line of his essay about Ivanov to sense the problem: 'Lev Ivanov—second balletmaster,
rehearsing old ballets with the artists, Petipa's soundless shadow . . .'.
Slonimsky's inference is that Ivanov was the Russian serf to Petipa's grasp-
ing, foreign overseer. The distortion here is passive: Slonimsky makes
nothing of Ivanov's contractual responsibility to be Petipa's deputy, which
is precisely what the Director of Imperial Theatres, Ivan Alexandrovich
Vsevolozhsky, specified in 1885 when recommending Ivanov for this lucra-
tive, career-extending job. Vsevolozhsky made his point without the least
condescension: Petipa was 67 years old, overworked, frequently ill, and
needed help. By then the elder man had forty-five ballets on the imperial
stage to his credit, including the iconic *The Pharaoh's Daughter* and *Le Roi
Candaule*, and the still-performed *La Bayadère*, whereas Ivanov, at 51, had
none. How could there not have been a difference in stature between them,
and how could we not expect their contemporaries to notice? Slonimsky's
disparaging critique of Petipa forms a dissonant counterpoint to the recollections of Ivanov's and Petipa's acquaintances.

Active distortions are no less troubling. Slonimsky's remark that 'Even a
few years ago Ivanov was not recognized as the producer of *Swan Lake*' (p.
188) is unruffled mendacity at its most transparent, refuted by abundant
documentary evidence. In fairness we must acknowledge that *Masters of the*

---

[1] Yu[rii Iosifovich] Slonimskii, 'Lev Ivanov', in *Mastera baleta* [Masters of the Ballet]
(Leningrad: 'Iskusstvo', 1937) [hereafter: *SlonMasters*], 171–99; trans. Anatole Chujoy in *Dance
Perspectives*, 2 (Spring 1959), 8–41.

Ballet was published in 1937 when a harsh political climate prevailed in the Soviet Union, and that in later essays Slonimsky revised some of his immoderate statements. All the same, his remains the only substantial study of Ivanov available before now in English.

Vera Mikhailovna Krasovskaya's account of Ivanov in *Russian Ballet Theatre of the Second Half of the Nineteenth Century* is more comprehensive than Slonimsky's,[2] but she too advances an undifferentiated stereotype of Ivanov the downtrodden. A disparity in salary between Petipa and Ivanov as teachers in the theatre school in 1858 cannot stand as evidence of discrimination at a time when Petipa's accomplishment far outweighed Ivanov's, and no account is taken of teaching effectiveness.

Ivanov's symbiotic relationship with Petipa was the central dilemma of his professional life, and for historians a source of vexation and mischief. It makes Ivanov difficult to assess outside Petipa's shadow, yet if assessed within it, his virtues are subject to challenge for their autonomy, his defects subject to dismissal on the basis of Petipa's selfish motives. The inextricability of the two men's contributions to the same ballet, given the lustre of Petipa's reputation and the obscurity of Ivanov's, deepens the enigma surrounding Ivanov still more.

Soviet historians have played upon this distinction to Petipa's disadvantage. Is it a valid approach? Ivanov was hardly petulant, nor inevitably meek. He was assertive in his correspondence with administrative superiors, never overlooking an opportunity to remind them of his worth. For reasons not altogether clear, he was in debt for long periods of time, yet his pleas for money are no less demeaning than the ones Petipa made, and the possibility is never broached that petition of this kind, in a broader perspective, was routine in an age before artists' management.

As Petipa's assistant, Ivanov did work on projects which Petipa had begun, subject to Petipa's final approval. This is comparable to Joachim Raff's drafting or orchestrating the compositions of Franz Liszt, and yet music history does not make of Raff the martyr that ballet history makes of Ivanov. The celebrated ballerina Mathilde Kshesinskaya wrote that Petipa reigned with almost limitless power from the middle of the nineteenth century onwards, and 'subordinated to himself even such a remarkable balletmaster as Lev Ivanov', reiterating a few pages later that 'the ballets of even such a remarkable balletmaster as Lev Ivanov had to receive Petipa's approval'.[3] But is this even a criticism, and if so, is it just? If Petipa invari-

[2] 'Lev Ivanov's Creative Journey', *Russkii baletnyi teatr vtoroi poloviny XIX veka* [Russian Ballet Theatre of the Second Half of the Nineteenth Century] (Moscow and Leningrad: 'Iskusstvo', 1963) [hereafter: *Krasovskaya*], 337–401.

[3] Matil'da Kshesinskaya [Mathilde Felixovna Kshesinskaya], *Vospominaniya* [Recollections] (Moscow: 'Artist, Régisseur, Theatre', 1992) [hereafter: *Kshesinskaya*], 107, 122.

ably 'corrected' Ivanov's work (Slonimsky's term), the nocturnal scenes of
Swan Lake might never have survived. Petipa acknowledged the perfection
of the first lakeside scene as it stood (implying thereby the damage which
his intervention would have caused it) when he embarked on the celebratory scenes of that ballet. We know this from an artless note he made in his
sketches: 'The second act is already composed.'

In his later years Ivanov did in fact suffer financial and personal problems. Yet no quarter is given in the literature to the theatre direction, which
by any rational standard would have been justified in questioning Ivanov's
work performance, but which rarely turned him away when he requested
money, continued to support him after it was clear that he would never repay his debts, and gave money to his family for years after his death as they
repeatedly based claims for additional remuneration on the strength of his
legacy. Such generosity is unthinkable in today's artistic world.

Seeking a well-rounded picture of Ivanov is complicated by the present
state of his official service record.[4] This fundamental source, located at the
State Central Historical Archive in St Petersburg, is now sequentially foli-
ated but curiously inconsistent in the type and amount of information it
contains. There is no indication of Ivanov's matriculation into the theatre
school, and no entry of any kind between March 1852 and February 1858,
between June 1863 and October 1864, or between November 1893 and 18
September 1895. It strains credibility to believe that a highly paperwork-
oriented bureaucracy found nothing to report about Ivanov in these
periods, in particular that his staging of the second act of *Swan Lake* in 1894
for a concert in memory of Tchaikovsky, a deed of historical importance
accomplished under trying circumstances, was too insignificant to warrant
mention. It contains nothing, moreover, about Ivanov's reputed alcohol
addiction (except by inference from doctors' reports late in his life), or
about trips away from St Petersburg which we know from other sources
that he took. Myriad routine documents—residence permits, reports of departure and return from official travel, which one would expect to clutter
such a record—are also in short supply. Is this to be explained by sloppy
administration, the legacy of a revolution and two world wars, or wilful
tampering?

From the unilateral Soviet and understated imperial approaches to
Ivanov a reasonable conclusion emerges: there were dimension and texture
in Ivanov's life. It was not marked by absolutes. A reassessment of Ivanov
is thus in order, which tempers outsized Soviet claims and supplements the
major imperial-period histories. Among other tasks, his professional ac-

---

[4] St Petersburg, Historical Archive, 497.5.2106, 'On the Service of the Chief Régisseur of the Ballet Troupe Lev *Ivanov*, 10/II/50 to 11/XII/01' [hereafter: Ivanov Service Record].

complishment must be clarified. Slonimsky's attribution of twelve productions to Ivanov in *Masters of the Ballet* is inaccurate; a tally based on
imperial-period sources increases that number to fifteen, accepting
Slonimsky's questionable attributions and not counting two extensive opera ballets, for Alexandre Borodin's *Prince Igor* and Nikolay Rimsky-
Korsakov's *Mlada*. Two of Ivanov's new ballets were produced for the
imperial summer theatre in the village of Krasnoe Selo (of which Slonimsky
says nothing), where he worked from 1885 to 1900, and where his revivals of
earlier repertoire—partial or complete stagings of Petipa, Saint-Léon, and
Perrot—defy accurate count.

Implicit in his accomplishment is a fresh view of Ivanov's relationship to
the theatre direction. Why would a 'second balletmaster', hired as an assistant, be entrusted with such responsibilities as those just described, including sole authorship of two expensive grand ballets, if the direction
considered him inferior or untrustworthy?

Ivanov the person also invites closer scrutiny. He commands interest as a
creator and a member of the community of Russian artists, though little
apart from his memoirs illuminates his personality. Should he have become
a composer, as some of his contemporaries maintained in light of his prodigious musical talent? Was the inflexible classification of students in the
theatre school responsible for misdirecting his vocation? Why did not
Ivanov press, even as a student, to become musically literate? What of his
family life, of being married to a talented artist whose star was rising faster
than his was? Reducing myth to man may demote veneration to respect,
and make us acknowledge that Ivanov, no less than his situation, was responsible for both good and bad that he encountered in professional life.

Some notes on procedure: dates are Old Style, twelve days behind the
Western calendar in the nineteenth century, thirteen in the twentieth. Frequently cited sources are identified with an abbreviation after the first
reference; these are listed at the beginning of the book. Russian names in
the text have been spelled without English counterparts of the Russian
soft sign, except where this is considered standard (i.e. Prokofiev, not
Prokof'ev). Christian names have been changed to their English or French
counterparts, whichever seemed better suited to English prose (e.g. Claudia
for Klavdia, Alexandre for Aleksandr); occasionally a Russian name has
been kept (Pyotr instead of Peter, Fyodor instead of Theodore). Forenames
not present in a quoted text have been supplied within square brackets,
when known, on first occurrence of a name, and thereafter included as
appropriate to the context.

Many individuals and institutions have contributed to the efforts of data
collection, translation, and the editing of the present volume. Research for
this book was supported in part by grants from the International Research

and Exchanges Board (IREX), with funds provided by the National Endowment for the Humanities, the United States Information Agency, and the US Department of State, which administers the Soviet and East European Training Act of 1983 (Title VIII). In the United States grateful thanks are also extended to the Library of Congress; the Harvard University Libraries, especially to the Harvard Theatre Collection and Dr Jeanne T. Newlin; and to the late George Verdak of the Indianapolis Ballet.

In Russia I am indebted in St Petersburg to Mr Igor Stupnikov and to the patient and helpful staff of the Library of the Academy of Sciences, the State Historical Archive, the St Petersburg Museum of Theatrical and Musical Art, the St Petersburg Theatrical Library, the Central Music Library, the Library of the All-Russian Theatre Society, and the Public Library named after Saltykov-Shchedrin; in Moscow to the Russian National Library and the most accommodating staff of its Newspaper Division at Khimki, to the Central State Archive of Literature and Art, and to the Library of the Bolshoy Theatre.

With special thanks I acknowledge Mrs Natalia Challis of Ann Arbor and Mr Clement Crisp of London for reading the manuscript and, as ever, making helpful suggestions, Professor William P. Malm, Mrs Elizaveta Yakovlevna Surits of Moscow for lively discussion and much archival assistance, Mr Valery Vladimirovich Gubin and Mrs Inessa Sergeyevna Preobrazhenskaya, the Director and Chief Manuscript Archivist respectively of the State Theatre Museum named after A. A. Bakhrushin in Moscow, for placing the truly extraordinary resources and thoughtful staff of that institution at my disposal, for their unfailing collegiality, and for innumerable other kindnesses.

Closer to home, I wish to thank my wife Jitka for enduring the strains and privations of bookwriting yet again.

Questions about Ivanov will doubtless remain after this essay is finished. Meanwhile, there is much to tell.

ROLAND JOHN WILEY

Ann Arbor, Michigan

Contents

List of Illustrations

I Of Lev Ivanovich Ivanov

1. Lev Ivanov in Mexican costume for Mazilier's *Jovita* (Bakhrushin State Theatre Museum, Moscow)

2. Lev Ivanov, possibly in the 1860s (private collection)

3. Maria Granken and Lev Ivanov in Russian costume, late 1860s (Bakhrushin State Theatre Museum, Moscow)

4. Lev Ivanov as Solor in Marius Petipa's *La Bayadère*, 1877 (private collection)

5. Lev Ivanov as Milon, the dancing master, in Petipa's *L'Ordre du roi*, 1886 (private collection)

6. Lev Ivanov in his later years (Bakhrushin State Theatre Museum, Moscow)

II Of Vera Lyadova (Ivanova)

7. Vera Lyadova in ballet costume, mid-1860s (Bakhrushin State Theatre Museum, Moscow)

8. Vera Lyadova as Helen in Offenbach's *La Belle Hélène*, c.1868 (private collection)

9. Vera Lyadova as Helen, and Nikolay Sazonov as Paris in Offenbach's *La Belle Hélène*, c.1868 (private collection)

III Of Russian Dancers who Performed in Ivanov's Works

10. Maria Anderson (Bakhrushin State Theatre Museum, Moscow)

11. Anna Johanson (Bakhrushin State Theatre Museum, Moscow)

12. Alexandra Vinogradova [Petrova] (private collection)

IV Of Lev Ivanov's Works

Abbreviations

Borisoglebsky	M. Borisoglebskii, *Proshloe baletnogo otdeleniya Peterburgskogo teatral'nogo uchilishcha, nyne Leningradskogo Gosudarstvennogo Khoregrafisheskogo uchilishcha. Materialy po istorii russkogo baleta* [The Past of the Ballet Division of the Petersburg Theatre, now the Leningrad State Choreographic School. Materials Relating to the History of Russian Ballet], 2 vols. (Leningrad: Leningrad State Choreographic School, 1938–9).
Demidov	A[leksandr Pavlovich] Demidov, *Lebedinoe ozero* [Swan Lake]. Masterpieces of the Ballet (Moscow: 'Iskusstvo', 1985).
Fille	*La Fille mal gardée*, Famous Ballets, no. 1, ed. Ivor Guest (London: The Dancing Times, 1960).
Gaevsky	Vadim Moiseevich Gaevskii, *Divertisment* [Divertissement] (Moscow: 'Iskusstvo', 1981).
Ivanov Service Record	St Petersburg, Historical Archive, 497.5.2106, 'On the Service of the Chief Régisseur of the Ballet Troupe Lev *Ivanov*, 10/II/50 to 11/XII/01'.
Khudekov	S[ergei] N[ikolaevich] Khudekov, *Istoriya tantsev* [The History of Dances], vol. iv (Petrograd, 1918).
Krasovskaya	Vera Mikhailovna Krasovskaya, *Russkii baletnyi teatr vtoroi poloviny XIX veka* [Russian Ballet Theatre of the Second Half of the XIX Century] (Moscow and Leningrad: 'Iskusstvo', 1963).
Kshesinskaya	Matil'da [Feliksovna] Kshesinskaya, *Vospominaniya* [Recollections] (Moscow: 'Artist, Régisseur, Theatre', 1992).
Kshesinsky	Ios[if] Fel[iksovich] Kshesinskii, 'Several Extracts from my Memoirs Touching on Reminiscences of Marius Iv[anovich] Petipa', 2 vols., Moscow, Theatre Museum named after A. A. Bakhrushin, *fond* 134, no. 2.

MarPet	*Marius Petipa. Materialy, vospominaniya, stat'i* [Marius Petipa: Materials, Recollections, Articles], ed. Yu[rii Iosifovich] Slonimskii *et al.* (Leningrad: 'Iskusstvo', 1971).
Pleshcheyev	Aleksandr [Alekseevich] Pleshcheev, *Nash balet* [Our Ballet], 2nd, supplemented edn. with foreword by K. A. Skal'kovskii (St Petersburg: Th. A. Pereyaslavtsev and A. A. Pleshcheyev, 1899).
Shiryaev	A[leksandr] V[iktorovich] Shiryaev, *Peterburgskii Balet. Iz vospominanii artista Mariinskogo teatra* [The Petersburg Ballet: From the Recollections of an Artist of the Maryinsky Theatre], ed. Yu. O. Slonimskii (Leningrad: All-Russian Theatre Society, 1941). NB: this volume was typeset, but the only surviving copy in this form seems to be a photocopy preserved in the St Petersburg Public Library Is70 G-3/21.
Skalkovsky	K[onstantin] A[pollonovich] Skal'kovskii, *V teatral'nom mire; nablyudeniya, vospominaniya i rassuzhdeniya* [In the Theatre World: Observations, Recollections, Discourses] (St Petersburg: A. S. Suvorin, 1899).
SlonChai	Yu[rii Iosifovich] Slonimskii, *P. I. Chaikovskii i baletnyi teatr ego vremeni* [P. I. Tchaikovsky and the Ballet Theatre of his Time] (Moscow: State Music Publishers, 1956).
SlonMasters	Yu[rii Iosifovich] Slonimskii, *Mastera baleta* [Masters of the Ballet] (Leningrad: 'Iskusstvo', 1937).
Solyannikov	N[ikolai] A[leksandrovich] Solyannikov, 'Recollections', ed. N. A. Shuvalov; literary working-out by Nonna Solyannikova (typescript). St Petersburg, Library of the St Petersburg Branch of the All-Russian Theatrical Society, Inv. no. 35-R2.
Tchaikovsky–Jurgenson	[Petr Il'ich Chaikovskii and Petr Ivanovich Yurgenson], *P. I. Chaikovskii. Perepiska s P. I. Yurgensonom* [P. I. Tchaikovsky: Correspondence with P. I. Jurgenson], 2 vols. (Moscow and Leningrad: State Music Publishers, 1938, 1951).
Tchaikovsky's Ballets	Roland John Wiley, *Tchaikovsky's Ballets* (Oxford: Clarendon Press, 1985).
TMB 205	Moscow, Theatre Museum named after A. A. Bakhrushin, *fond* 205, archive of documents pertaining to the work of Marius Petipa.
Vaganova	[Agrippina Yakovlevna Vaganova], *Agrippina Yakovlevna Vaganova. Stat'i, vospominaniya, materialy* [Agrippina Yakovlevna Vaganova: Articles, Recollections, Materials] (Leningrad and Moscow: 'Iskusstvo', 1958).

Vazem

Ekaterina Ottovna Vazem, *Zapiski baleriny Sankt-Peterburgskogo Bol'shogo teatra, 1867–1884* [Memoirs of a Ballerina of the St Petersburg Bolshoy Theatre, 1867–1884] (Moscow and Leningrad: 'Iskusstvo', 1937).

Wiley

Roland John Wiley, trans., *A Century of Russian Ballet: Documents and Eyewitness Accounts 1810–1910* (Oxford: Clarendon Press, 1990).

I
The Life of
Lev Ivanovich
Ivanov

1

Ivanov's Memoirs

To all appearances, Lev Ivanovich Ivanov was a quiet, introspective man. Unlike his elder colleague Petipa, or any number of famous dancers, he never granted an interview with the press. An obligation to speechmaking came with his promotion to second balletmaster, when he would salute the artist of the hour at benefit performances. Even here emotion or shyness could render him mute. Thus, at the farewell performance of ballerina Evgenia Sokolova,

When *Trilby* was over the curtain swept up and the moment came to honour Evgenia Pavlovna Sokolova by her colleagues, artists, and deputations from the companies of the other Imperial theatres.

On behalf of the ballet troupe balletmaster M. I. Petipa turned to the celebration's recipient with a brief, sincere, and touching greeting.

Then the balletmaster L. I. Ivanov began to speak, but broke off his address from emotion, begging E. P. Sokolova's pardon, and presented her a wreath from the ballet company.[1]

If Ivanov was not given to public speaking, neither did he write much about himself. The regulation whereby artists whose contracts were expiring had to request a renewal from the Director of Imperial Theatres produced a number of letters by Ivanov in which he emphasized his value to the company. He did not shrink from this task, but apart from communications to administrative superiors, the only significant writing by Ivanov about himself came in his memoirs.

In *Masters of the Ballet* Slonimsky persistently refers to Ivanov's memoirs as a 'diary' [*dnevnik*], which suggests that they were written systematically, day by day over a long period. Nothing about their organization and content supports the use of this term. Ivanov's manuscript appears to have been improvised (his widow referred to it as a 'draft'). The date on the title-

---

[1] *Peterburgskii listok*, 26 Nov. 1886, p. 3.

page, 2 February 1899, suggests a connection with his half-century anniversary of service to the theatre, publicly celebrated later that year. Moreover, Ivanov may have written it at the behest of historian Alexandre Pleshcheyev, for when Pleshcheyev published part of the text two days after Ivanov's death, an editor mentioned it being written in Ivanov's own hand, 'and before the last benefit performance given by him to A. A. Pleshcheyev, who gave it to us'.[2] The manuscript passed to the St Petersburg Museum of Theatrical and Musical Art in 1940 as part of the collection of theatre historian Lyubov Dmitrievna Blok.

In the absence of this source we would know virtually nothing about Lev Ivanov's life up to the age of 26. His service record contains but one document pertaining to the period before his career officially began in 1850. A certification from the Imperial Foundling Home in St Petersburg indicates that Ivanov's birthdate was 18 February 1834, that he was taken into the home on 22 January 1835, and was returned to his mother, Tio Adamova, on 25 November 1837.[3] Yet even this unexceptional bureaucratic report offers a hint of Ivanov's ancestry. In imperial times Russian children were named after saints in the Orthodox calendar, where a Georgian saint bears the name 'Shio' (or possibly 'Tio'—from an alternative reading of the Russian letters). Ivanov's mother was probably not Russian. Hers is a Georgian name, possibly a variant of 'Theodora', a saint much venerated in Georgia. This would make Ivanov, on his mother's side, a forebear of Balanchine in nationality as well as art.

Ivanov's memoirs speak of his devotion to the artistic community he is addressing. He dedicates them to his comrades and co-workers, his unstated purpose to confirm the continuity between his and later generations. So strong is this sense of community—of artists linked by training and tradition—that we need not puzzle over why he makes so little reference to foreign celebrities. Implicit is the solidarity of Russian dancers

    [2] 'The Autobiography of L. I. Ivanov (My Little Reminiscences)', *Peterburgskaya gazeta*, 13 Dec. 1901, p. 5. They were published again, still incomplete, in the journal *Sovetskii balet*, 32 (Jan.–Feb. 1987): 37–43.
    [3] Ivanov Service Record, fo. 16. Without citing a source, the compiler of a history of the St Petersburg/Leningrad Theatre School writes: 'There is information that Ivanov up to the age of 8 was brought up in a merchant family. Then he was put in a private boarding-school, where he spent two years, in the course of which he was matriculated into the Petersburg Theatre School' (see M. Borisoglebskii, *Proshloe baletnogo otdeleniya Peterburgskogo teatral'nogo uchilishcha, nyne Leningradskogo Gosudarstvennogo Khoregraficheskogo uchilishcha. Materialy po istorii russkogo baleta* [The Past of the Ballet Division of the Petersburg Theatre School, now the Leningrad State Choreographic School. Materials Relating to the History of Russian Ballet], 2 vols. (Leningrad: Leningrad State Choreographic School, 1938–9) [hereafter: *Borisoglebsky*], i. 191). The source not cited is, of course, Ivanov's memoirs; by omitting to mention this Borisoglebsky implies that Ivanov was not brought up in his own family.

trained in the theatre school, a corporate identity which is shared by other memoirists of the same estate.[4]

Ivanov also reveals to us much of his inner self. On the surface we are reading the words of an old man recalling his youth. The voice is childlike. Is the man behind it likewise, or are Ivanov's simplicity of expression, his delight in remembrance, the naïveté of his approach—informal, unsystematic, digressive, anecdotal—the attributes of someone who has endured much while charting the 'sea of life'—the *zhiteiskoe more* hymned in the Orthodox funeral service? Does a *fin de siècle* nostalgia seek a utopia in the past, or indeed, might Ivanov's lack of concern for recognition reflect his putting aside the tribulations of this world in favour of contemplating the next?

Throughout the text the reader senses Ivanov's underlying modesty. His exhortations to young artists to revere their art are the province of a senior artist, the advice of an uncle or brother. A staunch anti-chauvinist, he makes no mention of his lasting accomplishments, but only of application and diligence. If Ivanov ever amounted to anything, he claimed, these virtues were responsible.

In sum, the memoirs project a complex personality—capable of subservience and authority, affection and reproach, practicality and daydream, all wrapped in a beguiling artlessness. They constitute a first look at Ivanov's life. A second, drawn from diverse sources, will deal in Chapter 2 with the central issues in that life, many of which Ivanov does not even mention here.

The following is a translation of the complete text of Ivanov's memoirs, based on his manuscript and a typewritten transcription in the St Petersburg Museum of Theatrical and Musical Art, filed under shelf number KP 7154/76. Additional data, including words Ivanov omitted, which are necessary to the sense of a passage, have been added within square brackets.

MY RECOLLECTIONS
Dedicated to my comrades and co-workers

Foregone years flashed by in an instant,
And shades of the past fly before me,
Comrades of childhood, artists of the ballet,
Long since departed this earthly life.

(L. Ivanov 2 February 1899)

---

[4] See e.g. 'Recollections of T. A. Stukolkin, Artist of the Imperial Theatres. Copied from his account by A. Valberg', *Artist* [The Artist], no. 45 (Jan. 1895), 126–33; no. 46 (Feb. 1895), 117–25;

As much as I remember of myself in childhood is from the age of 6 or 7. I was born in 1834, in February. My father was quite a strict and serious man, my mother the kindest and most tranquil soul. Our family consisted of me, two brothers, and a sister; true, my parents had other children but I don't remember them, as they died in childhood. My father was a merchant of the first guild; he was involved in contracting—he built houses, roads, and the like. He was not, like most contractors, of simple stock, but rather was intelligent and educated. I recall that first we lived in a rather modest flat. Then, probably with an improvement in our situation, we moved into a large and expensive flat, and, finally, two or three years later, my father acquired his own stone house and carriages. At about the age of 8 I was sent to boarding-school, and after passing two or three years there entered the theatre school, and this is how it happened. My father loved the theatre very much, especially the Alexandrinsky, where he once took all of us to watch a performance from box seats. On that occasion the programme consisted of several one-act plays and *Don Juan*, a short, one-act ballet [by Blache, to music of Sonné, first performed in Russia in 1832, revised in 1840]. This ballet made a great impression on me, and especially the play *The Schoolteacher* [a vaudeville translated from the French by Pyotr Andreyevich Karatygin], in which, as we all know, young actors participate, students of the theatre school. On the way home, my father asked me what I had liked about the theatre—and I began to praise the ballet and especially *The Schoolteacher* with such enthusiasm, and said that I would like to be a young actor like those who took part in it. I was made gentle fun of, and my dear mother commented that it was a very difficult art, one had to study it a great deal. But my father took it differently and said: 'And why would we not send him to the theatre school? Perhaps this is his destiny and career.' And so I was put into the theatre school, and my father's words were vindicated, as I turned out not the worst of artists.

After entering the school, I went first of all to dance class, to Frédéric [Valette Malavergne]'s assistant instructor, [Alexandre Ivanovich] Pimenov. It must be said that then, according to school regulations, every person entering was required to study dance. After that, depending on one's capabilities, one stayed in this class or was transferred to classes in drama or music, or even the decorative arts. Metamorphoses would happen, such as the well-known, celebrated, brilliant [actor Alexandre Evstafievich] Martynov, who was trained as a decorator and became an artist of genius.

[Ivan Ivanovich] Sosnitsky, who was trained for the ballet, turned out to be a wonderful dramatic actor.

I began to show great capability for ballet, and for that reason after a year was taken from the ranks of external students and placed among the state-supported students. For the whole time of my stay in school my teachers were: Pimenov, Frédéric, [Émile] Gredlu, and finally [Jean Antoine] Petipa, not the present balletmaster but his father.

My life in school was very merry; everyone was an excellent and good comrade; true, some were scoundrels, but any family can have its black sheep.

These dear comrades come to mind spontaneously: [Vasily Romanovich] Shemaev, Malyshev, [Ivan Egorovich] Chernyshyov, [Alexandre Dmitrievich] Dmitriev, [Gavriil Nikolaevich] Zhulev, [Alexandre Alexandrovich] Nilsky, and finally [Nikolay Timofeyevich] Ilyin, who was especially friendly with me; he was a distinctive original. We very much loved to read novels translated from French, especially the works of Dumas: *Monte Cristo*, *The Three Musketeers*, *Queen Margot*, and others. He was a frightfully pensive character, and especially liked to dream about being in love.

We would return from the theatre at one o'clock in the morning, and he often invited me after dinner into the dark auditorium to indulge in a bit in reverie. As he had a speech defect, he pronounced 'p' instead of 'b', and 'f' instead of 'v', and 'k' instead of 'r'. It came out like this: 'Lyofa, let's go build castles in the sky.' We often mocked him gently, but he was nevertheless a fine and good chap, a man with soul; I was very fond of him.

In earlier times we had leave to stay with our parents on Sundays only until 9.00 p.m., or only until 6.00 p.m. for those who were needed at the theatre; and even during summer holidays, although academic classes had ceased, we stayed in the school in order to take art classes.

When refurbishing was under way and they were painting our immense dormitory, they put us on mattresses on the floor of the dance rehearsal hall to sleep, an experience which was a great pleasure for us since we engaged in various pranks and foolishness there. It would happen, for example, that after dinner our duty supervisor put us to bed in the hall and would stay until we calmed down, then go to have tea or his own dinner. (Almost every supervisor had an apartment in the school.) No sooner had the supervisor left than all manner of pranks and foolishness would begin. For example: several people would represent an orchestra, others horses, horsemen, clowns; we'd begin playing horses jumping over barriers with various leaps and somersaults; the orchestra of course would play on its lips, window frames would serve as drums. Such noise and uproar could, I think, have wakened the dead.

Since the supervisors mostly lived in our part of the building, directly above the hall, this unimaginable din would reach them. The duty supervisor would run in, just to find everyone sleeping quietly on his mattress; this of course was quite astonishing to him. We managed this as follows: we posted one of the young students to guard the stairs, and just as the door above opened he would tell us, and we would instantly jump into bed. This would happen several times: but once we were caught and punished by being denied permission to go home for a whole month. For this we got revenge on the supervisor who caught us in our minor pranks. Our supervisors were each funnier than the last; there were five of them, some we loved and others not, and we played various jokes on them. For example there was a certain Knapiche, a Greek by birth, who besides being a supervisor was an arithmetic teacher in the junior class.[5] What a joke we played on him! He always wore galoshes with cleats; we once took it into our heads to nail these galoshes to the floor, and again were punished. We played many such pranks, and I cannot remember them all now.

In earlier times our school was very rarely visited by any highly placed person, let alone a minister, for example, and almost never by the Sovereign Emperor. But once it happened that the Sovereign Emperor Nikolay Pavlovich thought to visit our school unexpectedly, without warning our supervisors. His Imperial Majesty, having caught the school unawares, found various deficiencies in it, especially as regards cleanliness; he was extremely displeased and angry, as a result of which many supervisors left.

In place of the ousted supervisor of the school, F[yodor] N[ikolaevich] Auber, there came P[avel] S[tepanovich] Fyodorov, who was also appointed manager of the repertoire division. Although he was strict he was fair. Subsequently many reproved and blamed him, but these were all his enemies, unhappy with his strictness.

Then also I spontaneously recall my older brother, N.I., who took it into his head to request P. S. Fyodorov to enlist him in the service of the theatre.

At that time he told of an incredibly funny quid pro quo. It went like this: when he appeared before P[avel] S[tepanovich] with his request, the latter received him very cordially and announced that he personally could not accept him without [the approval of] the Director, Alexandre Mikhailovich Gedeonov. He advised him, in addition, to write his request, addressed to the Director, and to appear before him in his office, having discussed the matter in advance with his secretary, E. M. Simonov, and during this discussion to give him his calling-card. On the next day my brother went to see the Director and gave the request and his calling-card to P[avel] S[tepanovich's] secretary. No sooner had [my brother] begun to speak with

---

[5] Citing additional sources, Borisoglebsky indicates that Knapiche was a Bulgarian, and that he taught Russian grammar (*Borisoglebsky*, i. 139, 175).

him than the Director's loud and angry voice issued from his office; he was reproaching someone vehemently. Suddenly a small, dark-complexioned gentleman flew out the door of his office, ejected by the Director himself, who stayed in the doorway and continued to yell and swear. Seeing my brother caught unawares, he turned to him angrily and asked, 'What do you want?' My brother had no choice but to explain his purpose, whereupon A[lexandre] M[ikhailovich] began to yell at him and call him a drunk and a scoundrel. Listening to this abuse, my brother answered him modestly: 'Your Excellency, I am not as yet in service, and you already deign to swear at me . . .' At that point Gedeonov clearly thought better of it, ordered my brother to leave his request with the secretary and return for an answer the next day. The next day, upon receiving a satisfactory answer from the secretary, my brother made his way to P. S. Fyodorov to thank him for the petition, and when he was exchanging bows upon departure they butted foreheads, since they were both tall. Laughing, P[avel] S[tepanovich] noted that this was a sign they would be friends. In less than a year P[avel] S[tepanovich] took my brother as his secretary, since he had beautiful handwriting and was able to put together service papers well, and P[avel] S[tepanovich] was very fond of him.

In Lent, beginning the second week, they staged student performances twice a month in the school theatre, for drama as well as ballet and music students. The Director was present at them, together with the entire management, and students' parents were also admitted. During his reign Alexandre II graced these performances with his presence, and since then we have had the high attention of other emperors.

Drama students performed mainly classical plays, and sometimes comedies and vaudevilles, ballet students small ballets and divertissements, music students played concertos on various instruments in the intervals, and even an orchestra of students was assembled, led at that time by old Mauer, whom everyone knew, the supervisor of all theatre orchestras. Professors of the drama class were famous artists of different eras: I. I. Sosnitsky, P. A. Karatygin, P[yotr] I[vanovich] Grigoriev, and V[asily] V[asilievich] Samoilov II. Subsequently this class passed to the *littérateur* Vasilko-Petrov, and still later to the teacher of dramatic reading N. I. Svedontsov. Vasilko-Petrov often enticed and tried to persuade me to transfer from ballet to drama, observing my good appearance and excellent readings of dramatic works (at that time all students had to take a course in dramatic reading), but I could not in the least agree, loving the balletic art too much.

How simple and excellent was everything for us then! If, for example, we wanted to put on a ballet rehearsal in the evening after classes, we announced this forthwith to the supervisor of the day, who sent a messenger to the girls' dormitory, and sometimes went himself and brought the ones we needed. We would begin the rehearsal, everything would go well and decorously (not without flirting with the girl students of course), since the supervisor, seeing us seriously occupied with our business, went back to his duties. But all this was so proper and moral: one but kissed the girl students' hands. In our time they courted in a somewhat knightly fashion, profoundly respecting the lady of one's heart, without allowing oneself the least liberty.

In the summer holiday we spent nearly the whole day in the open air. In our large courtyard there were grounds where we played ball, *lapta* [a type of baseball], and most of all *bory* [a game of tag]. This was a most entertaining game, full of motion, which develops the lungs, because the whole time is taken up in running about; twenty or thirty people play, divided evenly, half standing on one side of the grounds, half on the other. The set-up looked like this:

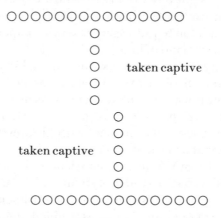

Play begins as follows: one person runs out from one side and one from the other, they must catch each other and tag each other, that is, one hits the other on the shoulder, and whoever manages to do this first takes the other captive on his side, and so forth, continuing to run out by twos. But those running out from the side where there are captives must try not only to avoid being tagged, but also must come to the aid of his man who is a captive, running up to tag him. And thus the game sometimes continues for two hours and more, until one side or the other has taken all the other team prisoner. We had such good runners it was simply amazing. There was one student, Timofeyev, who almost never allowed himself to be tagged; but whomever *he* tagged fell down for sure! The girl students always watched this game from their windows, and we, like knights at a tourney, tried not to fail in the eyes of our beloved ladies.

In the wintertime there were always skating and slides on these grounds. We were all excellent ice-skaters.

How pleasant to me are these reminiscences of childhood and youth; they somehow put one into a poetical mood, which make the words from [Glinka's] opera *Ruslan and Lyudmila* come to mind: 'O lovely shades, fly not away, fly not away!' The time and years passed unnoticed; so it was that 1852 came—the year of my graduation from the school. I graduated as a first dancer with a salary of 360 roubles a year, which for that time was considered the best of salaries.

Upon entering the service [of the theatre] I did not reside with my parents in their home because it was quite distant from the school, where I had to be every day for practice in my art. Rather I lived in my brother's flat, which was located very near the school. At that time my brother lived with the two Maximov actors, brothers of the famous artist Alexey Mikhailovich Maximov. The flat was pleasant enough and spacious. A footman served us, one Chrysanth; he was our cook and valet and laundryman—in a word, a jack of all trades. He was Siberian by origin and a seminarian, but expelled from a religious seminary after a prank on the rector, whom the seminarians wanted to drown. After that he came to Petersburg on foot, hungry, cold, and sick. One of the Maximov brothers, seeing him on the street in such a state, out of mercy brought him home to warm and feed, and from then on Chrysanth stayed with us, working as a valet. Although he was quite a clever fellow, he was a serious drunk.

Finally my service began, and I was set free. How pleasant the words 'set free' were to someone who had spent eight years in a closed institution. My service, however, had begun before graduation; I had danced from the age of 16 when still in school in the ballets *Caterina*, *Esmeralda*, and *La Filleule des Fées*, staged by the balletmaster [Jules] Perrot with the celebrated Fanny Elssler.

My participation in them was in the corps de ballet of course, because I was still very young and a student; this, however, continued for several years after my graduation. I explain it by the fact that our balletmaster Perrot was not too fond of us Russian artists, and all [important] roles and leading parts were assigned to foreigners. I set out on my real path [partly] by my own efforts and partly by accident, and this is how it happened. In daily exercises in the class of Petipa-*père* the Russian first dancer Tatyana Petrovna Smirnova, subsequently Nevakhovich by marriage, always took part with us.

Seeing me in class, always so able and well prepared in dances, she once asked me why I never danced separate *pas* on stage, but always in the corps de ballet. To this of course I could only answer that such roles were not given to me. She then proposed that I dance a *grand pas de deux* with her in her forthcoming benefit performance in the ballet *La Fille mal gardée*, which would take place in three months.

Being a modest, shy, and reticent young man I at first declined, but she persuaded me and I agreed. Soon after that we began to rehearse together and to prepare this *pas de deux* under the observation of Petipa-*père*. Having studied the *pas de deux* for fully three months, I made my début as a first dancer with great boldness and assurance at her benefit performance [on 3 November 1853], and my début was quite successful, as the public received me warmly. From that time our balletmaster Perrot began to give me small solo parts and various *pas*.

Also by accident I became a first mime and *jeune premier*, and a substitute for [Marius] Petipa, our present balletmaster. I attended every rehearsal and performance, even those in which I was not taking part, and by observation studied the mimed scenes and dances in all the ballets; my memory was excellent. The mime and acting of Mr [Nikolay Osipovich] Golts and Mr Perrot made a great impression on me. These were such immense talents in mime, from which one could gain much.

Here I shall make a small digression.

In my time at the school we were permitted into almost every rehearsal, even though we were not involved, thus taking advantage of [the opportunity of] constantly following the acting and dances of our best artists, and also the productions of that most talented balletmaster Perrot. All of this, I am sure, brought immense benefit to my service. Now we are not permitted this, which is most unfortunate because [withholding] it is a great loss to young people who are learning. They could gain much from direct observation.

Once, on the day of a performance when *La Vivandière* was scheduled, Mr Petipa sent word that he was ill. Someone had to replace him or the performance had to be cancelled, and the theatre was sold out. Our régisseur [Ivan Frantsevich] Marcel, knowing me well, proposed that I stand in for my ill colleague, to which I immediately agreed. Although Perrot winced somewhat, he nevertheless gave his consent. They immediately sent for Miss [Anna Ivanovna] Prikhunova, who was performing the ballerina's role, and I went through our roles and dances with her. Thus I performed my role that evening without mistakes, for which, by command of Director Gedeonov, I received 100 roubles as a reward. On another occasion, but without any rehearsal, I played the role of Phoebus in the ballet *Esmeralda*, since Petipa let his illness be known in the evening just before the performance.

Subsequently, and also impromptu, I played through several roles, namely: Claude Frollo in *Esmeralda*, for [Felix Ivanovich] Kshesinsky; Valentine in *Faust*, for [Christian Petrovich] Johanson; Coppélius in *Coppélia*, for [Timofey Alexeyevich] Stukolkin, and many other small roles which I cannot even remember. From that time I established a reputation as an excellent *jeune premier*. When Mr Petipa took the post of balletmaster, I replaced him completely in the roles of first mime and dancer.

In February 1855 the Sovereign Emperor Nikolay Pavlovich died, and the next year in August the coronation of the Sovereign Emperor Alexandre Nikolaevich took place in Moscow. A part of our ballet troupe was sent to the celebration, another part remained in Petersburg, where during the celebration there would be several performances of opera and ballet. According to the management's decision I was to remain here in the capacity of régisseur and balletmaster. This assignment was frightfully unpleasant for me, first because it was not at all in keeping with my character, and second because I very much wanted to visit Moscow. Thus I asked my colleague [Alexey Nikolaevich] Bogdanov if he would replace me here, to which he joyfully agreed; it was in keeping with his character, since he always strove to supervise and command. My brother organized it with P. S. Fyodorov, and I was delighted. Only one thing was unpleasant for me, that my passion and love remained here, the student beauty S——; it was sad for me that I was not to see her for a long time, yes and besides, my rival, the young actor M——, also remained here. This of course was a schoolboy's passion, not a genuine one.

They brought us to Moscow, gave us ample travelling expenses, hired Raevsky's entire house on the Dmitrovka for our lodgings, assigned us the whole first floor, while the women were put on the second, and began to feed us magnificently. Living there was marvellous, friendly, and merry. In the house where they put us, although they offered me, as befits a first dancer, a special room to share with someone else, I refused and was put in the huge communal hall; my colleagues were all young, happy, and wonderful people, playing pranks and causing the same mischief as the schoolchildren had. It would happen that most would leave for rehearsal, while those staying at home would get up a surprise for those who had left. We would remove the boards from beneath the mattresses on the beds, and those returning from rehearsal would immediately want to lie down and rest, and would throw themselves on their beds just to have the beds immediately collapse. Uproarious laughter would ensue, and no one would take offence at the surprise. And there was another prank: among our comrades was one Efimov, whom for some reason they called 'Itzak the Jew'; he was pure Russian, [but] they got it into their heads to baptize him, acquired from somewhere a huge tub with water, stocked up on syringes, and when he returned from rehearsal they refreshed him [with towels], undressed him, put him in the tub and began to spray him from all sides with the syringes. And he took no offence whatever, but said, laughing: 'Thank you, gentlemen, I wanted to have a bath, but now I needn't go because you have refreshed me excellently well.' There were many other similar japes, all lost to memory.

In our free time we went to the Sparrow Hills to admire the views of Moscow. In several carriages we went to the Monastery of St Sergius [Zagorsk], which was located about 60 versts [about 39 miles] from the city, and spent a whole wonderful day there. This trip to Moscow left a most gratifying and pleasant impression on me. We had several performances before the sacred coronation; there was a gala performance three days after the sacred coronation at which I danced a *pas de deux* with the beautiful dancer Zinaida Richard, who subsequently went to Paris, married the first dancer Mérante, and became a wonderful teacher of dances.

I was corresponding, of course, with my brother and with my parents. In one letter from my brother I found out that my passion and love was frightfully attracted to my rival, and that they were getting along very well. This very much angered me and saddened me such that I wanted to cry, but I contained myself and resolved to take vengeance on her by flirting here with somebody else. They also brought several girl students from Petersburg, among whom was Verochka Lyadova, a very nice-looking blonde whom I began to court and subsequently married. It began with foolishness and ended seriously. Thus it pleased the fates. Finally at the beginning of September we returned to Petersburg. There our rehearsals and performances began, and I undertook to court Verochka Lyadova in earnest, who graduated from the school in 1858. I immediately got acquainted with her family, and married her in 1859.

My wife's father, Alexandre Nikolaevich Lyadov, was a ballet conductor here. He was an exceptional person in all respects—good, honourable, big-spirited, and a magnificent artist. At rehearsal he played the violin with such spirit and expression that everyone would be delighted. During the reign of Emperor Nikolay Pavlovich, Lyadov was much favoured by Empress Maria Feodorovna, spouse of the Sovereign Emperor: he and his orchestra were always playing at court balls. Once it happened that Lyadov, because of illness, could not appear at a ball, whereupon the Sovereign Empress commanded that it be put off until his health was restored.

I do not remember on what occasion, at the command of the Sovereign Emperor N[ikolay] P[avlovich] three celebrations were scheduled at Peterhof: a ball, a performance, and a masquerade. The performance included a ballet. The first day the ball took place, on the second the performance was scheduled, during the morning of which we had a rehearsal with orchestra; almost half-way through the rehearsal a messenger came for Lyadov, whom the Sovereign Emperor commanded come to him at his palace. When he got there he was led directly to the Emperor's apartments. On seeing Lyadov the Emperor asked him a question: did he not have with him such and such a waltz, which he named, and which the Sovereign Empress, when still a bride, loved to dance and which had long fallen out of fashion? Lyadov, to his horror, admitted that he did not have it. 'Well then, don't you remember the first two motifs of this waltz?' asked the Emperor. Still more horrified, Lyadov said that he didn't. Then the Emperor asked him if he didn't have some music paper. Fortunately he did. At that point the Emperor commanded him to sit at a table and write, and that he would whistle these two motifs of the waltz. The Emperor began to walk around the apartment and whistle, and Lyadov to write, and in some fifteen or twenty minutes all was ready. Satisfied, the Emperor ordered him to orchestrate this for the next day's masquerade, and to introduce these two motifs into some waltz when he began to dance with the Empress. 'I want to have a surprise for the Empress,' said the Tsar, 'and you will provide me the great pleasure, I hope, that this be ready for tomorrow.' 'I shall obey, Your Imperial Majesty,' answered Lyadov, with a low bow. The Emperor slapped him affectionately on the shoulder and said: 'Now be off!'

When Lyadov returned to the English Palace, where lodgings had been arranged for us, he was as red as a crab. Telling us everything, he added what a fright he had suffered. Lyadov orchestrated these thirty-two bars the whole night; he had two assisting musicians, who wrote out everything into orchestral parts. The next day at the masquerade everything turned out well, the Emperor and Empress were very pleased, and Lyadov received there and then from the Emperor's hands a ring worth 1,500 roubles.

There was yet another very funny occasion which I cannot but relate, it is etched so in my memory, all the more that I was witness to it. It is well known that the Sovereign Emperor N[ikolay] P[avlovich] loved ballet very much, and we often took part in performances at court. Thus once in the Hermitage Theatre there was a ballet rehearsal, I don't remember which work, and I, still a student, was taking part. The rehearsal had only just begun; I and one other student, Sokolov, were standing in the second wing. You should know that Sokolov was very tall and had a large nose, such that in school we called it 'the tsar of noses'. Suddenly the Sovereign Emperor N[ikolay] P[avlovich] entered this wing (as he often attended rehearsals). We, bowing low, huddled up against the wing in fright. Seeing us, the Emperor paid special attention to Sokolov's nose, took it with two fingers and said, laughing: 'What a huge nose you have!' Meanwhile the rehearsal had come to a halt, all had bowed low, the Director Gedeonov and the balletmaster Perrot had approached the Emperor, who began to converse with them, without, however, letting go of Sokolov's nose, who was frightfully timid; I could not be frightened at all, seeing the smiling Emperor. After some time the Emperor drew back his hand and said, merrily: 'Why have you attached yourself to me with your nose? Begone!' Then, having bowed to the Emperor, we rushed to the partition of the wings. It was clear that the Emperor was in high spirits; he went up to several women dancers, spoke with them a little, and then returned to his palace.

In 1858 I received two intermediate classes of girl students, replacing their former teachers, the coryphée [Severian] Gorinovsky and the dancer [Varvara Petrovna] Volkova, and combined them into one class.

How poorly they paid us for our work in those days! Before the transfer of the class into my hands I was receiving 600 roubles a year in all, for the class they added 400 and, as I recall, 5 roubles per-performance fee. But at that time I had just married. Let us suppose that life in general back then was not so expensive, and my wife and I occupied only a small flat with two rooms and a kitchen, adjacent to the flat of my father-in-law Lyadov, who assisted us a little. This very adjacency of flats brought unhappiness to my family life, since my mother-in-law, a nasty old woman, was always coming between me and my wife. She constantly harped at her to pay me no heed, to take advantage of life while she was young, and to have a good time.

We had three sons. The first died in infancy, and two remained; the younger was a deaf-mute, who died some three years ago. I lived with my wife for ten years and we finally separated, since I at that time was enduring many mental shocks and much unpleasantness. I do not blame her, however, as much as I do her mother. In 18— [Ivanov left the last two digits blank] I received a full salary of 1,140 roubles, 10 roubles per performance and a half-benefit.

My life among comrades and artists was most cordial and pleasant; my colleagues were such people as Stukolkin, [Alexandre Nikolaevich] Picheau, Golts, Johanson, Kshesinsky, Chistyakov, [Fyodor Fyodorovich?] Geltser, [Nikolay Petrovich] Troitsky, [Gustav Ivanovich] Legat, [Nikolay Ivanovich] Volkov, [Teodor?] Ledé, [Alexandre Emelyanovich] Prosbin, Leonov, [Lev Petrovich] Stukolkin II, [Konstantin Panteleimonovich] Efimov, [Vasily] Thomas, [Pyotr Fyodorovich] Diering—all of whom completely deserved to be remembered as wonderful, spiritual people and good comrades. And our former régisseur Marcel—he was a kindly man, always fair, honourable, and humane, especially in dealings with our younger brothers, the corps de ballet and artists of lesser rank. Not in vain under his supervision was our troupe considered a model; if a disagreement or argument arose with someone, he was always able somehow to restore harmony and make peace. He and I always enjoyed the best of friendships, he always called me simply 'Lyova' and would get angry with me because I did not address him in the familiar second person, as I was very young compared to him and it was frightfully awkward for me to address him in this way. He was a profoundly cordial and good person. Rest in peace, unforgettable comrade! . . . Upon his demise the post of régisseur passed to Bogdanov, who had often taken over this responsibility when the late Marcel went somewhere or was ill. He was quite a good régisseur as regards authority, but for that reason in regard to comradeship and friendship everything changed under him.

With the death of P. S. Fyodorov, Lukashevich replaced him as head of the repertoire division, and the retired Colonel A[lexandre] P[etrovich] Frolov was made supervisor of the school. Before that all the companies answered to the supervisor of the repertoire division; with Frolov's arrival, Director I[van] A[lexandrovich] Vsevolozhsky assigned him to supervise our ballet troupe. Two or three years later, something did not go well between him and régisseur Bogdanov, who as a result had to give up his post. At that time they proposed that I take his job. For me this was a quite unpleasant turn of events, since I never reckoned myself to be either a régisseur or a balletmaster, knowing my too kindly and weak character; but then our balletmaster Petipa began to persuade me, and said that if I went hand in hand with him, things would go well with us. For about three days I thought about it, and decided to agree to the proposal. This was in 1882. Three years passed and what then? . . . It was Mr Petipa who went against me first and began to complain to Frolov and the Director that I was weak of character and was spoiling the entire company. This was not true; the troupe did its job as it always had done before. At that time [Alberto] di Segni took the post of régisseur, a former assistant régisseur of the Italian [opera] company, which had been abolished. They made me second balletmaster, with which I was quite content, because the post of régisseur was most disquieting; although being a balletmaster was not especially calm, it was altogether better.

In 1869 my wife Lyadova died, and after seven years as a widower I married a second time.

The coryphée Varenka Malchugina had been transferred from Moscow— she was a very nice young lady, I liked her very much, and I began to pay court to her. After a time I married her, and so to this day we are living out our time together with three children: a son and two daughters. In 1883 I received my first imperial award, a large gold medal on the Stanislav ribbon, to be worn around the neck; in 1891 I was awarded the Order of St Stanislav, 3rd degree; in 1896, during the coronation of the presently felicitously reigning Sovereign Emperor Nikolay Alexandrovich, the Order of St Anne, 3rd degree. In the course of my service I have several times been sent by the direction to Moscow to produce ballets and dances in operas. In 1897 I was invited privately to Warsaw, where I staged three ballets: [Petipa's] *The Parisian Market*, [Ivanov's own] *The Magic Flute*, [Petipa's] *The Halt of the Cavalry*, dances in [Anton Rubinstein's] opera *The Demon*, and several numbers for divertissements, for which I received a generous honorarium.

And so now, feeling quite strong and robust, I am continuing my not unuseful activity as balletmaster, and onwards as God grants. We ballet artists, by means of constant movement, always attain a healthy and sturdy old age. Old age is as it should be, but may the Lord keep us from senility. I have served during the time of three Emperors, four Ministers of Court, and am now serving during the time of my fourth Emperor and fifth Minister and sixth Director of Theatres. Our present Director, I. A. Vsevolozhsky, during whose time our service has been very easy and excellent, one can say without any flattery is a fair, cordial, and humane man; I am sure that all my colleagues agree with me.

Having written these recollections and read them through, the thought came to me: 'My God, my God, how much strength has been expended, how much deeply felt bad blood over wounded pride, over degraded human dignity'—but of such is the life of an artist generally, and nevertheless this glance back and these reminiscences are very pleasant to me and provide great delight.

You see, my good comrades and co-workers, like a good soldier I have passed through the stages of my service beginning with foot soldier and ending up as general, from dancer in the corps de ballet to coryphée, first dancer in *jeune premier* roles, played character parts, danced character and classical *pas*, was made a teacher of dance, régisseur, and finally balletmaster. I have danced with practically all foreign and Russian women dancers except Fanny Elssler, and that because I was very young at the time; I have performed many ballets and now stage ballets myself; although I do not possess a talent such as Mr Petipa's, I nevertheless stage ballets no worse than many other balletmasters. Please do not, my amiable comrades, take everything I have said as boasting. I only wanted to prove by it that with patience, effort, persistence, and with fervent love for one's art, one can achieve anything. I turn especially to you, my young comrades whose career is still ahead of you, [with advice to] love your art as fervently as I do, and all will go beautifully. I shall permit myself some more advice: don't be too proud, don't consider yourself better than others, be modest, since with great pride, which leads to egoism, everything can be lost. This can be compared with a worker's physical labour, who expends his strength through excessive burden and effort; likewise superfluous vanity can destroy your talent. I ask you, my good comrades, not to call to account my perhaps not altogether literary work; for I have made no pretence of writing literature. These are simple notes and reminiscences which I wanted to share with you, and with my young colleagues as if to give them counsel and put them on a true path. And so I remain in the hope that you will look upon me favourably, my dear friends, comrades, and co-workers.

Having finished my recollections I wanted to speak a little, my good and kind male colleagues, and especially with you, my charming ladies, and ask you to hear me out and accept my well-meant counsel on your relationship to your service and your art. Your cold and negligent response to it has always amazed me, and still does. Let us take, for example, our rehearsals: you always arrive later than you should, with the preconceived notion of ending and leaving as soon as possible, thinking nothing of forcing the balletmaster and régisseurs to wait for you for a half hour and more, and taking no interest in your profession. At rehearsals you do anything that suits you: you chatter, walk about, fool around, and joke, and do not do what you came for. Why is this? Because you are not men and women artists but mannequins, which until someone pulls a string will not move from their places. You rehearse without relish, lazily, you pay no attention to what you are doing; consequently the same holds true at a performance. Indeed, from this our common task suffers. Of course there are those among you who do not behave this way, but they are very few. Even if you are the last dancer of the corps de ballet, you should perform everything the balletmaster has staged, study, and then you would fully be considered artistes. All this results from your petty vanity. Each of you considers herself more talented than she really is, and whoever among you is put in the last line [of the corps de ballet] takes it as a right to be lazy and to perform as she pleases. Kindly understand, acting in this way, that you sin against the service, against art and even against your self-worth, because the public sees this and laughs at you; not in vain does it call you dancers 'by the water' and in this way slights your worth. Sometimes it happens that you perform some corps de ballet [dance] beautifully, as if a ray of light reached you, but the meteor has sparkled and disappeared. You will answer that the *pas* was not staged well, and that is not true; there are no bad *pas*, everything depends on execution, if it is performed well and artistically, an excellent *pas* has been presented to the stage.

Forgive me, my good and dear comrades, men and women, that I am perhaps so sharp, [but] I speak the truth. For this you will surely not take umbrage at me, an old man. But I wanted you not to be such rigid statues, I wanted to inspire the soul and energy in you, that you not look upon your art as no more than a trade which feeds you, and that you love it with all your soul and would hold its banner high. Second dancers suffer especially from this petty vanity. Should one of them replace a first dancer, she immediately forms a high opinion of herself, that she has in fact already become a first dancer, and the next thing, returning to her original place, performs her *pas* in an uninspired way, any old way she pleases. This is very unfair and illogical if she truly loves her art, and indeed the balletmaster sees this petty vanity, and will be unwilling next time to have her stand in for a first dancer. Is it not better, remaining in her place, to continue to perform her duties as she ought, without caprice? One must believe that with patience and effort one can achieve a promotion to first dancer.

How excellent, if you, my dear women comrades, were to take my advice and were to accept it as a rule. Then our common task would be better; even now our ballet stands high in comparison with foreign companies, but then it would stand even higher. I ask you again to excuse me for speaking out to you in this way, and for often getting angry with you during rehearsals; but it is all because I so love my work and art, and I wish it to flourish to its furthest extent, and for you I wish great successes and all the best in it.

[Further on in Lev Ivanov's memoirs is a note dating from the year 1901:]
(Already ill, but loving art, I took upon myself to stage *Sylvia*.)

In 1901, the first of October on a Monday I began to stage the ballet *Sylvia*. Of the first numbers 148 bars were produced. The second of October, although a rehearsal was scheduled, it did not take place for the lack of a place and musicians. The ninth, tenth, and eleventh (of October) were rehearsals of the b[allet] *Sylvia*, the twelfth and thirteenth as well; on the fourteenth and fifteenth Act I was almost completed, on the twentieth . . .'

[With this L. Ivanov's memoirs cease, and a notation of V. Ivanova (Malchugina) follows:]

The twentieth of October was the first attack of asthma, and until the eleventh of December 1901 he was at home, suffering from sclerosis of the lungs; and all the time he kept on speaking of and grieving over the ballet.

He died peacefully of a heart attack, instantly. He bore much injustice from Petipa Marius, and contracted heart disease from stress.

This is a rough draft, consequently, it represents the most personal [thoughts].

V. Ivanova. 1911, December 11. Ten years later.

2

Lev Ivanov's Life

His First Ten Years of Service

Lev Ivanov was 11 when he entered the theatre school on 3 April 1845.[1] His professional life officially began when he turned 16, on 18 February 1850. To count the onset of service from a student's sixteenth birthday was an administrative policy of the time; Ivanov did not graduate from the theatre school until 20 March 1852, the last event recorded in his service record for the next six years.[2]

There is a reason why the first decade of Ivanov's career is so obscure. It was a period of obligatory service: he was expected to perform any duties asked of him in return for the cost of his education. Thus no reference is made in his service record to substituting for Petipa on short notice and being rewarded for it (above, p. 12). Exceptional achievements were treated as routine under these circumstances, though Ivanov would remind the direction of them in negotiations once his obligation had been met.

Vera Krasovskaya has culled various sources for the first signs of Ivanov's celebrity. She reports a public stage appearance by Ivanov as early as 1850 (in the ballet *The Millers* at the Alexandrinsky Theatre on 7 June), and the distinction of his being the only student in the first performance of *A Peasant Wedding* the next year on 27 April. In 1853 he appeared with two Russian ballerinas, first in Charles Didelot's *The Hungarian Hut*, revived for Elena Andreanova's benefit performance on 22 February, and then as Tatyana Smirnova's partner at her benefit performance on 3 November, the occasion which he described in his memoirs. The next year

[1] St Petersburg, Historical Archive, 498.1.1143, 'On the Placement of the state student *Lev Ivanov* in the School'.
[2] Ivanov Service Record, fo. 14.

Perrot assigned Ivanov small solo parts in his ballets.[3] In 1854 a critic wrote, again of *The Millers*:

This ballet produced the most pleasant impression on me personally, and on the public too, so far as I could tell. The ballet is not great, and is distinguished neither by its story nor a magnificent production nor by its music. What about it then, you ask, could please the public? That only young artists took part, and almost all performed extremely conscientiously. Mr Ivanov danced so well that it strikes me only Mr Johanson could execute this *pas* on our stage with greater precision and ease.[4]

Three points about Ivanov's first ten years on stage rise above the everyday: he decided against music as a profession, he became a teacher, and he married.

For a time, Ivanov's remarkable musical ability challenged dancing as a career. As a student he revealed an extraordinary ear, scorned by his superiors but praised by the Director of the Petersburg Musical Society, who spoke of Ivanov as a genius and urged him to leave the theatre school.[5] In time he won renown for composition and musical memory, and had his works performed in public. In 1858 his mazurka, 'Pétulance', was danced at the Théâtre-Cirque by his bride-to-be, Vera Lyadova, with Alexey Bogdanov. Later he composed a hymn in honour of the visit in 1867 of King Otto I of Greece, an orchestral march played at Pavel Gerdt's benefit performance in 1875, a new variation for Evgenia Sokolova to dance in Arthur Saint-Léon's *The Little Humpbacked Horse* at her benefit performance (1878), and other dances.[6]

A major obstacle to Ivanov's prospects as a composer was his inability to notate music. A memoir by the dancer Nikolay Solyannikov, who happened unexpectedly on Ivanov late in life when he was improvising, says as much:

Once after a rather long rehearsal I stayed around the school. The grey dusk fell rapidly, and just as quickly it changed into the thick darkness of a rainy, snowless autumn. Passing one of the classrooms I heard the sound of a piano. I was astonished. At such a late hour it was not usual to be coaching somebody, and besides, the music, full of original touches, spoke of the player's great artistry. Ballet rehearsal pianists did not play for dances this way. I softly opened the door. In the near-complete darkness, dimly outlined, was the hunched silhouette of Lev Ivanov: he played the last chord, which sounded heart-rending, full of suffering in

---

[3] *Krasovskaya*, 340–2. Concerning Ivanov's early appearances on stage, Borisoglebsky writes: 'While still a student he distinguished himself in a *pas de deux* with M[arfa] N[ikolaevna] Muravyova in the ballet *La Péri* and also by his appearances with Fanny Elssler in *Caterina*, *Esmeralda*, and in *La Filleule des fées*' [*Borisoglebsky*, i. 191]. Ivanov's reference to not dancing with Elssler (above, p. 18) is probably a reference to not partnering her.

[4] *Sanktpeterburgskie vedomosti*, 19 Sept. 1854, p. 1.

[5] *Borisoglebsky*, i. 191.

[6] See *Novoe vremya*, 11 Jan. 1875, p. 2; *Krasovskaya*, 343, 347–8.

this solitary room, inclined his head pensively, his fingers tossing off some absent-minded, half-conscious arpeggio. I was a bit afraid of distracting him from his compositional meditations, and wanted to close the door quietly. But a little strip of light had slipped into the room from the corridor, and Lev Ivanov raised his head.

'Is that you, Nikolasha? Come in, come in, don't be shy.'

'Lev Ivanovich, I did not know that you played this way! Play a little something more, it gives me such great pleasure,' I beseeched him.

'I can't . . . I can't . . . I have forgotten . . .'

'But you were just playing!'

'I have forgotten what I just played, just now I cannot remember anything,' Ivanov muttered with a sad, sad smile. 'There is nobody to take it down . . . there is nobody to help . . . And so many ideas . . . so many thoughts. And it is thus that I pour out my heart: flaring up and dying down. It is hard, Nikolasha . . . very hard . . .'[7]

Ivanov's extraordinary musical memory also finds witness in anecdotes from his contemporaries, of which one, transmitted by the dancer Alexandre Shiryaev and the ballerina Ekaterina Vazem, describes him at his most prodigious:

Ivanov's musical abilities were phenomenal. Once, I recall, Anton Grigorievich Rubinstein played through his ballet *The Grapevine* in the rehearsal hall. The composer had hardly left the hall before Ivanov sat down at the piano and reproduced by ear practically all of Rubinstein's music.[8]

The most elaborate account of Ivanov's musicality, probably apocryphal in some of its details, came from Josef Kshesinsky, who like Solyannikov knew Ivanov later in life:

His calling was not to follow along this path [to become a dancer] but to be a musician and in this sphere to be great, but the genius in him was broken by the coarseness and loutishness of people at that time. . . .

In childhood, as a 9-year-old little boy he entered the theatre school and there attracted attention, for no sooner did the child see and hear a piano than he would avidly begin to listen to the melody, and gaze at the fingers playing on the keys. After that, coming into a classroom where no one was, he would sit down at the piano and with his own tiny hands, without any knowledge, without any textbook, would repeat the melodies he heard. The little boy's ambition for music was so great that at night he would quietly get up from his bed and in his nightshirt steal into the hall and improvise wonderful melodies at the piano. But the management in those years, as I said, was loutish: instead of attending to the heart of the matter and making a Russian genius out of the child, the now-departed Director Gedeonov cried

---

[7] N[ikolay] A[leksandrovich] Solyannikov, 'Recollections', ed. N. A. Shuvalov; literary working-out by Nonna Solyannikova (typescript, St Petersburg, Library of the St Petersburg Branch of the All-Russian Theatrical Society, Inv. No. 35-R2) [hereafter: *Solyannikov*], 44–5.

[8] Shiryaev's account, quoted in *Krasovskaya*, 347.

out: 'Knock the music out of this little brat with a strap! Look—such a musician out of the blue! And if, you little scoundrel, you ever sit down at a piano here again, if you play a single note you'll get a whipping. But now, for the time being go without lunch, and no holiday at home on Sundays.' And Levushka, a quiet, modest little boy, hid somewhere in a corner and calmly sat down, weeping bitterly. Nevertheless he finished school, becoming an artist despite the fact that Gedeonov at his graduation cautioned that he would not let him advance, saying 'Your business is to dance, not to make music.' All the same, immediately upon receiving money for equipping himself and with his first salary he bought a piano on instalments and in his free moments gave himself over with all strength to the passion of his favourite art. Of course to become a musician, to begin study at the age of 19 or 20 is already late, but that's our Levushka (he was called this up to the point he was named chief régisseur, after which he was immediately rechristened Lev Ivanovich). As soon as he noticed that rehearsal hadn't yet begun, or in the intervals, he sat at the piano and not knowing a single note would play any melody, any ballet as from written music, and would accompany without a single error.[9]

Ivanov was appointed teacher in the theatre school on 14 November 1858,[10] an activity that would continue to the end of his career. By the time of his fiftieth anniversary jubilee, Pleshcheyev could list a Pleiad of Russian dancers Ivanov had taught:

Of his students, one may name [Alexandra Fyodorovna] Vergina, [Evgenia Pavlovna] Sokolova, [Ekaterina Ottovna] Vazem, [Varvara Alexandrovna] Nikitina, [Maria Nikolaevna] Gorshenkova, [Zinaida Vasilievna] Frolova, [Anna Alexandrovna] Noskova, [Olga Iosifovna] Preobrazhenskaya, and others.[11]

Along the way, as dancers passed a milestone, Ivanov would also be remembered. At Sokolova's farewell benefit in 1886, one critic explained Ivanov's inability to complete his address to her (above, p. 3) by pointing out that he had been the ballerina's first teacher.[12] When Alexandra Shaposhnikova retired a year earlier, a similar observation had been made.[13]

When his students did well, Ivanov would be credited. In part of the *Grand pas Lydien* in Petipa's *Le Roi Candaule*, for example, 'Two talented young girls were applauded, the students [Vera Vasilievna?] Zhukova and [Antonina?] Petrova, pupils of L. Ivanov; they very nicely performed their short adagio of some 16 bars'.[14]

---

[9] Ios[if] Fel[iksovich] Kshesinskii, 'Several extracts from my memoirs touching on reminiscences of Marius Iv[anovich] Petipa', 2 vols., Moscow, Theatre Museum named after A. A. Bakhrushin, *fond* 134, No. 2 [hereafter: *Kshesinsky*], ii. 19–20.

[10] Ivanov Service Record, fo. 18.

[11] *Novoe vremya*, 3 Dec. 1899, p. 3.

[12] *Novoe vremya*, 27 Nov. 1886, p. 3.

[13] *Peterburgskaya gazeta*, 20 Jan. 1885, p. 3.

[14] *Golos*, 19 Oct. 1868, p. 1.

In the last act of Petipa's *Don Quixote* in St Petersburg (1871), children from the theatre school portrayed cupids who freed a captive from a castle. In a notice of the fourth performance, for Ivanov's benefit, a critic remarked,

Mr Ivanov is a most excellent teacher of dances, of which it was easy to make certain, watching the dances in Mr Petipa's new ballet which were performed by little children of the theatre school, and who were, for the most part, students of the benefit artist.[15]

Testimony from the other side of the footlights is quite different. Ekaterina Vazem, who would have been a student in Ivanov's classes soon after his appointment, later wrote: 'Lev Ivanovich Ivanov was never an excellent pedagogue—chiefly because of his innate gentleness and the antipathy of his character. He was not able to compel study and could not enforce discipline.'[16]

A generation later Mathilde Kshesinskaya was Ivanov's student, and went on to recall his teaching in a similar way:

When I entered the theatre school, my first teacher was Lev Ivanovich Ivanov, a notable balletmaster, of whose works have remained the matchless second act of *Swan Lake* and *The Nutcracker* by Tchaikovsky. . . .
Lev Ivanovich himself accompanied on the violin, and as it sometimes appeared to us, loved it more than us. . . . He taught beginning exercises, the alphabet of ballet as it were, but this could not captivate me very much since I had been through it all at home. Sometimes, it seemed to me, he dictated movements to us, and made observations almost by inertia. In a lazy voice he told us: 'Pliez', 'Straighten your knees', but he never stopped, he would never correct, would not hold up the class over some student's incorrect movement. It seemed to me then that he did not create in class, that he was not inspired and was not inspiring us, but was, machine-like, only fulfilling his obligations.[17]

Later still Agrippina Vaganova, a respected artist before and after the October Revolution, referred to the 'antipathy and complete indifference' of Ivanov's classes.[18]

The year 1858 began and ended with a flourish. On 28 February Ivanov received a rise (from 360 to 600 roubles per year) 'in recognition of his gift and successes on the stage'. His appointment in the theatre school brought

---

[15] *Peterburgskaya gazeta*, 21 Nov. 1871, p. 3.

[16] Ekaterina Ottovna Vazem, *Zapiski baleriny Sankt-Peterburgskogo Bol'shogo teatra, 1867–1884* [Memoirs of a Ballerina of the St Petersburg Bolshoy Theatre, 1867–1884] (Moscow and Leningrad: 'Iskusstvo', 1937) [hereafter: *Vazem*], 29.

[17] *Kshesinskaya*, 22–3.

[18] *Agrippina Yakovlevna Vaganova. Stat'i, vospominaniya, materialy* [Agrippina Yakovlevna Vaganova. Articles, Recollections, Materials] (Leningrad and Moscow: 'Iskusstvo', 1958) [hereafter: *Vaganova*], 37.

another rise of 300 roubles.[19] And on 6 December he petitioned the direction for a certification, which he received the next day, that it had no objection to his marrying Vera Lyadova. He also requested, according to custom, a one-time marriage allowance from the Director of Imperial Theatres. The newly-weds were given 350 roubles—nearly the amount of Ivanov's annual salary just a year before.[20]

Ivanov's bride, Vera Alexandrovna Lyadova, was born on 15 March 1839 to an important family of musicians.[21] Her father Alexandre Lyadov, about whom Ivanov wrote in his memoirs, was principal conductor of the Petersburg Imperial Ballet. Her uncle Konstantin was a conductor of the Imperial Russian Opera there, and a second uncle, Mikhail, inspired great hopes as a musician before his early death. Like Ivanov, Lyadova was a prodigious child, perhaps even more so than her fiancé. And like Ivanov, her talents pressed her in more than one direction. She was a dancer, actress, and singer.

Lyadova entered the theatre school at the age of 10, and (exceptionally) took singing lessons in addition to classes in acting and dance. At 12 she sang couplets in the opera *Lesta, Rusalka of the Dnieper* seventeen times in three months. At her graduation in 1858 she was at a crossroads, having to decide which path to take. At the urging of her relatives, she chose ballet.

As a student Lyadova occupied a noticeable place in the Petersburg company, and as an artist a prominent one. She and Ivanov made frequent appearances on stage together, as on 3 December 1857 in the bolero from Auber's *La Muette de Portici* which Ivanov staged—possibly his earliest composition—and on 29 April 1858 in a waltz in the ballet *Robert and Bertram, or The Two Thieves*, produced in St Petersburg by Felix Kshesinsky.

Early in her career Lyadova danced in the summer theatre at Krasnoe Selo.[22] 'On Thursday Miss Kosheva danced, then Miss Lyadova, as is her custom, with the same lovely grace and airiness as always. Miss Lyadova was especially well applauded, who in recent times decidedly stands in the first ranks of the Petersburg ballet.'[23] On 12 April 1860 she and Ivanov appeared in a dance, 'La guirlande de fleurs', at the first performance of

---

[19] Ivanov Service Record, fo. 17.   [20] Ibid., fos. 20–5.

[21] The biographical account of Lyadova which follows is taken from *Borisoglebsky*, i. 237–8; *Krasovskaya*, 342–3; P. Medv., 'Vera Alexandrovna Lyadova. Biographical Essay', *Vsemirnaya illyustratsiya*, vol. 3 (issue for 4 Apr. 1870), 247–8, 250; Alexandre Alexeyevich Pleshcheyev, *Nash balet* [Our Ballet], 2nd edn. (St Petersburg: Pereyaslavtsev and Pleshcheyev, 1899) [hereafter: *Pleshcheyev*], 190–1, 197; S[ergei] N[ikolaevich] Khudekov, *Istoriya tantsev* [The History of Dances], vol. iv (Petrograd, 1918) [hereafter: *Khudekov*], 82, 100; V. A. Bryanskii, 'V. A. Lyadova (1870—Mar.—1920)', *Zhizn' iskusstva* [Life of Art], nos. 419–21 (1920); and other sources as noted.

[22] On this theatre see Roland John Wiley, 'The Imperial Theatre at Krasnoe Selo', *Dancing Times*, 82/988 (Jan. 1993), 352–4.

[23] *Teatral'nyi i muzykal'nyi vestnik*, 22 June 1858, p. 287.

Marius Petipa's *The Blue Dahlia*; barely two weeks after that, 'The benefit artist Mr Kshesinsky danced with Miss Lyadova the mazurka *Souvenir de Varsovie* with such animation that the auditorium, electrified, demanded an encore and showered the dancers with deafening applause.'[24] Later still in that year Lyadova appeared as Lise in *La Fille mal gardée*.

Lyadova's ballet repertoire was diverse, but probably most celebrated for two works by Arthur Saint-Léon. In the concluding divertissement of nationalities in *The Little Humpbacked Horse* (1864) she and Alexey Bogdanov represented the Ukraine in a scene and dance. Sergey Khudekov remembered her as

especially pleasing. The originality of her costume, the graceful swishing of her apron, and finally the unexpected kiss at the end called forth a storm of applause. This dance was always repeated, and Miss Lyadova, as if to call attention to it, always kissed her partner in an especially juicy fashion, audible throughout the hall.[25]

The other ballet, *Graziella* (1860), came to Lyadova after Carolina Rosati, who first performed the leading role, had left the stage. Again Khudekov:

Her face was lively, her gesture beautiful. She successfully performed the leading role in the short ballet *Graziella*, where together with [Lyubov Petrovna] Radina she danced the light cancan with a swishing of the skirts, staged by Saint-Léon. Pedant balletomanes reproached the balletmaster for this light-minded dance, inappropriate to the 'model classical' stage. But the entire auditorium relished the gestures of these two artists, who strove to give the 'cancan' a gracefully tender style, completely free of boisterousness.[26]

By choosing ballet as a career, Lyadova did not overcome the sense that a future on the lyric stage might still be hers. In 1864 she performed Fenella in Auber's *La Muette de Portici*, a role which called not for singing but for a superior actress, as it traded heavily in mime. An important date in Lyadova's reassessment was 25 October 1865, when at the request of the actress Elizaveta Matveyevna Levkeyeva she sang and acted in a vaudeville at the Alexandrinsky Theatre. Though she continued to dance for the next few years, the turning-point came in 1868. At the beginning of that year she was still drawing favourable notice at Adèle Grantzow's benefit performance: 'Among the other dances [in *Le Corsaire*], "Les Forbans" warranted the public's special approval, a very playful *pas* in which Miss Lyadova excelled, spryly fencing with sabres. . . .'[27] But the summer again

[24] *Severnaya pchela*, 23 Apr. 1860, p. 362.
[25] 'The Petersburg Ballet During the Production of *The Little Humpbacked Horse* (Recollections)', *Peterburgskaya gazeta*, 21 Jan. 1896, p. 5; trans. in *Wiley*, 274.
[26] *Khudekov*, 100.
[27] *Golos*, 27 Jan. 1868, p. 2.

found Lyadova testing her skills in drama and song at Krasnoe Selo, and in the autumn, after an extraordinary success as Helen in Offenbach's *La Belle Hélène* on 18 October, she decided that operetta was her true calling, and left the ballet.

The record will show that she was right. As a dancer Lyadova never received the extremity of adulation that was hers in operetta. In the spring of 1869, for example, so great was the demand for her performances that after carnival, with the theatres closed, Lyadova in regular dress appeared in Lenten concerts singing excerpts from her repertoire. 'When she sang the couplets [from Offenbach] beginning with the verses:

> I was a dancer,
> But there was much talent in me . . .

the public responded to this truthful *à propos* with an outburst of thunderous applause.'[28]

Her popularity continued that autumn, but she suddenly fell ill after the new year and died on 24 March 1870, at the age of 31, of now mysterious causes. Her eulogist in *World Illustration* suggests that overwork was a factor, but pleads ignorance of the medical reason. Borisoglebsky, on the other hand, reports that she died of an overdose of powerfully acting medication.[29] 'All Petersburg attended her funeral,' Khudekov recalled, 'those services are probably remembered to this day by the many literary people who took part in them during the funeral procession along Millionnaya Street.'[30] 'So great was her popularity', according to one writer, 'that many simple folk, encountering her funeral procession, said, "Look, they are burying *La Belle Hélène*!".'[31]

It is easy to imagine how Lyadova and Ivanov, who separated in July 1869, could have had a troubled marriage. The intrusive mother-in-law of

---

[28] *Vsemirnaya illyustratsiya*, vol. 3 (issue for 4 Apr. 1870), p. 248.

[29] Borisoglebsky goes on to relate a curious incident which may have contributed to Lyadova's early death and strained relations between her and Ivanov. Lyadova, it seems, had insignificantly discoloured teeth but perceived this problem to be a serious obstacle to her success in *La Belle Hélène*. As a result, 'Lyadova decided to have false teeth put in. Not every artist would have the resolve and the courage to replace natural teeth with false only to give pleasure in a role being performed. Enduring twelve agonizing operations and having experienced a multitude of worries at rehearsal, the artist made her appearance in a great fright, but was rewarded with extraordinary success—after each of her arias, after each of her appearances, the auditorium shook with thunderous applause. . .' (*Borisoglebsky*, i. 237). We can only wonder what medical complications would ensue from such a procedure performed in 1868, and whether a less drastic remedy might have been preferred, especially for a singer.

[30] 'The Petersburg Ballet During the Production of *The Little Humpbacked Horse* (Recollections)', *Peterburgskaya gazeta*, 21 Jan. 1896, p. 5; quoted in *Wiley*, 264–5. Lyadova's father followed her to the grave a year later to the day; among the handful of mourners who bade him farewell were Lev Ivanov and Marius Petipa.

[31] *Vsemirnaya illyustratsiya*, vol. 3 (issue for 4 Apr. 1870), p. 260.

whom Ivanov complained in his memoirs may have exacerbated personality differences between them. There were probably clashes of ambition
and rank as well: she was clearly driven to fame while he was not; she
enjoyed a higher social position than he did, based on the prominence of her
family in the artistic circles of St Petersburg; Ivanov may have objected to
her giving up ballet.

Lyadova's celebrity in operetta prompted the printing of a letter to her in
The Saint Petersburg News on 17 October 1868.[32] The writer, who signed
himself 'The Stranger', begins a harangue by acknowledging Lyadova's
quick rise to stardom in *La Belle Hélène*. His subject is not, however, her
portrayal of Helen in the theatre, but two posed commercial photographs of
scenes, ostensibly from the operetta, which the critic claimed exceeded the
bounds of discretion imposed by the public stage. Both are love scenes of
Helen and Paris. In one, the writer claims, Lyadova has bared her leg to the
last possible degree; the other depicts Menelaeus interrupting the lovers *in
flagrante delicto*. 'If I wrote here *how* he holds you,' the writer continues,
'*how* his hands are situated on your body, the editor of *The Saint Petersburg
News* would probably strike out this passage.' While Ivanov's name is not
mentioned, he enters the discussion indirectly when 'The Stranger' goes on
to compare Lyadova's unseemly poses with the elegance of groupings found
in Petipa's *Le Roi Candaule*, first performed the week before, in which
Ivanov had taken a leading role.

It is difficult to assess the validity of these complaints today (Plate 9).
'The Stranger' goes on to mention more extreme commercial photographs
which any society would find pornographic. As a self-appointed arbiter
of public life, he may have simply been the counterpart, as a music critic,
of the pedantic balletomanes who objected to Lyadova's dancing the
cancan in *Graziella*. In any event, one can imagine the effect of such a re-
buke on the virtuous Ivanov, given the Victorian public mores of the day.
That he was scandalized is hardly speculation; that he rued his wife's
change of career, and that it affected their marriage, are eminently plausible contentions.

The strain of raising a family, which is extraordinary for professional
artists, was increased in the case of Lyadova and Ivanov by the
tragedy of the couple's second surviving son, Mikhail, who could neither
hear nor speak. He was born on 21 November 1867, a year and a half before
his parents separated, when Lyadova must have been debating her career
change. One can only ponder the impact of raising this child on Ivanov's
muse, especially at those moments in his choreography where wordless
movement attains its greatest poignancy.

[32] 'Letters to Contemporaries. To Vera Alexandrovna Lyadova', *Sanktpeterburgskie vedomosti*,
17 Oct. 1868, p. 2.

First Contract to First Dancer

On 22 March 1860, his period of obligatory service completed, Lev Ivanov
sent a letter to the Director of Theatres, Privy Councillor and Cavalier
Andrey Ivanovich Saburov. He wrote in the bureaucratic jargon expected
at the time:

Serving as a dancer in the Imperial St Petersburg Theatres from 18 February 1850,
and always occupying first roles in ballets, I have continuously tried to execute
them and to perform, as is not unknown to Your Excellency, with zeal and in a satisfactory manner despite a limited salary, which at the present time does not exceed
900 r[oubles] silver per annum, although I also fulfil the duties of teacher of ballet
dances of female students in the Theatre School. And as at the present time the ten-
year period of my obligatory service has ended, I make bold to trouble Your Excellency with the most humble request, to address your kind supervisory attention to
all set forth above, and to order the concluding of the hoped-for contract with me for
the next three years, designating my full prior salary and a corresponding per-
performance fee, with one half-benefit yearly, and properly for the post of Teacher
to fix a special fee, at a level with that enjoyed by the other teachers; by such command Your Excellency will permit me still more zeal to the execution of my responsibilities, significantly relieving me of cares about my domestic needs.[33]

A notation in the upper left corner, possibly by Saburov, assigns Ivanov
the same salary as received by Alexey Bogdanov, namely 1,143 roubles per
year plus 5 roubles per performance. Ivanov was thus granted everything
he asked except a half-benefit, in a contract not for three years, but for one.

Because artists were required to indicate, six months before the expira-
tion of their contracts, their intentions about continued service, we know
Ivanov's subsequent requests from the direction. In the next three years he
asked for the following:

24 November 1860: the same salary for 3 years, 10 roubles per performance, and a
half-benefit; receives the same salary for one year, 10 roubles per performance, no
half-benefit.

23 November 1861: renewal 'with the best and [most] advantageous conditions'
without specifics; receives the same terms as the preceding year.

23 October 1862: a full salary, 10 roubles per performance, a half-benefit 'as my
colleagues and co-workers receive', and special pay for teaching duties of 800
roubles; receives a two-year contract and a rise of 400 roubles for teaching.

How are we to interpret these data? How were diligence and dedication
assessed? Understanding Ivanov's remuneration is a more complex matter
than can be accounted for in the simple résumé of a ritual negotiation. We
must pause to investigate the fiscal implications of being a Russian artist.

[33] Ivanov Service Record, fo. 27.

Ten years of obligatory service were required of graduates of the theatre school in return for their education. Because young students took part in productions, the direction began to collect its debt long before its charges graduated, under the guise of providing practical experience.

This policy was seen not as a fiscal sleight of hand, but as part of a familial approach to management. The Director of Theatres, typically a nobleman or person of high civil rank, was patriarch over a large company of artists who were perceived as his family. As a system of management, patriarchy had its drawbacks and advantages. It permitted an extraordinary measure of indulgence, ensured job security, protected laggards, forgave debt and irresponsible behaviour, and launched many marriages which took promising women artists away from the stage before their potential had been reached. It also shielded Russian artists from the vagaries and pitfalls of life in the ruthlessly competitive world where foreign stars had to find their way.

Among the drawbacks pay was low, and subject for decades to an iron-clad salary schedule based on rank. Yet progress through the ranks was slowed by elder colleagues remaining in service as long as possible, a particular frustration for dancers whose physical prime was harder earned and sooner passed than that of actors and musicians. Incentive was easily blunted under these circumstances. Another drawback was the expectation that artists should not complain about the flaws of patriarchy. This would be an affront to solidarity, to the providers of free education.

The administration of the imperial theatres succeeded with this approach as long as the theatre school could supply most or all the talent required to operate its companies. Paying the occasional specialist foreigner—a conductor or choreographer—a very large salary was acceptable. But the appetite of Russian audiences for foreign celebrities, whetted by the phenomenal success of Italian opera throughout much of the nineteenth century, introduced market pressures into the system with which it was not equipped to deal. Highly touted visitors with international reputations commanded princely fees which habitually placed the theatre budget in deficit. The problem, however, was not purely budgetary. As the number of foreign artists increased, the disparity between their salaries and the salaries of native artists produced a polarized system of compensation discriminatory to Russians whose talents were separated from the imports by a far narrower margin than their pay. The later nineteenth century witnessed the gradual breakdown of Russian artists' passivity to this problem, acknowledged by the administration in the reforms of the 1880s, which doubled and tripled their salaries. Later still, artists like Mathilde Kshesinskaya and Anna Pavlova officially retired soon after they had met their service obligation so they could negotiate with the direction to return to their own theatre as touring artists, for fees similar to those paid to foreigners. By then, Russian artists had become unabashedly entrepreneurial when their obligatory service was completed.

Russian balletic entrepreneurship was just beginning when Ivanov drafted his first contract in 1860. The Director, Saburov, if ever the question crossed his mind, would surely have concluded that Ivanov was no entrepreneur. Was then his treatment of Ivanov prejudicial? Was his failure to grant all of Ivanov's requests evidence of discrimination?

In fact, Saburov responded in a favourable way. Having no warrant to treat Ivanov as a foreign celebrity, he paid the young man a compliment by linking his salary to that of Alexey Bogdanov. While Bogdanov's later history in the company is undistinguished—he was arrogant, an indifferent performer, and fancied himself Petipa's rival as a choreographer—for Ivanov to be compared with him in 1860 was a recommendation. Bogdanov was Ivanov's senior by four years, and by 1860 had outperformed him on several fronts. Ivanov danced a *pas de deux* with Tatyana Smirnova in 1853; the year before Bogdanov had toured with her through the provincial towns of Russia. When Ivanov was offered the régisseurship of the company which stayed in St Petersburg during the coronation of Alexandre II—itself an approving sign from the direction—Bogdanov not only took the job, but also demonstrated his capacities as a producer by reviving a ballet, putting together several divertissements and dances for six operas. Bogdanov, moreover, had proved his worth outside the Petersburg ballet community, receiving 1,700 roubles a year in the employment of a Russian prince.[34] In effect, Ivanov was being paid like an entrepreneur without having to be one.

For a time the linkage continued. The increase in Ivanov's performance fee in 1861, for example, coincided with a similar increase for Bogdanov. Yet Ivanov pressed his own terms, apparently hoping that persistence would be rewarded. In time he received a long-term contract and a benefit performance. The exception apparently proved the rule. The year Ivanov did not specify his wants, the tone of his request was more emphatic:

With the coming of 1 April 1862 the term of my contract is ended. Wanting to renew the same for the future, I make bold most humbly to ask Your Excellency to turn Your gracious attention to my diligent service; for, as it is well known to Your Excellency that I fill two posts: as Dancer in ballets and as teacher of the art of dance in the Theatre School; besides that I have always tried to be useful to the Direction in the production of dances for various operas and was always punctual in my service; as a consequence of this I most humbly ask Your Excellency to renew my contract

---

[34] *Borisoglebsky*, i. 182.

with the best and [most] advantageous conditions for me; for such will compel me to be ever more diligent in my service, and useful for the Direction.[35]

This effort having gained him nothing, we are left to wonder where Ivanov's dealings about salary might have led had no new circumstance intervened to force a change in the direction's response. But something did happen, in which Ivanov had no part, yet which enhanced his stature and altered the course of his professional life. The direction's action on this occasion, given the options at its disposal, may be seen as another testimonial to Ivanov's worth.

In March 1862 Marius Petipa was appointed balletmaster of the Russian imperial theatres after the extraordinary success of his ballet *The Pharaoh's Daughter*. He gave up dancing as a result, and Ivanov took his place as first dancer and mime. This substitution made Ivanov the leading male dancer of the Petersburg ballet in the 1860s, and continued as his principal appointment before becoming régisseur of the company in 1882. A subtle implication in this promotion is easily overlooked. As Petipa withdrew from dancing, management broke with long-standing policy. Petipa, a foreign dancer, had been called to Russia to replace another foreign dancer. When the need arose to replace him, the opportunity to search for a new foreigner and to pay accordingly was again at hand. The direction declined to do this, putting its faith instead in Lev Ivanov.

In the Public Eye: Ivanov on Stage

Ivanov's situation in the 1860s and 1870s was comparable to Petipa's in the 1850s: however indispensable first male dancers may have been, their history is obscure if no one writes about them. Petipa and Ivanov were much before the public eye in the periods indicated—partnering, miming, dancing—but these were times when choreographers attracted more attention. Ivanov's star was obscured in the 1860s by the rivalry of Petipa and Saint-Léon, and by the lustre of ballerinas, who, aligned with one or the other choreographer, nourished the balletomanic instinct for noisy rivalry.[36]

In his time Ivanov danced with an impressive roster of ballerinas: 'He took part as an artist', Pleshcheyev wrote, 'in a number of ballets, performing classical and character roles with the ballerinas [Fanny] Cerrito, [Henrietta] Dor, [Amalia] Ferraris, [Adèle] Grantzow, [Marfa Nikolaevna]

---

[35] Ivanov Service Record, fo. 39.

[36] These rivalries are described in Khudekov, 'The Petersburg Ballet during the Production of *Little Humpbacked Horse* (Recollections)', *Peterburgskaya gazeta*, 14 Jan. 1896, p. 5; trans. in *Wiley*, 252–60; excerpts from various Russian sources on the same subject are translated in Wiley, *Tchaikovsky's Ballets* (Oxford: Clarendon Press, 1985), 10–17.

Muravyova, [Maria Sergeyevna] Petipa, [Ekaterina] Vazem, [Alexandra Nikolaevna] Kemmerer, [Evgenia] Sokolova and others.'[37] The arch of Ivanov's dancing career (detailed in Appendix A) spanned his student days in 1850 to an appearance in the Hermitage Theatre in 1900; it began in obscurity, grew ascendant in his competition with Alexey Bogdanov, and reached its high point with the call to replace Marius Petipa. After 1882 and 1885, Ivanov's duties as régisseur and balletmaster reduced his performance activity, though he continued to take mimed roles well into the 1880s.

Finding evidence of Ivanov's activity as a dancer requires searching a vast literature for the merest references. A substantial first-performance review of the period would give the story of a ballet, praise the ballerina, and refer to male dancers in passing. The following account of the first performance of Petipa's *La Bayadère* (1877) is typical. After a long paragraph of adulation for Ekaterina Vazem as Nikia, and two more devoted to the other women in the cast, the men are given a remark apiece in approximate order of seniority:

Of the performers of the men's roles, Mr [Christian] Johanson, who represented the Rajah of Golconda with purely oriental seriousness and suavity of gesture, was very fine, and the veteran of our ballet stage Mr [Nikolay] Golts, who transmitted, with his customary talent for mime and nobility of gesture bequeathed by the traditions of the old classical school, the mental agitations of the enamoured brahmin. With great animation and even drama Mr L[ev] Ivanov performed his customary role of balletic *jeune premier* and Mr [Pavel] Gerdt I, as before, brought forth thunderous applause for the lightness and precision of his dances.[38]

The public record of Ivanov's dancing career is a chronicle of such ritual mentions. Most were neutral, as this remark about Petipa's *A Regency Marriage* (1858): 'The characters of these dancers [that is, Anna Prikhunova, Marfa Muravyova, Nadezhda Amosova II, and Maria Sergeyevna Petipa] are still more clearly displayed in the very nice *pas de sept*, which they dance with Mr Johanson, Mr Petipa, and Mr Ivanov.'[39] Ivanov might reflect the ballerina's glory by being the other person on stage. In Saint-Léon's *The Lily* (1869), 'Miss Grantzow's best is the *grand pas* in the second act, which she performs with Mr Ivanov. . . .'[40] Or he might contribute to breakthroughs of technique, as at Grantzow's benefit performance in January 1868:

During the *chanson à boire* [from Saint-Léon's *Fiammetta*], Miss Grantzow stands on a little stool, supported by Mr Ivanov, and makes a double pirouette on one pointe; Miss Muravyova and Miss Lebedeva did the same, but to execute this

---

[37] *Novoe vremya*, 3 Dec. 1899, p. 3.   [38] *Golos*, 26 Jan. 1877, p. 3.
[39] *Teatral'nyi i muzykal'nyi vestnik*, 28 Dec. 1858, p. 605.
[40] *Golos*, 23 Oct. 1869, pp. 2–3.

choreographic difficulty they required the assistance of two dancers, Mr Ivanov and Mr Bogdanov.[41]

Whether by directive or out of lifelong dedication to the advancement of Russian artists, Ivanov would partner students making important débuts. 'I cannot remain silent about the charming student Muravyova, who has already managed to attract widespread attention,' wrote the critic Mavriky Rappaport in 1856 of Saint-Léon's *La Vivandière*, 'She performed "La Diablotine" with Mr Ivanov, and created an absolute delight.'[42] At a performance of *Le Corsaire* in 1868 he brought forward Alexandra Shaposhnikova in a similar way, who went on to distinction as classical solo-ist: 'Miss Shaposhnikova, a student of the theatre school who was making her début on that evening, with great precision danced a quite difficult *pas* with Mr L. Ivanov.'[43]

Ivanov's record as a mime is mixed. Occasionally he could not overcome his demure personality to project a role forcefully and was called to ac-count, as in his portrayal of Count Milenne in Petipa's *Camargo* (1872):

Mr Ivanov is a most proper but too modest Count Milenne, as this Don Juan of the court of Louis XV was said to be a desperately frivolous and foppish man who plumed himself with aristocratic ways, riches, conquests over the fairer sex, and his active participation in the royal orgies of Versailles.[44]

When Virginia Zucchi made her début in the imperial ballet in *The Pharaoh's Daughter*, one reviewer quipped in passing that 'Mr Ivanov, in the role of the Pharaoh, suffered from a lack of magnificence'.[45] Yet in Petipa's *Zoraya* (1881), 'Mr L. Ivanov excellently performed the role of the chief of the tribe of Almagadases (?!) He had dignity, and in addition he dis-played significant energy in a scene of the sixth tableau.'[46] Another critic of this ballet included Ivanov among artists who magnificently conveyed the dramatic side of their roles, and who were in no need of praise.[47]

When mime and dance were both required, Ivanov performed the first and excelled in the second. He was at his best while dancing, and loved it most. His role in Petipa's *Le Roi Candaule* comprised both arts, with a pre-dictable result. Vazem recalled:

Speaking of *Candaule*, I cannot but recall how L. I. Ivanov, who held the post of *premier*, rehearsed the role of King Candaule's retainer, Gyges. In the first act a good half of his role was reduced to striding back and forth in front of the tent of

[41] *Peterburgskaya gazeta*, 23 Jan. 1868, p. 3.
[42] *Muzykal'nyi i teatral'nyi vestnik*, 29 Apr. 1856, p. 326.
[43] *Novoe vremya*, 30 Jan. 1868, p. 1.
[44] *Peterburgskaya gazeta*, 19 Dec. 1872, p. 3.
[45] *Peterburgskaya gazeta*, 12 Nov. 1885, p. 3.
[46] *Peterburgskaya gazeta*, 3 Feb. 1881, p. 2.   [47] *Golos*, 3 Feb. 1881, p. 3.

Queen Nisia, from whom he later fends off barbarians. Astonishingly modest in his nature, he stubbornly performed this function of a simple extra. Petipa understood the awkwardness of the situation thus created.

'Don't worry, Ivanov,' he told him in his broken Russian, 'In last act you will have large mimed scene.'

We rehearsed to the last act. It turned out that all of Gyges's large scene consisted of his making an entrance [and] sitting on a throne, whence he watched the divertissement. For a long time we made jokes over this episode. . . .[48]

The press critique of Ivanov as Gyges affirms this backstage view. Sergey Khudekov, early in his career as a journalist, observed in an extensive notice of *Le Roi Candaule*, 'As for Mr L. Ivanov (Gyges), I would advise him to put more energy and life [into his portrayal] and not to be so antipathetic on stage.'[49] Ivanov was on stage again in the third scene of this ballet, less active still, lost in the spectacle:

Of the scenes *à grand spectacle* the triumphal procession (in the third scene) deserves mention, in which Candaule and Gyges ride in a golden chariot drawn by a pair of white horses. Queen Nisia, led in on an elephant, with horsemen astride it, the king's captives, men and women slaves, vestals, young girls scattering flowers about the stage—more than 200 persons—artists, dancers, students, extras.[50]

When Ivanov danced in this ballet, the critical tone warmed: 'Miss Kantsyreva, this *ingénue* of our ballet troupe, with her innate playfulness and wholly childlike naïveté, performed a shepherds' dance with L. Ivanov which recalled a pastoral scene in the genre of Watteau.'[51]

By many accounts, character dancing was Ivanov's great strength, variously praised but generally adding a flourish to Petipa's first decade as chief balletmaster. As Basile to Alexandra Vergina's Kitri in *Don Quixote*, Ivanov performed a Spanish Dance, 'La Morena', in Act II. According to one reviewer it was 'not bad at all and colourful, but executed rather flabbily'.[52] In Act II of *The Adventures of Peleus*, 'Miss Kemmerer performed an "Infernal Dance" with Mr L. Ivanov, with such genuinely demonic shadings that it caused spontaneous applause.'[53] In *The Daughter of the Snows* (1879), the 'Norwegian Wedding Dance executed by Miss Kemmerer and Mr Ivanov was covered in applause'.[54] According to Borisoglebsky, Ivanov and Nikolay Golts were Alexandra Kemmerer's best cavaliers.[55] Of *Roxana* (1878) a critic noted: 'The ballet ends with character dances, all of which produced the grandest effect, especially "la

---

[48] *Vazem*, 69.   [49] *Peterburgskii listok*, 19 Oct. 1868, p. 1.
[50] *Golos*, 19 Oct. 1868, p. 1.
[51] Ibid.
[52] *Golos*, 14 Nov. 1871, p. 1.
[53] *Peterburgskaya gazeta*, 20 Jan. 1876, p. 1.
[54] *Journal de Saint-Pétersbourg*, 12 Jan. 1879, p. 1.   [55] *Borisoglebsky*, i. 242.

Raviola", performed by the corps de ballet headed by the impetuous Miss Radina, perfectly seconded by Mr Ivanov. This dance was encored. . . .'[56] In *Mlada*, the same two dancers performed a gypsy dance 'in the costumes of the gypsies one can see in suburban restaurants; Mr Ivanov assimilated all their manners and gestures, and Miss Radina—she is fire, attractiveness, life itself, languor and unrestrained passion'.[57]

It is easy to extend the list. Ivanov played Brighella in a *commedia dell'arte* scene in Petipa's *The Parisian Market* (1859); he was the leader of the gypsy band in Saint-Léon's *The Pearl of Seville* (1862); he jauntily slapped heel to heel in a series of Cossack cabrioles in the divertissement of Saint-Léon's *The Little Humpbacked Horse* (1864); he made (as Vazem recalled) 'a very beautiful jump from the hills to the stage' in the same choreographer's *The Lily* (1869), which left a great impression on the spectators; and as the dancing master Milon in Petipa's *The King's Command* (1887), he conducted a lesson with his violin, as he did in real life (Plate 5). 'I remember L. I. Ivanov long ago,' Pleshcheyev recalled, 'He was indisputably an outstanding artist, and in character dances virtually the best.'[58]

While memory, diligence, and musicality all enhanced Ivanov's artistry, these virtues were offset by a serious physical drawback: Ivanov was nearsighted. Vazem wrote of this:

Ivanov was a first-class, artistically polished, extremely experienced classical dancer-soloist, with dancing that was very pleasant for the eye, calm, and correct; he was also an excellent partner for a ballerina. Unfortunately, in the latter capacity he was hampered by his short-sightedness. I do not recall any particular brilliance in Ivanov's classicism; he managed all his dances equally well, never spoiling anything. He loved to dance in the character genre, was very effective and elegant in it, but could not, of course, compare with Petipa in this regard. As a mime artist he played the longest list of roles in the course of his service, and was always in his place in them, imposing and fairly expressive, but of the roles of his broad repertoire none is engraved with particular clarity on my memory. His gift shone with an even light, without flashes.

Deeply devoted to his art, Ivanov was a model of an uncommonly honourable artist, conscientious about his art and profoundly disturbed if he thought that something had gone wrong in a performance because of him. I shall give one extremely revealing example. Once in the ballet *Don Quixote* the ballerina [Alexandra] Vergina, who was dancing with him, made a turn too early. Ivanov with his myopia did not immediately notice this, did not manage to catch her, and she fell. The cavalier here was not at fault. Very musical by nature, he knew that according to the music the time for this ill-starred turn had not yet come, and that nothing could be done about the ballerina's self-willed haste. In the company and the public, however, under the influence of the 'Verginist' party, a voice was raised

---

[56] *Journal de Saint-Pétersbourg*, 4 Feb. 1878, p. 2.
[57] *Peterburgskaya gazeta*, 4 Dec. 1879, p. 3.   [58] *Novoe vremya*, 3 Dec. 1899, p. 3.

against Lev Ivanovich, who was made to shoulder all the blame for this incident. Having utterly lost his head, the unhappy dancer truly thought himself guilty and did not want to endure the shame. Rushing home, he took a revolver and was at the point of putting a bullet into his brain. Fortunately his wife rushed over to him, wresting the weapon from his hand.[59]

Vazem's account is inaccurate in one detail: this performance, which took place on 24 October 1872, occurred while Ivanov was a widower; whoever saved him could not have been his wife.

A reviewer provided further details of the incident. The fall left Alexandra Vergina bleeding from her left elbow and leg. The curtain was lowered, Act II not completed, and later scenes were omitted if they involved complex dances for the ballerina, causing the ballet to be shortened by half. To that writer there was no question of responsibility:

While sympathizing sincerely with Miss Vergina, we observe nevertheless, in the name of fairness, that the cause of this unfortunate event was the ballerina herself. The fact is that Miss Vergina sometimes has the unfortunate habit of dancing counter to the beat, of not completing a step, and in general of displaying superfluous haste. Thus, even in the incident at hand, Miss Vergina sped up somewhat and finished her *enchaînement* a whole bar ahead of the orchestra. Mr Ivanov, not expecting such inexcusable haste and knowing well the music of the adagio, did not manage to support in some impromptu fashion the ballerina who had left the orchestra behind. . . .

. . . [W]e have attended ballet performances for several years and have seen Mr L. Ivanov hundreds of times in various *pas de deux*. Mr Ivanov, even when dancing with first-class European ballerinas, has always distinguished himself as an adroit partner in supporting the *danseuse* during the performance of the most difficult adagios. . . . [H]e knows dance rhythm down to the finest details.[60]

The composite of Ivanov's honourable mentions over the years supports the conclusion that he was a competent, dependable mime, a deft partner, and a superior, occasionally stellar dancer. In the year of his appointment as second balletmaster, he is still described by the dutiful cliché as 'indisputably an adornment of the ballet',[61] and counted as one of 'the greatest strengths of our ballet', who contributed to harmonious artistic ensemble.[62] Sergey Khudekov concurred:

As a dancer, as a mime, L. Ivanov did not stand out for any special features; he did not move to the fore, he was considered of great 'usefulness'. Not one role did he

---

[59] *Vazem*, 116–17. Khudekov also referred to Ivanov's vision problems: 'L. Ivanov was very near-sighted. He acknowledged that this defect much hindered him on stage, both during the supporting of women dancers during their risky combinations and in the performance of mimed scenes. In exchange for this limiting defect, nature rewarded him with a musical memory which gave him good service in the composition of classical dances' (*Khudekov*, 172).

[60] *Peterburgskaya gazeta*, 26 Oct. 1872, pp. 2–3.

[61] *Peterburgskaya gazeta*, 9 Feb. 1885, p. 3.   [62] *Novosti i birzhevaya gazeta*, 10 Oct. 1885, p. 3.

spoil, nor did he ever bring one role created by him into the spotlight. Everywhere he was a seemly, elegant partner of women dancers, trying always to remain in the shadows. Modesty was the outstanding characteristic of this artist, who always danced 'properly', 'correctly', without resorting to virtuoso feats characteristic of the Italian school.[63]

Ivanov had hardly begun to flourish as Petipa's successor when a rival came upon the scene whose rise to prominence coincided with his own decline. Of German extraction, the son of a guildmaster, Pavel Andreyevich Gerdt was born in 1844, graduated from the theatre school in 1864, and went on to one of the most distinguished careers in the history of Russian ballet, performing from his student days in the 1850s until November 1916. The end of Gerdt's obligatory service in 1870 coincided with Marius Petipa's advance to sole balletmaster of the Petersburg company, for whose works he became the most eloquent spokesman. In 1870 Ivanov's wife died, and he first began to draw a pension.

Ivanov and Gerdt had much in common. They served the same company for over forty years, and also shared personality traits: both were gentle, even-handed, and somewhat stubborn. Both were fine artists utterly devoted to ballet but lacklustre teachers. The difference between them lay in the margin that separates a star from an eminently capable artist. Expressed in terms of their parts in Petipa's *The Two Stars*, Ivanov was Endymion to Gerdt's Apollo.

From the beginning of Gerdt's dancing career, he was consistently praised in the press where Ivanov drew no more than polite notice. Despite Ivanov's superior rank, some kind of competition was bound to develop between them, and it took on a distinctive pattern. As early as *Le Roi Candaule* (1868) and continuing with *Don Quixote* (1871) and *Camargo* (1872) and *The Butterfly* (1874) to *La Bayadère* (1877), Ivanov played the leading male part in the drama while Gerdt was the ballerina's anonymous partner in classical dances unrelated to the narrative. (When his own time came, Gerdt was treated in a similar way: in the first lakeside scene of *Swan Lake* the young Alexandre Oblakov rendered the *pas de deux à trois* by partnering Pierina Legnani while the 51-year-old Gerdt mimed.) In a given *pas* Gerdt would demonstrate artistry superior to Ivanov's in difficult, beautifully executed variations.

For a time Ivanov was protected in this arrangement by his rank and ten years of seniority over Gerdt. In the 1870s, however, containing Gerdt's extraordinary talent for the sake of Ivanov's rank became increasingly untenable. The reasons were plain enough: Gerdt's youth, his talent, and his peak physical conditioning. A photograph of Ivanov as Solor in *La Bayadère*

[63] *Khudekov*, 172.

makes clear to the inexperienced eye how he had lapsed in this regard (see Plate 4). The consequences were predictable. In an early cast list for *A Midsummer Night's Dream* (1876) Petipa crossed out Ivanov's name as the artist to portray Oberon, and wrote Gerdt's name in its place.[64] By the end of the decade, Gerdt had taken over as first dancer in fact and name. Ivanov was thenceforth cast in mimed parts and in character dances. While he still enjoyed the title of 'first dancer', his dancing career was on the wane. By the end of the century, Gerdt's elegance as a classical dancer, Christian Johanson's class of perfection, and Enrico Cecchetti's infusion of acrobatic technique had produced a renaissance of male dancing in Russian ballet.

Ivanov as Dancer and the Direction

Had the competition between Gerdt and Ivanov gone no further than how they were treated in reviews, it would hardly warrant mention. By all accounts free of malice and jealousy, Ivanov doubtless applauded Gerdt's rise to stardom as a colleague, but it must have affected his own artistic 'I' as a dancer. It also reckoned in his dealings with the direction when Ivanov, perhaps injudiciously, would justify a request for some amenity by pointing out that Gerdt was already receiving it.

In his memoirs Ivanov wrote that he advanced 'by accident'. Apparently offered in innocence, this remark obscures a complex and not altogether clear relationship between Ivanov and the direction from the 1860s to his appointment as régisseur. It is the period from which accusations of discrimination against him are most easily justified.

For someone advanced by accident, Ivanov became an increasingly inventive agent for himself as the years passed. On 11 October 1864, for example, he replaced Petipa as Taor, the leading male part in *The Pharaoh's Daughter*; his request to the Director for a new contract, sent two months later, includes an increase of 10 roubles in his per-performance fee and a paid leave in the summer.[65] A similar request two years later shows a considerable advance in sophistication over his prior effort. This letter reads in part:

As a consequence of repeated testimonials of supervisory persons, and also of Your Excellency, that the designation of per-performance fees and benefit performances is an extreme burden on the Direction, I agree to the continuation of service in the Direction, without receiving per-performance fees and benefits, but with the condition that a contract be concluded with me for three years, with a salary of 4,000

[64] Moscow, Theatre Museum named after A. A. Bakhrushin, *fond* 205 [hereafter: *TMB 205*], Inventory no. 541.

[65] Ivanov Service Record, fo. 54.

roubles per annum (which constitutes nearly the salary I am presently receiving), and the designation of time in the summer after the example of my co-workers, a contractual three-month leave with the retention of pay.

The petitioning of Your Excellency concerning the concluding of a new contract with me on these conditions gives me the means to serve three years, in the course of which the completion of my twenty years of service with the Direction will occur; for my part I shall attempt still more to devote myself and my labours to the benefit of the Direction.[66]

In this case, the direction should not be faulted for refusing Ivanov (which it did), having reason enough on the basis of simple arithmetic. At the time he wrote this letter Ivanov was making 1,140 roubles as a dancer, 400 roubles as a teacher, 10 roubles per performance, and he had just been granted his first benefit. In the two calendar years preceding his letter there had been sixty-five and sixty-eight ballet performances in the regular season; taking sixty-seven as an average, and assuming that Ivanov performed in all of them, this added 670 roubles to his income. The average return to Ivanov in the first three benefit performances for which his service record contains figures (1866–8) was 438 roubles. He was thus asking for 4,000 roubles and a paid summer leave when his income was about 2,650 roubles. The effective increase of 50 per cent amounts to even more when the value is added of services from which he is asking to be exempt. Far from being 'nearly the salary' he was already receiving, this figure represented a grandiose rise, and the direction responded accordingly.

A summary of Ivanov's remuneration during his heyday as first dancer shows him achieving mixed results. He had some successes, to be sure. He requested and was given a benefit performance to mark fifteen years of service, after which a yearly benefit was included in his regular contract. He managed after several years to increase his fee per performance from 10 to 15 roubles. But two points, one fiscal, one administrative, do not accord with Ivanov's stature as principal dancer and mime. The first is that between 1860 and 1882 his salary as a dancer was never raised. The affirmation of his abilities implicit in his replacing Petipa had no corresponding fiscal expression. Perhaps it was entangled in an inflexible pay scale. Ivanov suffered further indignity when he applied for a pension after twenty years of service. The pension was granted, in the amount of Ivanov's salary (1,143 roubles per year), but by administrative policy the next two years of service were construed as 'free' labour which Ivanov donated in 'gratitude' to the state. In other words, he received a pension but had to work for it. His salary was thereby reduced to 400 roubles for teaching, per-performance fees, and benefit receipts. For two years he could not draw his pension plus an additional salary for continuing to work.

[66] Ibid., fo. 68.

The second point, also curious, represents more an affront to Ivanov's ego than to his pocketbook. In the entire run of his contracts during this period, all but one ran for a single year (the exception, for two years, came at the beginning of his appointment as principal dancer in 1863). Yet Ivanov repeatedly asked for three-year contracts, which were normal for Petipa and others, including Bogdanov. Advanced by accident? Possibly, but through no lack of personal effort. Ivanov tried to further his cause, but the direction responded to its own prerogatives.

Discrimination is one but not the only explanation for this treatment. Fiscal economy—a perennial concern of theatre managers—was a preeminent goal in these years. In 1867 a new Director of Theatres was appointed, Stepan Alexandrovich Gedeonov, son of Alexandre Mikhailovich Gedeonov, who had served in this capacity between 1833 and 1858. This change alone does not explain the management's lack of generosity towards Ivanov. From Borisoglebsky we learn that Gedeonov *fils*, though an able administrator, was especially devoted to pictorial art (he had been appointed Director of the Imperial Hermitage in 1863), and deferred to his assistant, Baron Karl Karlovich Kister, in the administration of the ballet.[67] Kister succeeded Gedeonov in 1875, and gave vent to a mania for economy so extreme that Alexandre III, ascending the throne in 1881, appointed Ivan Alexandrovich Vsevolozhsky to clear the wreckage left in Kister's wake. This wreckage was beginning to collect during Gedeonov's tenure, and may explain the increasingly sharp tone of instructions to issue Ivanov contracts 'with prior clauses'. During this period Petipa appealed for increases as well, all denied. He and Ivanov were surely not alone in being treated in this way.

Economy seems to have had no bearing on the management's decision to rehire Ivanov year by year. It is difficult to believe that he petitioned with no other purpose than to pester the administration. There is no indication that his job was ever in danger, but perhaps it was, or he might have thought so. Was there friction between Ivanov and the direction? The withholding of an amenity so easily granted suggests that Ivanov's seniors were dissatisfied with him. Perhaps it was discrimination, but that explanation clashes with Ivanov's stature in the company. Perhaps some aspect of Ivanov's work or personal situation about which no information survives made the direction cautious about guaranteeing his salary for periods longer than a year. Perhaps the one-year contracts were reprimands, pressure to overcome a reputed attachment to drink.[68] Or they may have been a response to another problem, evidence of which first appears in Ivanov's service record in 1863.

---

[67] *Borisoglebsky*, i. 375.   [68] *Krasovskaya*, 347.

At first glance, the letter dated 29 January of that year from 'honourable Citizen Vasily Nikitin Kovmovskoi' seems almost comical. He is a vegetable seller, and Ivanov has defaulted in payment of 17 roubles silver, 85 copecks for goods received. At a time when one could survive if modestly on 500 roubles a year, the sum in question represents a small mountain of vegetables. Ivanov's income was around 2,500 roubles and Lyadova's at least 600 at the time—certainly enough to pay for food. Something was diverting their money. The proud Lyadova may have been making inordinate demands on the family budget, or one can easily imagine problems with the children, or illness.[69] A eulogist hinted at another possibility, namely Ivanov's falling prey to hustling friends:

As a person, the late L[ev] I[vanovich] was distinguished by a rare goodness. Articulate, responsible, soft-hearted, always cheerful, he was an artist in his soul, and as an artist of the good old days was always in need of money, which he was unable to keep track of. Anybody who was broke and down on his luck took from the departed's pocket as if it were his own.[70]

By any reasonable standard Ivanov was earning enough to live comfortably, barring catastrophe, from this time until the end of his life.

Régisseur

Two other events contribute to the picture of Ivanov's life before his appointment as régisseur, one happy, one sorrowful. In 1873, two coryphées were transferred to St Petersburg from Moscow, and both ended up marrying balletmasters. Lyubov Leonidovna Savitskaya became Marius Petipa's second wife, and Varvara Dmitrievna Malchugina became Lev Ivanov's. On 19 July 1876 Ivanov again asked the direction to certify that it had no objection to his marrying, and again requested a financial allowance. The certification came two days later; he seems not to have received another marriage allowance.[71] On 6 August 1876 *The Petersburg Gazette* announced:

In our little balletic world a few days ago the wedding took place of the first dancer Mr L. Ivanov, husband of the late V. A. Lyadova, and the ballet dancer Miss Malygina [*sic*], who some two years ago was transferred to Petersburg from the Moscow ballet troupe.

[69] In the direction's contract with Ivanov that became effective on 7 Mar. 1872, the standard clause on illness, whereby it reserved the right to withhold pay if a debilitating illness kept him from performing more than three months, has been changed to three weeks (Ivanov Service Record, fo. 107).

[70] *Peterburgskii listok*, 14 Dec. 1901, p. 3.

[71] Ivanov Service Record, fos. 129–30.

Three children were born of Ivanov and Malchugina: Serafima on 29 July 1877, Alexandre on 20 August 1878, and Maria on 24 March 1883. At Alexandre's baptism, Lyubov Savitskaya stood as godparent, and at Maria's Fyodor Ivanovich Bazilevsky, a balletomane celebrated for his wealth.[72]

The assassination of Alexandre II in March 1881 was a shock to the Russian nation. The official mourning closed the theatres until the autumn, giving the company a respite from regular performances. The succession brought momentous change, benefits to the ballet, and fortuitous opportunities to Ivanov. The new Director Vsevolozhsky's mandate for reform took years to implement, but soon after the beginning of his term the artists must have known that their lives were going to change. One might suppose that Ivanov, who by 1881 had trod the boards for over thirty years, would seek some activity outside performance, disengage from his competition with Gerdt, and perhaps even retire.

A newspaper account hints at this. On 4 November 1881 the St Petersburg Society of Lovers of Theatrical Art began giving drama classes. After a year the Society had acquired patronage, expanded its course offerings, and published a report of its activities. Among the subjects and instructors listed we read, 'for the class in dancing the famous artist L. I. Ivanov'.[73]

This post may have meant no more to Ivanov than supplemental income, or a strategy to make himself more attractive to the direction. Whatever it was, by the late summer of 1882 another promotion 'by accident' had come his way in the imperial theatres, which effected the best kind of compromise: a higher salary, with performance activity reduced but not eliminated.

What happened was by no means an accident, though Ivanov was not directly involved. Alexey Bogdanov again, as twenty years earlier, helped shape Ivanov's future. Having been chief régisseur of the Petersburg ballet since 1873, the petulant Bogdanov had a falling out with Alexandre Petrovich Frolov, supervisor of the ballet company. It was one burnt bridge too many. On 24 August 1882 Frolov informed the Bureau of the Imperial Theatres that Vsevolozhsky was appointing Ivanov to fill the duties of chief régisseur.[74] In another report from Frolov, sent four days later, we read:

The Chief Régisseur of the ballet troupe Bogdanov requests release from his duties; as a consequence, proposing to designate the dancer Lev Ivanov as the person to carry out the duties of Chief Régisseur of the ballet troupe, I have the honour to re-

---

[72] Ivanov Service Record, fos. 165, 168.   [73] *Novoe vremya*, 9 May 1882, p. 3.
[74] Ivanov Service Record, fo. 153.

quest the petition of Your Excellency to present the same to the resolution of His Excellency, Mr Minister of the IMPERIAL Court.[75]

This request received favourable action, and Ivanov's salary as of 1 September 1882 was set at 5,000 roubles plus 1,000 rubles for teaching. Bogdanov was transferred to the Moscow ballet as régisseur in 1883. After six more years of wilful, at times scandalous behaviour, he retired.

Little can be said for or about Ivanov's new appointment. In passing Vazem remarked, 'Compared with Bogdanov's seething energy, Ivanov was a very sanguine, calm régisseur; he performed his duties conscientiously, and that was all.'[76] 'As régisseur he deserved the widespread, sincere sympathy of his comrades,' Pleshcheyev recalled.[77] Ivanov's temperament was mismatched with his new responsibilities, the enforcement of discipline in particular a task for which he showed little inclination.

More than at any time as a dancer, success in Ivanov's new occupation depended as much on personality as talent. His memoirs revealed that personality to be complex: affectionate, volatile, quirky. His acquaintances fill out the picture. Mathilde Kshesinskaya recalled his innocent pleasure in food:

Later, when I was already a ballerina and he would be visiting us, I discovered in him a passion not only for the violin [the playing of which had seemed to preoccupy Ivanov in class]: like many artists, he loved to eat, and unfolding his napkin would say, 'Let's have a bite.'[78]

Vazem described him as

an amazingly modest, undemanding, weak-willed, very fine, forgiving, although at times hot-tempered man. In the theatre 'Levushka' Ivanov was friend to everyone, and no one could help but be friends with this fine comrade and, as they say, 'nice man'. In private life Lev Ivanovich was not without a certain originality. Thus for example, his whole life he did not own a staff uniform other than of greenish-khaki colour, and, when it wore out, he immediately ordered for himself another just like it. Next, although he was always a family man . . . he almost never ate at home, but passed the time in restaurants. He especially liked the Restaurant Dominique on the Nevsky, across and down the street from the Kazan Cathedral. When he was régisseur, artists who wished to see him on various matters went to the Dominique, knowing fair well that they would find Ivanov there, and they were rarely mistaken.[79]

Josef Kshesinsky described Ivanov as 'beloved of all, a great talent, the best of people and a great eccentric. . . .'[80] A friend of the Kshesinsky family,[81] Ivanov would visit in the summertime:

[75] Ibid., fo. 155.   [76] *Vazem*, 130.   [77] *Novoe vremya*, 3 Dec. 1899, p. 3.
[78] *Kshesinskaya*, 23.   [79] *Vazem*, 118.   [80] *Kshesinsky*, ii. 12–13.
[81] Felix Ivanovich Kshesinsky was Ivanov's senior colleague in the company. When it was clear that he had an irrepressibly balletic daughter in Mathilde, Felix summoned Ivanov. What hap-

[A]fter lunch no one felt like going for a walk: [it was] too hot. The youths began to play *bik*,[82] croquet, lotto: the women occupied themselves with *mushki* [Russian for the English card game 'loo'], some with vint [a game like auction bridge]. L[ev] I[vanovich], my deceased brother (by my mother) Felix Teodorovich Ledé, A. A. Oblakov, the wife of Professor-Doctor O. F. Borgenhagen, and I played thus: my brother with Oblakov, and L. I. with the doctor's wife; I was an extra player and sat next to her, and the game had already been going on for an hour; everything was proper and going along happily. But then: Lev Ivanovich begins to get excited with each new hand, pulling at his cards and whispering something to somebody, getting more nervous by the minute. Then the doctor's wife says to him: 'Two hearts.' And he answers: 'I have nothing.' She shows him aces, he answers, already quick-tempered: 'I have just plain nothing,' and he did not play his hand. A new hand. L. I. looks at his cards, gets red in the face and says: 'Just you wait!' And the doctor's wife says to him: 'L. I. has no trump' (that is, three aces were out), and he suddenly threw down his cards and shouted, 'I'll get you, you abomination, you'll remember me!'

The doctor's wife was nearly in a swoon, close to tears, but then he said, utterly calmly, across the table, 'Madam, it is not you (addressing her with his hand), not you, not you. I, I, you see, here, this vile hand.' He turns up his cards, takes the queen of spades and tears it to pieces. 'Aha! I warned you!' And then, quite coolly he adjusts the pince-nez on his nose [and] turns to me: 'Joinka, pet, give us another pack of cards or find another queen of spades. Or take one from the *mushkists*. They can play *mushechka* without it, for this one really got me down.'

It turns out that the queen of spades came to him in every hand, and the other cards one could simply throw away. That's why he got boiling mad.[83]

Pleshcheyev's characterization of Ivanov as enjoying the sympathy of colleagues was seconded to a person by others who remembered him on cer-emonial occasions. 'The revered jubilee artist, loving his art, has served it honourably his whole life without ever pursuing any egotistical goal, and therefore has always enjoyed the widespread love and affection equally of artists and all others who have had occasion to get well acquainted with him.'[84] 'The honouring of L. I. Ivanov had an especially heartfelt charac-

pened next comes down to us in Ivanov's words: 'Once after rehearsal F. I. Kshesinsky asked me to come to him, explaining that he wanted to show me his younger daughter and to advise what might be done with her. "She is mad about ballet; you don't take her to the theatre and she cries, you take her and she doesn't sleep the whole night, and the whole time she tries to make a ballerina of her-self." Coming to where he was, I soon saw a 7-year-old little girl dressed in ballet costume, who, never having studied classical dance, with remarkable agility and grace went through all manner of balletic *pas* and struck various, often difficult poses. Being astonished at such passion in a child, I looked at her more intently and decided that this was an undoubted calling and that an undoubted talent was hidden in the child. "She must study," I told her father, "and study without delay. Such a love for dancing is rare, it is undoubtedly a talent which must be developed. You will see that she will be a ballerina and a celebrity"' (E. E. Kartsov, *Nashi artistki. M. F. Kshesinskaya* [Our Artistes: M. F. Kshesinskaya] (St Petersburg, 1900), quoted in *Kshesinskaya*, 378).

[82] Kshesinsky's reference is not clear; perhaps *bik* in Russian is a short form for *bilboquet* or tiddlywinks.

[83] *Kshesinsky*, ii. 22–3.   [84] *Peterburgskii listok*, 6 Dec. 1899, p. 4.

ter,' wrote yet another, 'The sympathies of the ballet troupe were expressed in that noisy applause which drowned out each greeting addressed to L[ev] I[vanovich]. The public also applauded.'[85]

In the short term, Ivanov's gentility must have provided a welcome contrast to Bogdanov. Moreover, he brought to this post, as he would to the post of balletmaster, an extraordinary knowledge of the repertoire and a memory to match. These indisputable virtues were nevertheless diminished by Ivanov's conflicting personal traits—friendliness and irascibility, creativity and lack of focus, outward pliability and dogged stubbornness within. It is easy to imagine how Ivanov the person could endear while Ivanov the régisseur could falter.

Documents from this period offer no insight into Ivanov's capacities as régisseur, but rather address a miscellany of other matters. The first of many business trips took Ivanov to Moscow in March and April of 1883, in preparation for the coronation performances in May. On 15 May 1883 he won imperial recognition—a gold medal on the Stanislav ribbon. Several entries in his service record have to do with his children. A separate residency permit was requested and granted in November 1882 for young Lev, who following in his mother's footsteps went on to become an artist in operetta, and in his father's to become a régisseur.[86] In connection with Mikhail Lvovich, we encounter another sad indication of Ivanov's finances. On 14 December 1884, the Director of the Empress Maria School for Deaf-Mutes notified the theatre management that Ivanov was over a year behind in paying educational expenses for Mikhail, who by then had finished the course of instruction. The reason for this default, especially after the reform of theatre salaries, continues to be inexplicable solely on the basis of Ivanov's income.

Ivanov's dancing career was curtailed with his appointment as régisseur, and even more so with his appointment as second balletmaster. Yet he took new mimed roles. When *La Bayadère* was revived in 1884, the role of the rajah passed to him from Christian Johanson. 'Ivanov as rajah is immeasurably better than the previous performer Johanson. His talented acting brings a role to the forefront which had been left in the shadows, and the scene with the brahmin can now be considered a classic model of pantomime.'[87] A week later Ivanov was complimented again, if indirectly, when Nikolay Aistov, his replacement as the governor in *Paquita*, was found wanting by comparison.[88] In the autumn of 1891 Ivanov was still being complimented on his performance of the dancing master in Petipa's *The*

[85] *Peterburgskaya gazeta*, 6 Dec. 1899, p. 4.
[86] Ivanov Service Record, fos. 157, 159; *Borisoglebsky*, i. 192.
[87] *Novosti i birzhevaya gazeta*, 18 Sept. 1884, p. 3.
[88] *Novosti i birzhevaya gazeta*, 25 Sept. 1884, p. 3.

King's Command.[89] Ivanov's last appearance as a dancer, which the tsar attended, was at a compensatory benefit performance on 3 January 1893 which he had been granted for replacing Petipa as choreographer of *The Nutcracker*. 'The benefit artist harked back to the old days and danced with Miss Petipa I [Marius's daughter, Marie] the famous Spanish *pas* "La chica andalusa".'[90] The old days indeed: Ivanov and Marie had performed this dance together as recently as July 1891, but the reviewer may have been referring to the *chica* performed twenty years before that in *Don Quixote*. Lyubov Radina had danced it then, in a lively costume and with dishevelled hair, a number which Carlo Blasis had described as 'the most passionate and attractive of all existing national dances transmitted by the Moors into Spain', which the Creoles loved to dance, and with which even the Spanish monks in the middle ages 'on the eve of the Christmas holidays, in public view, expressed their delight on the occasion of the Saviour's birth'.[91]

On 18 February 1885 Ivanov celebrated his thirty-fifth year of service in the theatre school with the entire company assembled. A newspaper had announced the week before that his colleagues were preparing a valuable present for him,[92] a few days later that a committee had been formed to consider an appropriate programme for the occasion.[93] The celebration was reported in the press:

Three days ago, on 18 February, a celebration with a wholly familial character took place in the ballet troupe; at midday the entire company gathered in one of the halls of the theatre school to greet their sincerely beloved régisseur, L. I. Ivanov, on the occasion of the thirty-fifth anniversary of his service on the ballet stage. His comrades and co-workers presented the deserving jubilee artist with a box of enormous dimensions, with a silver service, and during this presentation the veteran of the troupe, Mr Kseshinsky [*sic*] gave a heartfelt speech; then from two other companies, the Russian and German [dramas], laurel wreaths were presented, on the ribbons of which there were inscriptions in gold. The régisseur of the latter, Mr Bock, greeted the jubilee artist warmly. After these fully warranted ovations, boy students of the school played a march on the piano, dedicated to L. I., and girl students sang a duet, which was concluded with a reading of warm-hearted verses composed by one of the dancers of the corps de ballet. To serve thirty-five years in the backstage world, with its hidden reefs and capricious, petty vanities, as L. I. Ivanov has served, is a feat in its own right, for which one may be envied. In general a genuine sympathy towards the jubilee artist was expressed in this honouring, both as to a talented artist and to a human being with a rare, beautiful spirit.[94]

A rival newspaper presented variants of detail:

[89] *Peterburgskii listok*, 2 Sept. 1891, p. 3.
[90] *Novoe vremya*, 5 Jan. 1893, pp. 3–4.
[91] *Peterburgskaya gazeta*, 11 Nov. 1871, p. 3.
[92] *Peterburgskaya gazeta*, 11 Feb. 1885, p. 3.
[93] *Peterburgskaya gazeta*, 15 Feb. 1885, p. 3.
[94] *Peterburgskaya gazeta*, 20 Feb. 1885, p. 3.

The *comradely honouring* of the most senior of our ballet artists, L. I. Ivanov, who has served the choreographic art *thirty-five years*, took place yesterday at noon in the 'ballet' hall of the theatre school.

L.I. requested the direction to give him a benefit performance, but received a refusal based on the fact that supposedly benefits are given only for 20, 25, 40, and 50 years of uninterrupted service, and since the number of years (35) served by Mr Ivanov in the ballet does not correspond with the numbers of years cited, he remains without a benefit performance.

The artist's comrades nevertheless wished to show him their sympathy, and for that reason gathered, without exception: present were first dancers and ballerinas, and coryphées, and corps de ballet, and even boy and girl students of the theatre school from ballet class with their mentors.

Mr Stukolkin and Mr Gerdt led the jubilee artist into the hall. The veteran of the ballet troupe, Mr Krshesinsky [*sic*], gave the first greeting speech, presenting L.I. with a silver wreath from his colleagues; then Mr Ivanov was favoured with wreaths from the Russian drama and the German troupes, represented by Mr Bock and Mr Fichtmann. Mr Bogdanov, dancer of the corps de ballet, recited greeting verses which were affectionate in the highest degree.

In general this honouring was purely comradely, showing marks and the stamp of profound esteem and sympathy towards Mr Ivanov not only from ballet artists, but also from the men and women of our other state companies.

Mr Ivanov was touched to the depths of his soul and could not find words to thank those honouring him.

A Russian artist and man, the jubilee artist responded by inviting all who greeted him home for a festive *pirog*.[95]

What stock can we take of Ivanov's career on the eve of his appointment as balletmaster? He had achieved an eminently respectable rank and remuneration. His dancing years, buoyed at the outset by the compliment of replacing Petipa, had brought him prominence on the stage. With salary reform, his appointment at 6,000 roubles per year seems fair in light of his thirty-five years of service and the cruder realities: that Pavel Gerdt was a better dancer, and Alexey Bogdanov a more effective régisseur.

Second Balletmaster

Three issues inform the last sixteen years of Ivanov's life: his ballets and their reception, to be taken up in the next chapters; his relationship with chief balletmaster Marius Petipa; and his life outside the theatre.

Ivanov's relationship with Petipa may be put in perspective with two points. The first is Ivanov's assessement of his own abilities, expressed in the memoirs: 'although I do not possess a talent such as Mr Petipa's, I

95 *Peterburgskii listok*, 19 Feb. 1885, p. 3.

nevertheless stage ballets no worse than many other balletmasters.' The second is the direction's utterly unambiguous purpose in promoting Ivanov: to help Petipa. In a request dated 1 March 1885—eleven days after Ivanov celebrated his thirty-fifth anniversary of service—Vsevolozhsky explained to the Minister of the Imperial Court:

The numerous responsibilities placed on the Balletmaster Petipa are especially intensified by continuous rehearsals of ballets and operas, caused by the replacement of indisposed artists; as a consequence the extreme necessity is recognized to name a second balletmaster to help Mr Petipa.

Presenting this to Your Excellency's consideration, I have the honour to solicit permission to designate as second Balletmaster Chief Régisseur of the ballet troupe Ivanov, and to assign as Chief Régisseur of the ballet troupe in his place the former Régisseur of the Italian opera company, di Segni. . . .[96]

There is no hint here of equal status with Petipa, or of any expectation that Ivanov is to create his own works. While some may construe 'second balletmaster' to mean that Ivanov was entitled to some autonomy as a choreographer, nothing in the appointment suggests this, nor does the term, here at its point of origin, connote anything demeaning. The relevant passage of Ivanov's first contract as balletmaster (which ran, incidentally, for three years) is only slightly more open-ended than Vsevolozhsky's request. It states that Ivanov 'is obliged to perform on the stage of the IMPERIAL Theatres in Petersburg and Moscow all roles assigned to him, as well as all those obligations which will be commissioned from him by the Direction as second balletmaster'.[97]

The opinions, mostly of artists who thought that Petipa maltreated Ivanov, must be considered in light of these duties. Ekaterina Vazem wrote:

A fine savant of balletic affairs and of classical dance in particular, Ivanov not infrequently produced separate dance numbers and even ballets for performances of the theatre school, and also for the large stage, especially when he was régisseur of the ballet company. Petipa did not give him much rein in this direction, however, wishing to avoid creating a rival. Later Ivanov was second balletmaster in Petersburg, but even in this post he did not manage to show his undeniable talent as a choreographer in full measure.[98]

Nikolay Solyannikov, twenty-five years Vazem's junior, concurred:

To work in the theatre in the atmosphere of Petipa's and Vsevolozhsky's absolutism was not easy. Talented but weak of character and indecisive, L. I. Ivanov felt this very strongly.

The most winning ballets Marius Petipa strictly reserved for himself to produce,

⁹⁶ Ivanov Service Record, fo. 170.   ⁹⁷ Ibid., fo. 172.   ⁹⁸ *Vazem*, 117–18.

and left Ivanov the right to take what the all-powerful balletmaster did not like, or to produce ballets during the latter's periods of leave abroad.[99]

The dancer Alexandre Shiryaev, who at one time or another served as assistant to Petipa and Ivanov, recalled that 'Petipa's monopoly was very powerful; to Ivanov, of course, he gave what was less desirable, or what he did not want to do himself.'[100]

These remarks are exaggerations to the extent they impute to Petipa particular spiteful or defensive motivations for treating Ivanov as an assistant. Viewing the situation as subordinates, the artists writing them (all in the Soviet era) had probably never read Ivanov's contracts. Moreover, to observe Petipa's treatment of Ivanov in such terms is misleading because Petipa could be arrogant towards any subordinate. That is not to be commended, but it is hardly exceptional.

Nor is it likely that Petipa considered Ivanov a serious competitor. The elder man knew competition when he saw it, and surely he saw nothing in Ivanov as he had in Arthur Saint-Léon in the 1860s, and as he would later in Enrico Cecchetti and Achille Coppini. In those relationships he competed, and he won.

There is another explanation for Petipa's attitude. His superiority of rank over Ivanov was hard-earned. Unlike Didelot, Taglioni, Perrot, and Saint-Léon, Petipa began work as a choreographer in Russia with no prior reputation for composition. He had served the imperial theatres for fifteen years before being named balletmaster, and had produced not only the successful revivals of Mazilier's *Paquita* and *Satanilla* at the outset of his stay, but also a number of short ballets staged between 1858 and 1862. Even so, it required a coup like *The Pharaoh's Daughter* to establish his credibility with the direction as a choreographer. Such an apprenticeship would make him jealous of his prerogatives, whereas Ivanov, who was being advanced to a rank just beneath his, had no more apprenticed for it than Felix Kshesinsky, Alexandre Shiryaev, or any number of other Russian dancers. That Ivanov was chosen speaks again of the direction's confidence in him, a choice that necessarily required Petipa's concurrence.

If Ivanov's apprenticeship was weak, what were his qualifications? Knowledge, performance experience, and musicality were his in abundance, and were recognized in the press a few months after he was promoted to balletmaster:

A few days ago, speaking of the present situation of our ballet, we gave full justice to the merits of the second balletmaster of the ballet troupe Mr Ivanov, who is con-

[99] *Solyannikov*, 45.

[100] A[leksandr] V[iktorovich] Shiryaev, *Peterburgskii Balet. Iz vospominanii artista Mariinskogo teatra* [The Petersburg Ballet. From the Recollections of an Artist of the Maryinsky Theatre], ed. Yu. O. Slonimskii (Leningrad: All-Russian Theatre Society, 1941) [hereafter: *Shiryaev*], 31.

stantly ready to replace, even without rehearsal, an artist who has suddenly fallen ill. There have been many such occurrences both in past and the present seasons. We cannot but point out that Mr Ivanov, possessing an extraordinary memory which amazes everyone in the ballet, is of great benefit in the revivals of old ballets. . . .[101]

Whatever his complaints with the management, Ivanov was also loyal. At a time when Russian artists were beginning to acquire reputations abroad, he was steadfast in his dedication to the Petersburg ballet. Improved morale and *esprit de corps* could be expected from having a balletmaster who was native born and well liked. Set against Petipa's arrogance, Ivanov's kindness could by itself explain the criticisms raised against his chief.

As régisseur, so again as balletmaster, Ivanov's lack of command instinct vitiated his strong qualities. Next to Petipa, accustomed to lead, Ivanov looked hesitant and equivocal. Kshesinskaya acknowledges the privileges of Petipa's superior rank, but mentions Ivanov's personality as a counterpoise:

His gift was not fated to be developed in full, and he did not create everything that he could have under other circumstances. His natural laziness hindered him at times, and at times his situation, in which the chief balletmaster Petipa governed everything and could always take a ballet of his and readily change it the way he wanted, such that it was then a ballet by Petipa.[102]

Alexandre Shiryaev recalled the distinction between Petipa's methods and Ivanov's:

Ivanov's technique in production work was much weaker than Petipa's. He improvised a production in the process of rehearsing, was unsure of himself, and sometimes repeatedly changed what he had first decided.

M. I. Petipa frequently taught me and others: 'One must proceed' with prepared material at rehearsal. On Petipa's advice, Lev Ivanov prepared his productions at home, but by nature very lazy, he often arrived at the theatre unprepared all the same. At that point he gladly permitted individual artists not only to rework something in his staging, but also to make whole dances themselves. He, it seems, was even happy on occasion that someone came to his assistance.[103]

There is evidence that Ivanov could not master the idiosyncrasies of his personality even in moments of creation. Cards are again at issue in this account of Ivanov at rehearsal:

L[ev] I[vanovich] is staging the ballet *The Nutcracker*; Pyotr Ilyich Tchaikovsky is at the rehearsal, sitting at the piano. Drigo is playing. Oblakov, Lukyanov, and I are standing near the piano. The conversation is about cards, about playing vint.

---

[101] *Peterburgskaya gazeta*, 30 Jan. 1886, p. 3.   [102] *Kshesinskaya*, 22–3.
[103] *Shiryaev*, 63.

Oblakov, in general always very reserved and quiet, says: 'I really don't understand why people argue, practically climb the wall. To my mind if it's a mistake, it's a mistake. So—take note of it and let it go.' Lukyanov and I agree, and say: 'For that reason, Sasha, we like to have you as our partner.' L.I., in the middle of the hall at the staging of some *pas*, peered over and clearly was listening to our conversation, and then as quietly as a cat came up to us, adjusting his pince-nez on his nose, and asks: 'What is this talk about vint?' (for he was an inveterate vint player). 'Well, L.I., we were just commenting on how people play cards and that there's no reason to get upset.' The blood rushed to Lev Ivanovich's face: 'I heard, I heard. Be calm! Don't get excited! In that case I would rather not sit down to cards, I'd rather not play at all!' Then he struck the piano with his fist, such that the strings all began to vibrate, and then, utterly calmly, went back to the centre and continued to stage the ballet, as if his work had not been interrupted. 'Now then, mesdames, *pas de bourrée, balancé, et jeté en tournant* . . . and these three say "Be calm"—it's a pity, for they *are talented*: take Kshesinsky for example, how he played [the role of] Phoebus! By himself he is worth ten others—the girls will remember him to their dying day, and he goes on about "calmly". Now then, *jeté en tournant* and so on, so on, what do *you* think? And so on . . .' The production proceeds. . . .[104]

Petipa's irritation with Ivanov can be explained by the indolence, distraction, and resistance to advice of someone he had chosen to undertake important responsibilities. Given Ivanov's lack of experience, Petipa might feel obliged to oversee his work and to look in at rehearsals. Seeing Ivanov permitting anyone who wished to make a dance might inspire him to supervise and make changes, whatever the appearance of wilfulness. Yet to the extent we know the circumstances, Borisoglebsky's remarks that the bulk of Ivanov's work is attributed to Petipa and that Petipa interfered in Ivanov's compositions only to have the moral right to name himself as producer, seem biased.[105]

Ivanov's strengths and weaknesses are important for what they say about his works. The reception of his ballets seems perfectly aligned with the vagaries of a talent so little groomed for the responsibilities of composition. The direction's alleged prejudice against Ivanov need not have played a part, and is nonsensical on its merits: why would the direction have placed its faith in Ivanov if it intended to neglect him, why would it invest such sums in his grand ballets if it was plotting his failure? Knowing Ivanov's personality puts his great accomplishments into proper perspective. They were singular feats inexplicable by reference to his other works, not glimpses at some level of accomplishment that would have been routine had he not suffered discrimination. Tamara Karsavina summarized:

Had Ivanov's talent been given an unchecked course, could he have become a representative of an epoch such as Petipa had been? Perhaps not. His inspiration

---

[104] *Kshesinsky*, ii. 21–2.   [105] *Borisoglebsky*, i. 192.

welled up richly, but it was undisciplined and moody. Artists coming into a rehearsal might find him playing the piano, improvising. He hardly noticed them and
continued playing. Sometimes, becoming aware of their presence, he would get up
from the piano and dismiss them. More often, though, his creative mood fertile, he
might go on composing, keeping the artists beyond all reasonable time. It is doubt-
ful if he would have left behind him anything like the consistent, highly polished
output of Petipa, but he might have left to us many unfading flowers of poetic inspiration, far deeper and of broader vision. In his use of integrated dance as distinct
from mere uncoordinated steps, he was the precursor of Fokine.[106]

The debate over his abilities aside, Ivanov got right down to work in his
new post. We do not know the specifics of his initial duties, which probably
involved assuming Petipa's burdensome rehearsal schedule. Whatever this
meant for opera, managing the ballet must have been bedlam: Petipa was
indisposed; Evgenia Sokolova fell ill in the autumn of 1885, which caused
Virginia Zucchi to début early, in *The Pharaoh's Daughter*, which had to be
revised for her; a change of venue of ballet performances from the Bolshoy
to the Maryinsky Theatre was under way (the Bolshoy having been declared unsafe earlier in the year), with attendant rehearsals for a grandiose
féerie, *The Magic Pills*, to mark the move; a new production of *La Fille mal
gardée* with Zucchi was in preparation for Pavel Gerdt's twenty-fifth anniversary benefit; and Zucchi's own benefit was to be celebrated early in 1886
with a new ballet by Petipa, *The King's Command*, also in its planning
stages during the autumn. After less than four months on the job, Ivanov
felt entitled to special compensation. On 19 December he wrote to
Vsevolozhsky:

Your Excellency!
I turn to you with a most humble request that you petition on my behalf with His
Excellency the Minister for a benefit in compensation for my fulfilling of the responsibilities of balletmaster during the rather prolonged illness of Balletmaster Petipa
which has taken place.[107]

Ivanov's service record contains no response to this request, though
Borisoglebsky states that it was refused.[108] If that is true, all the more pecu-
liar the seconding of his request in the press a few weeks later. Ivanov, a reporter contended,

not only works during the course of the winter season, but also invariably in the
summer producing ballet performances at Krasnoe Selo. Having served thirty-five
years honourably and with utter diligence, Mr Ivanov fully deserves a benefit performance, not for the thirty-five years of course, since jubilee benefits are quite

---

[106] ' "La Fille mal Gardée" at the Maryinsky,' in *La Fille mal Gardée*, ed. Ivor Guest, Famous Ballets, No. 1 (London: The Dancing Times: 1960) [hereafter: *Fille*], 29.
[107] Ivanov Service Record, fo. 173.   [108] *Borisoglebsky*, i. 192.

properly given only for twenty-five and fifty years of service. But he unquestionably deserves a so-called bonus benefit, as we see in other companies. The present direction always sympathetically and justly responds to the conscientious labours of outstanding artists, and we are certain it will devote its attention to the indisputable merits of a theatre man like Mr L. Ivanov.[109]

Once the madness of that first season had passed, Ivanov found a great deal to do in the workaday. Repeatedly in his last sixteen years he was on the road, mostly to Moscow to mount dances. As régisseur he had been to Moscow in connection with Alexandre III's coronation in 1883,[110] and was involved again at Nicholas II's coronation in 1896; the particulars of this contribution are obscure, but he received imperial recognition again.[111] In August 1889 he went there as a temporary replacement for Alexey Bogdanov, who had retired,[112] and again in October to cover until the arrival of Bogdanov's successor, José Mendes. In the autumn of 1891 he returned to mount the dances in Tchaikovsky's *The Queen of Spades*,[113] and early in 1898 to produce the Petipa-Ivanov-Cecchetti *Zolushka* (Cinderella). In 1897 he was invited to Warsaw, where he staged Petipa's *The Halt of the Cavalry*, *The Parisian Market*, his own *The Magic Flute*, and Petipa's dances for Anton Rubinstein's opera *The Demon*.[114] When Petipa was away, Ivanov was in charge of the company in St Petersburg.[115]

Ivanov's knowledge and memory also served him well in his post as balletmaster of the Imperial Theatre at the village of Krasnoe Selo. Built in the 1850s, this theatre was staffed by artists of the state drama and ballet companies (occasionally by private troupes hired to perform there) but was administered by the military, who attended it in the summer when manœuvres were conducted nearby. Performances would be given two or three days a week in July and early August, consisting of comic plays or vaudevilles followed by a short ballet or divertissement. In the early days admission cost a rouble and a half in silver, we learn in a report which continued:

The theatre at Krasnoe Selo does not yield in size to the Mikhailovsky [Theatre in St Petersburg]. This year [1858] it was refurbished and some significant extensions were made in it: a winged approach in front by the entrance and winged galleries along the sides (on the outside). These constructions impart no little beauty to the building. Inside is a very comfortable stage with men's and women's dressing-rooms along the sides. There are two rows of boxes, twelve rows of stalls (up to 150 places), places behind the stalls, three entrances for patrons below, and two above. Next to the theatre is a beautiful little park and garden; further on is a hotel with

---

[109] *Peterburgskaya gazeta*, 30 Jan. 1886, p. 3.   [110] Ivanov Service Record, fos. 160, 184*b*.
[111] *Novoe vremya*, 23 May 1896, p. 4.   [112] *Novoe vremya*, 23 Aug. 1889, p. 3.
[113] *Syn otechestva*, 5 Sept. 1891, p. 3.   [114] *Moskovskie vedomosti*, 18 Dec. 1901, p. 5.
[115] *Syn otechestva*, 28 Feb. 1896, p. 3.

rooms for new arrivals, and an open dining-room for artists; before this year a table and tea were prepared for the artists; now they are given a daily allowance of three roubles' silver besides a performance fee. Performances are given three times a week: on Tuesdays, Thursdays, and Fridays.[116]

For artists, performances at Krasnoe Selo were virtually paid holidays. Josef Kshesinsky left a charming reminiscence:

In the summers, during the military encampment at Krasnoe Selo, dramatic performances and ballet were staged in a theatre that belonged to the military, under the patronage of the elder Grand Duke Nikolay Nikolaevich and its directors, his adjutants General Krylov and Colonel Andreyev. There was a time, before the railroads were built, when artists went there in the so-called Court Singers' carriages. These were high, long carriages which held twenty to twenty-four persons, drawn by a foursome of sprightly horses from the court stables driven by formally dressed coachman. Some of the artists gathered at the theatre school, while others were picked up along the road at their dachas, as participants in these performances lived in dachas along the Narva highway, in the village of Ligovo [and] the estate of Countess Kusheleva-Panova. They would sit by their gates awaiting the *dolgusha* [long carriage]. These performances were a kind of picnic, beloved by all: our favourite Levushka headed the ballet; his assistant was régisseur K[onstantin] P[anteleimonovich] Efimov. That was all; otherwise there was neither clerk nor supervisor. Those two ran the entire balletic part of the operation.

Upon arrival at Krasnoe Selo we immediately went to a rehearsal with orchestra: the conductor was A[lexey] D[mitrievich] Papkov. Then we would all be invited to lunch in the pavilion next to the lake opposite the theatre; lunch was taken in a very lively and merry way. In a word—it was a community of artists. After that everyone dispersed, some boating on the lake, some fishing; those who wished to go for a ride around the encampment were given a sprightly troika.

Before Lev Ivanovich the balletmaster there was Alexey Nikolaevich Bogdanov, a mean and spiteful man who advanced only those who gave him gifts. He was in no way a balletmaster, and for Krasnoe Selo would only rehearse works already mounted on the large stage by Marius [Petipa] or Lev Ivanovich, or Saint-Léon or Perrot of fond memory. The theatre at Krasnoe Selo and the pavilion were very beautifully constructed in the purely Russian style outside and in—the auditorium, drawing-rooms and boxes. Illuminated in the evening, the hall had an effective and elegant appearance. The parterre glistened with white, high-collared uniforms, gold epaulettes and medals, while the boxes were filled with women in bright dresses and stunning hats; behind the ladies the high collars and medals gleamed again; the first row was occupied only by grand dukes, the second and third by the retinue and the officer corps, while the Tsar and the Tsarina and their children were in a box on the side, built in the shape of a small Russian peasant's cottage. Opposite, in the same kind of box, sat the Minister of Court and the Minister of the Military with their families. No one was to applaud anyone before the first

---

[116] *Teatral'nyi i muzykal'nyi vestnik*, 22 June 1858, p. 287.

handclap by the Tsar. I am describing this in such detail because further on it will have a bearing on Lev Ivanovich's eccentricity.

After the performance there would be dinner, then the horses took us back to Petersburg (30 versts) and delivered us to our homes along the road. Later, when the railroad was built to Oranienbaum and Narva, these performance trips lost their picnic-like charm; we were provided free passes: artists of the highest rank in first class, corps de ballet and orchestral players in second, and service personnel in third. Also, instead of supper and dinner each received, regardless of position, an additional 3 roubles each performance as a subsistence allowance. By then artists were living not only in Ligovo but also Oranienbaum, Sergeyevo, Strelna, who all came to the station at Ligovo, whence the trains departed.[117]

Krasnoe Selo provided a steady exercise of Ivanov's régisseurial skills and an apprenticeship for his original essays in choreography. As a producer he reached back into otherwise forgotten repertoires, giving his audiences their first look in decades at parts of Taglioni's *La Fille du Danube*, Perrot's *Faust* and *La Fille du marbre*, Saint-Léon's *The Golden Fish* and *The Nymphs and the Satyr*, and Petipa's *Trilby* and *A Regency Marriage*, among many others. Complementing these revivals were excerpts from ballets recently performed for the first time on the official stage. Here follow, as examples, lists of dances in two divertissements compiled by Ivanov for Krasnoe Selo. The years of first production in Russia are provided within parentheses. On 28 July 1889 the evening performance began with a comedy-farce in three acts called *The Process of Divorce*, and was followed by a divertissement which included the following dances:

1. *Pas de deux* from Perrot's *Gazelda* (1853)
2. *Pas de quatre* [no other identification; possibly new]
3. *Valse folie* from Mazilier's *Paquita* (1847) [one couple]
4. Obertas from *Esmeralda* (1849) [4 women, 2 men]
5. *Folichon* (possibly from Perrot's *Marcobomba*, 1854) [one couple]
6. *Chardache* by Ivanov to music by Drigo [5 couples]
7. *Les Mantilles* from Petipa's *The King's Command* (1886) [8 women].

Four days later the non-danced part of the programme was more diverse. A comedy in one act, *The Night after the Ball* opened the performance, followed by a short vaudeville, *The Dress Uniform*, and 'a scene of military camp life in one act' called *The Secret Order*. Ivanov was ready with a new divertissement to round off the evening:

1. *La Bernoise* from Petipa's *Trilby* (1870) [one couple]
2. *Pas de Corbeille* from Saint-Léon's *Météora* (1861) [female solo]
3. Russian dance from Petipa's *Camargo* (1872) [one couple]

[117] *Kshesinsky*, ii. 16–18.

4. *Chardache* by Alfred Bekefy [one couple]
5. *Grand pas* from Perrot's *La Filleule des fées* (1850) [3 couples]
6. Mazurka from Mazilier's *Le Diable amoureux* (1850) [3 couples]
7. *Vilano* from Petipa's *Zoraya* (1881) [8 women, 3 + 'other' men].

Who danced at Krasnoe Selo depended on the availability of artists; what was danced seems to have been decided with the same informality that pervaded the atmosphere there and made it a pleasure for artists to visit. This brings Josef Kshesinsky to his anecdote about Ivanov's eccentricity:

But I return to Lev Ivanovich, and give way to his eccentricity. This summer, in the régisseur's room . . . once were sitting: L.I., régisseur K. P. Efimov, [and] several of us artists, deciding the repertoire for the next performance at Krasnoe Selo: Lev Ivanovich is designating numbers for a divertissement, and Konstantin Panteleimonovich blurted out: 'But you see, L.I., this is boring.' Suddenly our L.I. blushed, looked wide-eyed at Efimov and said, almost in a whisper: 'What is it with you, Kostya—the auditorium is lit, elegant women are in the boxes, charming hats on their heads, the music is playing, on the stage there is dancing, and it is boring,' then pounds his fist on the table and cries out: 'It is merry, gay, cheerful!' and stormed out of the régisseur's office. And in no more than two minutes he returned and said, utterly calmly: 'So then, Kostya, what numbers would you advise?' and all proceeded agreeably.[118]

One number in the programmes at Krasnoe Selo was predictable. At the end of the last performance each season all the dancers would to come together for what was known as 'the infernal galop'. Mathilde Kshesinskaya recalled:

In accordance with an old tradition the last performance of the summer season at Krasnoe Selo ended with a grand galop, the *Galop infernal*, in which all the artists appearing that evening took part. We had only just begun the rehearsal when completely unexpectedly Grand Duke Nikolay Nikolaevich the Elder, who was long since retired, arrived at the theatre. In his youth he was very attracted to the ballet artist Chislova and had two sons by her, who received the surname Nikolaev and later served in the Life Guards Horse Grenadiers regiment, and two daughters, of whom one, a real beauty, married Prince Cantacuzène.

Many years later, when they were refurbishing the theatre and put up scaffolding, it was prescribed that one of the women's heads drawn into the medallions was Chislova, and one could even read the inscription beneath her image, which earlier it had been impossible to make out from a distance. The Grand Duke was very fond of my father and the balletmaster Lev Ivanovich Ivanov, used the familiar form of address with them, and they often paid calls on him without formalities.

When the rehearsals for the galop began, the Grand Duke was sitting in the tsar's box, when suddenly he stopped the dance and began to try to prove to Ivanov that he had staged the galop incorrectly. Lev Ivanov began to object, but the Grand Duke leapt out onto the stage and himself began to demonstrate how the galop should be performed.[119]

Ivanov composed many individual dances and three short ballets for Krasnoe Selo, two of which were never seen anywhere else. Of another significant task Ivanov might have carried out there nothing remains but enticing hints. Early in 1886 the Petersburg direction was apparently considering the revival of one act of Tchaikovsky's *Swan Lake*, which had last been performed in Moscow in 1883. Our knowledge of this project is limited to an exchange of letters between Tchaikovsky and his publisher, Pyotr Ivanovich Jurgenson. On 27 March 1886 Jurgenson wrote:

Today Altani [conductor of the imperial opera in Moscow] was here. He or Pchelnikov [Intendant of the Moscow theatres] received a private letter from Vsevolozhsky, in which he asked that I send him the score and parts of one act of your ballet. He requests further that this act be designated by you. He wants to give one act this summer at Krasnoe Selo before the tsar, and, understandably, he wants to give the best one.[120]

Jurgenson suggested Act IV, but Tchaikovsky in his reply rejected this suggestion, insisting that Act II, 'the best in all respects', be sent instead.[121] We know nothing further about this project,[122] though the possibility is fascinating. Could Ivanov have known this music, and pondered how it might be choreographed, eight years before it fell his lot to stage it?

Composing opera dances was another of Ivanov's regular duties as balletmaster. Krasovskaya reports his contributions in works as stylistically diverse as Verdi's *La Traviata* and Wagner's *Tannhäuser*, Rossini's *William Tell* and Bizet's *Carmen*. Petipa deferred to him when Russian dances were required, which brought Ivanov into contact with the music of his leading contemporaries. *Prince Igor* has already been mentioned, to which may be added Rimsky-Korsakov's *Mlada* and *Christmas Eve*, and prior to Ivanov's work on *The Nutcracker* and *Swan Lake*, Tchaikovsky's music in the dances for *Mazepa*, *Evgenii Onegin*, and *The Enchantress*.[123]

Serving as balletmaster also had its ritual component. We have seen that

[119] *Kshesinskaya*, 31–2.

[120] *P. I. Chaikovskii. Perepiska s P. I. Yurgensonom* [P. I. Tchaikovsky. Correspondence with P. I. Jurgenson], 2 vols. (Moscow and Leningrad: State Music Publishers, 1938, 1952) [hereafter: *Tchaikovsky–Jurgenson*], ii. 37.

[121] *Tchaikovsky–Jurgenson*, ii. 39.

[122] Yury Slonimsky remembered hearing, when young, reports of veteran balletomanes that Act II of *Swan Lake* was performed not in the 1880s but in the early 1890s, on an island of one of the lakes either at Peterhof or Tsarskoe Selo; see his '*Lebedinoe ozero*' *P. Chaikovskogo* [P. Tchaikovsky's 'Swan Lake'] (Leningrad: State Music Publishers, 1962), 40. Of these there is no other confirmation either.

[123] *Krasovskaya*, 55–8.

Ivanov often found himself at benefit performances making addresses on behalf of the Petersburg ballet and presenting gifts to artists. He was first to speak at the celebration of Marie Petipa's twenty-fifth anniversary jubilee.[124] He and Marius Petipa presented the conductor Papkov with a silver coffee service at the informal celebration of that conductor's fortieth anniversary.[125] More than once Petipa himself was the honoree. At his fortieth year of service,

First A[lexandre] P. Frolov made a heartfelt speech, an appreciation of the jubilee celebrant as an artist-poet. Then, with a warm, sincere greeting attributing the beauties of our ballet to the recipient of the celebration, Mr L. Ivanov observed that Petipa's former, inexhaustible inspiration had not abandoned him after a mass of artistic creations and of course will not leave him for many years to come. Deeply touched, surrounded by professors of the school and students, all of whom had studied with him, Marius Ivanovich [Petipa] . . . thanked them all from his heart. . . .[126]

At Petipa's half-century jubilee, Ivanov was again first to offer greetings, and to review his chief's accomplishments for the audience.[127]

Often Ivanov presided at farewell benefits, though he never took one himself. 'If farewell benefits have the look of celebrations,' a reviewer wrote when one ballerina retired,

in their festive staging, ovations, addresses, flowers and gifts, for the men and women honoured at these triumphant celebrations, they must be very sad episodes of a long artistic career. Indeed, put yourself in the artist's position, what she has been accustomed to for twenty years, not to mention the artistic milieu, and the stage on which life's best years have passed—and you will sense that pensive mood with which an artist *comes out for the last time* before the public which has provided the best moments of success; *for the last time* one occupies the centre of attention in a crowd of a thousand people; *for the last time* one hears the applause, without which an artist finds it as hard to live as for a fish out of water![128]

Sometimes Ivanov himself was the recipient of ceremonial honours, marks of esteem from the state, comparable to modern honours lists. For 'excellently diligent service' Ivanov was awarded the Imperial Order of St Stanislav, 3rd degree, on 21 April 1891; made a Cavalier of the Order of St Anne, 3rd degree, on 14 May 1896; and awarded the Imperial Order of St Stanislav, 2nd degree, on 1 April 1901.[129]

Three footnotes to Ivanov's official service deserve mention. In the spring of 1887 a newspaper reported as rumour that Ivanov would succeed Frolov as supervisor of the ballet troupe and director of the theatre

---

[124] *Sanktpeterburgskie vedomosti*, 23 Jan. 1896, p. 3.
[125] *Peterburgskaya gazeta*, 6 Oct. 1886, p. 3.   [126] *Peterburgskaya gazeta*, 7 May 1887, p. 3.
[127] *Peterburgskaya gazeta*, 9 Dec. 1896, p. 3.
[128] *Novosti i birzhevaya gazeta*, 27 Nov. 1886, p. 3.   [129] Ivanov Service Record, fos. 308–10.

school.[130] In the late summer of 1888, with the death of Alberto di Segni, who had replaced Ivanov as ballet régisseur in 1885, another rumour circulated that Ivanov was to be reappointed chief régisseur.[131] Given the zest with which newspapers reported activities of the so-called balletic anthill, and the backstage connections of reporters, the possibility that Ivanov was being considered for these posts cannot be dismissed, though we have no other trace of them. On 9 April 1888 Ivanov wrote to the Bureau of the Imperial Theatres:

I am requesting the issuance to me [of a copy] of my service record and a testimonial of my service, which are required for presentation to the Governing Senate, Department of Heraldry, in connection with receiving [the title of] Honoured Citizen for the serving out of my years in the St Petersburg Imperial Theatres.[132]

We have no knowledge of the outcome of this effort.

On 5 December 1899 Ivanov celebrated fifty years of service in the imperial theatres with a benefit performance. The principal roles in Perrot's *Esmeralda* were taken by the Kshesinsky family: Mathilde performed the title role, her brother Josef that of Phoebus, and their father Felix that of the syndic Claude Frollo. The honouring of Lev Ivanov began with a presentation by the Director of Imperial Theatres, Prince Sergey Mikhailovich Volkonsky:

Between the second and third acts, with the curtain down, the Director, Pr. Volkonsky presented the jubilee artist with a diploma conferring the title, 'Merited Artist of the Imperial Theatres', and a gold medal, studded with diamonds, with the number 'L'. Then the curtain was raised, and endless greetings, presentations, and telegrams commenced. Gifts were presented until 11 o'clock.[133]

In connection with Ivanov's new title a letter to him from Volkonsky dated 4 December 1899 reads:

Respected Sir, Lev Ivanovich!

In consequence of my petition has followed the resolution of His IMPERIAL MAJESTY to award you the honour, established by IMPERIAL command on 25 February 1895 for merited artists of the IMPERIAL Theatres.

Responding to such IMPERIAL wish, I have the honour to forward herewith the prescribed gold medal.

Accept, Kind Sir, assurances of my complete esteem and devotion.[134]

Ivanov's response to this recognition was the expression of 'one desire—to serve art until the grave'.[135]

Of the remaining ceremonies Pleshcheyev wrote:

[130] *Peterburgskii listok*, 29 Apr. 1887, p. 3.   [131] *Novoe vremya*, 22 Aug. 1888, p. 3.
[132] Ivanov Service Record, fo. 183.   [133] *Novosti i birzhevaya gazeta*, 6 Dec. 1899, p. 3.
[134] Ivanov Service Record, fo. 259.   [135] *Moskovskie vedomosti*, 18 Dec. 1901, p. 5.

After the third scene of the ballet *Esmeralda* the ballet company gathered on stage, with representatives of the opera and drama troupes and other deputations. The régisseur Mr Aistov, announcing and greeting Mr Ivanov, asked that he accept a medal, presented on a pillow by his comrades Mr Gerdt and Mr Lukyanov.[136] The drama company, represented by Miss Dyuzhikova, Miss Levkeyeva, Mr Shemaev, and Mr Osokin, expressed their greetings and presented a wreath. The opera company also made a presentation and Mr Stravinsky [the composer's father] gave a short speech. The Moscow ballet sent a laurel wreath, given to Mr Ivanov by the dancers Miss Bakerkina and Miss Mosolova, who had previously served on the Moscow stage. From the public the benefit artist received a massive gold cigar case with his initials in diamonds. Then followed an address by members of the production staff of the Maryinsky Theatre; the artists of the orchestra gave L. I. Ivanov another medal. The French drama company sent a laurel wreath. After that telegrams were read from E. P. Sokolova, E. N. Zhuleva, and K. A. Varlamov. Finally the theatre carpenters presented bread and salt to the benefit artist. The public greeted L. I. Ivanov, led onto the stage by Miss Petipa I and Mr Aistov, with a roar of applause. The ovation lasted a long time and the curtain was raised several times. The balletmaster Mr Petipa was absent due to serious illness. Nor was Miss Legnani on stage, from whom the benefit artist received a wreath. L. I. Ivanov does not look like a master jubilee artist; he looks exactly the same as he did several years ago on stage—spry, vivacious, merry.[137]

Other accounts fill in details. Aistov's address was apparently inscribed, with decorations in water-colour: at the top a lion, referring to Ivanov's Christian name, and beneath this the roman numeral 'L'; it was accompanied by a similar numeral fashioned in silver and studded with diamonds. Stravinsky's speech was accompanied by a gold medal with diamonds from the opera company.[138] Legnani's wreath was accompanied by yet another gold piece with inscription, 'De la part d'Odette'.[139] The orchestra presented him with yet another gold medal, and the theatre decorators a ceremonial mead cup.[140] The reviewer for *The Petersburg Gazette* correctly estimated that the receipts from this performance reached nearly 6,000 roubles. The takings of the actual house were 5,786.63 roubles; after expenses of 3,088.43 roubles were deducted and other adjustments made, Ivanov took just over 2,837 roubles from his half-century benefit performance.[141]

---

[136] Other accounts mention the warmth of Aistov's address. 'The chief ballet régisseur spoke a heartfelt word, in which he characterized the entire *simpatichnyi* [likeable] side of L. I. Ivanov's long service, and his relationship to his comrades on the stage' (*Peterburgskaya gazeta*, 6 Dec. 1899, p. 4); 'N. S. Aistov, presenting the jubilee artist with an address, wreath, medal, and a valuable present from the ballet troupe, delivered a warm speech in which he clearly oulined L. I.'s activity' (*Peterburgskii listok*, 6 Dec. 1899, p. 4).

[137] *Novoe vremya*, 6 Dec. 1899, p. 5.

[138] *Novosti i birzhevaya gazeta*, 6 Dec. 1899, p. 3.

[139] *Peterburgskaya gazeta*, 6 Dec. 1899, p. 4.

[140] *Novosti i birzhevaya gazeta*, 6 Dec. 1899, p. 3.

[141] Ivanov Service Record, fo. 260.

Some twelve days later, Ivanov's anniversary was celebrated in the ritual way:

Yesterday the circle of ballet lovers and admirers of the talent of the balletmaster L. I. Ivanov honoured the latter on the occasion of his fiftieth year of stage activity. Around seventy people gathered for dinner in the Restaurant Cubat; among the ballet artists were Miss Kshesinskaya I and Miss Kshesinskaya II [Julia and Mathilde], Legnani, Preobrazhenskaya, [Marie] Petipa, Leonova, Pavlova I and II [the latter being Anna], Sedova, Egorova, Rykhlyakova, Ogoleit, Borkhardt, Vasilieva, Tatarinova, Makhotina, Kulichevskaya, Bakerkina, Andreanova, Vaganova, Grupolion, and others. Mr Ivanov was greeted at his appearance with applause. Two orchestras played during dinner—Romanian and Italian. There was, of course, no lack of toasts and speeches addressed to the jubilee artist, who thanked those present. The honouring was marked by liveliness, and bore a sincere character.[142]

This was, to all appearances, a celebration of the community of Russian artists. 'Among the ballet artists there' only one, Pierina Legnani, was an outsider.

Nine weeks after his half-century jubilee, on 14 February 1900, Ivanov performed in Petipa's *Les Élèves de Dupré*, a reworked excerpt from *L'Ordre du roi*, first produced in 1886. The performance took place in the tsar's private theatre in the Hermitage, a circumstance which placed the focus of most press reports on the guest list and the ceremonial aspects of the evening. Ivanov played the part of the Comte de Montagnac, father of daughters Rose (Varvara Rykhlyakova), Violetta (Olga Preobrazhenskaya), and Daisy (Evgenia Obukhova). Together with these and four other dancers, men and women, Ivanov took part in 'La Révérence perdue' in the first act.[143] At one point Petipa had considered having Ivanov play the role of King Louis XV.[144] This was, in all probability, Lev Ivanov's last appearance on stage.

Ivanov's Personal Affairs

For two years after Ivanov's appointment as balletmaster, his service record gives no indication of domestic problems. On the last day of 1887, however, we see the first sign of a plague upon his house that would ravage it until well past his death. On that day he sent a petition to Vladimir Pogozhev, Supervisor of the Bureau of the Petersburg theatres:

Finding myself in straitened financial circumstances on the occasion of the serious illness of my wife and children, I request you, Vladimir Petrovich, in all humility,

---

[142] *Novoe vremya*, 19 Dec. 1899, p. 5.   [143] *Peterburgskaya gazeta*, 16 Feb. 1900, p. 3.
[144] *TMB 205*, no. 402.

concerning the obtaining for me of 600 roubles, to be paid back over 4 months, 150 roubles monthly, from my salary.[145]

The condition which afflicted Ivanov's family is not specified, but the financial drain required to deal with it was apparently devastating. Illness of his family and himself, educational expenses, and general indebtedness are Ivanov's justification for fourteen similar requests to follow (one for a fortieth anniversary benefit, rationalized as a reward for honourable service), each coming soon after the last was repaid (barring a respite during 1894 and 1895), the latest eight months before Ivanov's death. Interspersed with these requests for money are eleven others asking that his family, and sometimes Ivanov himself, be permitted to reside elsewhere than in St Petersburg for various periods of time, though Ivanov seems not to have taken all the leaves he was granted. The purpose of these dislocations is never explained.

The direction's overall response to Ivanov's petitions was laudable. The outcome of some requests is not clear from Ivanov's service record, but the evidence it provides shows that only once did the Ministry of the Imperial Court deny Ivanov, perhaps because on this occasion he did not specify a reason for the advance; only once was less than the full amount requested granted—900 roubles instead of 1,200. Only once did Vsevolozhsky fail to give a favourable endorsement. On this occasion Ivanov had requested a compensatory half-benefit for his production of *The Mikado's Daughter*. Vsevolozhsky, in a letter to the Minister of the Imperial Court, explained:

Fearing that the designation of a benefit for the balletmaster Ivanov after the successful production of a ballet can serve in the future as a precedent for others, I do not find it possible to approve this petition, but taking into consideration the continuously diligent performance by Ivanov of his service responsibilities, his prolonged useful service and real financial problems, I consider it my duty to petition before Your Excellency to provide Mr Ivanov, instead of the half-benefit he is asking for, a one-time allowance from the funds of the Minister of the IMPERIAL Court, concerning which I have the honour to add that Ivanov has been with the Direction since 18 February 1850, [and] receives a salary of 5,000 roubles per annum.[146]

The Minister gave Ivanov 1,500 roubles, a figure quite possibly higher than the proceeds of a half-benefit.

Twice during these troubled years the Director of Theatres took action on Ivanov's behalf without prompting. After his successful staging of *The Nutcracker*, Vsevolozhsky volunteered a half-benefit for him; Volkonsky interceded with the Minister to increase Ivanov's fiftieth anniversary benefit from half to full.[147]

---

[145] Ivanov Service Record, fo. 177.
[146] Ibid., fo. 257.   [147] Ibid., fos. 210, 258.

On 26 April 1898 Ivanov missed a rehearsal of Gounod's *Romeo and Juliet*, a rare instance of absenteeism and a harbinger of serious health problems. The medical report sent to the direction three days later found Ivanov to be suffering from 'irregular digestion and catarrh of the gastro-intestinal canal'. Ivanov called it 'an illness of the liver'.[148] The doctors advised him to take the waters, to pay for which an advance of 1,200 roubles was necessary.

Ominous notes are struck here for the first time. The loan was guaranteed by three of Ivanov's fellow artists—the conductor Riccardo Drigo and balletmasters Enrico Cecchetti and Marius Petipa.[149] On a similar request of 28 April 1900, the Director indicated in his endorsement, 'In the event of the death or retirement from service of Lev Ivanov, the sum being asked for by him is guaranteed by two warrantors, artists of the ballet troupe A. Shiryaev and E. Cecchetti.'[150] The last such request Ivanov made, received by the Direction on 19 January 1901, was guaranteed by Drigo again, and by Petipa, Ivanov's allegedly spiteful chief, nearly 83 years old and himself ailing at the time.[151] Since the term of this repayment extended to thirteen months after Ivanov died, one must assume that Petipa and Drigo paid off Ivanov's final earthly debt.[152]

In March 1901 Ivanov was again seriously ill. On the 13th the Director requested for him a one-time allowance for illness, based in part on a certification by Ivanov's doctor, who diagnosed influenza complicated by a catarrhal inflamation of the lung with symptoms of fluid retention.[153] The debilitating illness was exacerbated by fatigue. Ivanov wrote to the Minister of the Imperial Court:

During all of last winter season I was obliged to work alone, to prepare and rehearse the entire winter repertoire every day, and in addition to revive the long-unperformed ballet, *Camargo*. The balletmaster Petipa revived only one ballet this season, *La Bayadère*. Being fatigued and having caught a cold, I fell ill with influenza, complicated by inflammation of the right lung. I thought that I would not survive this illness and it would put an end to my existence, but fortunately I came upon an excellent doctor who saved me. Now, upon the instructions of that doctor, for my fullest recovery, I must repair somewhere to a warm climate, but since con-

---

[148] Ibid., fos. 244–5.   [149] Ibid., fo. 244.   [150] Ibid., fo. 264.   [151] Ibid., fo. 268.

[152] Nikolay Legat recalled: 'When Johannsen's friend and colleague, Lev Ivanoff, instructor of the Junior Class, died at the age of about 70, I came to tell Johannsen the sad news. Instead of saying "Oh, how sad," he burst out laughing. "Ha, ha, ha," he exclaimed, shaking a forefinger, "it must have been his debts strangled him!" (Nicolas Legat, *The Story of the Russian School*, trans. Sir Paul Dukes, K.B.E. (London: British Continental Press, 1932), 40).

[153] To put Ivanov's request in some perspective, it is well to realize that the direction received many others like it. In 1901, for example, before Ivanov's request on 13 March, Georgy Kyaksht had requested an allowance to pay for his wife's protracted illness (17 Jan.), Ekaterina Geltser an allowance to offset the expenses of illness and recovery (26 Jan.), and Olga Preobrazhenskaya, on 6 March, an allowance while she was recovering from illness (St Petersburg, Historical Archive 468.14.373, fos. 1, 5, 27).

siderable means are necessary for this, I make bold to turn to Your Excellency's good heart with my most humble, most respectful request to permit me a benefit performance, at the end of Easter Week, that will enable me to follow my doctor's advice and recover fully, thereby to rededicate all my labours to the benefit of the Direction.[154]

On 4 April Ivanov modified this request, asking for a benefit performance in the winter season and an immediate advance against it. The Ministry responded by adding 900 roubles to the 400 already given him as an illness allowance. Formal action on Ivanov's request, which for years had been taken within days and sometimes hours of his petition, in this case inexplicably took months. Only on 3 December 1901 did the Director endorse the request to grant Ivanov a benefit enabling him to take sick leave. By then, Ivanov had eight days left.

On 12 December 1901, the ballet régisseur Aistov sent a message to the Bureau of the Imperial Theatres that could hardly have been a surprise: 'I have the honour of reporting that yesterday, 11 December, the balletmaster Lev Ivanov died; I most respectfully ask for an allowance for his burial.'[155]

On 15 December *The Petersburg Gazette* reported the details of Ivanov's funeral:

It was yesterday at the Smolensk Cemetery, where they buried the merited artist, the balletmaster L. I. Ivanov. The ballet troupe, which had gathered the day before, decided to place a modest wreath on their comrade's grave, and to erect a monument above it with the money raised. No few of Lev Ivanov's comrades were at the cemetery, since they were present at the conducting of the coffin from his apartment. In the church gathered the Director of Imperial Theatres V[ladimir] A[rkadievich] Telyakovsky, Supervisor of the Theatre Bureau V. P. Lappa-Starzhepetsky, St Petersburg Commandant N. S. Krylov, [artists] M. N. Gorshenkova, Ev. P. Sokolova, A. N. Bogdanov, F. I. Kshesinsky, I. F. Kshesinsky, O. I. Preobrazhenskaya, N[adezhda] A[lexandrovna] Bakerkina, Yu[lia] N[ikolaevna] Sedova, E[lena Karlovna] Ogoleit, M. A. Alexandrov; the conductors Mr Drigo, Mr Papkov, and Mr Rosenfeld, several representatives of the press and others. The deceased's family and male students of the Theatre School, headed by its supervisor, accompanied the coffin.

There were quite a number of wreaths: from the ballet troupe . . . from the artists of the Russian opera, and others.

Kshesinsky *père*, sighing, told me: 'Few, very few of us oldsters remain . . . myself, Petipa, Johanson, the régisseur Efimov, and that, perhaps, is it.'

. . . F. I. Kshesinsky relates that he was with Lev Ivanov a week before his death and the latter, in response to 'How are things with you?', said 'It's all

---

[154] Ivanov Service Record, fo. 274.   [155] Ibid., fo. 281.

right, something's the matter with my stomach, but it's all right.' Having seen Ivanov almost the day before his death, his friend I. F. Nesterov said that Lev Ivanov gave the impression of being unwell, but to expect death so soon was impossible.[156]

The Smolensk Cemetery, the reporter continues, is well kept, and someone approaching it does not sense the proximity of a necropolis, as at others, whose entrances are lined with sellers of wreaths and monuments. Vera Lyadova was also buried at the Smolensk. 'They wanted to bury Lev Ivanov next to her, but found that this location was expensive. Ivanov is buried along the same pathway as Lyadova-Ivanova, but a few graves further along.'

The hyperbole of Ivanov's financial need did not end with his death. His widow, in an age without government benefits, continued petitioning the direction for help. Eleven days after Ivanov's death she asked that his pension be continued, claiming that Serafima, though 24 years old and having just been given a separate residency permit, suffered a physical defect which made her unfit for work, and that Maria had not yet finished her education. The request was justified on the insufficiency of her own pension as an artist, and 'in the memory of the services of my deceased husband, who irreproachably served the Direction of the IMPERIAL Theatres fifty-two years'.[157]

The Ministry of the Imperial Court hesitated for a time. On 4 January 1902 it granted Varvara Ivanova an exceptional allowance of 300 roubles 'in view of her straitened circumstances'.[158] She must have petitioned again, for the Minister wrote a long report to the Director of Theatres on 4 February about her financial problems, and on 27 February granted her an increase in pension from 500 roubles to 1,070 roubles. At the end of March Serafima applied for a separate pension, on the basis of her father's long service and 'in view of her extreme need and situation of illness'. The direction recommended favourable action on this request as well, though in the modest amount of 192 roubles per annum.[159]

Documents in Lev Ivanov's service record are dated as late as 1912, and continue to include, though less frequently after his death, requests for money. The Bureau of the Imperial Theatres acted on the last of these on 1 July 1910. That was the day Marius Petipa died.

Pleshcheyev recalled Ivanov as 'one of the most talented Russian artists . . . a magnificent colleague, free of all intrigue . . . a rare man in his goodness of spirit and gentle character, who in fifty-two years of activity never made an enemy'.

---

[156] *Peterburgskaya gazeta*, 15 Dec. 1901, p. 3.
[157] Ivanov Service Record, fo. 297.   [158] Ibid., fo. 301.   [159] Ibid., fo. 304.

My personal acquaintance with Lev Ivanovich compels me to say that in the theatre milieu there are few such people, sincere and in general attractive for their spiritual qualities. He was a good-natured person, who never had any secret and evil schemes backstage; he stood apart from every theatrical type. Artists loved him because he, having lived to almost 70, remained and died a comrade, a sincere comrade who recommended himself not in words but in deeds. . . . [160]

[160] *Novoe vremya*, 13 Dec. 1901, p. 4.

II
The Ballets of
Lev Ivanov

Introduction

The choreographic works of Lev Ivanov, apart from individual dances and dances for operas, may be classified in various ways. The most obvious is to distinguish the famous from the obscure, which is tempting but misleading. Ivanov's career was more than *Swan Lake* and *The Nutcracker*; knowing his other works enriches our perspective, and gives us a closer look at what the Petersburg ballet was like during his time.

The easiest classification is by genre, namely short ballets which were extended divertissements in a popular vein, anacreontic divertissements in the spirit of the late eighteenth century, or grand ballets based on fantastic stories. Ivanov's short ballets were creations of circumstance; when they came into the repertoire of the official stage, as distinct from the school theatre or the theatres at Krasnoe Selo or Peterhof, it was after being tested in those venues.

The most problematic classification also illuminates historical reality with the greatest force: the ballets Ivanov shared with Marius Petipa. These collaborations, which include Ivanov's most celebrated works, were the expected consequence of his appointment as second balletmaster. In many cases it is difficult to know who did what. Petipa on occasion counted *The Tulip of Haarlem* as his own, though it appears he took no significant part in its production; he published a strongly worded claim to authorship of *Flora's Awakening*, virtually excluding Ivanov, yet official documents attribute the ballet to both men.

The following account of Ivanov's ballets will be chronological except for generic groupings (ballets at Krasnoe Selo, major operatic projects) which interrupt the exact sequence of composition. It is based on published libretti, newspaper reports, and archival data. Of these sources, press notices are at once the most numerous and the least reliable. Like modern reportage, they have the virtue of eyewitness accounts and the defects of slanted opinion and unliterary prose. Something may be learned from the opinions; otherwise, the notices have been summarized as appropriate to avoid redundancy, and edited for clarity.

3

Ivanov's First Ballets

La Fille mal gardée

Known by any other name, such as 'Lise and Colin', 'The Deceived Old Woman', or 'Vain Precautions', and despite local variants in matters of names and staging, Dauberval's ballet has always turned on the same plot. Girl loves boy, but is engaged by her avaricious mother to a rich but foolish rival. Mother berates daughter for persisting in her love, and keeps her locked up to protect her virtue. This is *the* vain precaution (in Russian the title is in the singular), for when the mother lets down her guard, which allows the beloved to enter the house and hide, it leads to a tryst. The couple are discovered, and the hint of compromise implicit in their meeting confounds the matchmaking, whereupon girl and boy are allowed to marry.

A revival of *La Fille mal gardée*, which had last been seen in St Petersburg on 28 February 1880, was mounted for the twenty-fifth anniversary jubilee of Pavel Gerdt's artistic activity on 15 December 1885. It was remembered more for being the second work Virginia Zucchi performed in the imperial theatres (after *The Pharaoh's Daughter*, in which she replaced the indisposed Evgenia Sokolova). Zucchi had first appeared in Petersburg on 6 July 1885 in a private theatre, an event zestfully described by Konstantin Skalkovsky.[1] On 6 August she danced with state artist Sergey Litavkin at Krasnoe Selo in a *pas de deux* from *A Journey to the Moon*, the *féerie* which she had been performing that summer.[2] She enjoyed a phenomenal success, which caused the emperor to command his theatre direction, not without misgiving, to invite her to the official stage. By 26 August Zucchi had left St

---

[1] K[onstantin] A[pollonovich] Skal'kovskii, *V teatral'nom mire; nablyudeniya, vospominaniya i rassuzhedniya* [In the Theatre World: Observations, Recollections, Discourses] (St Petersburg: A. S. Suvorin, 1899) [hereafter: *Skalkovsky*], 121–6; trans. in *Wiley*, 314–20.

[2] *Pleshcheyev*, 271–2.

Petersburg, but plans to revive *La Fille mal gardée* for her were announced in the press that day.[3]

This would be the first new production in the Petersburg ballet since Lev Ivanov was made second balletmaster. In characteristically declarative voice, but citing no external authority, Slonimsky claims for him an important part in the new staging:

L. Ivanov's first significant labour was the revival of Dauberval's ballet *Vain Precautions* with new music by Hertel (1885).

With this spectacle L. Ivanov passes his examination in three subjects. In danced-acted scenes preserved from the celebrated balletmaster of the eighteenth century Dauberval and edited by J. Perrot, L. Ivanov shows that he is well in command of the traditions of pantomime dance. He stages this ballet, transformed in Berlin into a sentimentally comic pastorale, as a brilliant dance spectacle, which gives him the right to the title of master of divertissement numbers. Finally and principally, from the viewpoint of the management of the imperial theatres and Marius Petipa, he makes it through (not, however, with a mark of 'outstanding') the examination in abolishing sharp angles and social accents in the redaction of Dauberval's ballet *Vain Precautions*, which is the rarest reflection in the ballet theatre of the fomenting class struggles of the French Revolution of 1789.[4]

Slonimsky is no less certain of Ivanov's involvement, now shared with Petipa, in a later study of the ballet:

L. Ivanov and M. Petipa revived the production on the basis of G. [i.e. Peter Ludwig] Hertel's music.

The work accomplished by the the balletmasters was called on *affiches* a revival of the production. Dauberval was, as before, declared its author. Petipa only advised on the production and composed the 'pure' dances. The burden of the reconstruction of the spectacle to new music fell to L. Ivanov. Once having played the role of Colin side by side with Perrot, Ivanov possessed a phenomenal memory: he knew *Vain Precautions* as it had been seen in the forties, when the spirit of Dauberval/Didelot had not yet disappeared from it. Ivanov's rare musicality allowed him without particular losses to produce the 'grafting' of Dauberval's *mise-en-scène* onto new music. But the original scene of the harvest was unknown to Ivanov.

Whether Petipa and Ivanov wanted to or not, they could not but follow Hertel. In particular, they had to 'stuff' the performance with divertissement dances. The public of the capital was clamouring for this, and foreign touring artists also wanted it. Zucchi also brought in her crowning numbers, which she performed in *Vain Precautions* as well.[5]

---

[3] *Novosti i birzhevaya gazeta*, 26 Aug. 1885, p. 3.

[4] *SlonMasters*, 176.

[5] Yu[rii Iosifovich] Slonimskii, *Tshchetnaya predostorozhnost'* [The Vain Precaution] (Leningrad: State Music Publisher, 1961), 56. Krasovskaya, possibly following Slonimsky, also attributes the revival to Ivanov without citing evidence (*Krasovskaya*, 351), while Ivor Guest attributes it to Petipa, also without verification, in *The Divine Virginia: A Biography of Virginia Zucchi* (New York: Marcel Dekker, 1977), 84–5. Given the contention of Soviet historians that Ivanov was a neglected genius, one would expect them to document his productions more rigorously than this.

In sources from the time of the revival, Ivanov's contribution is not so clear: none available to this study attributes any part of *La Fille mal gardée* specifically to him. Only from his appointment as second balletmaster and the frantic schedule that autumn may we infer his involvement. Imperial-period historians are vague on the matter. Khudekov in the *History of Dances* does not list *La Fille mal gardée* among the productions of 1885, but remarks elsewhere that Petipa staged it.[6] Pleshcheyev reports on Gerdt's jubilee and Zucchi's débuts but mentions no producer,[7] an omission echoed in official lists of dances, cast, and costumes submitted to the direction on 23 and 28 November 1885 by régisseur Alberto di Segni.[8]

Reviewers tended to slight the producers in favour of more newsworthy aspects of the performance: Gerdt, the recipient of honour, and Zucchi, the recipient of glory. The following account gives us a sense of a jubilee evening in the imperial theatres: at some break in the performance a ritual hyperbole of tribute would come, enlivened in this instance by the ballerina.

After the third scene the curtain swept up and the jubilee artist, surrounded by the ballet company and deputations from the other theatres, was presented to the public. The first to speak was second balletmaster L. Ivanov on behalf of his colleagues, who presented the jubilee artist with a silver wreath from the ballet company. 'Accept, dear comrade, this wreath as a tribute to your talent!' L. Ivanov said; the jubilee artist wanted to respond, but overpowering emotion kept him from speaking. Then balletmaster M. Petipa said a few heartfelt words; he was, as we know, Mr Gerdt's teacher, and after this, boy students of the theatre school presented a wreath to Mr Gerdt, who at present is their teacher. The Russian opera troupe also sent greetings with a wreath and an address by Mr Koryakin, which ended with words to the effect that these 'first twenty-five years of service to art weren't the last'. On behalf of the Russian drama troupe a wreath was presented to the jubilee artist by Miss Strepetova, who spoke several sympathetic words in honour of Mr Gerdt's talent. Nor did the German company forget the jubilee artist and presented a wreath. Only the French shone by their absence. After these ovations, Mr Gerdt recovered somewhat and turned to the audience with a speech, which, however, because of the powerful agitation he felt, he broke off after hardly a word, and left incomplete. It began thus: 'It is strange that in ballet, where mute language reigns, I shall speak in real words. Although mute balletic speech is accessible to all, understandable to all, since it has no nationality, for which reason our art is the property of all nations. . . .' With these words Mr Gerdt finished. They were, apparently, translated for Miss Zucchi, taking part in the ovation, who sincerely applauded the jubilee artist; she ran up to Mr Gerdt and kissed him on the cheek before the public. After this the audience roared. *Russian choreographic art and the Italian school flowed together in a friendly kiss* in an overflowing hall.[9]

---

[6] *Khudekov*, 119, 162.
[7] *Pleshcheyev*, 274–5.
[8] St Petersburg, Historical Archive, 497/18/605, fos. 2–3ᵛ.
[9] *Peterburgskaya gazeta*, 16 Dec. 1885, p. 3.

Zucchi's performance in the ballet was no less impressive, and the focus of critical attention:

[In] . . . the 'Dance with the Ribbon' and in two *pas de deux* with Mr Gerdt, the theatre shook with applause. . . . In all her dances, in all her graceful, elegant movements there was something new, fresh, distinctive . . . in everything lay the stamp of originality and living truth. Dancing, she acted with her face and her expressive, continuously eloquent eyes. . . . What a marvellous transition from tears to joy, how subtle and artistically handled the scene in the cottage during the mother's nap—all were pearls of the choreographic art![10]

Skalkovsky recalled Zucchi's acting with similar warmth:

With astonishing delicacy Zucchi represented the varied scenes of girlish innocent jests and foolishness, then fright, passion, despair, and finally repentance. The extraordinarily agile mime of her face transmitted the tiniest shades of the role with amazing precision, and if one may, as the Greeks, call mime 'mute poetry', then Zucchi's acting fully corresponds to this term.[11]

Such data as the press provides—usually no more than a line or two— suggest that Petipa and Ivanov worked on the revival together. 'All of Dauberval's dances are preserved; the music is completely new and eminently melodious. The ballet is produced by L. Ivanov, but Mr Petipa gives the final *coup de maître*.'[12] Other reports are vaguer. Skalkovsky wrote, 'The balletmasters Mr Petipa and Mr Ivanov also worked a great deal on the production of the ballet.'[13] A review of the second performance ended with a remark still more noncommittal that 'Generally the efforts of our balletmasters M. Petipa and L. Ivanov are fully rewarded by the success of their compositions'.[14] Yet *The Petersburg Gazette*, whose critics seemed well informed about such matters, implied that Petipa alone staged the revival:

Rendering Mr Petipa full justice in the production of the ballet, which so clearly proclaims a *coup de maître*, we candidly admit the last act was manifestly composed in an offhand way; there is nothing outstanding in the dances, and the ballerina finished the work with an insignificant *polka de caractère* and a merry enough general dance, a *bourrée*. The dance with the bouquets, newly staged for the corps de ballet, turned out quite graceful, a joining of flowers in costumes and charming groupings with the dancers' garlands, pointing to the balletmaster's great taste.[15]

---

[10] *Peterburgskaya gazeta*, 17 Dec. 1885, p. 3.   [11] *Skalkovsky*, 139.
[12] *Peterburgskii listok*, 15 Dec. 1885, p. 5.   [13] *Novoe vremya*, 17 Dec. 1885, p. 3.
[14] *Novosti i birzhevaya gazeta*, 20 Dec. 1885, p. 4.
[15] *Peterburgskaya gazeta*, 17 Dec. 1885, p. 3. The same newspaper on 30 Nov. 1885, p. 3, tends to corroborate that Petipa might have worked alone: 'The work of Mr Petipa and Miss Zucchi at the present time is simply amazing: besides the performance of a ballet twice a week, every day morning to evening are prolonged rehearsals of the two new ballets and the *féerie*, *The Magic Pills*.' In this context the 'two new ballets', which the writer goes on to mention, would be *The King's Command* and *La Fille mal gardée*.

Reasons for this muddle are not obscure. One is the custom of Russian writers to attribute any ballet to its original choreographer. Pleshcheyev and the press notices referred to *La Fille mal gardée* as Dauberval's. When Zucchi later performed Lise and the ballet was listed as Mendes's, one writer was taken aback:

This ballet, composed by Dauberval in the last century, for some reason has been transformed on the poster of the Arcadia Theatre into a ballet by Mendes, although only a few dances were produced by him, in the same form as they were composed by balletmaster Taglioni for the stage in Berlin.[16]

A second reason was that Zucchi herself contributed to the production. To call *La Fille mal gardée* an 'old ballet', a typical appellation in the 1880s, is ambiguous, for neither music nor choreography was old to Russian audiences. Since May 1876 Zucchi had been performing the Taglioni/Hertel version of *La Fille mal gardée*, and we may infer Zucchi's influence on the Petersburg revival in part from the direction's purchase of the rights to Hertel's music. Zucchi, it would appear, was not going to dance the version familiar to St Petersburg, but rather St Petersburg was going to dance the version familiar to her.[17] In November 1885, after correspondence between Zucchi and the balletmaster Joseph Mendes in Warsaw, the supervisor Frolov requested Vsevolozhsky's permission to pay Mendes 1,500 francs for the music.[18] By 23 November it had arrived in St Petersburg.[19] The strain on the company, its other responsibilities notwithstanding, of performing a ballet on 15 December to music it had not yet heard three weeks before, can only be imagined.

If Zucchi danced to familiar music in the Petersburg revival, it follows that she would have danced familiar steps as well, Taglioni's or her own; Petipa or Ivanov would not have choreographed everything afresh.[20]

---

[16] *Novoe vremya*, 27 May 1889, p. 3.

[17] That Zucchi danced some version of Paul Taglioni's setting of *La Fille mal gardée* makes Slonimsky's apostrophe to Ivanov as producer more equivocal than it sounds. What possible use would Ivanov's knowledge of Dauberval's work 'edited by J. Perrot' be in this situation? Slonimsky's contention that Ivanov's musicality allowed him to graft Dauberval's *mise-en-scène* onto new music seems far-fetched as a practical matter.

[18] St Petersburg, Historical Archive 497/10/138, fo. 12. Guest relates an exchange about the music between Zucchi and balletomane Konstantin Skalkovsky which appears to have preceded the direction's payment of rights (*The Divine Virginia*, 74–5).

[19] *Peterburgskaya gazeta*, 23 Nov. 1885, p. 3.

[20] Certain exceptional features of the 1885 production point indirectly to Zucchi's influence by their recurrence in other productions of *La Fille mal gardée* in which she participated. The assignment of the role of Marcellina to a woman artist in 1885, for example, was a departure from a Russian tradition of casting that goes back to the first performance. In 1892, when Zucchi was again dancing Lise in St Petersburg (at the Maly Theatre as part of a touring company), a woman took the part—Zucchi's sister 'Miss Constan[tina]', if a press report is accurate (*Novoe vremya*, 26 Jan. 1892, p. 4).

Skalkovsky praised a *pas de deux*, presumably hers, in a production otherwise undistinguished:

La Fille mal gardée is not especially rich in dances, and one can only regret that for
unknown reasons the final ballabile was omitted, and as a result the last act seemed
short, somewhat cooling the impression of the first three charming scenes of the ballet. To increase the danced part, Miss Zucchi interpolated a *pas de deux* with Mr
Gerdt in the second scene, a *chef d'œuvre* of choreography in the full sense of the
word. The cleanness and lightness with which the artist danced the most difficult
pas on pointe were amazing—the *pas fouetté*, made in two turns, tipping over on the
third into her partner's arms; she maintained perfect balance in what would seem to
be impossible *attitudes*, and finished it all with an airy flight into Mr Gerdt's arms, a
worthy partner to the dazzling ballerina.

   Miss Zucchi danced the *pas de ruban* with Mr Gerdt in the first scene no less beautifully, and the 'characteristic polka' in the last. Beyond that one can praise, as
danced by others, the 'Gypsy Dance' and the 'valse with bouquets' in the second
scene and the 'galop' in the last. In general the corps de ballet danced not quite
evenly and was costumed without taste, and in dances *sujets* of second and third
rank took part. Why such disfavour towards the public from the *soloistes*—is not
known.[21]

   While Zucchi had an outstanding success, which 'forced even the most
severe spectators, who had responded sceptically to her appearance on our
state ballet stage, to be reconciled with her',[22] not all voices spoke in her favour. To one traditionalist, there was a defect in the allure of her mime and
staging. Lise, he claimed, was a classic type—naïve, primitive, and mischievous—an *ingénue*:

Miss Zucchi introduces much of her own into this role—which is *excellent* if you
judge by her success with our public, yet nasty and inartistic if judged from the

   The régisseur's report of 28 November 1885 also indicates that the 'Danse Bohémienne' performed in Act II was 'instead of the czardas that was designated according to the first list'. Though
omitted on the official stage in the end, the czardas was being considered for a time, and was rein-
stated in *La Fille mal gardée* when Zucchi performed it in the Hermitage Garden in Moscow in 1888
and at the Arcadia Theatre in St Petersburg in 1889. Both productions were supervised by Mendes,
and reinforce the supposition that Zucchi knew and preferred his version of the work.
   The régisseur's reports from 1885, finally, reveal signs of haste. There are many deletions and
other marks suggesting uncertainty. Three weeks before the first performance the *polka de caractère*
for Lise and Colin, and the *ensemble bourrée et final* of the last act were not listed among the dances,
and the *pas sabotière* was to be borrowed from Saint-Léon's *Pâquerette*.
   [21] *Novoe vremya*, 17 Dec. 1885, p. 3. The régisseur's reports (above, n. 8) tend to confirm
Skalkovsky's criticisms, especially the dearth of fresh costumes. According to the report dated 23
Nov. 1885, Marcellina was allotted one costume, Colin, Micheau, and Nicaise two apiece, 'one simple, one luxurious'. The notary was to wear '[Vasily] Geltser's costume from *Coppélia*'. Except
where certain members of the corps de ballet had to represent gypsies, there is no alternative to
their peasant costumes, which they wore from act to act without change. In contrast, Zucchi was
assigned four costumes, one for each scene.
   [22] *Suflyor*, 19 Dec. 1885, p. 5.

point of view of art. In a clear, eminently expressive, and talented way Miss Zucchi transmits a type—a cunning, spoiled, passionate girl—but the image of Lise in her performance is missing.

All the unexpected changes—fear to passion to the ecstasy of love, which vanquishes shyness and shame—are beautifully transmitted in Miss Zucchi's mime, but nevertheless it is not Lise, and as such, it is a perversion of type. Of Miss Zucchi's dances nothing new can be said: the same limited stock of effects, the same unbeautiful manner of the Italian school in pointe work. Certain numbers the ballerina has staged anew, and for that reason all responsibility for their *composition* rests with her, not our balletmasters, who are not permitted such methods as the *pas de ruban*, where Miss Zucchi, at the end of a long ribbon held by Colin in the centre of the stage, makes a circle on pointe, as in the circus on a cord. Then Colin takes the ribbon by both ends, and Lise, 'champing at the bit', marks time in place, playing a mischievous little horse. Such an idea for a *pas* can be and is very playful, but one can hardly acknowledge artistic taste in it.[23]

Her own numbers apart, Zucchi may have demonstrated to the company, as Fanny Elssler had in 1848, other dances and mimed scenes. That she co-produced the revival on the basis of the Taglioni version may explain why the sources make such tentative reference to Petipa and Ivanov.

As long as Zucchi performed on the imperial stage, *La Fille mal gardée* was hers. At her first performance of Lise in the autumm of 1886, a critic noted that her entrance was applauded, but not as noisily as before, that she had grown thinner in the face and bust, her shoulders were more pointed, that it took until her mimed scene in Act III for the 'ice to break', and that a breach had opened among the balletomanes, some of whom preferred Antonietta Dell'Era and at times 'hissed like a snake'.[24] The 'Divine Virginia' danced the last of sixteen performances of *La Fille mal gardée* on the official stage on 2 December 1887. For the next five years she performed it in the privately owned theatres of St Petersburg and Moscow.

In Zucchi's stead, the role of Lise fell to her protégé Alexandra Vinogradova (Plate 12), who graduated from the theatre school in 1887.[25] Under Ivanov's supervision she prepared Act I of the ballet in the summer of 1888 at Krasnoe Selo, and performed it at the Maryinsky Theatre in October. There was no attempt to disguise her indebtedness to Zucchi:

Miss Vinogradova, successor to Virginia Zucchi in the role of Lise, although in her acting copied her predecessor down to the finest detail, did not let this keep her from

---

[23] *Novosti i birzhevaya gazeta*, 20 Dec. 1885, p. 4.
[24] *Peterburgskaya gazeta*, 16 Oct. 1886, p. 3.
[25] Alexandra Ivanovna Vinogradova-Petrova (1869–89) graduated from the theatre school with a certificate of merit and additional prizes. Her talent was so highly regarded that Alexandre Petrovich Frolov, supervisor of the school, requested that her initial salary be raised from 800 to 1,500 roubles per year. She studied with Marius Petipa and Christian Johanson and was coached by Evgenia Sokolova. While abroad she studied on one occasion with Jules Perrot, who rehearsed her in the role of Esmeralda (*Borisoglebsky*, i. 314).

taking the role very nicely and from dancing several demi-caractère dances with great taste.[26]

In the harsher scrutiny of the autumn season, the comparison was not so flattering:

What a difference, for example, in the performance of *La Fille mal gardée*, between Miss Zucchi and Miss Vinogradova, who danced on Sunday. The latter literally copied the former, but a student copy will never fully correspond to the master's original; for it is one thing to create a type and another to imitate it slavishly. Above all, in mime the facial expression, which depends on the acting of the eyes, has extraordinary importance. It is impossible to imitate this acting; nature bestows it, and for that reason it is impossible for Miss Vinogradova or even a more talented artist to copy Miss Zucchi.[27]

Fate kept Vinogradova from developing her potential: she died on 15 July 1889, at the age of 20. The plan to groom a Russian successor to Zucchi's Lise was effectively ended with her death. Ivanov kept the ballet alive in the summers at Krasnoe Selo, but no complete performance of *La Fille mal gardée* was given on the Petersburg imperial stage between Zucchi's last and 25 September 1894.

On that date the ballet was performed by Hedwige Hantenberg in a revival clearly attributed to Lev Ivanov.[28] Reviewers again focused on the ballerina to the virtual exclusion of the producer, only the balletomane-critic Nikolay Bezobrazov commenting that 'all the dances of *La Fille mal gardée* are staged by balletmaster L. I. Ivanov with taste, especially the ballabile for the corps de ballet'.[29]

Two questions may be posed about this revival. Why was it undertaken, and how much of it was Ivanov's?

Ivanov seems to have retained much of the 1885 production, including the game of horses in the *pas de ruban* associated with Zucchi. In the following list,[30] an asterisk marks dances referred to in the press or régisseur's reports nine years earlier:

ACT I, SCENE 1

1.* *Scène dansante*—Lise, Marcellina, and 8 peasant girls
2.* *Pas de ruban*—Lise and Colin

ACT I, SCENE 2

1. *Scène générale*—Lise, Marcellina, Colin, Nicaise, Micheau [his father] and all participants

[26] *Novoe vremya*, 4 Aug. 1888, p. 3.   [27] *Novoe vremya*, 4 Oct. 1888, p. 3.
[28] *Ezhegodnik Imperatorskikh Teatrov* [Yearbook of the Imperial Theatres], 1894/5, 196.
[29] *Peterburgskaya gazeta*, 27 Sept. 1894, p. 3.
[30] The list is taken from the *Ezhegodnik Imperatorskikh Teatrov*, 1894/5, 197–8.

2.* *Danse bohémienne*—a lead couple (Marie Petipa and Alfred Bekefy at the first performance), and four additional couples

3.* *Valse comique*—Nicaise and the 8 peasant girls from the *Scène dansante* in Scene 1

4. *Pas de deux*—Lise and another cavalier

5.* *Valse des bouquets*—32 women

6. *Galop comique*—Marcellina and Nicaise

ACT II

1. *Scène dansante*—Lise, Marcellina, Colin

ACT III

1. *Pas de cerises*—a solo couple (this *pas* was performed only at the first performance on 25 September)

2.* *Galop*—5 women

3.* *Polka de caractère*—Lise and Colin

4.* *Bourrée* and

5. *Finale*—Lise, Colin, 22 women, 4 men, 'and other men and women dancers'

To be sure, Ivanov made changes. He restored the role of Marcellina to a male artist, Enrico Cecchetti, and added a new named part, the tavernkeeper. The ballet was at first reconceived in four acts, but had reverted to three acts and four scenes by the first performance. A borrowed *pas sabotière* from 1885 was omitted, the *danse bohémienne* was recast for a lead couple and four additional couples, instead of a lead couple and eight women dancers, as before. To make the ballet richer in dances, a *pas de cerises* was added for a solo couple in Act III. Ivanov may have made other changes in details, or have retained more of the 1885 production than the sources illuminate. A review from 1897, for example, reports an amusing touch in his production: 'The fact is that the hens and cocks in the henhouse produced such a concert as nearly drowned out Mr Drigo's orchestra. Fortunately, these "disruptors of order" were soon removed from the stage.'[31]

Krasovskaya refers to the new staging as a 'regular' or 'periodic' revival, as if Ivanov were fulfilling a routine duty of his post. This term also downplays changes made between 1885 and 1894, allowing Ivanov's certain attribution of the later staging to extend by implication back to the earlier one.[32]

Other factors suggest that Ivanov's revival was substantially autonomous. For one, he had shown himself adept at comedy in *The Magic Flute*

---

[31] *Novosti i birzhevaya gazeta*, 30 Sept. 1897, p. 3.

[32] *Krasovskaya*, 351–2. Her logic here is slippery: the clarity of the attribution to Ivanov in 1894, set against the obscurity of attribution in 1885, argues against crediting him with the earlier production, and suggests that the new revival bore the stamp of his style.

the year before (see below), an obvious prerequisite for reviving *La Fille mal gardée*. For another, Zucchi had finally left Russia. She took her farewell benefit at a private theatre in St Petersburg on 4 February 1892, in the role of Lise, and a discreet interval had now passed since her departure. Observing a period of silence for her rendition of Lise would be diplomatic if the purpose of a revival were to make *La Fille mal gardée* a repertoire work again—suitable for any good ballerina, not the idiosyncratic vehicle of one artist.

The pull of the ballet's Russian tradition may also have been felt after Zucchi's departure, not least in the person of Evgenia Sokolova, who knew that tradition and had joined the company as a teacher and coach. According to Borisoglebsky, Alexandra Vinogradova went through various roles with Sokolova, though he does not name which ones.[33] Some idea of Sokolova's approach to *La Fille mal gardée* may be gleaned from a description she made of Lise's mime. The document is not dated, and could therefore relate to the part in 1879 or before, when she danced it, or to after 1886, when she taught it. It may describe some non-Zucchi variant of the role, judging by the absence of any reference to the game of horses within the *pas de ruban*. Yet the synopsis is not complete, the scene of the matchmaking being omitted, nor does it describe any dancing. The *pas de ruban* is simply mentioned, not parsed, at the point where it is to be danced. Her synopsis is translated in Appendix D.

The 1894 revival seems to represent a conflation of the most pleasing of Zucchi's dances and mimed scenes with numbers newly staged by Ivanov, in which Lise's principal dramatic shading reverted from Zucchi's allure back to the *ingénue* of the Russian tradition. Ivanov's redaction of *La Fille mal gardée* was the basis of the performing version in the Petersburg imperial ballet thereafter, which in time came to be modified by interpolations and reworkings made for various occasions, often first solo appearances of young dancers. After Hantenberg's appearance it was a début piece for other visitors, such as Maria Giuri (1899), and a repertoire work for ballerinas like Olga Preobrazhenskaya, Vera Trefilova, and Tamara Karsavina. Most of all, however, it was a vehicle for Mathilde Kshesinskaya.

The later history of *La Fille mal gardée* in St Petersburg is dominated by Kshesinskaya, whose task it was to take the Zucchi out of Lise, and create something just as effective in its place. This process, not to mention Ivanov's own preparation for the revival, may have started in the summers of 1891 and 1892 at Krasnoe Selo, where Kshesinskaya danced all of Act I.

Tamara Karsavina recalled the new staging enthusiastically, praising Pavel Gerdt, Kshesinskaya, and Ivanov's production.

---

[33] *Borisoglebsky*, i. 314.

The choreographer achieved integration of dance and action: the *pas de ruban* is a delightful interplay of the two, and the captivating youth and innocence of Lise and Colas, established from the first, disarms us against all their future transgressions. Indeed, the amorous game of the *pas de ruban* is but a children's game—'let's play horses'. The images of Mathilde Kshesinska and Gerdt in this dance are for ever in my memory. Gerdt's transformation from his habitual role of *jeune premier* into a rustic swain was admirable. Mathilde stamped the ground with her steel toes, worrying the reins, tossing her head like a high-mettled thoroughbred. In this type of *pas de deux*, belonging to the older ballets, there is no rigid division into four parts (adagio, two solos, and coda). It began by andante and passed into allegretto, during which, divided by the length of the ribbon across the stage, both dancers did identical *enchaînements* and pirouetted as if suspended to the air by the ribbon.[34]

When Kshesinskaya first performed Lise, the memory of Zucchi made for comparisons:

Zucchi moved the choreographic aspect of the role into the background—in general the dances here are not the most complicated—but her mime impressed with its artistry, its rare expressiveness, [and] sentimentality. The love and fear transmitted by Zucchi, brought on by the unexpected meetings with the man she loves, moved [the audience] to tears. Miss Kshesinskaya did not achieve this, but drew attention more to Lise's childlike qualities, to her mischievousness, charming coquetry and naïveté. The touching quality was not there, but the public saw instead a nice, poetical, youthful creation—merry, graceful, at times rather embarrassed. Fanny Elssler, judging from notices, made no attempt to be touching, and so one cannot reproach Miss Kshesinskaya 2 for the same understanding of the role. One watches the young ballerina with pleasure, and she had a positive success not with the claque, but with the public. She danced still better than she mimed.[35]

A year later Zucchi was still considered the better mime, but Kshesinskaya's superiority as a dancer was given more credit.[36] Five years later, memories of Zucchi had faded:

In this elegant ballet M. F. Kshesinskaya in the role of Lise is a genuine masterpiece. It is difficult to imagine more gracious and sensitive acting. A living person is before the audience the whole time, the delicate and expressive mime of the artist fully substituting for that mighty instrument of understanding—the human word. Miss Kshesinskaya performed several mimed scenes with rare artistic realism and produced a powerful impression on the public. In various ways Miss Kshesinskaya's dances in this ballet are distinguished by great brilliance. To please that part of the public which loves technical difficulties in its dances exclusively, our ballerina powerfully advanced the technique of her dances and obviously demonstrated that all the exceptional *tours de force* invented by the latest Italian school are accessible to her. Only our ballerina, during the execution of even the most dizzying

[34] *Fille*, 26.   [35] *Novosti i birzhevaya gazeta*, 14 Sept. 1896, p. 3.
[36] *Novosti i birzhevaya gazeta*, 30 Sept. 1897, p. 3.

technique, does not lose sight of the basic traditions of the old French school: gracefulness and ethereality. Thus, in the second scene of *Vain Precautions*, in one of her
variations, Miss Kshesinskaya performed those celebrated *fouettés* which were Miss
Legnani's war-horse. Our ballerina performed the same number [i.e. thirty-two]
with astonishing finish, assurance, and grace. Naturally with such a brilliant performance of the role, in both mime and choreography, Miss Kshesinskaya had success and was greeted unanimously by the entire theatre, without distinction of the
factions which exist in the ballet.[37]

For her farewell benefit performance on 4 February 1904 Kshesinskaya
chose Odette in the first lakeside scene of *Swan Lake*, and to begin, Lise in
Acts I and II of *La Fille mal gardée*. One reviewer lamented: 'She danced for
the last time. She danced and mimed amazingly, in the brilliance of her talent, elegance, beauty, and strength.'[38] It was, of course, neither the last time
Kshesinskaya danced nor the last time she danced the role of Lise. On 21
January 1907 she was in Moscow to perform Lise (with Fokine as Colin) at
the farewell benefit of Vasily Fyodorovich Geltser after fifty years of service. Later still, in December 1915, in the middle of the First World War,
Kshesinskaya, who at 43 was now seven years older than Zucchi when the
Italian first appeared in St Petersburg as Lise, could still draw favourable
notices. The loyal Pleshcheyev found that

Kshesinskaya in collaboration with Mr Vladimirov in fact underscores the naïveté,
the frivolousness, and coquettishness of the two figures Lise and Colin. A childlike
quality shows through in these love duets. . . . Kshesinskaya and Vladimirov perform the *pas de deux* so spontaneously, easily, effortlessly, that it fits in with the simple life [of the setting] and does not rend the general choreographic outline. The
execution is artistic and graceful.[39]

André Levinson commented: 'Only in the excellent *pas de ruban* and in
the *pas de deux* of *Vain Precautions* is their art materialized in its persuasive
fullness. Miss Kshesinskaya's success was great, as in former times. . . .'[40]

La Fille mal gardée was last performed in Petrograd before the Revolution on 27 September 1917. On that occasion, Elsa Will took the role of Lise.

The Enchanted Forest

Every year performances were given at the graduation ceremonies of the
theatre school, for which a new ballet might be staged. Composing *The En-*

---

[37] *Novosti i birzhevaya gazeta*, 10 Apr. 1901, p. 3. A review in the same newspaper on 1 May 1903
(p. 3) noted that Kshesinskaya/Lise had performed thirty-four *fouettés* in the last ballet performance of the season on 27 April.

[38] *Novoe vremya*, 5 Feb. 1904, p. 5.

[39] *Novoe vremya*, 22 Dec. 1915, p. 7.   [40] *Rech'*, 23 Dec. 1915, p. 5.

chanted Forest had nothing in particular to do with Lev Ivanov's appointment as second balletmaster; it was a routine function of his teaching.

The Enchanted Forest is based on a simple tale. Valeria has been separated from her friends in a storm; she grows distraught and faints. Genies and dryads discover her, take delight in her beauty, but frighten her when she awakes. The genie of the forest falls in love with her and and begs her to rule with him over this realm. Discovering that Valeria has a human fiancé, he threatens her, and she faints again. Mortals are heard approaching, and the forest creatures withdraw. Peasants enter and find Valeria. Petrus, her fiancé, revives her. She recounts her experiences, and the ballet ends with rejoicing and dances.

The new work was first staged on 24 March 1887 at the theatre school, with a public performance by the senior company in the Maryinsky on 3 May, the last day of the season. On the large stage Valeria's name was changed to Ilka, Petrus's to Josi, and the corps de ballet of dryads was expanded. The public début of Ivanov's ballet also marked the first appearance of the Italian virtuosa Emma Bessone in Jules Perrot's *The Naiad and the Fisherman*. The mix of favourable and unfavourable circumstances—the compliment to Ivanov implicit in committing the company to learning a new ballet late in the season, and the juxtaposing of his ballet with a much stronger attraction on the same programme—is of a kind he would experience again.

The critical response was mixed. There were quibbles about the ballerinas: Alexandra Vinogradova, who danced the leading role in the school performance, was found to be plump,[41] whereas Varvara Nikitina, her counterpart on the large stage, was declared lacking in aplomb.[42] The press critique ignored the official favour implicit in bringing the ballet to the Maryinsky, and focused instead on Ivanov's inexperience. 'This was Mr Ivanov's début as a balletmaster,' Nikolay Bezobrazov observed,

Up to now he was known only as an excellent dancer and mime artist; it happened that he sometimes had occasion to produce separate numbers of dances in operas, but in the production of ballets Mr Ivanov had not yet tried his powers. His first attempt turned out to be more than successful. *The Enchanted Forest* is a short piece, but in it the gifted artist was able to demonstrate much taste.[43]

Indulgence towards Ivanov as a beginner was sometimes offset by harsh complaint:

[41] *Sanktpeterburgskie vedomosti*, 28 Mar. 1887, p. 3.
[42] *Sanktpeterburgskie vedomosti*, 5 May 1887, p. 3.
[43] *Sanktpeterburgskie vedomosti*, 28 Mar. 1887, p. 3. Bezobrazov's recital of Ivanov's accomplishments makes an indirect statement about who revived *La Fille mal gardée*: if Ivanov had been significantly responsible for that staging, why would Bezobrazov not have given him credit in this circumstance?

As for the production and the dances, we must be lenient. Why? Because *The Enchanted Forest* is Mr Ivanov's first attempt as an independent balletmaster. If it were composed by a real balletmaster, we would declare it poor work, but it is acceptable for a débutant. Excepting one variation with classical shadings, there is absolutely nothing in the new ballet deserving of praise: there is neither beautiful grouping nor outstanding *pas*. There is a lot of running about, especially for young students of the theatre school.[44]

A colleague concurred: 'Of Mr Ivanov's first attempt at a balletic bagatelle,' he wrote,

we can only say that it is a quite graceful trifle with respect to dances, but its programme is too thin and insignificant, and offers absolutely no interest as a novelty. Mr Drigo's music, full of melody, helped it a great deal to achieve a certain success. In any event, Mr Ivanov, judging by this first attempt, as regards choreography can announce himself in future as an artist capable of creating more serious works.[45]

Suffering comparison with *The Naiad and the Fisherman*, Ivanov's effort was dismissed by one critic: 'Also given at the same performance was the little one-act ballet, *The Enchanted Forest*, which offered nothing outstanding amidst a series of mediocre choreographic trifles, in story, music, or execution.'[46]

Ballet conductor Riccardo Drigo garnered more praise for writing the music of *The Enchanted Forest* than Ivanov for composing the choreography. The critic for *The New Time* devoted a separate article to the composer, outlining the difficulties of composing for ballet, of finding the middle path between vulgarity and complexity, and concluded that

Mr Drigo passed between this Scylla and Charybdis quite adroitly. The music of his ballet, while not especially original, is outstanding in a symphonic sense, reveals an experienced composer, a man with taste, and an excellent orchestrator. There are beautiful melodies in it, its rhythms are not overdone, and everything is listened to with pleasure from beginning to end.[47]

Another reviewer found the music fresh and novel in its motifs. 'For Mr Drigo,' he continued, 'this was also a first effort at composing an entire ballet. We greet his success with pleasure, as we do Mr Ivanov.'[48]

Surveying the press notices of *The Enchanted Forest*, one senses that critics were swayed by the main attraction of the evening. A familiar Russian ballerina competing with a new Italian one, Lev Ivanov competing with Jules Perrot, a graduation piece competing with *The Naiad and the Fisherman*—all this disadvantaged the new work and produced perfunctory, dutiful assessments. This sense is strongest in comments about the

[44] *Peterburgskii listok*, 4 May 1887, p. 3.   [45] *Peterburgskaya gazeta*, 29 Mar. 1887, p. 4.
[46] *Novosti i birzhevaya gazeta*, 5 May 1887, p. 3.   [47] *Novoe vremya*, 5 May 1887, p. 3.
[48] *Sanktpeterburgskie vedomosti*, 28 Mar. 1887, p. 3.

czardas, which illuminate the opaque line between legitimate difference of opinion and lack of critical focus. Reviewers could not agree as to which element—music or dance—promoted its success.

Mr Drigo has written rather insipid music. As for the czardas, except for the appropriate rhythm, it more recalls the noisy finale of the overture than any kind of Hungarian dance. One is amazed that our ballet artists can dance this number.[49]

The review concludes by noting that the czardas, performed by the character dancer Alfred Bekefy, who specialized in Hungarian dances, was repeated by public demand, as if salvaged by the dancing. Another critic observed that Bekefy won rich applause for the czardas 'which he dances, as ever, with a perfection that admits of no comparison'.[50] The critic of *The Petersburg Gazette* came to the opposite conclusion, that the czardas was 'unsuccessful by its pallid performance', and yet as music 'produced a most pleasant impression for its spry rhythm and movement'.[51] In *Our Ballet* Pleshcheyev summed up the dance as 'masterfully staged by L. Ivanov'.[52]

The most extreme disparity between official and press responses to *The Enchanted Forest* came from the outspoken Bezobrazov. Whatever Petipa's attitude towards Ivanov over the years, he was doubtless shocked and somewhat wary of his colleague after reading Bezobrazov's assessment of the student production. Not only did the critic consider *The Enchanted Forest* 'more than successful', the work of 'a gifted artist able to show much taste', but also that Ivanov's success seemed to him especially precious,

that he represents a fresh element on our stage, foreign to all the routine which has settled on our ballet. Mr Ivanov can with ease gradually replace Mr Petipa. Our balletmaster's song is already sung, and since 'to everything there is a season', so the end is approaching for the masterful Petipa's choreographic composition.[53]

This has the look of faction, and Petipa might well have wondered if it were generated by his detractors, or if Ivanov had been organizing support in the press. In any event, Bezobrazov's counterpart at *The Petersburg Gazette* took umbrage at the assessment. He too complimented Ivanov, but continued:

Of course we shall not allow ourselves to pay him a compliment which insults, of the kind paid him today by the unceremonious ballet reviewer of *The Saint Petersburg Gazette*, who with some prejudiced, absurd assurance argues that Mr Ivanov easily can gradually replace Mr Petipa, whose creativity is coming to an end!!?? Nothing can be said for such excellent ideas about art, whence similar crazy and scandalous experts and judges are recruited![54]

[49] *Peterburgskii listok*, 4 May 1887, p. 3.   [50] *Novosti i birzhevaya gazeta*, 5 May 1887, p. 5.
[51] *Peterburgskaya gazeta*, 5 May 1887, p. 2.   [52] *Pleshcheyev*, 295.
[53] *Sanktpeterburgskie vedomosti*, 28 Mar. 1887, p. 3.
[54] *Peterburgskaya gazeta*, 29 Mar. 1887, p. 4.

In a touch no less acrid for the temptation, the critic made a pun on his rival's surname in the Russian word for 'scandalous' (*bezobraznyi*).

Criticisms aside, the new ballet was surely appealing. The choreography, especially of the ensemble dances, showed promise of sustaining repeated viewings, and the setting was attractive. The mysterious atmosphere of a forest populated by fairy-tale beings was reminiscent of romantic ballet, but was also related to the forest imagery, with profound psychological implications, of more recent works such as Wagner's *Siegfried*, to be produced in St Petersburg for the first time in 1889. In addition, Ivanov anticipated the imagery of other balletic forests—the one which overgrew the castle in *The Sleeping Beauty*, the one between the Christmas party and Confitürembourg in *The Nutcracker*, and the one where Siegfried would meet Odette in *Swan Lake*. The mystical ambiance of the ballet was clearly conveyed in Drigo's opening bars, where the gentle tremolos and stylized bird-song in the winds anticipate similar devices when the curtain rises on Fevronia's wooded domicile in *The Legend of the Invisible City of Kitezh*, though Rimsky-Korsakov would not compose his forest music, clearly derived from Wagner, for another fifteen years.

Some initial impressions of Ivanov's work remained in responses to his later ballets. While he was not expected to seek an imposing libretto for a student ballet, the criticism that his story was insubstantial and uninteresting will return. The positive observations were also early signs of tendencies: a flair for the well-made dance, and for working with competent composers.

The decision to include *The Enchanted Forest* in the regular repertoire could not have been taken without the concurrence of Ivanov's seniors in the theatre hierarchy, including Vsevolozhsky and Petipa, who must have believed in the ballet's future. But there were other reasons. Various small ballets, some composed for private state occasions, deserved to be shown to the regular public. Petipa's *A Midsummer Night's Dream* from 1876 was one, as would be his *The Seasons*, *Ruses d'Amour*, *The Pearl* (given at the coronation of Nicholas II in 1896), and Ivanov's own *Acis and Galatea* and *The Magic Flute*. In a repertoire dominated by grand ballets, it was difficult to schedule short ballets on a regular basis. An attempt to rectify this problem was made in the late 1880s.

Since grand ballets tended to be danced by visiting Italian ballerinas, there was also a need for pieces in which the leading role could be taken by Russians. Between Ekaterina Vazem's retirement in 1884 and Mathilde Kshesinskaya's rise to prominence in the mid-1890s, the multiple bill served as a proving ground for Russian ballerinas. It was a source of encouragement for the dancers involved, but mostly of disdain from critics, who tended to relegate Russian ballerinas to secondary status in their preference for Italians, or to rail against the direction for not giving native talent more substantial opportunities. The air of relegation associated with these ballets was exacerbated by the tendency to offer them at the very beginnings or ends of seasons, before the visiting celebrities arrived, or after their annual stay had ended, which was often the day before Lent.

The leading role in *The Enchanted Forest* was danced exclusively by Russians, many of whose careers were marred by official indifference or tragedy. Alexandra Vinogradova danced Valeria in the school performance; her early death has been noted. Varvara Nikitina, the first Ilka in the Maryinsky, retired without taking a farewell benefit, displeased with her treatment by the direction. Maria Gorshenkova took the role from October 1889; she was considered a martyr of discrimination, being sent on extended visits to Moscow to make room for visiting Italians in St Petersburg. Ilka passed to the promising young Maria Anderson in September 1892 (Plate 13), but she was injured at rehearsal the next year, and had to leave the stage after an agonizing convalescence. Claudia Kulichevskaya, a competent if not outstanding Russian dancer, took the role from April 1894, and Lyubov Egorova from May 1901.

These circumstances, together with the modest beginnings of *The Enchanted Forest*, make the ballet's survival all the more remarkable. But with survival came changes. In April and June 1889 the press announced a revival of *The Enchanted Forest* with new dances, including an interpolated divertissement, for a gala performance at Peterhof in July.[55] A régisseur's report from that year, probably prepared for this revival, indicates that forty dryads were now to dance in the ballet: two first dancers, four seconds, and thirty-four members of the corps de ballet. In addition twelve 'little genies' took part—children of the theatre school, and eighteen Hungarian couples in addition to Ilka and Josi.[56] The same report indicates a 'Petipa'— probably Marie—as 'Queen of the Dryads', a new character.

This information corroborates the claim of his detractors that Petipa intervened in the production of Ivanov's ballets. Petipa was much involved in the gala performances in the first half of 1889, for which he staged his *The Caprices of a Butterfly* and revised *A Midsummer Night's Dream*. Ivanov, moreover, was tied to his regular duties at Krasnoe Selo when *The Enchanted Forest* was due for production at Peterhof. This would not necessarily have precluded his participation, but the number of galas spread throughout the first half of the year makes Petipa's involvement likely. Moreover, three pages of notes in Petipa's hand, in French and undated, survive for 'La Forêt enchantée'.[57] A cast list geared to costume drawings

[55] *Novoe vremya*, 5 Apr. 1889, p. 3; 6 June 1889, p. 2.
[56] St Petersburg, Historical Archive, 497.8/2.431, fos. 64–5.   [57] *TMB 205*, no. 338.

calls for '23 personnes' led by 'Petipa' as 'La reine des Dryades', followed by six other dryads, performed by soloists including Anna Johanson, Maria Anderson, and Olga Preobrazhenskaya. The principal dancers he lists are the same as those on the régisseur's report just cited. Petipa's notes refer exclusively to a *pas* of dryads led by their queen—that is, it is probably a sketch for the new divertissement. An additional notation speaks of the protocols of imperial performance, namely a concern for time limits: 'Cela doit durer 12 minutes,' Petipa writes of his *pas*, 'Même un quart d'heure.'

Given the flexible performance tradition of the Russian imperial ballet, these changes were surely not the last. At some point, judging by its inclusion in the *répétiteur* (which in its present state is a mixture of various productions), a male variation was added to *The Enchanted Forest*, which Pavel Gerdt had danced in Ivanov's *The Tulip of Haarlem*.

When *The Enchanted Forest* was given as part of a triple bill in the autumn of 1889, one critic identified a problem with the one-act ballets on the programme (including *A Midsummer Night's Dream* and *The Caprices of a Butterfly*)—that they were too alike.

All three ballets are fantastic, all move in the magic world of insects, elves, flowers, and fairies, which requires a calm, poetical mood, wafted by the light grace and the ethereal, poetical quality of the story, images, and sounds. Today's spectator, used to powerful effects, to brilliant moments, to the dazzle and noise of magnificent spectacles, endures with difficulty the monotony of soft impressions, and one cannot insist that his attention be not blunted near the end of such a performance, nor that a prosey boredom does not somewhat displace poetical dreaminess.[58]

'*The Enchanted Forest*', we read in a review of the opening of ballet performances in the autumn of 1892,

strictly speaking is a wholly routine divertissement, which in its choreographic value and production is a negative phenomenon in its sphere, the inability to enchant even the undemanding spectator. Yesterday it offered a certain interest, for Miss Anderson attempted, successfully, to carry out the duties of first ballerina.[59]

The impression gained from the perusal of other reviews is that ballerinas performing the role of Ilka were praised, but the ballet itself was somehow nondescript, 'insipid', and 'colourless'. The only part of it to enjoy consistent success was the czardas, which was also performed at Krasnoe Selo. It was a portent of the czardas to Liszt's Second Hungarian Rhapsody that Ivanov would interpolate, late in his career, into Saint-Léon's *The Little Humpbacked Horse*.

The Enchanted Forest was last performed on 15 June 1907 at Krasnoe Selo. After sixty-one showings it had become dependable, of service, always

---

[58] *Novosti i birzhevaya gazeta*, 27 Oct. 1889, p. 2.   [59] *Novoe vremya*, 4 Sept. 1892, p. 4.

there, a metaphor of its choreographer. It began as a modest occasional piece. If its lot were that of most other ballets created for graduation festivities, its history would have ended with the first performance. Petipa's *A Magic Tale* (1893) never left the theatre school; Fokine's *Le Pavillon d'Armide*, which boasted far greater pretensions in the participation of Vatslav Nijinsky, did not enjoy the same longevity as *The Enchanted Forest* despite trips to Paris and London.

Composed for one performance, *The Enchanted Forest* held the stage for twenty years.

4

The Tulip of Haarlem

That *The Enchanted Forest* was incidental to Ivanov's duties as second balletmaster is implied by his work on another project whose origins were earlier, production later, and preparation concurrent with it. It was a grand ballet, and speaks yet again of the importance the direction attached to Ivanov within a year of his appointment as second balletmaster.

On 15 August 1886 *The Petersburg Gazette* reported:

According to the wish of Director of Theatres Mr I. A. Vsevolozhsky, the production of a ballet has been entrusted to the régisseur [*sic*] of the ballet troupe, L. I. Ivanov, on his own scenario. Mr Ivanov presented two scenarios to the direction, one of which was approved for production. Miss Zucchi has been named ballerina. The story indeed is still not known, and the production itself will not take place before January. The music will be commissioned from one of our best Russian composers, one with a solid reputation.[1]

The announcement raises several points. Ivanov was clearly not at liberty to devise any libretto he pleased and commit the resources of the imperial theatres to staging it, a fact which mitigates the criticism that his weak libretti were exclusively his own doing. Is it significant that Ivanov, not Petipa, was entrusted with a new ballet for Zucchi? Was this a compliment to Ivanov? A slight to Zucchi? Why did she never dance in it?

Two months later we learn a title and composer from the same source:

A bit of news: two acts of the music to Mr Ivanov's ballet *La Belle de nuit*, which probably will be performed in January, are already written, and a few days ago terms for obtaining it for the Imperial stage for three thousand roubles were agreed by the direction with the composer, Baron Fitinhof-Schell.[2]

---

[1] *Peterburgskaya gazeta*, 15 Aug. 1886, p. 3.

[2] *Peterburgskaya gazeta*, 14 Oct. 1886, p. 3. Of Baron Boris Alexandrovich Fitinhof-Schell (1829–1901) it may be said, as of most Russian ballet composers other than Tchaikovsky and Glazunov, that posterity does him a disservice in disregarding the significant credentials he brought to the

In respect to music, the new ballet was in the vanguard of reform. One of Vsevolozhsky's initiatives had been to develop new sources of ballet scores, principally from Russian composers. We owe Tchaikovsky's *The Sleeping Beauty* and *The Nutcracker* to this effort, but these were still in the future. Ivanov's new work was the first to come after the retirement of Ludwig Minkus, the last official composer of ballet music in the imperial theatres. This notice also signals Ivanov's tendency to collaborate with Russian composers. Except for music composed by the conductor Riccardo Drigo and Liszt's Second Hungarian Rhapsody, his original ballets were set to Russian music. In part the consequence of Vsevolozhsky's reform, this trend is seconded by Ivanov's choice of ballerina. Except for the Italian ballerinas who danced *The Tulip of Haarlem* and the works Ivanov staged with Petipa, all his ballets were produced for Russians. This accords with the sense of community expressed in his memoirs, though Ivanov in effect may have helped to create an enclave within the company of Russian artists secondary in importance to foreigners.

A scant two months later, we learn that *La Belle de nuit* was not to be produced that season for lack of time.[3]

Sometime before 23 July 1887 Ivanov changed the name of the ballet to *The Tulip of Haarlem*. This change need not imply a major reworking of the story, as the first title fits the final scenario. The censor approved the printed text on 28 September 1887, six days before the first performance.

The libretto opens with a recounting of the legend of the magic tulips. In the seventeenth century, near Haarlem, there was an enchanted tulip field where at night women spirits of the flowers would dance until sunrise. The mortal who kissed one of them would render her mortal as well. As his wife she would bring wealth and happiness to his house. This happened once, whereupon the tulip field lost its enchantment.

Pieters, long away on a journey, returns home and protests against his parentally arranged betrothal to Marianna. Both young people love someone else. Pieters's beloved, Emma, puts her trust in a gypsy whose talisman, a tulip, will guarantee his love. That night the gypsy takes Pieters to the magic field where tulips are transformed into young women. Emma is their queen. She confesses her love to Pieters but evades his embrace until dawn, when he manages to kiss her, and the lovers flee. The scene changes to show Marianna and Anders, her beloved, attempting to change their parents' minds. Pieters and Emma arrive, and only their threat to jump to their

---

task. A student of Field and Henselt, Fitinhof-Schell composed four operas and two ballets produced in the imperial theatres of St Petersburg—no insignificant accomplishment—together with some seventy songs and other works.

[3] *Peterburgskaya gazeta*, 9 Dec. 1886, p. 3.

deaths from a high window sways the parents into reconsideration. A double wedding ensues.

Ivanov's story is full of clichés. The female sprite who falls in love with a mortal man had been a staple of ballet stories since Filippo Taglioni; the woman as the spirit of a flower recalls *The Fern*, a ballet produced in Moscow in 1867; for one character to be interrupted by a second in pursuit of a third, as Pieters's is prevented by moths and butterflies and enchanted maidens from reaching Emma, recalls Solor's attempt to dance with Gamsatti, interrupted by the shade of Nikia in the last act of Petipa's *La Bayadère*; and the spirit maidens who disappear with the first ray of the morning sun echo the same device in *Giselle*, and in Petipa's *Roxana* of 1878.

Few data survive about the collaboration and production of *The Tulip of Haarlem*. The change of title was meant to focus but not to limit local colour. According to Nikolay Solyannikov, the final divertissement was to comprise national dances from many countries represented by merchants at the fairground where the weddings are celebrated. Supposedly under Petipa's nefarious influence, Vsevolozhsky objected to this plan, whereupon Ivanov, famous for his reticence, stood his ground. Solyannikov quotes his letter to the Director. 'Most esteemed Ivan Alexandrovich,' Ivanov wrote,

Platon Pavlovich informed me of your wish to maintain a purely Dutch style in my ballet, that is, not to introduce any other nationalities at the end.

It seems to me that if we do not fill up the divertissement with various nations, it will be very dry and boring,—all the more so because the character of Dutch dances is very heavy and the divertissement will be very wretched, as it will consist of only three numbers besides the finale, namely: the dance of the riflemen, the sailors' dance, and *La Belle Hollandaise* with Bessone and Gerdt; as regards the fairground procession it would also be necessary to abandon the merchants of various nations. . . .

[In its original conception] the ballet would be more interesting for the public. The first act is purely in the Dutch style, the second act fantastic, the third act first scene Dutch again, and finally, the last scene would be more varied and merrier.

Your Excellency, I most earnestly and most humbly request that you leave the ballet as it was proposed to you, and you will yourself then be convinced that it is better that way.

L. Ivanov[4]

The outcome of this request was apparently a compromise; a gypsy dance is the only component of a variegated divertissement of nations at the end of the ballet.

When substantial reference to the project next emerges in the press it is

---

[4] *Solyannikov*, fos. 47–8.

the autumn of 1887, and the sets of 'The Queen of the Tulips' are being described:

The first act decoration represents a suburb of Amsterdam and a view of the sea; ships and boats scurry about; from left and the right stretch out buildings more like huts than houses. The town has a festive look; it is decorated with flags, garlands, etc. In several places windmills are visible, thrusting out their wings. The decoration of the second act represents a broad field of tulips, with a hut in the foreground on the left. The entire landscape is effectively illuminated by the moon, since the action of the second act apparently takes place at night. The first scene of Act III represents a captain's room, where seafarer's accoutrements attract the attention, and finally the second scene of the last act transports us to a festive Amsterdam. A square opens up before the audience's eyes, surrounded by magnificent civic buildings, town hall, and palaces; the architecture of the houses is of the Flemish renaissance. At the right a barrel of extraordinary dimensions, with garlands of flowers cascading from it; at the left a row of booths, with acrobats, and canopied stalls overflowing with fruit. The dress rehearsal of the ballet is set for 2 October.[5]

The first performance of *The Tulip of Haarlem* took place on 4 October 1887. Let us look at the ballet's reception first, then investigate some of the questions surrounding its production.

That dancing should prevail over narrative and a narrative be filled with clichés were not necessarily faults. Yet Ivanov, it seems, paid too little heed to coherence. 'The story does not follow very clearly from the action,' one critic wrote, 'Without the libretto, even the habitués of the ballet will not know too much of what is happening.'[6] 'The subject is ordinary and simple,' wrote another, 'and of course cannot help but affect the entire ballet in an unfavourable way, even if considerable talent has been put into the dances.'[7] If *Giselle* was Ivanov's model, proposed a third, *Tulip* is a long way from its prototype. 'He did not achieve brilliance of fantasy, this necessary element in ballet, despite the fact that one can look at his entire ballet with pleasure, thanks to the tastefully produced dances for the ballerina.'[8]

On balance these criticisms seem just. *The Tulip of Haarlem* lacks dramatic tension. A wealth of dances in *Giselle* does not diminish the effectiveness of its plot. Pieters's arranged marriage, in contrast, is unprovoked by dire circumstance, strikes no chord, stirs no sympathy in the spectator, and is put right by the most mechanical of dénouements in the lovers' threatened suicide. The point of the piece lies in the dances; mime is secondary.

Praise for the costume designer, Evgeny Ponomaryov, was unanimous. The critic of *The Petersburg Leaflet* declared the ballet a success 'thanks chiefly to the truly luxurious, beautiful, and effective costumes', adding the

---

[5] *Novosti i birzhevaya gazeta*, 28 Sept. 1887, p. 3.
[6] *Journal de Saint-Pétersbourg*, 9 Oct. 1887, p. 1.
[7] *Novosti i birzhevaya gazeta*, 5 Oct. 1887, p. 3.   [8] *Peterburgskaya gazeta*, 5 Oct. 1887, p. 3.

next day: 'The entire ballet is supported exclusively by Miss Bessone, who managed the most difficult *pas*, and, however odd this seems, by the costumes.'[9] 'The costumes are positively magnificent,' wrote another, 'They are entirely free of that needless variety of colours of those . . . heavy costumes in which, for quasi-historical accuracy, the direction's prior artist loved to dress women dancers. Judging by the costumes of "Tulip", Mr Ponomaryov is an artist with fine and elegant taste.'[10] Skalkovsky concurred:

The costumes of the ballet, from drawings by Mr Ponomaryov, were magnificent, both in the successful combination of colours and in respect to authenticity; we were not expecting the clumsy Dutch, Zeelandish, and Frisian costumes and headwear to be made for the stage so elegantly and beautifully.[11]

Staging was a different matter. One critic found a set very fine, or executed in a strict, correct style, while another carped about the absence of any sense of water in a setting of maritime Haarlem. All agreed that the romantic ambiance of the second act—the field of magic tulips at night—was rent by the mishandling of the *mise-en-scène*. Complaints centred on the decoration, perspective, and lighting. This act 'suffered grievously from the semi-darkness in which the dances were performed. . . . We should add that the decoration of the second act was also quite crude, and in particular the cloudy sky was bereft of any element of naturalness, in a cut-out of which, too symmetrical and reminiscent of a window, the moon appears in the form of a twinkling electric lantern.'[12] The next day the same critic declared the decoration an utter failure, 'a field of tulips at night with a hole in the sky for the moon', adding sarcastically that the effect of lighting was true to life, 'it is dark on stage, as in a real night'.[13]

Skalkovsky charitably pointed out that the decorator's task was not easy in the Maryinsky Theatre, where the stage was not very deep and thus not altogether suitable for effects of perspective. His observation did little to stem the tide of complaint, which quickly flooded into derision.

In front there is a small field sprinkled with tulips; in the distance windmills are visible, of which the closer ones are three times smaller than those further away. They look as if they were glued to the stage. The field is illuminated by the moon. But what kind of moon is this?! It reminds one of an unripe watermelon floating in a pool intending to represent a cloud.[14]

'As for the tulip field in the moonlight, which prompted some applause,' noted the reviewer for St Petersburg's French language newspaper,

[9] *Peterburgskii listok*, 5 May 1887, p. 3; 6 May 1887, p. 3.
[10] *Sanktpeterburgskie vedomosti*, 6 Oct. 1887, p. 3.
[11] *Novoe vremya*, 6 Oct. 1887, p. 3.   [12] *Novosti i birzhevaya gazeta*, 5 Oct. 1887, p. 3.
[13] *Novosti i birzhevaya gazeta*, 6 Oct. 1887, p. 3.   [14] *Peterburgskii listok*, 6 Oct. 1887, p. 3.

it seems to us entirely botched. At first the spot of bright blue [the cut-out in which the moon was to appear?], which surrounds the moon and remains even after it has disappeared, is utterly inexplicable; the artificial tulips are poorly integrated with those painted on the backcloth; the windmills in the background of the tableau remind one of rabbits sitting on their hind legs. . . .[15]

Such reports led to adjustments. After the second performance, three days later, *The Saint Petersburg News* could announce:

The directing of ballet criticism at the unsatisfactory production with respect to decorations of the second act of *The Tulip of Haarlem* had its effect: both set and lighting are improved, and the moon is handled in a good-looking way. This act has much profited from the substitution of Miss Petrova, who with her portly dancing had rent the harmony of the ensemble of butterflies, with Miss Fyodorova II, who together with Miss Kulichevskaya, replacing Miss Vinogradova, are fully suited to the ethereal dances of the moths.[16]

Among the dancers, the occasional individual warranted attention. The performance of Zinaida Frolova in the *Danse des papillons* of Act II, staged for two soloists and girl students of the theatre school, was singled out for praise. She 'flew like a moth', dazzled with her elevation, and 'was covered with applause in her delicious *pas du papillon*'. The critic for *The Petersburg Gazette* summed up:

The dances of the butterflies are beautifully staged, and placed the ethereal Miss Frolova in the spotlight, who with each new season is having immense success, not to mention the correctness and finish of her dances; the young artist, one can say, is elegantly graceful, and any Italian ballerina can envy her *ballon*.[17]

The performance of Marie Petipa in the divertissement of Act III was a failure. Her dance, *La devineresse*, was a gypsy dance 'with oriental shadings', variously criticized as insipid, lacking sense, plastic movement, and gypsy temperament, and being staged in a completely inappropriate way. 'Miss Petipa in her Bohemian costume of rags and tatters did not produce much of an effect,'[18] and by the sixth performance, 'to the general pleasure, the inelegant and coarsely realistic dance *La devineresse* was omitted'.[19] It had been the only dance in the divertissement not on a Dutch motif.

The dancing of Emma Bessone (Plate 14) was the centre-piece of the ballet, about which much ink was spilled. Konstantin Skalkovsky, with his passion for Italian ballerinas, doted over her:

[15] *Journal de Saint-Pétersbourg*, 9 Oct. 1887, p. 1.
[16] *Sanktpeterburgskie vedomosti*, 10 Oct. 1887, p. 3.
[17] *Peterburgskaya gazeta*, 6 Oct. 1887, p. 3.
[18] *Journal de Saint-Pétersbourg*, 9 Oct. 1887, p. 1.
[19] *Sanktpeterburgskie vedomosti*, 30 Oct. 1887, p. 3.

The ballet was mostly Bessone's triumph. A certain segment of our small press for some reason did not like this talented dancer, who has enjoyed an immense success everywhere, and went to the point of calling her a half-ballerina. In *Tulip* Bessone showed that it would be more accurate to call her a 'ballerina and a half', since one can boldly claim that another first-class ballerina can scarcely be found in Europe who could perform in one spectacle but two-thirds of what Bessone did so perfectly. Her strength and stamina were simply astounding. True, on account of this strength one newspaper obligingly called her a machine, but we know that Patti is called a 'musical snuffbox' here, Zucchi 'Rag Doll' and 'bowlegged', etc. You can't please everybody.

Bessone repeated the most difficult and dizzying variations without the least sign of fatigue, and better even than the first time. At some groupings in *pas* and adagios the public literally gaped. Thus, turning quickly in an inclined position around the whole stage, Bessone every two steps managed to stop and perform a complete turn on pointe in a completely perpendicular position; she stood on pointe in a position of harmonious equilibrium until the male dancer, taking her by one hand, runs from one side to the other to take her by the other hand; and she performed, without stopping, eight turns on pointe now from right to left, now from left to right. One cannot enumerate all the choreographic *tours de force* that Bessone demonstrated. Without the least exaggeration one can say that in Act I alone Bessone danced enough, to be honest, for a whole ballet; furthermore she danced consistently, and at the end of Act III, when it would seem the ballerina should be exhausted, she performed a huge, most difficult *pas de deux*, the best number in the ballet, with such perfection as graphically elicited the public's delight. The ballerina's other *pas*, however, also had great success, and she was reproached only for the sturdiness of her legs; but that is interesting, as if she could perform all those miracles of balance if she had thin legs.

. . . It is unfortunate that there was no scope for the ballerina's mimetic talent, which is no less remarkable. As we said, her best variations were repeated by noisy public demand, and in the intervals she was given magnificent baskets of flowers.[20]

Bessone's adherents were content to be dazzled by her technique. This was properly appreciated only when she was dancing in the right genre, as in the present case:

The first dancer, Miss Bessone, was marked for glory in the new ballet. In the adagio and her numerous variations she performed absolute miracles of technique with remarkable simplicity and cleanness. Miss Bessone performs double turns on pointe to perfection, producing the fullest effect with them. This is Miss Bessone's ornament, and in this she has no rivals on our stage. The ballerina also shone by her perfection and aplomb in various groupings, which exploded all the customary notions of steadiness and balance. Miss Bessone had a firm and fully deserved success, which ought to renew her choreographic reputation, shaken by ballets unsuitable to the nature of her gift, such as *Naiad* and *Giselle*.[21]

[20] *Novoe vremya*, 6 Oct. 1887, p. 3.   [21] *Sanktpeterburgskie vedomosti*, 6 Oct. 1887, p. 3.

Another critic concurred in that *The Tulip of Haarlem* was Bessone's best performance yet:

Miss Bessone has been indefatigable, massing *tour de force* upon *tour de force*. Her specialities are *attitudes* and *tours sur les pointes*, on the pointe of a single foot, especially that on which she turns many times and takes poses which demand an extraordinary force of equilibrium. One time she even stopped a moment utterly without support, in the most difficult pose, while Mr Gerdt, whose skill and sureness are well known, let go one of the ballerina's hands in order to take the other. None of the great danseuses whom we have seen in recent years has done anything more amazing.[22]

While no one doubted Bessone's technical mastery, not everyone liked it. Complaints were raised about the physique that made it possible, and her tendency to stun and amaze at the expense of grace and charm. 'It must be acknowledged that the ballerina has little innate gracefulness,' one reviewer remarked, 'Her technique and the strength of her legs are astonishing, but in general Miss Bessone produces the impression of a dancing machine.'[23] He continued the next day:

There is no dispute that Miss Bessone does two and three turns extraordinarily purely, that her *jetés en tournant* and *pirouettes renversées* are dizzying. But one thing about them is boring: that she takes them with her everywhere, giving all ballets the same forms of her technique, exhausting with the same *tours de force*. It is strange that such monotony goes unnoticed by the same public and ballet criticism which reproached *our* balletmasters and dancers for monotony, who display incomparably more variety in the composition of dances and in their performance. Technical difficulties are fine when they are in harmony with the artistic circumstances of the dance. . . . [But] to be delighted at each fidget because it threatens a ballerina's life, without determining whether it is beautiful or suitable for performance by a woman, is to look at ballet as circus, not as art. Stupid examples are always more infectious than excellent ones. The success of acrobatics will undoubtedly lead to where our dancers, in the press for laurels and baskets of flowers, will begin to imitate the illustrious representatives of the new art, and to the degree that strength and possibility permit, will reject *the old manner*, taking no care for beauty of style and other outlived aesthetic requirements.[24]

The reviewer for *The Petersburg Gazette* criticized Bessone in unspoken comparisons with Virginia Zucchi. 'It is too bad that this artist lacks that artistic fire which promotes the development of an audience's sympathy,' he wrote. 'If this artist had a more likeable figure, she would indisputably enjoy a leading place among first-class ballerinas.'[25] In extended commentary the next day he somewhat softened his line:

---

[22] *Journal de Saint-Pétersbourg*, 9 Oct. 1887, p. 1.
[23] *Novosti i birzhevaya gazeta*, 5 Oct. 1887, p. 3.
[24] *Novosti i birzhevaya gazeta*, 6 Oct. 1887, p. 3.   [25] *Peterburgskaya gazeta*, 5 Oct. 1887, p. 3.

Miss Bessone's *scène dansante* and especially the *pas d'action*, as regards difficult technique, significantly enliven the action. One must observe that, discounting the ballet's extremely modest dimensions, the first dancer is given a rich fund of material, and she hardly ever leaves the stage. Act II stands out in its abundance of dances and groupings, where Miss Bessone's and Mr Gerdt's poetical *scène de séduction* attracted attention, distinguished by freshness and by having little in common with similar scenes in other ballets. . . . Miss Bessone's best number was the *pas de deux* with Mr Gerdt in Act III. Here the Italian ballerina amazed people by the difficulties, on pointe and in little *pas* and in fabulous triple turns, without misfiring. But nevertheless, we repeat, her inelegant form of execution and inartistic legs spoiled the general illusion.[26]

On balance, how did Ivanov fare in the rush of attention paid to Bessone? The press raised a number of points. The distribution of dances, for example, favoured the ballerina too much to the exclusion of first soloists, the *pas des papillons* being virtually the only opportunity for classical soloists to shine. 'First dancers take almost no part in this ballet,' one critic remarked, adding that the role of Pavel Gerdt, first male dancer and Bessone's partner, was 'reduced to that of a property for the prima ballerina'.[27] Another lamented, surely unaware of Ivanov's appeal to Vsevolozhsky for variety in the divertissement:

If Mr Ivanov had a store of creative choreographic imagination, he could have demonstrated marvels of beautiful groupings, separate dances, and *pas* in this last scene. Our ballet is rich in talents of the second rank, rich in such ensemble as one encounters nowhere else! One needs only to be able to make use of them, which he was unable to do.[28]

At the same time, some degree of 'creative choreographic imagination' was implicit in praise for Ivanov's artistry as a composer of dances. Various reports identified particular numbers in this regard, including the *Frison* (repeated at the first performance), *Danse des arbalètes*, *Néerlandaise*, and the *Matelots* in the last act (performed by women *en travestie*), the Dutch dances in the first, and various groupings of tulips. One report contained an oblique slight to Marius Petipa:

The groupings in the classical dances are distinguished by novelty and originality. They have none of those unchanging and endless arabesques, the constant content of which in a majority of our ballets make several classical dances intolerably boring. The ballabiles for the corps de ballet are very beautiful, but mainly they are lively.[29]

One critic twice suggested some social distinction in the acceptance of the new ballet between the upper and lower reaches of the theatre, the first,

---

[26] *Peterburgskaya gazeta*, 6 Oct. 1887, p. 3.   [27] *Novosti i birzhevaya gazeta*, 6 Oct. 1887, p. 3.
[28] *Peterburgskii listok*, 6 Oct. 1887, p. 3.   [29] *Sanktpeterburgskie vedomosti*, 6 Oct. 1887, p. 3.

populated by students and the less wealthy, calling for the balletmaster, while the *parterre* remained silent.

Two reports summed up Ivanov's accomplishment in *The Tulip of Haarlem*. The critic of *The Petersburg Gazette* concluded, without explaining his last sentence:

After the little choreographic scene *The Enchanted Forest*, insignificant in content, Mr Ivanov in his new three-act ballet took an important step forward. This first attempt, despite several gaps and shortcomings, demonstrated his excellent qualities in general production, the composition of groupings, quite original dances, and in the harmonious movements of the corps de ballet. Rendering the excellent its due, to Mr Ivanov's independent undertaking, we note without insulting his authorial self-esteem that *un coup de maître* of a first-class artist like Mr Petipa would bring great benefit to the new ballet—a point, however, that Mr L. Ivanov himself acknowledges.[30]

The critic of *The Saint Petersburg News* placed Ivanov's ballet in an even broader perspective:

The Tulip of Haarlem is L. Ivanov's first important work. Until now he was well known to the public as an outstanding ballet artist long unrivalled on our stage as a character dancer and a superb mime. Distinguished by a remarkable memory for dances, Mr Ivanov is a living reference book, to whose services are always turned in the revival of old ballets. Mr Ivanov had staged several *pas* in ballets and operas; he also composed the little ballet *The Enchanted Forest*. But *The Tulip of Haarlem*, a ballet in three acts, is his début as a balletmaster-choreographer. One cannot, therefore, be severe towards Mr Ivanov's new work.[31]

The main points of assessment of *The Tulip of Haarlem* are clear: the scenario was weak but the dances were strong; Emma Bessone was a superior technical ballerina unable to captivate her audience in other respects; Ivanov was obviously capable of putting together a grand ballet. The new work was, to all appearances, an acceptable if not stunning first effort.

Apart from content and reception, *The Tulip of Haarlem* poses two questions. First, what was Ivanov's relationship to Marius Petipa in the staging of the work? The ballet is attributed solely to Ivanov on the title-page of the libretto. Yet in his old age, when gathering data to dictate his memoirs, Petipa repeatedly included *The Tulip of Haarlem* in lists of his own ballets.[32] Reviewers of the first performance to a person attributed the ballet to Ivanov as author of the scenario, then indicated, typically without elaboration, that Petipa was involved with the staging:

[30] *Peterburgskaya gazeta*, 6 Oct. 1887, p. 3.
[31] *Sanktpeterburgskie vedomosti*, 6 Oct. 1887, p. 3. Observe that the critics reciting Ivanov's accomplishments still omit mention of him in connection with the 1885 revival of *La Fille mal gardée*.
[32] *TMB 205*, nos. 7–9.

'The dances in it were produced by Mr Petipa and Mr Ivanov' (*Novosti i birzhevaya gazeta*).

'The ballet was staged very effectively by Mr Ivanov with the assistance of Mr Petipa . . .' (*Novoe vremya*).

'They say that Mr Petipa corrected and smoothed over the ballet for Mr Ivanov' (*Peterburgskii listok*).

'All [the dances] are composed by Mr Ivanov, whom Mr Petipa assisted not a little in the final production of the ballet, very tastefully, and [they] show in the balletmaster a finely developed taste' (*Sanktpeterburgskie vedomosti*).

'Mr Petipa and Mr Ivanov composed [the dances], for which give these balletmasters their due . . .' (*Peterburgskaya gazeta*).

'The new ballet achieved a great success, and its merit comes down entirely to the choreographic part, very skilfully composed by Mr M. Petipa and Mr L. Ivanov and masterfully interpreted by Miss Bessone and the corps de ballet' (*Journal de Saint-Pétersbourg*).

The double attribution is affirmed by Pleshcheyev in *Our Ballet*, who wrote that Ivanov and Petipa 'were in charge of [*zavedyvali*] the production'.[33] He made a similar attribution when *The Tulip of Haarlem* was revived in 1903: 'The ballet was composed by the late balletmaster L. I. Ivanov, but M. I. Petipa collaborated [*sotrudnichal*] with him in the production.'[34]

Were these writers aping a rumour or describing a situation well known at the time? And if he did take part, was Petipa a predator, encroaching on Ivanov's territory, as Soviet writers suggest, making a change here and there that he might claim co-authorship? Did he contribute substantially, or was he merely superintending his assistant's first large project, attending rehearsals, trying to smooth over rough spots? In the latter case his contribution might become part of the lore of the ballet without warranting mention on the libretto's title-page.

The evidence is mixed. Certain passages in the libretto support an attribution to Ivanov. His devotion to familiar devices of narrative and the centrality of dance show his affection for the repertoire he had known his entire life. His retrospective leanings, so prominent in the memoirs, are further expressed in antique touches of *The Tulip of Haarlem*. The inclusion of a foreword which explains the basis in legend of the story to follow harks back to Taglioni's libretto for *La Fille du Danube*. Ivanov's libretto also echoes Taglioni's in its fussy division into scenes. Nor is it over-interpretation to perceive Ivanov's hand in the occasional turn of phrase which expresses his sense of social propriety or emotional tone as we know them from the mem-

[33] *Pleshcheyev*, 300.   [34] *Novoe vremya*, 9 Apr. 1903, p. 13.

oirs. At the beginning of Act III the secondary couple Anders and Marianna have a rendezvous, not to vent their passion, but more primly 'to discuss privately how they might prevail upon her father'. A passage like the re-union of Pieters with his parents echoes Ivanov's personal traits of sympathy and compassion. An outpouring on which the librettist paused for a moment even though the emotion involved was not critical to the plot, it rises above the clichés of the story: 'His father and mother, tears of joy in their eyes, incessantly embrace and kiss their beloved son. After such a long separation they cannot gaze at him enough.'

These Ivanovesque touches are nevertheless balanced in the libretto of *The Tulip of Haarlem* with much else of Petipian influence, in situations and devices familiar from the elder balletmaster's *œuvre*. Ivanov's 'kingdom scene'—the Kingdom of the Tulips in Act II—a fantastic tableau which serves as a show-case for classical dances, shares this identity and purpose with many similar scenes in Petipa, such as the 'Kingdom of the Rivers' in *The Pharaoh's Daughter* and 'The Kingdom of the Shades' in *La Bayadère*. The personification of flowers and butterflies, concordant as it is with the imagery of romantic ballet, was a favourite device in Petipa's ballets, of which he made much, for example, in his *Le Roi Candaule* and *A Midsummer Night's Dream*.

Critics of the first performance were quick to point out other similarities.

The arrival of the young sailor Pieters in the first act reminds balletomanes of the departure of the young sailor in the first act of *The Daughter of the Snows*. The dances of the tulips and butterflies of the second act remind all of the second and third [*sic*] acts of *Giselle*, *Roxana*, and other ballets where the ballerina is obliged to change from her earthly shell of Act I into some unearthly flower or insect.[35]

Another reviewer found a precedent in Petipa for the moment of greatest dramatic tension in *The Tulip of Haarlem*, when Pieters and Emma threaten to take their own lives:

Of two dramatic moments, the second (when Mr Gerdt wants to throw himself out of the window) is nothing other than a copy of the scene when the pharaoh's daughter in the ballet of that name is also at the point of throwing herself out of a window, for she is being pursued by the Nubian prince, who is spiteful towards her, in the person of Mr Kshesinsky.

The last scene, the 'Kermesse' on the town square, thanks to the masses, processions of various guilds, men and women, messengers, oarsmen, etc., provides rich material for devising groupings and dances. What did Mr Ivanov do? He composed (also unsuccessfully) a dance of his own messengers on the dance of similar young people from the ballet *Trilby*.[36]

[35] *Novosti i birzhevaya gazeta*, 6 Oct. 1887, p. 3.
[36] *Peterburgskii listok*, 6 Oct. 1887, p. 3.

That Ivanov should borrow from what he knew, and that what he knew should be Petipa, are not surprising. Intriguing about *The Tulip of Haarlem* is that Ivanov's borrowings seem to have inspired Petipa to rework them in his own later ballets. In *The Nenuphar* of 1890 the ballerina impersonated an animated flower encountered at night in the depths of nature. The gypsy, after she is changed into the benevolent Fairy of the Enchanted Field, is a stereotype similar in dramatic function to the Lilac Fairy (*The Sleeping Beauty*), the fairy godmother in *Zolushka* (Cinderella) of 1893, and the White Lady in *Raymonda* of 1898. Pieters's Lohengrinesque arrival in a boat will be used again in *The Sleeping Beauty* when the Lilac Fairy and Prince Désiré arrive at the sleeping castle, and in *The Nutcracker* when Clara and the prince arrive at Confitüremburg. *The Caprices of a Butterfly* of 1889 was populated wholly by dancers impersonating insects.

Perhaps most intriguing, however, are other anticipations in Ivanov's work of *The Sleeping Beauty*, which was in the early stages of planning and negotiation when *The Tulip of Haarlem* first saw the light. They take the form of choreographic details, such as the daring moment remarked by critics when Gerdt let go Bessone's hand as she balanced on one pointe, and walked around her to take her other hand—a foreshadowing of Aurora and the four princes in the Rose Adagio. To have seen *The Tulip of Haarlem* would have been especially intriguing for the scene of Pieters's pursuit of Emma. While the device, as already observed, recalls the last act of Petipa's *La Bayadère* in staging, it is much more poetical in effect, and for its poetry anticipates the vision scene in Act II of *The Sleeping Beauty*. In *La Bayadère* Solor is attempting to reach Gamsatti at their wedding feast, but is distracted by the shade of murdered Nikia. In *The Sleeping Beauty* Prince Désiré has just been taken on a journey by a benevolent fairy, as Pieters by the old gypsy; Désiré has been shown a vision of his beloved, as Pieters has been shown Emma, and Désiré, like Pieters, must kiss his beloved in order to break a spell. The Lilac Fairy's part in a danced trio is to keep Aurora just out of Désiré's reach, as Emma is kept from Pieters. The difference between the two scenes is symbolized by Ivanov's ceremonial kiss—on Emma's shoulder—as compared with Désiré's on Aurora's forehead.

Proving the artistic influence of one choreographer on another, difficult at any time, is impossible at this remove. These comparisons nevertheless raise questions of the direction in which influence might have passed. Petipa may again have sensed a rival in Ivanov, and felt challenged to answer Ivanov's effective devices, to put them to better account, or to assert his authority over them. In sum, Petipa's involvement in *The Tulip of Haarlem* seems likely but not extensive, his relationship direct and indirect, contributing to and drawing from it. The details and mechanism of his involvement, however, cannot be specified.

The second question posed by *The Tulip of Haarlem* has to do with the politics of the Petersburg ballet of the late 1880s. Was it a vehicle for official policy? This question is pointed by the fact that the theatre direction committed Ivanov to stage it in the first place, knowing that the ballet held fast to dramatic motifs and scenic devices that had sustained the company for decades. The ballet was incontestably *vieux genre*. Its love interest was polite and childlike; the point of the piece lay in the visual splendour of production and in providing a refined audience, through numerous dances, opportunities to savour the fine points of technique.

These features did not correspond with the preferences or strengths of the initially announced ballerina. Was assigning Virginia Zucchi the leading part in *The Tulip of Haarlem* a cunning way of alienating her? The libretto was not in her style. Whatever its shortcomings as a drama, more decisive faults were the scarcity of persuasive mime and the absence of sexual manipulation or coquetry in the ballerina's part. This deficiency could have been expected more in a libretto by Ivanov than one by Petipa, and explains more readily than reasons reported in the press—that she could not dance to the music—Zucchi's refusal to participate.[37]

If the critical response to Fitinhof-Schell's music is any indication, that excuse was ridiculous. There is little evidence that Zucchi possessed discriminating musical taste, and even less that the score of *The Tulip of Haarlem* was distinguished by it. Apart from the well-received concert numbers for solo violin and solo harp, written for Leopold Auer and Albert Heinrich Zabel respectively, the score was dismissed with quips. 'And the music?' wrote the reviewer for *The Petersburg Gazette*, 'On the one hand it is boring and does not always correspond to the character of the dances and action, and on the other it has nice little waltzes and galops! . . .'[38] Another heard it as a hodge-podge: 'Mr Schell's music goes hand in hand with Mr Ivanov's creation: a deft compilation of other mens' things, and nothing more.'[39] 'When the orchestration is not too noisy,' a colleague added,

it does not differ all that much from standard ballet music, and consequently pleases enthusiasts of this genre. Apart from the vulgar things, as for example the march in the epilogue, one sometimes encounters pieces of a type, if not most original, at least most delicate—the dance of the butterflies or the pizzicato of the last act.[40]

[37] Ivor Guest writes that Zucchi had been released from her obligation to perform in *The Tulip of Haarlem* in order to enable her to play the part of Pepita in a revision of Petipa's *The King's Command* (*The Divine Virginia*, 110). The *Birzhevye vedomosti* reported on 2 Oct. 1887 that 'The leading role was originally assigned to Miss Zucchi, but at the "diva's" refusal, Miss Bessone will represent the "Queen of the Tulips" '; the *Peterburgskii listok* for the same date indicated that 'Miss Zucchi's lack of inclination to take part in Mr Ivanov's ballet, according to rumours, was supposedly based on the impossibility of dancing to the music composed for *The Tulip of Haarlem*'.

[38] *Peterburgskaya gazeta*, 5 Oct. 1887, p. 3.   [39] *Peterburgskii listok*, 6 Oct. 1887, p. 3.

[40] *Journal de Saint-Pétersbourg*, 9 Oct. 1887, p. 1.

These descriptions characterize the kind of music that Zucchi would most have been accustomed to.

Zucchi's refusal to dance in *The Tulip of Haarlem* could be dismissed as a display of artistic temperament, but it may have involved motivations of greater import. She may not have fitted into Vsevolozhsky's vision of the Petersburg ballet as he wished to shape it over the next several years. Ivanov's ballet hints at that vision: a union of the dance-intensive grand ballet long favoured in Petersburg and the extraordinary *mise-en-scène* of the Franco-Italian *féerie*. This is not to suggest that the scenic element in the earlier Petersburg repertoire was deficient, but rather that Vsevolozhsky wanted to match the West European fashion for grandiose staging, then better it with elegant choreography and sophisticated music which the West European model lacked. This hypothesis is speculation, for the sources make no reference to a Vsevolozhsky/Zucchi intrigue. To pursue the hypothesis is to extend the speculation, though not without basis in the facts of the Petersburg company's repertoire and principal artists in the first decade of Ivanov's work as balletmaster.

Neither such a union nor an audience ready to accept it could be effected in a single work. Technical innovations in stagecraft notwithstanding, complicated in this case by the move from the Bolshoy to the Maryinsky Theatre, Vsevolozhsky's public included sophisticated adherents of the established repertoire and lovers of Italian virtuosity. Traditionalist disgust with Italophiles had led to what the press called 'the Italian question'— whether the art of Italian ballerinas would destroy the traditions of elegance and finesse in which Russian dancers, schooled in French technique, had been trained.

In addition, Vsevolozhsky had learned from experience that the typical *féerie*—a simple story with staging so elaborate as to overwhelm the choreographic element—would not serve as a model for the Petersburg ballet. *The Magic Pills*, with the best artists of drama and ballet taking part in an extraordinarily costly production, had been mounted to celebrate the opening of the Maryinsky Theatre after renovations, and had proved that grandness of effect alone would not fill the house.

Instead, the wished-for choreographic and scenic components were to be brought together gradually, in a series of ballets in the late 1880s which culminated in *The Sleeping Beauty* of 1890. *The Tulip of Haarlem* was the first step in the process (followed by Petipa's *The Vestal* of 1888, and *The Talisman* of 1889). Accordingly, Vsevolozhsky would not want to give up *Tulip* whatever its liabilities. These included the risk of irritating an audience in Virginia Zucchi's thrall by not making some concession to cast her in a new work, and the likelihood that the controversial 'Italian question' would fester if, after Zucchi's withdrawal from *Tulip*, he replaced her with another

Italian. This would be an affront to Russian chauvinists, pleased that Ivanov was being given an opportunity to stage a grand ballet. Yet from an artistic standpoint, the disjunction between Ivanov's old style and Emma Bessone's new virtuosity would serve neither very well. By juxtaposing them Vsevolozhsky may have been engaging in some purposeful contrariness: he could isolate the *vieux genre* as unsuitable for advanced technique, play on his public's obvious delight in the new virtuosity, and enhance the reasonableness of devising a new genre to reconcile the two without stylistic disparity. While a bold strategy was necessary to dislodge the status quo, the tensions in Vsevolozhsky's plan, if such it was, threatened the new ballet's prospects for success. Risk of failure may have brought the director to assign to Ivanov, not Petipa, the staging of *The Tulip of Haarlem*. In effect, the second balletmaster was available for sacrifice.

Predictably, a reprise of the 'Italian question' materialized. The critic for *The News and Commercial Gazette*, unsigned but possibly Dmitry Dmitrievich Korovyakov, unenthusiastic about gaudy if vapid European ballets, rehearsed the present situation in Russian ballet and how *The Tulip of Haarlem* fitted into it. His was the stance of a disenfranchised traditionalist:

It is well known that the establishments of summer entertainment for our public are the presenters of Western European ballet: the Arcadia, Livadia, and other semi-theatres, which have taken up the task of showing Petersburgers of what strength and beauty consist in contemporary choreography. The laurels of Mr Setov, Polyakov, and Alexandrov [proprietors of these theatres] pushed our theatre direction onto the path of blind imitation of foreign stages, where ballet has lost any artistic meaning, having turned into exhibitions of beautiful bodies, weapons, fabrics, and embroidery, flooded with electric light, in a spectacle which strikes only the senses—indeed, perhaps more the nerves of people who seek strong sensations, who have taken up betting, if they want, on whether an Italian ballerina will crack the back of her head while executing astonishing feats of tightrope walking and acrobatic virtuosity. Our public, in order to prove its 'Europeanness', immediately developed a taste for the new genre once they had been saturated with French operetta. Everything which delighted the aesthetically advanced spectator in our ballet before, everything which imparted artistic sense to ballet and justified that esteemed place which choreography enjoyed by right in the company of fine arts—to its credit turned out to be old, superfluous, and unnecessary, having yielded its place to the crowd's new idols. To put as little sense and subject-matter into a ballet as possible, and as many dizzying feats, without safety nets but directly on the slippery boards of the stage, as many women as possible, dressed as men or quite undressed, men adorned in plush, velvet, and satin, spangles, with multicoloured flags, elephants, camels, and horses, more extras got up as soldiers strictly dressed and aligned—all flooded with light and deafened by incoherent music—such is the recipe for a ballet after the taste of Mr Manzotti and our theatre Direction. . . .

The extremity of the writer's conservatism is revealed next when the recipe he has conjured up is not for *Excelsior* or *Sieba*, but a caricature of *The Tulip of Haarlem*, which his Italophile colleagues would find quite old-fashioned. He cites the ballet by name, and condemns the tendency of his fellow critics to place artists of the imperial ballet at a level below those of the New Village, a summer entertainment garden:

Looking at these ballets [*Tulip*, and Petipa's *Pygmalion*], one yearns for the time when the interest of a performance was concentrated not on the tailors but on artistically executed dances, on those *belles dames* of whom soon no memories will be left. For what use are our superb soloists any more, our strictly elegant school which has preserved the traditions of classical art for more than a century—when the crowd of newly arrived beautiful 'women' or peasant boys from the New Village delight the public, and the ballet critic, not standing on ceremony, declares that our dancers do not stand to compare with them?[41]

Was Vsevolozhsky facing a dilemma, or constructing one? It may be that condemnations of this kind were playing into his hand. He could affirm the traditionalist call for excellent dancing, and turn his attention to Virginia Zucchi in response, whose technique did not meet the standard. At the same time, Zucchi posed a problem for Vsevolozhsky: he must yield to the indisputable financial advantages of casting his lot with her, or stand his ground in the hope that his vision would prosper, at the risk of jeopardizing the popularity of ballet and plunging his budget deep into deficit.

He chose to stand his ground. Doing so, he was acknowledging the practical reality that the benefits of retaining Zucchi could only be temporary, since she was approaching 40. Moreover, he was committed to hiring other Italian ballerinas. Zucchi performed in the imperial theatres from the autumn of 1885 until the winter of 1888, in which period Bessone, Elena Cornalba, and the male dancer Enrico Cecchetti were invited to perform in the Petersburg ballet. After Zucchi's departure Carlotta Brianza, Antoinetta Dell'Era, and Pierina Legnani would dance there. Could Vsevolozhsky have guessed that so great an exposure of Russian artists to Italian dancers would have a salutary influence on their strict French training, then he was right.

Unverified newspaper reports hint that Vsevolozhsky, vision or no, still made efforts to come to terms with Zucchi. *Satanilla* (that is, Mazilier's *Le Diable amoureux*), with scenes of dramatic intensity suitable to Zucchi's gifts, was announced for her on 26 January and again on 29 March and 3 April 1886, but cancelled on 29 April; a production of Luigi Manzotti's popular *Excelsior* for Zucchi was announced on 17 July, but it was never

---

[41] *Novosti i birzhevaya gazeta*, 6 Oct. 1887, p. 3.

mounted; the next year, on 26 November 1887, it was reported that Zucchi had rejected Petipa's extravagant new *The Vestal*.

The newspapers report other signs of tension. On 27 June 1886, Vsevolozhsky is reported as having suffered a stroke; on 23 October Zucchi's displeasure with *The King's Command* is announced as the reason for cancelling a revival of it that season; and in November 1887 the direction refuses Zucchi's request for three Petersburg dancers to accompany her to Moscow. Relations between Zucchi and Vsevolozhsky may have been strained from the beginning by her going over the Director's head to secure an invitation to the imperial stage. In the process of doing this, she could easily have broken a taboo of protocol whereby artists, however influential, did business in the Russian imperial theatres. Having lost that battle, Vsevolozhsky set his sights on winning the war. In this construction, *The Tulip of Haarlem* was the first step in dislodging Zucchi, and the first milestone on the road to *The Sleeping Beauty*.

In the short term Vsevolozhsky was criticized for not renewing Zucchi's contract, but in time, his vision realized, he was vindicated. The mode for Zucchi ultimately passed, despite her frequent returns to Russia. When Carlotta Brianza created the role of Aurora, and Pierina Legnani that of Odette in the Petersburg revival of *Swan Lake*, there was neither call nor lament for Zucchi—nor could there have been. These ballets were a match of genre and Italian technique in which Zucchi had no part. The ballerina's roles in them lay outside her effective but comparatively restricted dramatic range, and demanded technique which she seems never to have had, least of all at the time they were produced. The fundamental incompatibility of Zucchi's art with Vsevolozhsky's vision is a fact that all parties, recriminations aside, must have realized.

Lev Ivanov was planning *The Tulip of Haarlem* in the midst of these tensions. Did he sense the political and historical import of this assignment? Though modern authorities look back upon *Tulip* as a footnote, as another ballet produced by the choreographer of *Swan Lake*, Ivanov created it during the most disruptive debate in late nineteenth-century Russian ballet, over the impact on it of Italian ballerinas.

Was it a failure? Already at the second performance the house was poor, but this was blamed directly on the management for raising ticket prices.[42] The ballet continued to please after five performances.[43] *The Tulip of Haarlem* was shown twelve times in its first season, five in its second, and six in its third. Its simple tale could easily accommodate an interpolated dance, omissions or abbreviations of existing dances, or the reworking of choreography for a new artist. Enrico Cecchetti made his début on the imperial

---

[42] *Sanktpeterburgskie vedomosti*, 10 Oct. 1887, p. 3.
[43] *Sanktpeterburgskie vedomosti*, 20 Oct. 1887, p. 3.

stage at the seventh performance of *Tulip*, on 4 November 1887; Bessone included Act II in her benefit performance eighteen days later; on 16 December 1890 two important soloists, Varvara Rykhlyakova and Georgy Kyaksht, made their débuts in a *pas de deux* interpolated into *Tulip*.

Ivanov's work also served ballerinas well. Elena Cornalba succeeded Bessone early in 1888, with changes in the choreography 'permitting her to flaunt her elevation; besides, newly written for her were the entrance in the first act and a variation added to the *grand pas de deux* at the end of the third; a variation was added here for Mr Gerdt as well, who with Bessone had only processed majestically about the stage, since the ballerina danced enough for two.'[44] Brianza took the leading role a year later:

Miss Brianza is a complete contrast to Miss Cornalba: she is a brunette, young, beautiful, graceful and well built. In technique, especially firmness of pointes and cleanness of turns, she yields to Miss Cornalba and Miss Algisi, but thereby draws attention to the elegance, brilliance, and warmth of her execution.

It is not easy to dance *The Tulip of Haarlem*. Miss Bessone, with her extreme strength of pointe and amazing balance put four adagios into it, one more difficult than the last. For Miss Brianza, with few rehearsals, it was not easy to master a completely new ballet with the hoped-for assurance. For that reason she performed magnificently, in the full sense of the word, her own variation to the music of Stefani, interpolated into the second act, freely making two turns on pointe without a cavalier and circling around the stage with astonishing speed. This brilliant variation created a furore and was repeated by unanimous public demand.[45]

A Russian, Anna Johanson (Plate 11), performed the role of Emma for the first time on 23 September 1892, and brought a different way of perceiving the ballet.

Prior to this the role was performed by Miss Bessone and Miss Brianza. Italian ballerinas introduced a special fire into it, characteristic of their southern nature. Miss Johanson in her external appearance is more suitable to the role of a young Flemish girl than Miss Brianza, and in my opinion, the role of Emma in her performance lost nothing whatever in comparison with her predecessor. As for the dances, Miss Johanson was very fine everywhere that requires ethereality, beautiful *attitudes* and poses, as these qualities are characteristic of her. In her cold, northern gracefulness there is an independent charm; almost all her poses are distinguished by finish, and several are even artistic, like bas-reliefs of dancing women on ancient vases. She managed the *pas d'action* of the first act and the *Scène de séduction* best of all. In the variations, especially in the fantastic act of the tulips, she was weaker than Miss Brianza, who amazed the audience with dizzying turns, *rondes de jambes*, etc., and particularly the liveliness of her performance, which is inherent in Italians generally. Miss Johanson shortened this variation. Perhaps these gaps in the variations were because Miss Johanson has not for a long time performed the leading role in a

---

[44] *Skalkovsky*, 174.   [45] *Novoe vremya*, 17 Jan. 1889, p. 3.

ballet, perhaps also because of Mr Petipa's illness the ballet was staged with insufficient attention. The latter is more probable, because the corps de ballet, in the dances of the tulips and in the *Kermesse*, were confused and did not dance with their customary clarity.[46]

Skalkovsky's appreciation of Bessone had been of a phenomenal dancer who happened to be appearing in *The Tulip of Haarlem*. When her role finally came to a Russian dancer, brought up in the same traditions as Ivanov, a balance in the work was struck for the first time between the ballet and its principal executant. By 1892, however, the combination of old genre and old-school ballerina was no longer right for the Petersburg ballet.

In all, *Tulip* received forty performances before the Revolution, including two by students of the theatre school. Thirty-two came in the ballet's first nine seasons, another seven between 16 April 1903 (soon after Marius Petipa's retirement, in February) and 7 December 1905. The ballet was effectively dropped from the repertoire thereafter, to emerge for one last performance twelve years later on 30 April 1917, the recollection of a vanished era.

On this occasion they [the students] appeared before the public as real flowers and butterflies, because such are the personages of the second act of the ballet *The Tulip of Haarlem*, revived for the examination performance.

Twenty young women—tulips, although not among those who graduated from the school this year—produced the impression of a proper corps de ballet, executing complex variations precisely on pointe. Now they intertwined themselves into beautiful groupings, now dispersed across the field, as flowers disperse from a loosely tied bouquet.[47]

Could Claudia Kulichevskaya, who produced the ballet on that spring afternoon, have recalled the little verse published in 1894, then in jest but now more serious?

> To replace the last despondent flowers
> Of the northern Flora, pale and withered,
> The springtime of Terpsichore comes and blooms:
> Two-legged butterflies joyfully fly to us
> Lighted with their irridescent light,
> And through the cheerless autumn haze
> They bring to us with kind and merry greeting
> The first tulip out of Haarlem's forest . . .[48]

---

[46] *Novoe vremya*, 26 Sept. 1892, p. 2.   [47] *Novoe vremya*, 2 May 1917, p. 6.
[48] *Peterburgskaya gazeta*, 1 Sept. 1894, p. 3.

5

Krasnoe Selo

Ivanov's duties in the theatre at Krasnoe Selo involved making ready two or three ballet presentations a week in a season which could last from late June to early August. They were typically divertissements made up of numbers from a broad repertoire, current to long unperformed, which drew on his extraordinary memory. As we have seen in the case of *La Fille mal gardée*, these summer performances were also a testing ground for dancers new to roles, and possibly for excerpts from ballets scheduled for revival. Ivanov created three short ballets for Krasnoe Selo, which constitute his output of new ballets between *The Tulip of Haarlem* and *The Nutcracker*, and span the change of decade from the 1880s to the 1890s. The informal atmosphere of Krasnoe Selo complicates the reconstruction of their content and history.

The Beauty of Seville

As early as 7 June 1888 a new one-act ballet by Ivanov was announced, but no title was given. Ten days later we learn that its story will be Spanish, that its music will be confected from Bizet's *Carmen*, and that Varvara Nikitina will take the leading role.[1] On 28 July, *The Petersburg Gazette* guessed the name of the new ballet, *Pepita*, reported that its music was to be taken from several operas, and that it would be performed in two days.[2] With the end of the season at hand, an announcement in *The New Time* on 29 July stated, 'L. Ivanov's new one-act ballet will be produced in a short time.' Two days later we read in the same newspaper that Ivanov has composed a little ballet called *The Beauty of Seville*. It is a divertissement of Spanish dances, 'excellently mounted, in so far as it was possible for the balletmaster to do this

---

[1] *Peterburgskaya gazeta*, 7 July 1888, p. 3.   [2] *Peterburgskaya gazeta*, 28 July 1888, p. 3.

in the absence of new, original music, fresh costumes and decorations, and mostly in the absence of ballerinas and women soloists *ins Grüne*.[3] 'There is no story,' another source reported, 'but rather a series of waltzes, polkas, and other dances tinged with Spanish coloration.'[4] *The Petersburg Gazette* provided more details:

Yesterday, 29 July, on the stage of the theatre at Krasnoe Selo, the new one-act ballet by the balletmaster Mr Ivanov, *The Beauty of Seville*, was given. Composed without particular pretence to being an outstanding manifestation of choreography, this short work is nevertheless composed with great taste, both in the variety of dances and the music, which has been borrowed extremely successfully from various operas and ballets. The tale of *The Beauty of Seville* is not particularly original; its whole point lies in the passion of two smugglers pursuing the beautiful Pepita, who is much in love with a famous matador and who in the end, after various turns of plot, is united in Hymen's bonds. But on this modest canvas Mr Ivanov has been able to sew beautiful patterns of poetical and graceful dances. Of seven irreproachably staged numbers, and a beautiful selection of music, the 'Ballabile' invites attention, staged to Glinka's *Jota aragonesa*, performed with fire by the corps de ballet; two scenes, 'Coquetterie' and 'Scène d'amour', both with Miss Nikitina, Mr Gerdt, Stukolkin, Karsavin, and Lukyanov; the *Mandolinata*, a charming dance in which our second dancers Miss Zhukova II, Kulichevskaya, Gruzdovskaya, Fyodorova II, Vorobyova, and Vishnevskaya flaunt their remarkable refinement and firm pointes. Miss Vinogradova and Mr Litavkin performed the *Valse Espagnole* very nicely. The pearl of the ballet was the *Manola*—a dance full of life and fervent passion, performed with fire by Miss Zhukova I, this first-class, charming adherent of character dances, with Mr Lukyanov and Mr Karsavin. Such grace and poetical languor, and with it what fervent temperament Miss Zhukova I put into this dance! . . .

Miss Nikitina and Mr Gerdt performed the final Spanish dance, *Sevilliana*, with the ardent passion and *brio* with which these public favourites are so generously endowed, perpetual adornments of our ballet. In this dance Miss Ogoleit III, Labunskaya, and Slantsova also especially stood out.[5]

Another critic found that Nikitina's dances were not so successful; she danced everything on demi-pointe and, 'as ever, lacked sufficient finish'.[6]

Two performances the next summer (17 July and 7 August 1889) produced a complete list of characters, most of whom had participated in the single performance the year before:

An Innkeeper	Mr Stukolkin
Pepita	Miss Nikitina [on 7 August: Maria Gorshenkova]
Cigarello	Mr Gerdt
Bandits	Mr Lukyanov
	Mr Karsavin

[3] *Novoe vremya*, 31 July 1888, p. 3.   [4] *Sanktpeterburgskie vedomosti*, 31 July 1888, p. 3.
[5] *Peterburgskaya gazeta*, 31 July 1888, p. 3.
[6] *Sanktpeterburgskie vedomosti*, 31 July 1888, p. 3.

The dances were the same, but with some substitutions of artists:

Coquetterie—Miss Nikitina, Mr Stukolkin, Mr Karsavin, Mr Lukyanov
Scène d'amour—Miss Nikitina and Mr Gerdt
Ballabile—corps de ballet
Valse espagnole—Miss Petrova [replacing Vinogradova] and Mr Litavkin
Mandolinata—Miss Anderson, Kulichevskaya, Gruzdovskaya, Fyodorova II, Vorobyova, Nedremskaya, Mr Voronkov I and Mr Voronkov II.
Manola—Miss Petipa [replacing Zhukova I], Mr Karsavin, Mr Lukyanov
Sevilliana—Miss Nikitina and all participants.[7]

From a report of the performance on 17 July 1889 it would appear that the story of *The Beauty of Seville* had been modified, though the change could as easily be explained, in the absence of a written scenario, as a second description of the same stage action. The ballet was now about 'the preparations and departure of a toreador (Mr Gerdt) for a bullfight in Seville and the amorous meeting with his beloved Pepita (Miss Nikitina)'. As for the dancers, the same report continued, Varvara Nikitina

with her innate gracefulness performed the *scène d'amour* with Mr Gerdt, and in a very sprightly way, with fire, danced the *Sevilliana* with the corps de ballet. Miss Nikitina has been resting for the summer and has gained a little weight, which goes well on her. . . . Miss Petipa was an effective Spanish girl in the *Manola*; she was, as ever, much applauded. The polka *Mandolinata* also very much pleased, danced by Miss Anderson, Kulichevskaya, Fyodorova II, Vorobyova and others. As regards composition and execution, this is virtually the best dance in *The Beauty of Seville*.[8]

Another notice reported that the costumes were new.[9]

On the surface, in this ballet Ivanov was just plying his trades as choreographer and specialist in character dances. Yet some deeper inspiration is sensed, in that Ivanov's *The Beauty of Seville* may have paid homage to Arthur Saint-Léon's *The Pearl of Seville* (1861), in which the young Ivanov danced the part of the leader of a gypsy band. That three-act ballet was described as 'made up primarily of episodical scenes and divertissements',[10] based on the flirtation of a Spanish girl with the men who came in contact with her. There is no question that Saint-Léon's ballets were on Ivanov's mind in the summer of 1889. He revived *The Nymphs and the Satyr* at Krasnoe Selo that year, and it cannot be an accident that the divertissement performed at Krasnoe Selo a week after *The Beauty of Seville* included an excerpt from *The Pearl of Seville*.

   [7] *Novoe vremya*, 16 July 1889, p. 3.   [8] *Novoe vremya*, 19 July 1889, p. 3.
   [9] *Peterburgskaya gazeta*, 19 July 1889, p. 3.
   [10] *Syn otechestva*, 29 Jan. 1861, pp. 150–1.

Moscow Interlude

When Ivanov returned to the Maryinsky in the autumn of 1889, one project dominated the schedule: producing *The Sleeping Beauty*. After months of extraordinary labour, postponement, and anxiety, that work received its first performance on 3 January 1890. Given the demands it made on the company, Ivanov was curiously uninvolved with the staging of Petipa's masterpiece. He did not appear in it, and Alexandre Shiryaev, not Ivanov, is known to have assisted Petipa in the production. There are two probable reasons for this: someone had to rehearse the ballets to be performed while *The Sleeping Beauty* was in preparation, and Ivanov was frequently dispatched to Moscow. His old colleague Alexey Bogdanov had retired as balletmaster there, and Bogdanov's replacement was not yet available. In August, September, October, and November Ivanov travelled to Moscow, missing rehearsals for *The Sleeping Beauty* when they were in full swing.

His main compositional duty in Moscow was to mount dances for a new production of Shakespeare's *A Midsummer Night's Dream* first given at the Bolshoy Theatre on 27 October. The ballet music, according to the theatre poster that evening, 'in the second act and the apotheosis, is compiled by Mr Bezekirsky exclusively from piano works of Mendelssohn-Bartholdy'.[11] Bezekirsky also conducted the orchestra. The dancers, representing elves, birds, and insects, were reminiscent of the characters in Petipa's balletic version of the play. In Act II, thirty-one women (including two female students) performed 'Dances of the Elves, [sixteen] Butterflies and [eight] Birds of Paradise'. Also on stage were eight grasshopper musicians and four bats, represented by boy students, and four solo parts for Peaseblossom, Cobweb, Moth, and Mustardseed. Among the butterflies was the future ballerina Lyubov Roslavleva; among the grasshopper musicians, Vasily Tikhomirov. In Act V, a Bohemian Dance was set for a solo couple, and many of the artists from Act II returned for the 'Games and Amusements of the Elves, Butterflies and Birds of Paradise'.

Such press response to the dances as we have is what might be expected from drama critics. 'Choreographic groupings of the dancers' were listed with other elements of production as 'excellent, elegant, full of grace, taste, and in the full sense of the word, artistic'.[12] 'The ballet is beautifully staged,' according to another notice, 'but unfortunately the direction did not devise more original costumes for it, more suitable to the production than those

[11] Moscow, Central State Theatre Museum named after A. A. Bakhrushin, Division of *Affiches*, *af* N 11431/48.
[12] *Moskovskii listok*, 28 Oct. 1889, p. 3.

hackneyed ones we are used to seeing everywhere.'[13] The dances of the last act were marred by 'noise and uproar on the stage during a scene change'.[14] Another account elaborated:

Least satisfactory is the staging of the last act, which takes place in the palace of Theseus. The court has barely managed to withdraw, the hall emptied, and the candles extinguished before the people are exchanged for elves. Oberon and Titania enter and locate themselves with their retinue in the gallery which just before was occupied by warriors, while below them a ballet begins.[15]

The dances were implicated in another criticism of the production, that it did not deal successfully with the integration of the real and the fantastic. 'The kingdom of the elves which appears before us amidst the radiance of a moonlit night must be ethereal and tender, corresponding to the music,' the same critic lamented, 'But in fact the element of fantasy is the weakest side of our contemporary Russian art.' The music, in turn, was found to hamper the fantastic effect. The ballet in the fairy-tale-marvellous forest of Act II, if it were not for Mendelssohn's music, would produce a much better impression:

It is the music that lulls not just Titania to sleep, but the whole audience; to watch our four excellent soloists is simply a pity. All their efforts to produce a lively impression on the audience turn out to be in vain and the curtain falls, arousing only scanty applause here and there.[16]

These remarks strike anyone familiar with Mendelssohn's incidental music for *A Midsummer Night's Dream* as odd, until reminded that this celebrated score was not used, but rather orchestrations of the composer's selected piano pieces.

As the 1880s drew to a close, it is clear that Ivanov was an asset to the direction, as measured by the sheer volume and versatility of his work. *The Enchanted Forest* had held the stage, as too *The Tulip of Haarlem*, whatever mischief lay beneath its surface. Ivanov was still performing, still able to substitute on short notice when a colleague fell ill (taking Felix Kshesinsky's part, for example, in the revival of *The Wilful Wife*), still able to create new roles, such as the dancing master in Petipa's *The King's Command*. In response to the charge of his initial appointment as balletmaster, he was lifting a weight from Petipa's shoulders across the board, not least in choreographing Russian dances for operas. His work at Krasnoe Selo demonstrated not only his fertility as a producer, but also his phenomenal memory. What more could Vsevolozhsky ask?

[13] *Russkie vedomosti*, 30 Oct. 1889, p. 2.
[14] *Teatr i zhizn'*, 1 Nov. 1889, p.1.
[15] *Moskovskie vedomosti*, 30 Oct. 1889, p. 4.
[16] *Teatr i zhizn'*, 1 Nov. 1889, p. 1.

Cupid's Prank

Once it was on the boards, *The Sleeping Beauty* swept all before it. There were fourteen ballet performances between 3 January 1890 and Lent, and *The Sleeping Beauty* was given on all of them. For its part, the direction was prepared to give as many performances of the new ballet as possible in order to recoup its immense production costs. Eight days after the first perform- ance Ivanov requested an advance on salary, and for the first and only time we can verify he was peremptorily refused. The deficit caused by *The Sleep- ing Beauty*, not the ill will of Ivanov's seniors, may have been responsible, just as the causes for the request in the first place, if we knew them, might further explain why Ivanov was so inconspicuous during the time the new ballet was being staged.

He did not return to composition until Krasnoe Selo that summer. There on 24 July 1890 (and again five days later) he staged a short anacreontic ballet in one act, *Cupid's Prank*, the scenario of which recalls Didelot or Noverre. Returning from the hunt Endymion, struck by Cupid's arrow, falls in love with Diana's favourite nymph. The goddess discovers what has happened, and, jealous, wants to punish Cupid, but Venus, ever tolerant of amorous mischief, defends the cherub. The lovers are restored, Cupid is for- given, and the work ends in general merriment. For music Ivanov turned to a talented amateur composer, Alexandre Alexandrovich Friedman, whose primary occupation was to dance in the Petersburg corps de ballet.

Cupid's Prank stirred no particular interest during the summer. The principal dancers were named in short reviews, but Friedman's score was praised.

The entire interest of the performance was focused on L. Ivanov's new ballet, *Cupid's Prank*, the music for which was written by Mr Friedman (artist of the ballet troupe), who also appeared for the first time on the conductor's podium of a state theatre. Very beautiful is the solo violoncello in the seduction scene (Miss Nikitina, Anderson, and Mr Gerdt) and the variation of Miss Kulichevskaya and Nikitina. The waltz, which occurs several times during the ballet, recalls something familiar. Miss Nikitina (a nymph), Johanson (Diana), Petipa (Venus), Anderson (Cupid) per- formed their variations with great success.[17]

In 1888, after *The Beauty of Seville* had been produced at Krasnoe Selo, one critic expressed confidence, given Ivanov's remarkable union of chor- eography with costumes and decorations, that the ballet would 'be received on the stage of the Maryinsky Theatre with the full sympathy of our strict and demanding public'.[18] *The Beauty of Seville* was never mounted on the official stage, but *Cupid's Prank* was, first performed on 11 November 1890

---

[17] *Peterburgskii listok*, 26 July 1890, p. 3.   [18] *Peterburgskaya gazeta*, 31 July 1888, p. 3.

with Petipa's *The Nenuphar* and Act II of Saint-Léon's *Fiammetta*. As with
the transfer of *The Enchanted Forest* from the theatre school, we can but
speculate that the direction found Ivanov's unpretentious ballet attractive, and useful in its effort to develop multiple bills.

The critical response to *Cupid's Prank* in November ranged from praise
to hostility, depending on whether a critic distinguished elegant dancing
from antiquated subject-matter. 'Extremely graceful' and 'carefully
staged', one observed. '*Cupid's Prank* was already produced during the
summer of this year in the theatre at Krasnoe Selo,' wrote another,

Transferred to the large stage with a large number of extras, the ballet is significantly improved. One can even say that it had an excellent success. . . . Mr
Friedman wrote the quite melodious music to this ballet, and Mr L. Ivanov composed the elegant dances and groupings. The grand adagio, the 'seduction scene',
and the finale are the best parts of the ballet. . . .[19]

The change of venue, and with it the change in context, worked to the
ballet's disadvantage. *Cupid's Prank* was composed to follow a spoken comedy in a small theatre at a military encampment in the summer. Expecting
it to compete for attention in a thriving theatrical season with capital works—Borodin's *Prince Igor*, just given its first performance,
Tchaikovsky's *The Queen of Spades* about to follow, Jules Perrot's
Esmeralda soon to be revived with the latest Italian virtuosa, and the
première of a new ballet by Marius Petipa on the same bill—was unrealistic.
This juxtaposition represented the same mix of favour and dismissiveness
as placing *The Enchanted Forest* on the same bill with Emma Bessone in *The
Naiad and the Fisherman*.

It should come as no surprise that Ivanov's new work was found to lack
grandeur and novelty. In weighty condemnation, the critic of *The
Petersburg Leaflet* declared Ivanov's ballet

insipid in all respects; the story is not very interesting and the music is ordinary,
boring, and moreover abundant in attempts at some kind of symphonic picture,
little suited for dances, which, however, did not prevent the composer (a dancer in
our corps de ballet), from coming out for a bow immediately after the end of the
ballet. *Cupid's Prank* is staged indifferently, and clearly in haste, the decoration is
poor, and the groupings and movements of the masses uncertain and routine.[20]

The critic of *The News and Commercial Gazette* attacked 'choreographic
trifles' in general as boring and trite. *Cupid's Prank*, he claimed, had neither
story nor concept nor anything new to offer in the dances. He praised
Ivanov's artists, again exclusively Russian, especially Maria Anderson as
Cupid and the composer Friedman:

[19] *Novoe vremya*, 14 Nov. 1890, p. 4.   [20] *Peterburgskii listok*, 12 Nov. 1890, p. 3.

The music of the ballet, by the young dancer-composer Mr Friedman, who completed a conservatoire course with Professor Rimsky-Korsakov, is very melodious, extremely suitable for dances and magnificently orchestrated. Mr Friedman, for his just desserts, was called for at the end of the ballet.[21]

Miss Anderson [Plate 10] is revealing her indisputable talent more and more. The ability to seize a role's artistic essence, unusual grace of execution, lively, expressive mime, lightness and precision in dances—were always this young dancer's inherent qualities; as Cupid she was able to display the liveliness, the mischievous grace, and the spry gaiety of the eternally young god. And without question, she alone redeemed the boredom and emptiness of the rest.[22]

The notice which appeared in *The New Time*, possibly by Konstantin Skalkovsky, praised Varvara Nikitina in similar language, hinting at the direction's neglect of her:

Miss Nikitina danced with great confidence, lightly and gracefully. In recent years she has had more successes, for which reason one can only regret that such a talented artist, who while still in school promised such great hopes, has been kept in the background for ten years when her talent could have been developed better than any other.[23]

Cupid's Prank was a period piece placed before critics and audiences not especially receptive to its period. Yet its failure was not fully attributable to that miscalculation. Being first shown after a run of performances of *The Sleeping Beauty*—on eight of the nine ballet nights before its première—called attention to the modesty of Ivanov's little ballet and sparked the anger of critics who decried multiple bills. It was given six performances in five months, then dropped from the repertoire.

The Boatmen's Festival

Ivanov produced his last original ballet for Krasnoe Selo in the summer of 1891. *The Boatmen's Festival* was given one performance, on 26 July. The music was again by Alexandre Friedman, who again conducted the performance, and Marie Petipa took the leading role. It is the least documented of Ivanov's three ballets in this venue. 'The new little ballet by L. Ivanov is a graceful piece, staged quite well,' a critic remarked,

There is a mass of effective character dances. Miss Petipa performed *La jalousie-polka* with great success, and danced through the final cancan in a lively fashion.

[21] Friedman was appointed second conductor of the ballet orchestra in the autumn of 1893 (*Peterburgskaya gazeta*, 10 Sept. 1893, p. 3).

[22] *Novosti i birzhevaya gazeta*, 13 Nov. 1890, p. 3.

[23] *Novoe vremya*, 14 Nov. 1890, p. 4.

Miss Petipa was presented a basket of flowers. The music of the new ballet is melodious.[24]

The Boatman's Festival seems to have had no story, or just enough of one to link the dances of a divertissement. We sense this from the disjointed remarks of another report:

Miss Petipa, appearing for the first time this season on the stage of the theatre at Krasnoe Selo, performed the role of the *grisette* Folichanette elegantly, and danced the *chanson à boire* and *La jalousie*, a polka, with great success. Miss Petipa was greeted with friendly applause, and after the polka was presented a basket of flowers.

The [most] beautiful number of the ballet is the Gigue, jauntily performed by Mr Shiryaev (the Englishman) and Mr Novikov (the Frenchman). The *Valse des Matelots* is very beautifully staged; Miss Kulichevskaya, Skorsyuk, [and] Kshesinskaya I are completely effective in sailors' costumes.

Mr Friedman's music was melodious and *dansante*. The overture is beautiful, in which 'The Marseillaise' is heard almost the whole time, the *Chanson à boire*, *La jalousie*, a polka with very effective trio (solo cornet) and the *Valse des Matelots*.

There are no classical *pas* in the ballet, and Miss Kshesinskaya II and Mr Legat performed an interpolated *pas* from the ballet *The King's Command* with great success.[25]

No extraordinary claim can be made for the theatre at Krasnoe Selo as advancing Lev Ivanov's career. He created no immortal work there. At the same time it was his studio, where he could experiment as he pleased in informal, collegial circumstances, away from the scrutiny of the direction and the chief balletmaster. He could nurture young talent, try out new compositions, and maintain contact with past repertoires which he held in high esteem.

[24] *Novoe vremya*, 28 July 1891, p. 3.   [25] *Peterburgskaya gazeta*, 28 July 1891, p. 3.

6

Operatic Interludes

─────

Prince Igor

Over two years separate *Cupid's Pranks* at the Maryinsky Theatre from Ivanov's next ballet there, *The Nutcracker* on 6 December 1892. It was not a rich period in his life or art. His finances were bleak, causing him to ask for advances on salary three times since the management's refusal of his request in 1890. Petipa, officially at the helm, was suffering health problems again, and found himself on the sick list three times between December 1891 and August 1892; in the autumn of 1892 the elder balletmaster submitted to exhaustive medical examination, whence a diagnosis of the debilitating skin lesions that would plague him to the end. Petipa's woes increased with the death of his daughter Evgenia on 26 August 1892.

With his two balletmasters in such a state, Vsevolozhsky sought assistance and found it in Enrico Cecchetti, appointed second balletmaster in 1892.[1] Cecchetti had been dancing in Russia since the 1870s, in the imperial theatres since 1887, and in 1888 had staged a revival of Perrot's *Caterina* for Luigia Algisi, whose stay in St Petersburg was brief and unremarkable. He was not immediately entrusted with another new production, but rather assisted at rehearsals, as Ivanov had done in his early days as balletmaster. Such new productions as we find in this period were revivals—of *La Sylphide* and of Petipa's *Le Roi Candaule*—the latest novelty being Petipa's *Calcabrino* of February 1891. 'The ballet season is beginning with illnesses,' we read in *The Petersburg Gazette* for 26 August 1892, 'The first balletmaster Mr Petipa is quite seriously ill, the second balletmaster L. I. Ivanov also fell ill, so that Mr Cecchetti is now conducting all ballet rehearsals.'

─────

[1] Alexandre Shiryaev recalled that Cecchetti had been appointed without Petipa's consultation, which led to the elder balletmaster's antagonism towards Cecchetti for the length of his stay in the imperial theatres (*Shiryaev*, 41).

Illness was not the only cause of this lack of productivity. Opera, which had always required choreographic services, was again making extra- ordinary demands, as it had in the months before Ivanov was appointed balletmaster in 1885. In the autumn of 1890 two important operas with elaborate ballets were staged which would receive their first performances barely a month apart. These were Tchaikovsky's *The Queen of Spades* and Borodin's *Prince Igor*. Although both works were Russian, the division of labour was easy to decide. Petipa took *The Queen of Spades*, the principal dances of which came in a pastoral *intermède* in the French eighteenth- century manner, and Ivanov took *Prince Igor*, given its première on 23 October 1890.

Prince Igor was Ivanov's first setting of music by the Russian national- ists, whose members included Modest Musorgsky, Mily Balakirev, and Cesar Cui in addition to Borodin and Rimsky-Korsakov. While he must have sympathized with their advocacy of Russian art, Ivanov's contribu- tion to nationalist opera brought mixed results.

Prince Igor was to all accounts a success. Based on the twelfth-century 'Song of Igor's Campaign', the opera is about the military campaigns fought between Russians and the Asian Polovtsians who aspired to conquer Rus. In the prologue Igor's army departs from the town of Putivl amidst bad omens; in Act I we see what happened there during his absence—Putivl be- ing ravaged by the debauched Galitsky, brother of Igor's wife Yaroslavna, and then being attacked by the Polovtsians. Act II is set in the Polovtsian camp, where Igor and his son are prisoners of Konchak, the Polovtsian khan. In Act III Igor escapes, and in Act IV he returns to Putivl amidst the rejoicing of his people.

The dances in *Prince Igor* are found in Act II. There is a brief dance early in the act by the girlfriends of Konchakovna, the khan's daughter who has fallen in love with Igor's son. But the centre-piece is an extended divertisse- ment, in the tradition of French grand opera, rationalized as an entertain- ment that Khan Konchak offers his princely captive.

It is ironic, given the continuing popularity of Borodin's Polovtsian Dances, that they left so little impression on the critics of 1890. Press no- tices lack the spirited opinions that Ivanov's earlier efforts had inspired. Even lengthy reviews make but passing reference to the dances, and rarely mention the choreographer: 'The dances also pleased, successfully pro- duced by Mr Ivanov in the finale of the second act, though one must say that almost the greatest success fell to the chorus, which has much to do in Borodin's opera.'[2] Tchaikovsky's friend Nikolay Kashkin did not mention Ivanov, but found the dances, which 'awakened universal delight', to be

---

[2] *Sanktpeterburgskie vedomosti*, 25 Oct. 1890, p. 3.

'amazingly original and magnificently produced'.[3] In a series of articles the unsigned reviewer for *The Petersburg Leaflet*, though hardly garrulous, was more forthcoming than the rest. 'Among the orchestral numbers the overture the Polovtsian March and the dances of the second act attract one's attention,' he begins.[4] This point is elaborated the next day:

In the eastern music of *Prince Igor* there is much languor, beauty, melodic richness, passion, and colour; these extend in equal degree to the drawing of characters or to the music of the dances, which are distinguished by brightness of hue and a purely elemental, irrepressibly headlong quality.[5]

A few days later still, we get as much a sense of the action of the dance sequence as critics of the time provided:

The dance of the Polovtsian maidens and also the Polovtsian Dance with chorus in the finale of the second act are brimming with vitality, energy, and wild rushing about, which correspond fully to the picture of eastern life unfolding before the audience. . . .

The concluding scene is very effective, of which the Polovtsian chorus serves as background, whose theme is distinguished by a wild, unbridled character, similar to cries, set to the words 'The captives praise the khan, their khan', built on chromatics. The dances of the Polovtsian maidens, warriors and boys complete the scene.[6]

After seven performances, another critic could list the dances among the public's favourite passages: 'But all else is as nothing before the success of the dances. True, they are produced very effectively and with talent. Here music is joined with a spectacle worthy of it.'[7]

We get some idea of the dances from backstage sources as well, such as the diaries of Gennady Petrovich Kondratiev, régisseur of the opera company. As part of his entry for the first performance of *Prince Igor*, Kondratiev wrote:

Dances end the act, beautiful in all respects. Music, production, costumes, execution, everything together beautiful in all respects, so much that they do not yield to the impressions created by *The Sleeping Beauty*—and this ballet can be considered the ideal which production and execution can attain. After the act it was not applause, but a veritable 'roar'.

In reference to the second performance, Kondratiev noted, 'The dances again created a furore'.[8]

---

[3] *Russkie vedomosti*, 29 Oct. 1890, p. 1.   [4] *Peterburgskii listok*, 24 Oct. 1890, p. 3.
[5] *Peterburgskii listok*, 25 Oct. 1890, p. 3.
[6] *Peterburgskii listok*, 27 Oct. 1890, p. 3.
[7] S.A.S., 'Petersburg', *Teatral'nyi, muzykal'nyi i khudozhestvennyi zhurnal 'Artist'* [Theatrical, Musical, and Artistic Journal 'Artist'], Year 2, Book 4, No. 11 (Dec. 1890), 182.
[8] 'The Diaries of G. P. Kondratiev', in *Muzykal'noe nasledstvo* [Musical Legacy], vol. iii, ed. M. P. Alekseev *et al*. (Moscow: 'Muzyka', 1970), 347–8.

Information from choreographic notations of the dances is enticing if fragmentary.[9] Even though the notations lack musical cues to permit co-ordination with the score, the dances were probably organized according to the music, which is arranged by theme into clear sections: the languid open-ing melody, the energetic motifs of the Polovtsian warriors and boys, and refrains for the whole chorus. There were eleven women in the opening dance, entering 4 + 4 + 2 + 1 in succession. After several figures, including some represented by pinwheel-like patterns, instructions follow for the completion of their *entrée*: 'They slowly sit down in the Turkish manner, and with their left hand cover themselves with a veil.' The women run off as a male soloist runs on, followed by four comrades, who 'strike the floor with their bows',[10] and then 'brandish their bows over their heads', holding them aloft and turning them with a rotary movement of the wrist. In the ensuing *danse générale* they continue brandishing and stamping. The closing sec-tions of the ballet were not as clearly notated as those at the beginning, possibly because prior sections were repeated with few changes when brought back later in the sequence.

Whatever the tendency of opera critics to disregard dances, attention was further deflected from those in *Prince Igor* for a number of reasons. Though French by tradition, the dances in *Igor* also conform to a Russian practice, familiar from Mikhail Glinka's *A Life for the Tsar*, the polonaise from Musorgsky's *Boris Godunov* and the waltz from Tchaikovsky's *Evgenii Onegin*, in being accompanied by a chorus, the text of which sus-tains the drama, and in being enlivened by a high degree of autonomous musical interest. These factors vie with choreography for the audience's at-tention, and to the degree they prevail, diffuse the focus on the dancers' steps and patterns. How different from the *Igor* dances, for example, is the celebrated 'Ballet of the Nuns' from Meyerbeer's *Robert le diable*. Here the music was trite and the narrative suspended, leaving nothing to distract the audience from the dances of Marie Taglioni and her colleagues.

That the Polovtsian Dances remain vital as music is clear from the in-terest they continue to generate among listeners who have no idea what

[9] These are preserved in the Harvard Theatre Collection, bMS Thr 245 (16) and (27). Of three settings of the dances, two are clearly inauthentic, being prepared for performances in Paris in the 1930s. There is no indication on the remaining setting if the choreography is Ivanov's or Fokine's for the latter's revival in St Petersburg in 1909.

[10] From Fokine's redaction of the Polovtsian Dances we are accustomed to see a traditional bow and arrow as the weapons of the Polovtsian warriors. But the notators of these dances used the Russian word *samostrel*, which in modern usage connotes a self-firing weapon, or in the case of a bow, one perhaps with some mechanical contrivance to enhance its accuracy. We know that Borodin displayed a precise, refined historical awareness of the connotations of ancient Russian words, and the chronicles which tell us of Igor's campaign, together with data about other Russian battles, speak to the superior effectiveness of the weapons of Russia's foes. It is unlikely that move-ment notators would choose such a term on their own, and we have nothing from Ivanov to indicate what property weapons the dancers should hold. The use of the term remains a curiosity.

they mean. Yet the fastidious Borodin took care to infuse the words with important connotations for the drama. The chorus and dances are divided into two groups: captive women, 'beauties from beyond the Caspian', and the khan's own warlike tribe. This division not only creates a musical contrast between the captives' mellifluous song and the provocative shouts of the khan's own people, but also a symbolic representation of Prince Igor's own situation in the opera at that moment: he is a captive among bellicose enemies. As he has sung of his desire for freedom earlier in the act, he may now hear the offhand words of the captives in this dance as an unambiguous invitation to escape. It is a kind of a sirens' song:

> Fly on the wings of the wind
> To our native land, sweet song,
> There where we sang without restraint,
> Where we and you were free,
> Where beneath the sultry sky
> The air is filled with languor,
> Where to the murmur of the sea
> Mountains slumber in the clouds:
> Where the sun shines bright
> Where beloved mountains bask in light,
> The roses blossom rampant in the vale,
> Where the sweet grapes grow,
> And nightingales sing in the green forests,
> There, song, you are free,
> There you must fly!

The dances stood even less chance of attracting critical comment because *Prince Igor*, together with *The Queen of Spades*, ignited a polemic in the press about the state of Russian opera. It was a variant of the long-standing debate about whether Russian culture should follow the West or be autonomous—and especially whether opera in its lofty purposes should stand apart from much in Western models thought to be unelevated. This was an issue of lively interest at the time, but produced more specialist essays than typical reviews which provide lore. 'The present moment in sound' (Gerald Abraham's apt phrase), that sense of immediacy which so preoccupied the nationalist composers as stylists, to say nothing of its visual counterpart on stage, which Ivanov brought to the dances, were shunted aside in favour of philosophy and aesthetics.

Mlada

In the autumn of 1892 another dance-laden opera went into production, Nikolay Rimsky-Korsakov's *Mlada*. Less well known than *Prince Igor*, its scenario was also based on ancient Slavdom. The action of *Mlada* takes place in the Baltics 1,000 years ago, where Prince Mstivoi contrives to marry his daughter Voislava to Prince Yaromir by killing Mlada, Yaromir's beloved, on their wedding day. Voislava invokes the assistance of Morena, goddess of the nether world, because Yaromir remains faithful to Mlada.

Slavic peoples come to celebrate Ivan Kupala, marking the summer solstice. In a dance where couples are expected to kiss, the shade of Mlada prevents Yaromir and Voislava from doing so.

At a demons' sabbath, Mlada's shade exhorts Yaromir to be faithful; Morena requests help from the satanic Chernobog, who divines that he will fail as long as Yaromir loves Mlada; Chernobog therefore calls forth a vision of ancient Egypt, where Cleopatra and her slaves try to seduce Yaromir. Yaromir awakes, and tells his experiences to priests at the temple of Radegast.

The priests advise Yaromir to await nocturnal visions, which tell him to avenge Mlada's murder. He stabs Voislava, whereupon Morena destroys the temple and causes the nearby lake to overflow. When the havoc subsides, the shades of Mlada and Yaromir rise up from the waters, united forever, while the shades of ancient Slavic princes and warriors are seen in the clouds.

By 1892 the scenario of *Mlada* had been set in various media for over twenty years. In about 1870 the Director of Imperial Theatres, Stepan Alexandrovich Gedeonov, its author, approached four of the nationalist composers to set an act of the libretto apiece, and Ludwig Minkus to compose the dances. This project was left unfinished. Marius Petipa used the scenario for a grand ballet in 1879, with Minkus composing the entire score. In this form *Mlada* was given fifteen performances in two seasons (one for Lev Ivanov's benefit), and revived in 1896. In 1889, to mark the second anniversary of Borodin's death, Rimsky-Korsakov and others gathered to play over the music that had been composed for the first *Mlada*. A friend suggested that he set the libretto as an opera-ballet, and he did. The first performance was given on 20 October 1892.

From a nationalist standpoint, complaints could be raised about Rimsky-Korsakov's work. His style at the time was susceptible to diverse non-Russian influences, including Richard Wagner (whose *The Ring of the Nibelung* had been produced in St Petersburg in 1889, with Rimsky-Korsakov following the score at rehearsal), Karl Maria von Weber's *Der Freischütz*, and Hector Berlioz, whose diabolical chorus in *La Damnation de Faust* may have inspired the nonsense language—equally silly in both works—that Rimsky-Korsakov put into the mouths of his demons in Act III.

More significant than these influences may be that Rimsky-Korsakov conceived and partly composed *Mlada* at the time he was completing *Prince Igor*, which Borodin left unfinished at his death. A comparison of the two suggests that *Mlada* may have been Rimsky-Korsakov's attempt to better his deceased colleague. Where Borodin had adapted a historical source for his libretto, Rimsky-Korsakov turned (as he often had) to folklore, whence the Slavic element could be projected with greater force. Whereas Borodin had based some of his melodies on folk tunes, no tune or dance in *Prince Igor* was Russian. In *Mlada* Rimsky-Korsakov reinforced the sound of folk music with the visual element of Russian and other types of Slavic dance.

To opera lovers in Petersburg in 1892, the merging of opera and ballet was the most controversial aspect of *Mlada*, and graphically illustrates the challenge Vsevolozhsky faced in his parallel attempt to merge the grand ballet with the *féerie*: the audience resisted mixed genres. The composer was criticized on all sides because *Mlada* was a hybrid:

Mr Rimsky-Korsakov's new work is not an opera in the direct and established meaning of this word, at which its very title points in part: opera ballet. In it a large place is allotted to dances and mimed scenes, which bring it close to a fantastic ballet or a *féerie*. The style of *Mlada* is mixed, and for the absence in it of clear, well defined forms, it would be more correct in our view to call it a symphonic poem. It presents a series of separate episodes, tableaux, scenes, on the background of a fantastic element, but not joined together by unity in the whole. . . .[11]

Another reviewer seized upon this point and reduced it to absurdity. 'If you take away from *Mlada*', he wrote, 'what is essential in a *féerie*—miraculous production—and exclude, for example, the purely féeriesque third act—then it turns out that there is neither opera nor ballet in it.'[12]

Mlada failed. It did not excite the debate that *Prince Igor* had, possibly because there was no second work in 1892, like *The Queen of Spades* in 1890, to sustain a polemic. Moreover, its faults were considered grievous. It may come as a surprise today that the invocation of Cleopatra by the Satan of the ancient Slavic pantheon was not thought bizarre. But this concept was not significantly remarked. Composer Mikhail Mikhailovich Ivanov, who had written *The Vestal* for Petipa and whom the nationalists disliked, found much else to criticize. To him as well *Mlada* was the work of a gifted musician but it was not an opera, so great is the weight of the mixed genre on the characters. Nor was the story very interesting, since it was so foreign to the spectator historically and ethnographically. This claim is just, he argued, even compared with stories as remote from the spectator's everyday experience as Tchaikovsky's *The Sleeping Beauty* and Wagner's *The Ring of the Nibelung*, the latter of which in particular is guided in its intricacy by a phi-

---

[11] *Peterburgskii listok*, 22 Oct. 1892, p. 4.
[12] *Sanktpeterburgskie vedomosti*, 22 Oct. 1892, p. 3.

losophy everyone can grasp. The characters of *Mlada*, moreover, do not move the heart.[13] Another conservative composer, Nikolay Solovyov, summed up: 'In general, despite certain successful places, this opera does not give the impression of an integrated, inspired work.'[14]

Dancing in *Mlada* was too prominent not to receive critical attention, virtually all of which was negative. One review reported that Petipa was to have been the choreographer, but illness forced him to withdraw, whereupon his deputies made 'the corps de ballet . . . run around instead of dance'.[15] Mikhail Ivanov ended his notice with a slap at Enrico Cecchetti, who had staged the demons' sabbath and the scene with Cleopatra:

The dances are poorly staged, especially the fantastic dances of the third act; there we clearly see already where our ballet is going after Mr Petipa: it is going directly along the path of Italian ballets, where dances are not in store for large groups, where the corps de ballet is replaced by extras and where the main thing is not the dances, but the number of people on stage.[16]

In complete contrast with the reception of *Prince Igor*, and exceptional in its day for any opera, the balletic part of *Mlada* was separately reviewed. In this article, Ivanov and Cecchetti were treated harshly, their work compared unfavourably with Petipa's setting of the tale. It gives the clearest idea of any notice of what the dances in *Mlada* were like, including an image of warriors brandishing weapons which recalls the choreographic notations of the Polovtsian Dances.

The balletic part of *Mlada* consists of one character dance in the first act, three in the second, and of classical dances and groupings in the third and in the apotheosis.

    . . . In the first act . . . eight couples dance the '*dynya* [literally "melon"] round dance'[17] or *Redova*, which also occurs in Mr Petipa's ballet. It is difficult to say how legitimate the *Redova* is for Baltic Slavs of the tenth century. . . . The movements of this dance are not especially graceful, and much balletic idealizing is needed to make it stageworthy. In his ballet Mr Petipa was incomparably more successful with this task than Mr Ivanov, the '*dynya* round dance' of his ballet being much better and more beautiful. . . .

    In general one must observe that Mr L. Ivanov on this occasion did not distinguish himself in the staging of character dances in *Mlada*. The 'Lithuanian War Dance' in Act II is utterly insipid and dead. In almost every previous ballet there

[13] *Novoe vremya*, 26 Oct. 1892, p. 2.
[14] *Novosti i birzhevaya gazeta*, 22 Oct. 1892, p. 3.
[15] *Novoe vremya*, 21 Oct. 1892, p. 3.   [16] *Novoe vremya*, 26 Oct. 1892, p. 2.
[17] This unusual name for a dance, *dynya ryadovaya* in Russian, may or may not have involved melons, as the modern English translation of *dynya* would suggest. The term *dynya* in Rimsky-Korsakov's score may have been a corruption of the ancient Greek *dina*, connoting 'circling' or 'rotation', or of the ancient Slavic *dynya*, possibly suggesting a ritual to describe a circling of a fire, or the Belorussian *dayniei*, a ritual wheel on a pole which was lit up during the festivities of Ivan Kupala. *Ryadovaya* refers to a dance in rows or in a circle.

were such military dances for the men, which always use the same formations, the sole difference being that in one ballet the soldiers brandish spears, in another cudgels, axes in another; sometimes they strike each other's shields, sometimes simply wave their weapons in the air, inevitably ending their dance with half of the soldiers lying on the ground and the other half standing over them in a victorious pose. The choice of image, as you can see, could not be difficult for the balletmaster, and he chose probably the most wretched, because of all the boring war dances, the 'Lithuanian' in *Mlada* is the most boring and colourless.

The 'Dance of the Indian gypsies' is in the same act. Again the repetition of trite gestures and the complete absence of invention. Dancing in front, Miss Skorsyuk ran about a great deal, fussed, but revealed neither oriental languor nor graceful passion in poses or movements: the whole dance bears a kind of hashed up, hurried, faint resemblance to something gypsy-Indian, generalized oriental or wild. . . .

The 'Slavonic kolo', which ends the second act, is fit to be any round-dance *kolo*— monotonous, endlessly repeating the same thing and owing absolutely nothing to the balletmaster's invention. The shade of Princess Mlada in the person of Miss Petipa I, who appears during the dance, fulfils her task beautifully. The beautiful artist mimes her role gracefully and expressively and constitutes the sole bright spot on the dark balletic background of the new opera.

The composition of classical dances and groupings, entrusted to Mr Cecchetti, was no more characteristic than Mr Ivanov's part. Each grouping perforce made one recall the work of Mr Petipa in his ballet *Mlada*, which bore the stamp of noble elegance and artistic invention of this talented representative of true art.

The appearance and groupings of the shades by Mr Cecchetti are amazingly muddle-headed and monotonously symmetrical. Wrapped in white veils, in half-length skirts, they are more like boarding-school girls running from corner to corner while being rescued from a dormitory fire at night.

. . . The dances and groupings of Cleopatra with her women slaves are also poor. Miss Skorsyuk, with her thin, frail figure, who to our balletic creators somehow personifies the Egyptian queen, is placed in the depth of the stage at the pedestal of a gigantic sphinx, while [her slaves] are removed from her at the front [Plate 16]. Bored with lying there, she jumps up and begins to run among her slaves, but probably for want of the habit tires quickly and runs back to her sphynx to lie down for several minutes by the golden horde. Then she jumps up, runs around and resumes her place again, proceeding thus several times in the course of one scene.[18]

For his part, Rimsky-Korsakov, no authority on ballet production, had few kind words to say about anyone. 'The production of the dances and mimed movement in general was unsuccessful,' he later wrote,

The balletmasters Ivanov and Cecchetti normally do not know the music which they set to dances, and if it is not routine ballet music, they don't understand it at all. Despite detailed instructions I made in the piano-vocal score, they glanced over it too late, it seems. Ballet rehearsals are usually conducted, as of old, to the music of two violins which are obliged to transmit the sense of the whole orchestra. That

[18] *Novosti i birzhevaya gazeta*, 30 Oct. 1892, p. 3.

makes it almost unrecognizable, not only for the balletmasters but even for the musicians; for that reason the character of the movements the balletmasters invent rarely corresponds to the character of the music. They produce gracious movements to a heavy *forte*, and heavy jumps to a light *pianissimo*. Little notes of melodic roulades are beaten out by the legs with a zeal worthy of a better cause. Among the dances only the Indian Dance succeeded, thanks to the dancer Skorsyuk, a lively and spry young woman of the Gypsy type, as too the groupings of the shades, planned with elegance by the balletmaster Cecchetti. But even so, in the end he did not manage well the dances and groupings in the Cleopatra scene. The combination of two simultaneous dances—one slow and passionate, the other fast and violent— did not come out well, for Cecchetti did not work out the combination of two opposed rhythms in the music. Nor did the *khorovod* (kolo) of Act II succeed, which was monotonous and boring. Cecchetti was amusing at private rehearsals of the ballet. He ran around, jumped about, grimaced to represent a little devil, having bound his head with a handkerchief which soaked up the perspiration which flowed from him thick and fast. I doubt that M. M. Petipa I, who performed the role of Mlada's shade, knew and understood her role or would remember the verses which clarify the substance of her mime.[19]

Are these criticisms fair? What basis in ethnographic accuracy could these dances possibly have had? What did Ivanov or his critics know of how the Baltic Slavs danced in the tenth century? Lacking the least element of authenticity, on what, other than whim, could the criticisms have been based? Moreover, what could Ivanov have done to offset the shortcomings in the drama of *Mlada*? How could the negative response to the whole work not be directed to some degree at the dances? How could they be set in other than the most simple fashion if the music was as complex as Rimsky-Korsakov described? Could Ivanov have been limited by a conception of ancient Slavic dances upon which the archaeologically inclined Rimsky-Korsakov insisted? In that case conventional choreography, however artful, might not suffice, and a critic seeing some hybrid style might be led, in ignorance of Rimsky-Korsakov's intention, to think that Ivanov's inspiration had run dry. This speculation is difficult to prove, but its credibility is enhanced by Solovyov's remark that the dances were not very good as music. The '*dynya* round dance', he claimed, produced an excellent impression 'in which the paltry theme was excellently worked out and brilliantly orchestrated'. He continued, in reference to the Slavic dances of Act II:

Of the two dances, the Lithuanian Dance and the Indian Dance, one must give preference to the second as more colourful, worked-out, and musically substantial. The Lithuanian Dance is insipid in musical thought and simply unbeautiful. The rest of the act is boring. The insipid *kolo*, with its constantly repeated short little theme, is

---

[19] N. Rimskii-Korsakov, *Letopis' moei muzykal'noi zhizni* [Chronicle of my Musical Life], 8th edn. (Moscow: 'Muzyka', 1980), 236–7.

boring; only during Mlada's appearance does her theme stand out, which is quite passionate and in addition sad and agonizing.[20]

The point is not simply that Rimsky-Korsakov shares responsibility for the criticism of the dances. These criticisms leave unanswered the difficult question of whether a movement or the music accompanying it is the problem. And dances which are monotonous, always repeating the same short little theme, simply unbeautiful, the dancers just running around—in a work where the same critics praise the music of Mlada's shade for its beauty? Is a lapse of inspiration really causing such a disparity of style, or is it a premeditated conception of ancient Slavic dances which passed totally over the heads of critics in 1892, and went on to receive its most notorious expression in *Le Sacre du printemps*?

It would appear that Ivanov was insufficiently recognized for his setting of the dances in *Prince Igor*, and too severely reprimanded for defects of the dances in *Mlada*. Some element of failed co-ordination or special artistic purpose in the latter work made them unacceptable to the critical awareness of 1892. Their reception aside, these operas were important occupations for Ivanov in the first years of the 1890s. But he had to move on: by the time the complaints about his dances in *Mlada* were published, he had just six weeks to make ready his next première.

[20] *Novosti i birzhevaya gazeta*, 22 Oct. 1892, p. 3.

7

The Nutcracker

The first half of the 1890s was a paradox in Ivanov's career. With the exception of two short ballets, he did nothing he could call his own. Yet two works that were partly his will be remembered as long as people think about ballet. His work on them was born of misery and sorrow. The misery was by now familiar—Petipa's illness—which brought Ivanov to the gates of Confitürembourg. The sorrow was unexpected—Tchaikovsky's death—and led to the meeting of a young prince and a bewitched maiden on the shore of an enchanted lake.

The popularity of *The Nutcracker* today is so removed from the negative response to its first production that we do not suspect, let alone are we concerned about, the work's long road to respectability. The ballet and the mores surrounding it have changed: it has become a Christmas ritual, an idea which had no particular currency in the imperial theatres, and we accept it in versions with significant adjustments in the story.

Surely no other ballet has had such a complex, curious history. Its conception was flawed with respect both to scenario and the mode of presentation planned for it, namely as an after-piece in the eighteenth-century manner, a ballet to conclude an evening's entertainment after a more serious opera. This choice seems to have been an attempt by the Petersburg direction to surpass the Paris Opéra, where such double bills were traditional, by commissioning both works new from one of Russia's finest composers. The linkage did not last: after eleven performances, *The Nutcracker* parted company with *Iolanthe*, the opera Tchaikovsky wrote to be performed with it.

Vsevolozhsky himself, it seems, adapted the scenario of *The Nutcracker* from E.T.A. Hoffmann's story *The Nutcracker and the Mouse King*. In 1894 Modest Tchaikovsky wrote to the music critic Herman Laroche that he 'set down in writing the story of *The Nutcracker* from Vsevolozhsky's words'.[1] Petipa's gloss on this scenario became the source of instructions for the composer, and presumably of the published libretto.

Act I takes place at a yuletide party. The children are brought in to admire the Christmas tree and are given presents. Counsellor Drosselmeyer, godfather of young Clara and her brother Fritz, brings them elaborate gifts—life-size dancing dolls—which are demonstrated, then put away to avoid harm. Drosselmeyer gives them a nutcracker in compensation. Clara is enamoured of the nutcracker and cares for it after Fritz breaks it.

When the guests have left, Clara comes to check on the nutcracker and is attacked by mice. She is terrified at this, and even more when midnight strikes and Drosselmeyer appears in the clock's face. The Christmas tree starts to grow, the toys beneath it come alive and engage the mice in battle; they are nearly routed when the Nutcracker comes to life and takes command. He too is at the point of defeat in single combat when Clara throws her slipper at his adversary, the Mouse King. The victorious Nutcracker is changed into a handsome prince, and invites Clara to Confitürembourg, his homeland. They depart, passing through the branches of the Christmas tree and across a wintry landscape of fir trees (Plate 18).

Act II takes place in Confitürembourg, where the Sugar Plum Fairy welcomes the Nutcracker and Clara, who is honoured for saving his life. An entertainment of dances follows in celebration, which culminates in a *pas de deux* of the Sugar Plum Fairy and her consort. The ballet ends with a general dance and apotheosis.

Vsevolozhsky's adaptation from Hoffmann was exceptionally loose, and produced a ballet with a number of dramatic issues unresolved. The battle of the mice and the transformation of a nutcracker into a young man just happen, whereas in the story both events were motivated by a long-standing grudge the Mouse King (and his mother before him) held against Drosselmeyer and his nephew, who had been changed into the Nutcracker by an act of vengeance. Nor is the outcome of Clara's visit to Confitürembourg explained in the ballet. Does she ever come back? Does she marry the Nutcracker? Do her parents worry about her? Hoffmann resolves all these issues. Moreover, the scenarist specifically ruled out the device which has been invoked so often by producers of *The Nutcracker*— that the marvellous events happen to Clara in a dream.

In addition to lapses of dramatic coherence, the scenario offered few opportunities for characters to reflect, which in turn precluded the spectator's developing a sympathy for them deeper than the surface action permitted. The lack of balletic arias, if the phrase be allowed, affects our perception of

[1] Letter preserved in the Tchaikovsky House Museum at Klin, quoted in *Muzykal 'noe nasledie Chaikovskogo* [Tchaikovsky's Musical Legacy], ed. K. Yu. Davydov, V. V. Protopopov, and N. V. Tumanina (Moscow: Academy of Sciences of the USSR, 1958), 175.

Drosselmeyer most of all, who is more than outwardly eccentric and frightening and whose affection for Clara is genuine, but also who in Hoffmann lives outside time, a condition which has made him wry and sage.[2] Problems of characterization are exacerbated by the virtually complete break in narrative between Acts I and II. Drosselmeyer, who seems capable of real development in Act I, makes no appearance in Act II; Clara's part is resolved dramatically by the end of Act I, and the Nutcracker, who does not become a real character until the battle scene, is left in Act II with nothing more to do but recount the battle and watch the divertissement.

A third problem with the adaptation is a disregard for the balletic medium. It is difficult to imagine how Petipa could accept *The Nutcracker* as set forth in the published libretto. The choreographic components of the acts were not in balance, the first scene being primarily mime, the second dance only, and Act II a divertissement after a few mimed links to Act I at the beginning. There was no part for the ballerina in Act I, and when she finally danced in the penultimate number of the ballet, her appearance had the look of expediency, justified by the merest connection with what had happened earlier in the story.

It is ironic that the dances added to the scenario—the divertissement and the Waltz of the Snowflakes—have nothing to do with Hoffmann and yet are the numbers for which the ballet is most remembered. Considering that *The Nutcracker* was commissioned as *part* of an evening's entertainment, we may err in focusing on narrative coherence more intensely than Vsevolozhsky intended. The whole of *The Nutcracker* stood as a divertissement at the end of *Iolanthe*, and may not have been expected to meet the standard of an independent work.

How was the ballet perceived in its time? To dancer Nikolay Solyannikov, the conceptual problems of *The Nutcracker* were perfectly clear:

They attempted to make a somewhat simpler and more graphic ballet for children, but the absence of central danced parts for the ballerina and the first *danseur*, and also the absence of a story line, [made the ballet] fall apart after the first scene into a series of little pictures and divertissement numbers, and was reflected in a fateful way on the success of the performance.[3]

Solyannikov's colleague Alexandre Shiryaev found that Ivanov did well given the challenge he faced:

---

[2] Yury Slonimsky wrote: 'The mysterious conjurer Drosselmeyer turns out to belong to the same world as the Fairy Carabosse, and the rats from the fairy's retinue grow into a powerful force which comes out against the heroes of *The Nutcracker*.' This statement, discounting certain grotesque musical intonations that the two characters have in common, goes directly against the letter and sense of Hoffmann's story (Yu[rii Iosifovich] Slonimsky, *P. I. Chaikovskii i baletnyi teatr ego vremeni* [P. I. Tchaikovsky and the Ballet Theatre of his Time] (Moscow: State Music Publishers, 1956) [hereafter: *SlonChai*], 248).

[3] *Solyannikov*, 76.

The second balletmaster L. Ivanov produced [*The Nutcracker*] after a programme of Petipa, who at that time was ill. Bearing in mind the dramatic defects of this programme, one must admit that Ivanov unquestionably succeeded with the production of *The Nutcracker*. The individual numbers Ivanov staged were masterpieces in the full sense of the word. Such, for example, were the massive Waltz of the Snowflakes in the second scene, full of poetry, the comic Chinese dance, 'Tea', the languorously plastic dance, 'Coffee', and finally, the effective adagio of the Sugar Plum Fairy at the conclusion of the 'Kingdom of the Sweets'. True, certain of Ivanov's conceptions did not work: unsuccessful, in my view, was the battle of the mice and the toy soldiers, and the Spanish Dance, 'Chocolate', came out rather colourless. As regards 'Chocolate', Ivanov himself confessed that he did not understand the music.[4]

There is evidence of discord between Vsevolozhsky and Petipa. In a letter of 15 February 1891 to Tchaikovsky, Vsevolozhsky was candid about his differences with the balletmaster. He wrote to offer 'some thoughts about the ballet which do not agree with Petipa's opinions . . . He is what the French call *vieux genre*. All the solos and variations which he has conceived for Act I are without interest for the public. It is necessary now to compose a *grand ballabile* and *pas* for the ballerina, and all the variations for the various Johansons, Zhukovas, Nedremskayas only weary the majority of the public.'[5]

This smacks of dissimulation. Of all people, Petipa would have noticed and objected to the very choreographic imbalances which Vsevolozhsky claimed the balletmaster was disregarding.

For a time, Tchaikovsky also had difficulties with *The Nutcracker*. A complex of woes in the spring of 1891—umbrage at the removal of *The Queen of Spades* from the repertoire in St Petersburg, an imminent trip to America about which he felt little enthusiasm, and his sister Alexandra's unexpected death—distracted him in the attempt to compose music for Confitürembourg. It would appear that the ballet's faulty scenario played a part, at least initially, in Tchaikovsky's inability to come to terms with his task. He was at the point of withdrawing from the collaboration, but Vsevolozhsky's diplomatic encouragement kept him in the fold.[6] Numerous speculations have been put forward to explain how Tchaikovsky resolved the scenario's problems to his satisfaction, which all involve considerable leaps of faith.[7]

---

[4] *Shiryaev*, 48.   [5] Quoted in *SlonChai*, 241.

[6] For a fuller account see Roland John Wiley, *Tchaikovsky's Ballets* (Oxford: Clarendon Press, 1985) [hereafter: *Tchaikovsky's Ballets*], 193–7.

[7] Soviet authorities have developed a hypothesis according to which Tchaikovsky carried forward in the music of *The Nutcracker*, irrespective of its scenic formulation, the theme of childhood. In this view, Clara is the centre of the work. On stage she is seen in a static condition of childhood, but in the music Tchaikovsky bursts this limitation and shows her transition from childhood into young womanhood, and the development of her personality in the process of experiencing genuine love. The following writers subscribe in principle to this hypothesis: Slonimsky in *SlonChai*, 243–9,

Lev Ivanov had no part in any of this. *The Nutcracker* began as another collaboration of the artists who produced *The Sleeping Beauty*. Petipa was to be the choreographer, and went so far as to set the order of the dances and write instructions for Tchaikovsky concerning the musical requirements for each number.[8] When Petipa fell ill in the autumn of 1892—as of 12 August, according to his service record—Ivanov fell heir to his plans. The scenario, music, and choreographic layout were already set; Ivanov's task was to compose the dances in accordance with them.

It is possible that Ivanov was again, as he might have been when assigned *The Tulip of Haarlem*, being made to assume responsibility in a bad situation. If this is true, it speaks to the degree to which Petipa's illness was an expression of his belief that the new ballet could not be salvaged. In 1909 a reviewer of *The Nutcracker* recounted the early history of the work and suggested, with no apparent malice, that illness might not have been Petipa's reason for passing the torch:

The abuse of the ballet critics began when M. I. Petipa was still producing the scenario for *The Nutcracker*, which by the way is quite weak. Thinking himself less capable than Tchaikovsky and Vsevolozhsky to penetrate the reveries of children, Petipa, scenting failure, transferred the production of the ballet to L. I. Ivanov, his self-sacrificing, disinterested assistant. The first balletmaster had done such things earlier, but on this occasion the blindness of the criticism and the balletomanic rut helped show the public that the first Russian balletmaster, Lev Ivanovich—was just as esteemed as the talented creator of the dances in *The Snow Maiden* and other operas.[9]

From press reports in the autumn of 1892, it is clear that Petipa's illness did not prevent him from taking a hand in the staging. Throughout much of September, when *Mlada* was taking up Ivanov's time, Petipa remained housebound. But on 29 September we get hints of his involvement, providing 'counsel and instructions':

Second balletmaster L. I. Ivanov is staging *The Nutcracker* according to the counsel and instructions of M. I. Petipa, whose prolonged illness deprives him of the possibility of supervising rehearsals personally.[10]

citing a fulsome array of parallels from Tolstoy to Chernyshevsky; Krasovskaya in *Krasovskaya*, 364–5; Yuliya Andreevna Rozanova in *Simfonicheskie printsipy baletov Chaikovskogo* [Symphonic Principles of Tchaikovsky's Ballets] (Moscow: 'Muzyka', 1976), 107–13, who makes a convincing argument for intonational parallels between passages in *The Nutcracker* and from earlier works of Tchaikovsky dealing with childhood. For a different explanation of Tchaikovsky's motives, see Roland John Wiley, 'On Meaning in *Nutcracker*', *Dance Research*, 3/1 (Autumn 1984), 3–28.

   [8] *Tchaikovsky's Ballets*, 371–82.
   [9] *Novoe vremya*, 15 Dec. 1909, p. 6; Agrippina Vaganova wrote, without elaboration, that *The Nutcracker* 'was transferred to L. I. Ivanov, since Petipa was little interested in it' (*Vaganova*, 43).
   [10] *Birzhevye vedomosti*, 29 Sept. 1892, p. 3.

Who did what in *The Nutcracker*? The title-page of the libretto credits Petipa with the programme of the ballet and Ivanov with its production and dances. Sergey Khudekov questioned this division of labour:

The production of the ballet *The Nutcracker*, with music by Tchaikovsky, has been attributed to L. Ivanov. This is not true. This ballet was mounted by Marius Petipa. Only one act was assigned to L. Ivanov, who dealt beautifully with his task, staging several grandiosely poetical dances for the corps de ballet in this work, obviously meant for the amusement of children at matinee performances in Butter Week [the week preceding the beginning of Eastern Orthodox Lent].[11]

Khudekov's attribution of Act I to Petipa accords with the claim, reported by Slonimsky without citation, that Petipa began rehearsals and had roughed out the first scene before he fell ill.[12] Ten days before the première of *Mlada*, we learn that Act I is already staged, as if to imply that Petipa had been busy with *The Nutcracker* while Ivanov was working on the opera:

Rehearsals of P. I. Tchaikovsky's ballet *The Nutcracker*, which the balletmaster L. I. Ivanov is producing, are in fact moving forward: the first act of the ballet is already staged. P. I. Tchaikovsky visited one of the latest rehearsals of *The Nutcracker*. The composer was greeted with the applause of the whole ballet troupe, and we hear is fully pleased with the production of this part of the ballet.[13]

Rehearsal visits apart, Ivanov seems not to have enjoyed Tchaikovsky's systematic personal collaboration, in contrast to Petipa's experience with *The Sleeping Beauty*, where frequent meetings of composer and balletmaster can be documented. As a result, there were no adjustments in the music of *The Nutcracker* of the kind that we know were made in *The Sleeping Beauty*, aimed at a closer fit of note and step. Being committed to Petipa's choreographic plan may have involved Ivanov in profound differences of approach. 'All of L. Ivanov's attention was directed at the development of the danced action,' Solyannikov recalled,

the dances were produced with his characteristic mastery—musically, elegantly, distinctively . . . But whether Petipa constructed the libretto unsuccessfully, or whether the régisseur's contrivances were alien to Ivanov's creation, saturated with soft lyricism, there was little theatricality or humour in the performance, and without them it was impossible to justify the stage realization of a fantastic tale.[14]

We have few glimpses of Ivanov rehearsing *The Nutcracker*. Josef Kshesinsky's anecdote about Ivanov's preoccupation with cards has been quoted (above, pp. 52–53). Alexandre Shiryaev recalled:

[11] *Khudekov*, 172.   [12] *SlonChai*, 270.   [13] *Peterburgskaya gazeta*, 10 Oct. 1892, p. 3.
[14] *Solyannikov*, 77.

It also fell my lot to participate in the production of *The Nutcracker*. In the score of this ballet among the divertissement numbers of the last act there is a so-called 'trepak'. Ivanov composed a Russian dance to this music, which he assigned me to dance. At rehearsals, however, he himself did not like the staging and the costumes, and called the artist Ponomaryov into consultation, [who] proposed to remake my costume into that of a clown with a hoop (*cerceau*) in his hands. Ivanov agreed with this, and I was called upon to compose a new dance, which I quickly did. My staging so pleased the balletmaster that he immediately approved it and fixed it within the ballet. Of course, on the *affiche* my name as composer of the dance was not noted. At that time the regulation was strictly observed to place on the *affiche* only the name of the principal producer.[15]

We have some idea of the performing forces involved in *The Nutcracker* from a cast list of 1897, which gives details omitted in the published libretto. There were twelve pairs of children in the opening scene, to perform the dances and the galop, and a sizeable cast for the battle scene:

2 dolls	2 dancers
2 fife players	2 drummers
6 little soldiers	1 sentry
4 students in the retinue of the Mouse King	1 drum major
	3 additional soldiers
1 set of officer + 6 soldiers	1 gingerbread officer

The list still does not indicate the number of mice and gingerbread soldiers, whose parts were taken by students not from the theatre school, but from the Life Guards Finnish Regiment.

For the Confitürembourg tableau, in addition to the principals, there was one artist representing each of the fairies listed in the libretto, two sisters of the Nutcracker, two each of the ten confections listed except for one 'Biscuit', four emerald and four ruby pages, four moors and one brocade boy. In the apotheosis, eight students represented bees.[16]

The Nutcracker was presented to the public for the first time on 6 December 1892. The leading dramatic roles in the ballet were taken by Stanislava Belinskaya (Clara), Vasily Stukolkin (Fritz), Sergey Legat (the Nutcracker)—all students at the time (Plates 17, 19). The venerable character dancer Timofei Stukolkin, St Petersburg's first Dr Coppélius and Don Quixote, took the role of Drosselmeyer. The leading danced parts were per-

[15] *Shiryaev*, 48–9.

[16] St Petersburg, Historical Archive, 497.8/2.467, fos. 3–5, 8–9. These figures may not represent exactly the numbers of personnel of the first performance, which differ slightly in the number of confections (see Appendix C). The cast list gives fifty-six snowflakes to fifty-nine for the first performance, and in the Waltz of the Flowers six soloists and sixteen couples instead of the eight soloists and twenty-four couples listed in the 1892 programme.

formed by Antonietta Dell'Era (Sugar Plum Fairy), visiting from the Royal Theatre in Berlin, and Pavel Gerdt (her consort).

The first performance was subject to a torrent of criticism. To get a sense of the ballet's reception, let us begin with two reviews, given almost complete. The first is moderate in tone and rich in descriptive details, and provides an impression of what the spectacle was like.

Given on Sunday, 6 December, at the Maryinsky Theatre, the two-act (three-scene) ballet by Petipa and P. I. Tchaikovsky, *The Nutcracker*, from Hoffmann's tale of the same name, begins with a scene of the lighting of the Christmas tree in the home of the president and his wife and with the giving of toys to the children. Students of the theatre school receive the gifts very naturally and with animation, and dance a galop holding their gifts pleasingly. The appearance of several pairs of *incroyables* and *merveilleuses* in whimsical costumes of the French revolution sustains the liveliness of the scene, and their dances, involving the showing-off appropriate to these dandies, are original and rather piquantly over-affected, in which the beautiful Miss Petipa, with great style, makes much ado with her lorgnette and the train of her dress.

The entrance of 'godfather' Drosselmeyer brings to little Clara and her brother Fritz the presentation of mechanical dolls, which servants bring in wrapped up in paper and tied in ribbons and place in the middle of the stage. Beneath the wrappings are a sutler, a soldier, a Columbine, and a Harlequin. The dolls stand immobile as long as the 'godfather' does not wind them with a key, but then the mainspring is snapped and the dolls begin to move automatically, to turn and to dance. Although this scene closely recalls *Coppélia*, it is not without original interest, thanks to the talented Miss Anderson, who imitates the movements of a mechanical doll in an extremely typical and comical way. Mr Litavkin is also excellent in this regard; Mr Kyaksht is somewhat weaker, and Miss Preobrazhenskaya completely insipid.

The dance of student Belinskaya with the injured nutcracker, in the manner of a *berceuse* and polka, is quite unsuccessful both in composition and in execution, while the antique *Grossvater*, performed by old and young, is very original and probably started the hearts a-beating of older members of the audience with recollections of long-past youth.

The guests disperse, the fires die out. In the dark corners of the room squeaking breaks out and mice, armed with sharp daggers, begin to appear on stage. Through the window the moonlight silvers the darkened Christmas tree, beneath which several toys remain, including a sentry in his box and a rabbit with a drum. The crowd of mice grows and takes on a threatening aspect; the sentry in the booth comes to life and fires his musket, announcing the danger; the rabbit beats the alarm on his drum, the roofs fall away from the boxes and from them jump out gingerbread soldiers one by one: grenadiers, hussars, artillerymen. A battle begins, one side led by the King of the Mice, the other by the courageous Nutcracker, who has been transformed into a prince. The mice are defeated, and their conquerer—the Nutcracker—kneels before his beloved Clara and leads her to the fairy-tale world.

The appearance of the mice and the little soldiers and the battle itself are not altogether successful: there are many disorderly tangles and much unnecessary running about. It would be incomparably better if the formations were correct and intelligible and the whole scene significantly shortened.

The second scene—a snowy forest—is not connected in any way with the story of the ballet and could also be omitted and interpolated into any other ballet. In itself this picture is extremely effective, thanks as much to the charming set as to the costumes of the corps de ballet, which very successfully represent snowflakes. The downy pompons on the white tunics, and on the headwear in the form of rays of stars, and in fluttering little clusters on the wands, represent the movements of snowflakes completely and picturesquely, the original grouping producing an elegant allegory of a snowdrift. Something similar to it was presented in the ballets *Camargo* and *The Daughter of the Snows*, but our new balletic winter far exceeds its predecessors in beauty. The Waltz of the Snowflakes offers nothing new, perhaps with the exception of the backstage chorus, a novelty unprecedented in ballet up to now.

The third scene represents the 'Kingdom of the Sweets' in the original decoration of Mr [Konstantin] M[atveyevich] Ivanov, consisting of such an abundance of fruit drops, confections, and gingerbreads that just looking at it is cloying. Strictly speaking, there is no ballet in this scene, but only an exhibition of costumes which flaunt luxury and their more or less remote likeness to caramels, sugarplums, mint cakes, and other products of the properties-confectionary art.

Dances are introduced in a divertissement, in which chocolate dances in the form of a Spanish *pas* headed by Miss Petipa I—a dance little successful in its composition or with the audience—coffee in the form of an Arabic Dance, full of eastern languor and plastic poses, for which Miss Petipa II is little suited—and tea, in which the graceful Miss Anderson turned out best of all, performing her Chinese *pas* so characteristically and nicely that it had to be repeated. The jesters' dance—where boy students of the school serve only as a background for Mr Shiryaev's complicated *pas*, difficult and executed remarkably precisely—and the dances of the mirlitons are beautiful only for their music. The dance of the polichinelles, led out by their merry aunt (*mère* Gigogne) is a copy of the children's harlequinade beautifully composed and staged by balletmaster Petipa for the revival of *The Wilful Wife*. The *grand ballabile* of the gilded sweetmeats [i.e. the Waltz of the Flowers, in which the dancers were costumed in gold] is not bad as regards groupings, but the excellent soloists are completely lost in the mass. Miss Dell'Era dances an utterly insignificant *pas de deux* with Mr Gerdt which nevertheless gives her a chance to display her superb *attitudes* and brilliant pointes, and her cavalier his positively unfading youth and incomparable gracefulness. In general, the new ballet is produced primarily with children for children, and for everything that can have value in their eyes as regards external brilliance; for the woman dancer there is very little in it, for *art* precisely nothing, and for the artistic fate of our ballet—it is yet one more step downwards.[17]

[17] *Novosti i birzhevaya gazeta*, 8 Dec. 1892, p. 3; this translation has been edited to remove verbal clutter and the citation of many artists' surnames.

1. Lev Ivanov in Mexican costume for Mazilier's *Jovita*

2. Lev Ivanov, possibly in the 1860s

3. Maria Granken and Lev Ivanov in Russian costume (late 1860s)

Гранкина и Иванов

4. Lev Ivanov as Solor in Marius Petipa's *La Bayadère* (1877)

5. Lev Ivanov as Milon, the dancing master, in Petipa's *L'Ordre du roi* (1886)

6. Lev Ivanov in his later years

7. Vera Lyadova in ballet costume (mid-1860s)

8. Vera Lyadova as Helen in Offenbach's *La Belle Hélène* (*c*.1868)

9. Vera Lyadova as Helen, and Nikolay Sazonov as Paris in Offenbach's *La Belle Hélène* (*c*.1868)

10. (*above*) Maria Anderson
11. (*above right*) Anna Johanson
12. (*right*) Alexandra Vinogradova
(Petrova)

13. Maria Anderson as Ilka in Ivanov's *The Enchanted Forest* (*c.*1892)

14. Emma Bessone, who created the role of Emma in Ivanov's *The Tulip of Haarlem* (*c.*1887)

15. Maria Anderson in Ivanov's *The Tulip of Haarlem* (c.1892)

16. Maria Skorsyuk as Cleopatra in Rimsky-Korsakov's *Mlada*

17. A scene from *The Nutcracker*: Stanislava Belinskaya as Clara, probably with Vasily Stukolkin as Fritz, and Lydia Rubtsova as Marianna, President Silberhaus's niece

18. *A Forest of Fir Trees in Winter*: set design by Mikhail Bocharov for *The Nutcracker*, Act I, Scene 2

19. Stanislava
Belinskaya as
Clara, and Sergey
Legat as Prince
Nutcracker in *The
Nutcracker*, Act II
(1892)

20. A drawing
depicting the
enforced dancing in
Ivanov's *The Magic
Flute* (1893)

21. A grouping from Petipa's *The Sacrifices to Cupid* in Lev Ivanov's revival (1893)

22. The Throne Room. Set decoration by Matvey Shishkov for Act II of *Zolushka* (1893)

23. Anna Johanson, possibly in her costume as the Fairy
Godmother in *Zolushka* (1893)

24. A collage of sketches for set designs by Mikhail Bocharov; those on the right are for *Swan Lake*, Act I, Scene 2 (1894)

25. The set design by Mikhail Bocharov for *Swan Lake*, Act I, Scene 2

26. Alfred Bekefy and Marie Petipa as the lead couple in the Hungarian Dance, staged by Ivanov in Act II of *Swan Lake*, 1895

27. Mathilde Kshesinskaya as Galatea, and Sergey Legat as Acis in Ivanov's *Acis and Galatea* (1896)

29. Olga Preobrazhenskaya as O-Ioshi, and
Claudia Kulichevskaya as O-Tama in
Ivanov's *TheMikado's Daughter* (1897)

28. Title-page of the libretto of
Ivanov's *The Mikado's Daughter* (1897)

30. Drawing of a procession from Act III of Ivanov's *The Mikado's Daughter* (1897)

The critic who signed himself 'Domino' responded very differently. His unsparing attack takes aim at the new ballet's weakest points, genre and libretto.

First of all, *The Nutcracker* cannot in any event be called a ballet. It does not satisfy even one of the demands made of a ballet. Ballet . . . is mimed drama, and consequently must contain all the elements of regular drama; on the other hand, a place must be found in ballet for plastic attitudes and dances, the essence of classical choreography. There is nothing of this in *The Nutcracker*. Nor does it have a story, but rather a series of unconnected scenes, recalling the latest pantomimes which the boulevard theatres flaunt. In the first act there is not one classical *pas*, and the music is such that whatever the balletmasters' desire, it would have been impossible to stage one classical variation. In the second act there are several character and demi-character dances and one classical adagio for Miss Dell'Era. But in any case, to repeat, *The Nutcracker* cannot pretend to be a ballet, but constitutes 'spectacle', which can be given with success on the summer stages of our small theatres. For our first-class ballet the production of such 'spectacles' is an insult. We have the best corps de ballet in the world and first-class soloists, for whom the most difficult classical ballets are accessible, and it is a pity to take offence at them when they are obliged to play mere supernumeraries in a pantomime absurd in conception and execution, which could please only the most uncultured spectators. The only thing left in our state theatres from colossal sums expended is the ballet, of which Petersburg can be proud; but the production of ballets like *The Nutcracker* can quickly and easily lead to the company's downfall. Why study dance, why maintain the traditions of classical choreography, when artists seem to be no more than *figurants*, portraying roles fully accessible to any supernumerary? We repeat: the production of such ballets as *The Nutcracker* constitutes death for the company. In conclusion let us add, that having elicited the general disapproval of balletomanes, *The Nutcracker* failed with the public as well, who found it boring with good reason. God grant that similar failed experiments do not happen often.[18]

Other critical responses fell between these extremes. 'Two or three more such "Nutcrackers" and of our model ballet company . . . only a pleasant memory will remain,' one wrote.[19] There were many complaints about the scenario. 'The librettist apparently was not able to take full advantage of the subject matter or, perhaps, this story is too fantastic and complicated for pantomime. Almost all the story is placed in the first scene . . . and the remaining two are divertissements with new decorations and costumes.'[20] A colleague concurred, adding that 'for a *féerie* it has too little action and machines, whereas for a ballet there aren't enough dances . . . .'.[21]

Reviews were rich in comments about the production and the artists. The opening scene stood in distinctive contrast to the entrance of the parents *en incroyables*:

[18] *Birzhevye vedomosti*, 8 Dec. 1892, p. 3.   [19] *Peterburgskaya gazeta*, 7 Dec. 1892, p. 3.
[20] *Novoe vremya*, 8 Dec. 1892, p. 3.   [21] *Journal de Saint-Pétersbourg*, 9 Dec. 1892, p. 1.

In the first scene the entire stage is filled with children, who run about, blow their whistles, hop and jump, are naughty, and interfere with the oldsters dancing. In large amounts this is unbearable. . . . The dance *des incroyables* is very beautiful, much complemented by elegant costumes.[22]

In contrast to our reviewer who found her dances insipid, others found Olga Preobrazhenskaya superior in the dances of the mechanical dolls. Solyannikov recalled:

Particular success came the way of Preobrazhenskaya, the enchanting, elegantly flirtatious little doll Columbine. Preobrazhenskaya danced the entire number on pointe: this produced the character of a doll-marionette; she is pulled by her string, and she bobs up and down, barely touching the floor of the stage with her pointes. Columbine's dance enjoyed a noisy success, and Preobrazhenskaya always had to repeat this number.[23]

'Miss Preobrazhenskaya was charming in this role,' Bezobrazov noted in his review, 'and her light blue costume went very well on her.'

With great art she transmitted the automatic movements of a doll, maintaining this manner until the end. Columbine's entire *pas* was staged on pointe. Having elegantly danced her *pas*, Miss Preobrazhenskaya called forth friendly applause in the audience. To this dancer belongs the best success of the first scene of *The Nutcracker*.[24]

To introduce a complex battle scene at the height of an act, to be executed by children in semi-darkness, was at best experimental and at worst courting trouble, especially since many of the children were from a regimental school, and lacked the stage experience of the children of Theatre Street. On all sides it was declared a failure. 'The mice, in a muddled way, bustled around the stage, blocking the direction whence the Nutcracker's soldiers came,' wrote the critic for *The New Time*, 'Who was victor over whom was also unclear.'[25] Bezobrazov saw enough to know that the mice fought the gingerbread soldiers first and the tin soldiers second, but concluded that 'there was much turmoil and running about, and nothing more'.[26] This complaint persisted; three years later a critic would write, 'No few errors creep into the production, as in the first act during the appearance of the battling gingerbreads and mice, etc.; there is great confusion and chaos on the stage.'[27]

Ivanov enjoyed an undisputed triumph in the Waltz of the Snowflakes, the sheer beauty of which could not escape notice. 'The ballerinas are in white dresses, adorned with ostensibly real puffs of snow, with snowy

[22] *Novoe vremya*, 8 Dec. 1892, p. 3.   [23] *Solyannikov*, 76.
[24] *Peterburgskaya gazeta*, 7 Dec. 1892, p. 3.   [25] *Novoe vremya*, 8 Dec. 1892, p. 3.
[26] *Peterburgskaya gazeta*, 7 Dec. 1892, p. 3.   [27] *Novosti i birzhevaya gazeta*, 2 Oct. 1895, p. 3.

boughs which they gently shook, and with snowy rays about their heads; when they sat down and lay down they formed, beckoning, a pleasant and even warming mound of snow.'[28] 'Mr Bocharov's décor was much applauded,' another critic wrote,

and yet more the sparkling waltz, so original in rhythm and orchestration, which raises up a cloud of dancers dressed in white, with starry coiffures, adorned with white balls simulating snowflakes. The final grouping, on which electric light is suddenly made to fall, is truly a magical effect.[29]

Watching a revival in 1912, Andrey Levinson could still find that 'The dances of the snowflakes, accompanied by the singing of a distant chorus, this most popular of the balletmaster Lev Ivanov's compositions, preserved their somewhat lightweight charm even in the indifferent hands of the official "reviver", Mr Sergeyev.'[30]

If part of the effect of this dance had to do with costumes and properties and the effect of falling snow, part of it had to do with the movements and designs made by groups of dancers which imitated the shapes of windblown snow, as well as geometrical designs which the dancers formed from time to time, including a cross rotating in one direction within a circle moving the opposite way, and a pattern resembling a snowflake. In connection with these designs, Agrippina Vaganova recalled:

The snowflakes circled in a whirlwind, scattered as if windblown, and joined up again. The scene turned out marvellous. Not in vain did admirers go to the top, the fourth balcony, whence this scene could be viewed particularly effectively, specifically to admire the production.[31]

The national dances of the divertissement were written about more for their performers than their choreography. Singled out were Maria Anderson in the amusing Chinese Dance, and Alexandre Shiryaev in the athletic Russian Dance. 'Miss Anderson, dancing in the Chinese manner, was best of all. What a charming Chinese girl she was!'[32] Her dance was encored. The next day the Dance of the Jesters was praised, 'in which Mr Shiryaev very adroitly jumped through a hoop'.[33] Still another commented: 'Mr Shiryaev made one think of Mr Cecchetti in his dance of the buffoons, so much did he deploy the vivacity and flexibility of his limbs.'[34] In contrast, the Waltz of the Flowers or 'Golden Waltz', as it came to be called, failed to please: 'The *Grand Ballabile* has no success whatever, although the entire corps de ballet was dressed in gold cloth and even carried

[28] *Novoe vremya*, 7 Dec. 1892, p. 3.
[29] *Journal de Saint-Pétersbourg*, 9 Dec. 1892, p. 1.
[30] *Rech'*, 30 Oct. 1912, p. 5. [31] *Vaganova*, 43.
[32] *Novoe vremya*, 7 Dec. 1892, p. 3. [33] *Novoe vremya*, 8 Dec. 1892, p. 3.
[34] *Journal de Saint-Pétersbourg*, 9 Dec. 1892, p. 1.

in a huge gold vase with golden flowers, which turned out quite unbeautiful but was probably expensive.'[35]

It was approaching midnight before Antonietta Dell'Era performed her *pas de deux* with Pavel Gerdt. Musically, her solo variation within the *pas* was famous for the obbligato celesta. Opinions about Dell'Era's dancing differed depending on the side of the footlights from which they came. She had made a powerful impression on critics a month earlier in her début as Aurora. 'This dancer is completely serious,' reads one notice of that occasion, 'with a beautiful school and complete assurance in performance. The ballerina especially flaunted the strength of her pointes and in this respect can perform the most difficult variations. Her turns are smooth and elegant.'[36] 'Her technique is a model,' another notice reads, 'each movement, the most difficult *pas* is easily performed with that noble simplicity which compels one to forget physical difficulties. One need hardly add that Miss Dell'Era is beautiful in all three scenes in which she dances. . . .'[37]

In *The Nutcracker* the praise was not so lavish. 'Miss Dell'Era began to dance at half-past eleven in the evening. Despite the awkward and insipid music of her *pas* and the carelessly composed variation, Miss Dell'Era danced it magnificently and at the end of the performance was called out five times.'[38] Solyannikov, ill-disposed towards foreign dancers, thought that Dell'Era's engagement was a scandal:

The ponderous, coarse, unbeautiful, ungraceful dancer was much to the taste of the Germans and was firmly settled in at the Royal Theatre in Berlin. But the power of a foreign name turned out so great that the Petersburg press immediately went to pieces in delighted notices and did not spare epithets such as 'light', 'ethereal', 'astonishing', and the like, in spite of the dancer's sizeable weight. First she wanted to make her début in the part of Aurora in *The Sleeping Beauty*, but changed her mind and decided to wait for the new production of *The Nutcracker*, where the role of the Sugar Plum Fairy was especially composed for her. Although this was contrary to good sense, Lev Ivanov was too good-humoured and indecisive to go against the direction, and Petipa agreed compromisingly that 'Madam not so very good', but in a month her tour ended, so that there was no point, in his opinion, to objecting. . . .

Other than a quite good dance technique, Dell'Era possessed absolutely no merits whatever, and, prudently not staying to the end of her tour here . . . returned to the bosom of the Berlin theatre.

. . . Neither the corpulent, podgy Dell'Era nor her bearded partner who had put

---

[35] *Novoe vremya*, 8 Dec. 1892, p. 3. Bezobrazov observed that 'All the women soloists and second dancers take part in the *grand ballabile*, and a large golden vase figures in it, supported by caryatids. In ballet this is a novelty . . .', adding that no small sum was probably spent on the golden costumes in the third scene (*Peterburgskaya gazeta*, 7 Dec. 1892, p. 3).

[36] *Birzhevye vedomosti*, 10 Nov. 1892, p. 3.

[37] *Novoe vremya*, 10 Nov. 1892, p. 3.   [38] *Novoe vremya*, 8 Dec. 1892, p. 3.

on weight could produce model fairy-tale characters, and thereby did not contribute to the success of the performance.[39]

The staging itself almost escaped notice in the early reviews. 'Poor as usual were the machines,' wrote Bezobrazov, to whom they operated in a clumsy, noisy manner. 'The illumination was primitive; the fountains in the last scene were most wretched, the production officials have obviously never seen *fontaines lumineuses*.'[40]

There were, finally, conflicting views of Tchaikovsky's music. As was true of *The Sleeping Beauty*, *The Nutcracker* stirred some discontent, but it was outweighed by the praise. Because the music was not *dansante*, Bezobrazov argued that the balletmaster could not compose anything excellent, and the dancers, despite their fine performance, produced a mediocre effect.[41] 'P. I. Tchaikovsky has illustrated this *simple* tale with beautiful original music . . . the mimed scenes . . . are perhaps the most beautiful, characteristic, original, and interesting,' adding the next day that 'everything from beginning to end is beautiful, melodious, original, and characteristic'.[42]

The critic of *The New Time* was decidedly balletomanic:

[T]he ballet produced on me the same incoherent and unsatisfactory impression that its libretto did. Discounting for the moment that fact that the composer did not transmit the fantastic mood of the story into his music, in the first scene especially there sounded something sombre and burdensome. The *Grossvater* of the first act was heavy and wooden, unworthy even in texture of such a highly gifted composer as Tchaikovsky. The same impression stayed with me in the grand waltz of the snowflakes in the forest, accompanied by a distant chorus of voices which probably represents the howling of a blizzard. This waltz is closer to the Wolf's Glen scene in *Der Freischütz* than to a children's tale.

. . . As for the *Grand ballabile* and especially the music of the *pas de deux* to which Miss Dell'Era and Mr Gerdt danced, it is not interesting in any respect and is quite simply boring, and most important, it is unsuitable for dancing.[43]

'The howling of a blizzard'? The 'Wolf's Glen' scene? Foolish epithets. Even the balletomane Bezobrazov pointed out that the accompaniment of an offstage chorus had been used in ballet before, in Ambroise Thomas's *La Tempête*.[44] Vladimir Sergeyevich Baskin, Bezobrazov's colleague at *The Petersburg Gazette*, gave a more reasoned assessment: '[S]uch a great composer should not have taken upon himself such a trifle and such nonsense as the story of this ballet. But if the nonsense which Tchaikovsky's music illus-

[39] *Solyannikov*, 73–4, 76. [40] *Peterburgskaya gazeta*, 7 Dec. 1892, p. 3.
[41] Ibid. [42] *Peterburgskii listok*, 6 Dec. and 7 Dec. 1892, p. 3.
[43] *Novoe vremya*, 8 Dec. 1892, p. 3. [44] *Peterburgskaya gazeta*, 7 Dec. 1892, p. 3.

trates is forgotten . . . then the music itself, it can be said, is beautiful, and astonishingly rich in inspiration.'

Baskin continued with a discussion of the first scene, contending that the music improved throughout Act I. By the Waltz of the Snowflakes,

the composer gave full rein to his imagination and the scene turned out beautiful; the music before the waltz (this scene makes up the second part of Act I), and the waltz itself leave nothing to be desired; one can listen to such a musical picture with pleasure even without a stage, but it is all the more effective amidst live and poetical illustration.

The scene in the forest is in our view the best part of *The Nutcracker*; there in fact Mr Tchaikovsky stands at his full height: he ceased entertaining children, and provided the grown-ups with a poetical picture.

Baskin found it more difficult to assess the music of Act II with respect to the stage action, but found that number for number, Tchaikovsky's inspiration was still running high.

The divertissement consists of several numbers small in size but remarkably characteristic in content and instrumentation: a Spanish Dance, Arabian, Chinese, jesters, and others. Each of them is a completely finished work and amazingly self-possessed.

As for the the *pas de deux*, it is in form at least (theme and variations) also normal. Miss Dell'Era once told us that this number is not *dansant*, the music is too 'symphonic'; but if it is, we hope the symphonic nature of the music does not apply to the main theme, on which the ballerina builds her 'classical' patterns.

In sum: it's a pity that so much good music is expended on such nonsense, so unworthy of attention; but the music in general is excellent: that for dances is *dansante*, and that designated for the ear and for the fantasy will be heard accordingly. Of Mr Tchaikovsky's three ballets (*Swan Lake, The Sleeping Beauty*), *The Nutcracker* is the best, its music indeed not for the normal ballet audience.[45]

For all the complaints about *The Nutcracker*, it was given the lion's share of ballet evenings from the night of its first performance to the end of the spring season—eighteen showings—and supplied dances for divertissements the following summer at Krasnoe Selo. Five more performances followed in the 1893/4 season. Among the highlights of the ballet's first run is the appearance of Varvara Nikitina in the role of the Sugar Plum Fairy at the fourth performance:

On Sunday, 13 December, our graceful ballerina Miss Nikitina, who will dance in this ballet in alternation with Miss Dell'Era, appeared in place of Miss Dell'Era in the role of the Sugar Plum Fairy. Despite the achievements of the Italian ballerina, Miss Nikitina produces a more suitable impression. She resembles as does no other the light, fairy-tale content of *The Nutcracker*, and in her slender, graceful figure,

---

[45] *Peterburgskaya gazeta*, 9 Dec. 1892, p. 4.

in her ethereal dances, the Sugar Plum Fairy is realized incomparably more successfully.[46]

These successes apart, *The Nutcracker* did not play well during its first eight years. Already in the autumn of 1893 critical opinion had further soured: 'It is difficult to imagine something more boring and foolish than *The Nutcracker*,' we read in response to the opening performance of that season.[47] Even Anna Johanson's fine performance of the Sugar Plum Fairy 'could not conquer the fatal melancholy which reigned in the auditorium'.[48] Except for a performance on 19 February 1897, at which the size of the cast was reduced, it was not given at all between 15 October 1895 and 23 April 1900—dropped from the repertoire for nearly five seasons. The ballet was given a new lease on life on the latter date when Olga Preobrazhenskaya took the ballerina's role. 'In the famous *pas de deux*, with Mr Legat I, Miss Preobrazhenskaya enchants with her gracefulness and nobility of poses and movement. She performed the variation on pointe (to the celesta) irreproachably.'[49] Twenty-one performances were given between April 1900 and December 1905.

An extraordinary sidelight on the history of the work was reported by the ballerina Tamara Karsavina, who had been engaged to perform *The Nutcracker* in Prague. Distant from Petersburg, the producer there dealt unceremoniously with the ballet's defects, this being perhaps the first of many modified versions which come down to the present day.

The programme of the ballet is significantly broadened, and closer than ours to Hoffmann's *The Mouse King*. Since the ballet *The Sleeping Beauty* is given there to the music of the famous composer Nedbal, part of Tchaikovsky's music for this tale is added to *The Nutcracker*, which begins with the prologue from *The Sleeping Beauty*. Instead of the inevitable fairies, five beings figure there with the corresponding attributes. Miss Karsavina with a mirror, for example, represented Vision.

It is curious to observe that mimed roles are performed in the ballet by artists of the drama, which avoids the necessity of watching ballet dancers' conventional and boring mime. The beautiful dramatic actress Sedlachkova, for example, played the role of 'The Sugar Plum Fairy'.[50]

Soon after this in St Petersburg, régisseur Nikolay Sergeyev mounted a revival of *The Nutcracker*. It was an attempt to return to the original production as it began to recede from memory, rendering the problems at the heart of the work no less clear in 1909 than in 1892:

[46] *Novosti i birzhevaya gazeta*, 15 Dec. 1892, p. 3.
[47] *Peterburgskaya gazeta*, 6 Sept. 1893, p. 3.
[48] *Peterburgskii listok*, 7 Sept. 1893, p. 3.
[49] *Novosti i birzhevaya gazeta*, 11 Sept. 1901, p. 3.
[50] *Novoe vremya*, 26 Aug. 1908, p. 4.

The Nutcracker is indebted for its popularity exclusively to Tchaikovsky. It draws the public, one must hope, only for its music and *in spite of* its *mise-en-scène*.

Ballet production customarily suffers from the lack of a unified, conscious thought. In *The Nutcracker*, by contrast, one feels most acutely the non-coordination between a precise thought, the divine music, and the endless feebleness and dullness of producers who must create a stage realization for *this* conception to *such* music. *The Nutcracker must* be readapted for the stage.[51]

The first performance of this revival came on 13 December 1909. Vsevolozhsky had died a fortnight earlier, which gave critics pause to recall his artistic (as distinct from administrative) contribution to the work. A year later his authority was still being invoked:

The late director of theatres illustrated the gentle work of the composer's muse with 101 water-colour drawings of costumes, having them, according to Hoffmann, coincide in period with the Directory. All the characters are dressed and coiffured in the fashion of the end of the eighteenth century, including the eccentrics, the *incroyables* and *merveilleuses* with capricious veils and classical tunics, *fichus* and *dormeuses* on their heads, from under which show long curls and locks. Even the tin soldiers who do battle with the Mouse King—the infantry and artillerymen—wear the uniform of soldiers of the First Consul. Precious albums of Vsevolozhsky's drawings are preserved by his son-in-law, Count Grabbe, and N[ikolai] G[rigorievich] Sergeyev, recognized for the revival of *The Nutcracker*, would do well to have another look at them: the *incroyables* would probably not be permitted on stage in today's absurd and distorted coiffures. The gifted artists Makhotina, Eduardova, Leonova, and others perplexed the audience with such a coarse offence against the history of costume.[52]

Changes in this production were the omission of *La mère Gigogne*, and a reduction in the number of snowflakes from fifty-six to thirty-six.[53] *The Nutcracker* was to be staged in Moscow in 1913, but this plan was postponed for a year,[54] and in fact the ballet was not produced there until 1922.

By the time of its first revival in Leningrad in 1923, staged by Alexandre Shiryaev and Fyodor Lopukhov, Ivanov's choreography had lapsed beyond the physical memory of dancers, a loss much lamented by spectators familiar with the first production.[55]

The Nutcracker was last performed before the Revolution on 25 October 1917, with Tamara Karsavina as the Sugar Plum Fairy. This occasion

[51] *Rech'*, 28 Dec. 1909, p. 5.

[52] *Novoe vremya*, 31 Dec. 1910, p. 6.

[53] According to a programme of *The Nutcracker* for the performance of 9 Jan. 1911, preserved in the Harvard Theatre Collection, bMS Thr 245 (247). See also *Novoe vremya*, 30 Dec. 1909, p. 5.

[54] *Moskovskie vedomosti*, 11 Jan. 1913, p. 5; 21 Apr. 1913, p. 4.

[55] See e.g. excerpts from Akim Volynsky's critique of the 1923 production, translated in *Tchaikovsky's Ballets*, 388.

marked the twenty-fifth anniversary of Tchaikovsky's death, a fitting commemoration of the collaborator whose contribution, more than any other, had sustained the ballet through the first, fitful period of its stage life.

8

Between *The Nutcracker* and *Swan Lake*

The Magic Flute

On 12 December 1892, six days after the first performance of *The Nut-cracker*, Vsevolozhsky sent a memorandum to the Minister of the Imperial Court:

Because of the illness of balletmaster Petipa, the production of the ballet *The Nut-cracker* was transferred by me to second balletmaster Lev Ivanov, who performed this assignment with success, as a consequence of which I consider it my duty most respectfully to petition Your Excellency for permission to designate a compensatory half-benefit for Lev Ivanov similar to the one granted to balletmaster Petipa for the ballet which he produced, *The Talisman*.[1]

The Minister concurred, and the benefit performance was set for 3 January 1893. At first *Iolanthe* and *The Nutcracker* were to be performed, but the programme was changed to a mixed bill of ballet. It was a hail and farewell: the last performance on the imperial stage of Antonietta Dell'Era, and the first appearance of Mathilde Kshesinskaya in the role of the Sugar Plum Fairy. For his part, Ivanov had little time to prepare for his benefit: three days after Vsevolozhsky's request he was sent to Moscow until Christmas to revive Saint-Léon's *Fiammetta* for the ballerina Lydia Nikolaevna Geiten.[2] Even so, 'The revered benefit artist put together a quite interesting programme,' a reviewer observed,

[F]irst the ballet *The Nutcracker* was given, in which, because of Miss Nikitina's illness, Miss Kshesinskaya II performed the role of the Sugar Plum Fairy, from which the second act of the ballet lost nothing whatever. The young and talented ballerina

---

[1] Ivanov Service Record, fo. 210.   [2] Ibid., fo. 211.

danced the *grand pas de deux* very well, and had great success. Then the first act of *The Sleeping Beauty* and a divertissement were given. Mr A. [*sic*] Ivanov was called for in the second intermission and was presented with a valuable gift and two wreaths. Miss Dell'Era was given an ovation after the first act of *The Sleeping Beauty* by the numerous admirers of her brilliant talent: the artist was called several times and presented with about a dozen luxurious bouquets and baskets of flowers.[3]

For the next few months, Ivanov was involved in two projects for the theatre school, the first being the preparation of a new ballet. The story of *The Magic Flute*, the instrument which compelled all within earshot to dance, had been the basis of ballets produced in Russia since at least 1818, when the leading female part in a production at Moscow had been taken by Adam Glushkovsky's wife in a staging by Bernadelli, after which it was periodically revived from the 1820s to the 1860s.[4] Ivanov probably took the cue for his revival from productions he recalled as a young dancer: on 9 December 1865 Alexey Bogdanov had staged *The Magic Flute* with students of the theatre school for his benefit performance; a second performance followed on 27 January 1866, also by students, for Christian Johanson's benefit. In Moscow it was performed at the Bolshoy Theatre as late as 1878.

The scenario of *The Magic Flute* has points of contact with *La Fille mal gardée*. The young peasant Luc loves the charming Lise, daughter of a rich farmer, and she loves him. But Lise is being wooed by a rich, decrepit old marquis whom her ambitious parents hope will marry her. The marquis's wealth and station appear to be winning out over Luc's true love when the benevolent spirit Oberon intervenes. In the guise of a pilgrim he knocks at the farmer's door but the farmer's wife, entertaining the preferred suitor inside, drives him away. Luc, in contrast, receives him cordially, and is rewarded with a magic flute before the pilgrim vanishes. Luc plays the flute, and at its sounds Lise runs to him, then her parents with the gouty marquis—all compelled to dance (Plate 20). Furious, the marquis wants to wrest Lise from Luc's embrace. He calls the superintendent, the village judges, and soldiers to seize and punish the impertinent lad, but Luc again begins to play, and the judges, the soldiers, the marquis's footmen, Lise's relatives—everybody dances. Oberon enters again, this time in the form of

[3] *Novoe vremya*, 5 Jan. 1893, p. 3.

[4] The 1818 production is noted in 'A List of Ballets Given in the Imperial Moscow Theatres', *Ezhegodnik Imperatorskikh Teatrov* 1900/1, Supplement 2, p. 78; performances in 1829, 1841, and later are noted in 'A List of Ballets Given in the Imperial St Petersburg Theatres From the Year 1828', *Ezhegodnik Imperatorskikh Teatrov* 1899/1900, Supplement 3, p. 60; newspaper reviews and announcements of spectacles for a given day make us aware of other performances, such as e.g. the *Severnaya pchela* [The Northern Bee], 1 Jan. 1825, 8 Jan. 1825, 3 Dec. 1834, and 18 Dec. 1834. P. Shpilevskii reviewed a performance by actors in 1857 (*Muzykal'nyi i teatral'nyi vestnik* [Musical and Theatrical Messenger], 20 Jan. 1857, p. 35).

a good spirit, and decrees that Luc is to have Lise, and the marquis his gout. The curtain falls amidst the approving applause of the witnesses.[5]

The school performance took place on 10 March 1893, with a cast of important young dancers: Lise was Stanislava Belinskaya, who three months earlier had created the role of Clara in *The Nutcracker*, Mikhail Fokine was Luc, Sergey Legat the old marquis, and Agrippina Vaganova the farmer's wife. There were four danced numbers:

Danse villageoise for Lise, Luc, and eight other couples;
Pas d'action for Lise, Luc, the Marquis, and the eight women who had danced the preceding number;
Scène et danse forcée for Lise, her mother and father, Luc, the Marquis and his messenger, a Commissaire, and two judges;
Grand ballabile for all participants.

The programme began with excerpts from Ostrovsky and Molière, and ended with two more dances: a *pas de deux* from Perrot's *Caterina* and the *pas hongrois* from Petipa's *Camargo*.[6]

Later in life, Fokine remembered his participation in *The Magic Flute*. It was, he claimed, the first time he had taken part in an examination ballet:

I was about 11 when I appeared in this kind of performance, in *The Magic Flute*. This was a new ballet, specially staged by L. I. Ivanov. I played the part of Luc, a poor peasant lad in love with the peasant lass Lise (student Belinskaya). Her parents, of course, wanted to marry her to a rich old marquis (the 14-year-old S. Legat). But a fairy assisted me, giving me a magic flute. Playing the flute, I forced her parents and the marquis to dance. They called a judge. I exhausted him with dances too. They prepared me to be hanged, and had already put my head in the noose when the good fairy appeared again, and everything ended with dances in which I performed entrechats and turns. The end was of the happiest sort. After that this ballet was included in the repertoire of the imperial theatre, and A. Pavlova many years later gave it abroad.[7]

Hardly a month after the student performance, *The Magic Flute*, like *The Enchanted Forest*, had been transferred to the Maryinsky stage, where it was well received:

One must give Mr Ivanov his due—he has managed this little ballet extremely well. Not counting the incredibly funny scene of forced dancing, the remaining numbers are beautiful and as original as possible in the limited framework of a peasant ballet.

    [5] This synopsis was conflated from reviews of the public performance in *Peterburgskaya gazeta*, 13 Apr. 1893, p. 3, and *Novosti i birzhevaya gazeta* for the same date, pp. 2–3.
    [6] *Novoe vremya*, 12 Mar. 1893, p. 4. For the programme of the student performance see *Borisoblegsky*, ii. 46.
    [7] M[ikhail Mikhailovich] Fokin, *Protiv techeniya. Vospominaniya baletmeistera. Stsenarii i zamysly baletov. Stat'i, interv'yu i pis'ma* [Against the Current. Recollections of a Balletmaster. Scenarios and Projects of Ballets. Articles, Interviews, Letters] (Leningrad: 'Iskusstvo', 1981), 46.

In the *danse villageoise*, the *pas d'action*, and in the concluding *grand ballabile* he found several fresh constructions, and to Mr Drigo's melodious waltzes and polkas made beautiful dances for the corps de ballet of the loveliest coryphées, and for Miss Johanson, who performed the role of Lise with her inherent grace and lightness. Her variation in the *pas d'action* and dances with the eternally young Gerdt as Luc are models of elegant softness and noble style. Very fine are the second dancers who performed in the *ballabile*: Ivanova, Tistrova, Fyodorova, and Noskova simply fly, and stand out for their purity and graceful airiness in the lovely background formed by galaxies of peasant girls in the persons of Rubtsova, Pavlova, Kuskova, Tatarinova, Ogoleit III, and others.

Needless to say, Mr Stukolkin was an incomparable comic as the marquis, and Miss Ogoleit I dealt very well with the role of the farmer's wife, showing that the Direction acted wisely, assigning her mimed roles, for which she is wonderfully able, in her second term of service.[8]

After criticizing the new ballet for aping *The Nutcracker* in its appeal to children, the reviewer for *The Petersburg Gazette* continued to be grudging in his praise:

The Magic Flute is staged and the dances composed by the balletmaster L. I. Ivanov. The beginning of the ballet, at times in its story resembling *Giselle*— whence the set was taken—is not very interesting, indeed and the dances in it are quite simple, and go no further than *balonné* and *balancé*. The scene of the comic dances and the *grand ballabile* (which are strongly reminiscent in their groupings of the final ballabile with the hay from *La Fille mal gardée*) are successfully mounted, and to this part of the ballet *The Magic Flute* is obliged for the success it had at the first performance on Sunday, 11 April.

. . . Mr Drigo wrote the music for *The Magic Flute*. After *The Nutcracker* the orchestration seems rather thin, but several waltzes are pretty, dance tempi are sustained—in a word, this is genuine *musique dansante*. The best numbers are the adagio which Mr Auer played, and the ballerina's variation accompanied by the harp. *The Magic Flute* is a small ballet—it takes less than an hour—but it pleased very much. It had a fine success and of course is watched with greater pleasure than that most boring *Nutcracker*. The producer of the ballet, Mr Ivanov, and the composer Drigo were called for several times.[9]

The justification for mounting *The Magic Flute* on the large stage seems once again to have been part artistic, part practical. As a comedy it would make a pleasing contrast to fantastic ballets on a multiple bill. Moreover, Petipa continued to be indisposed, and any novelty would be welcome to vary the repertoire.

In the month between the school performance and its première at the Maryinsky Theatre, *The Magic Flute* was given a more numerous cast.[10] The

[8] *Novosti i birzhevaya gazeta*, 13 Apr. 1893, p. 3.   [9] *Peterburgskaya gazeta*, 13 Apr. 1893, p. 3.
[10] St Petersburg, Historical Archive, 497.10.388, fos. 12–12ᵛ, contains a cast list for *The Magic Flute*.

soldiers were increased from four to six, and the *Valse villageoise* was aug-
mented by four second dancers, namely those whom our critic observed
simply flew.

After a felicitous beginning, the critical reception of *The Magic Flute*
soured as this ballet, in another parallel with *The Enchanted Forest*, was associated not so much with any defect of staging or performance as from
other problems which the Petersburg ballet suffered. It was not inventively
programmed. As if to spite critics who complained of its similarity to *The
Nutcracker*, those in charge of scheduling placed *The Magic Flute* alongside
The Nutcracker and later alongside Nikolay and Sergey Legat's *The Fairy
Doll* as an evening's entertainment. In its first year *The Magic Flute* was
paired with *The Nutcracker* in seven of its ten showings. Like *The Enchanted
Forest*, *The Magic Flute* was given most often at the beginning of the autumn or in the spring, those margins of the theatre season where the absence
of star ballerinas and the direction's willingness to reduce expenses were
most acutely sensed. This complaint was voiced throughout much of the
ballet's run of performances, beginning in the autumn of 1893:

To whom is it not known that the beginning of the season, that is, the entire month
of September, is a time of poorest receipts, and to attract the public the economy-
minded director should make all efforts to increase interest by new productions or
the participation of artists who enjoy the greatest success? On our ballet stage it is
just the opposite. Instead of producing some new ballet, especially easy after the
long summer break, only old, exhausted ballets are given; nor can the best of the old
ballets be shown for the absence of ballerinas to dance them, who avoid appearing in
September, which the direction dooms to neglect. Our public's favourites, Miss
Nikitina and Miss Kshesinskaya II have been on leave up to now; an Italian ballerina is invited only in October; this leaves Miss Johanson, who dances only one
ballet and at that the worst—*The Tulip of Haarlem*, which has never brought in receipts. That leaves *The Nutcracker* from last year, which requires no ballerina, and
The Magic Flute in one act, with the very same Miss Johanson—and that is all of
September![11]

The Magic Flute was given thirty-four performances on the Maryinsky
stage between 11 April 1893 and 3 April 1904, with subsequent revivals at
Peterhof (23 July 1906), Krasnoe Selo (13 July 1906, 19 July 1912), the
Maryinsky Theatre (1 May 1914), and the A. S. Suvorin Maly Theatre (21
March 1916). Anna Johanson kept the role of Lise until she retired in 1898,
after which it was taken by Anna Pavlova and Lyubov Egorova. On 5 May
1902, the last performance of the spring season that year, the Petersburg
public bade farewell to Enrico Cecchetti, who appeared as the Marquis in
The Magic Flute. His first and last appearances on the imperial stage had
been in ballets by Lev Ivanov.

---

[11] *Novosti i birzhevaya gazeta*, 7 Sept.1893, p. 3.

Stepanov Dance Notation

Three days after the first performance of *The Magic Flute* the second project with which Ivanov had been associated that spring came to a successful conclusion. It was the final test of a system of notating dances invented by Vladimir Ivanovich Stepanov, a graduate of the theatre school in 1885 who had advanced to first coryphée by 1889.[12] In that year the industrious Stepanov began to attend courses in anthropology and anatomy at the University of St Petersburg, where he started to develop a method of movement notation using signs analogous to those of musical notation. By the spring of 1891 his method was sufficiently refined to warrant an official demonstration:

Artist of the ballet troupe Mr Stepanov has devised a method of notating bodily movements as they apply to choreography. At the beginning of this year the system he invented of notating ballets with the aid of musical signs was presented to the theatre direction. The proper authorities formed a commission of specialists, chaired by the Director of the Theatre School, to become acquainted with Mr Stepanov's invention. As a practical examination of his theory, he was to give a series of lectures in the theatre school before the artists and the commission. Mr Stepanov's system is deemed practical and readily adaptable for the notation of ballets. As a result of the examination, the commission deemed necessary a special protocol [expressing] its candid declaration that Mr Stepanov's system renders exceedingly great services to the choreographic art.[13]

Based on this demonstration, Stepanov was given leave to study anatomy in Paris. There he published an exposition of his system, *Alphabet des mouvements du corps humain. Essai d'enregistrement des mouvements du corps humain au moyen des signes musicaux* (M. Zouckermann, 1892). This book, announced in the Russian press as early as February of that year,[14] appears to have prompted a series of testimonials by officials of the Petersburg ballet. Pavel Gerdt was succinct: 'Mr Stepanov's work for the notation of dances is fully deserving of attention.' Petipa's report, dated 10 February 1892, contained mixed signals; while he was convinced that balletmasters of merit would not be served by Stepanov's notation, he wished the young artist success in the future.[15] Lev Ivanov's testimonial, undated, reads as follows:

[12] The discussion of Stepanov and the development of his notation system is drawn, in addition to other cited sources, from his death notice in the *Ezhegodnik Imperatorskikh Teatrov*, 1895/6, 504–5; *Borisoglebsky*, i. 308; ii. 37–8; *Krasovskaya*, 446–8; *Two Essays on Stepanov Dance Notation by Alexander Gorsky*, trans. Roland John Wiley (New York: Congress on Research in Dance, 1978), pp. ix–xix. For an introduction to the Stepanov system, see Ann Hutchinson Guest, *Dance Notation: The Process of Recording Movement on Paper* (London: Dance Books, 1984), 72–6.

[13] *Novoe vremya*, 10 Mar. 1891, p. 4.

[14] *Novoe vremya*, 21 Feb. 1892, p. 4; *Moskovskie vedomosti*, 25 Feb. 1892, p. 5.

[15] St Petersburg, Historical Archive, 497.6.4102, fo. 2 (Gerdt's testimonial), fos. 3–3ᵛ (Ivanov's), fos. 8–8ᵛ (Petipa's). Petipa's letter has been translated into Russian in *Marius Petipa. Materialy,*

Reading Mr Stepanov's book about the notation of ballet dances by means of signs he has conceived, thereby to preserve for a long time excellent ballets and various successful *pas*, I find Mr Stepanov's idea highly successful and useful for balletmasters, to whom, of course, it would be of great interest to preserve their best compositions for posterity. It is true that his idea is not new, because before him at various times many balletmasters devised similar signs; but I do not know why they have not been employed up to now, perhaps because then this idea was looked upon as awkward because of its complexity, or simply ignored. Mr Stepanov's merit is that he has greatly simplified the idea, and thereby helped it apply at the present time to our ballet. Of course his idea can persuade us of its usefulness and applicability only in actual practice.

Giving Mr Stepanov's work its due, I for my part respond favourably to his idea.

Balletmaster L. Ivanov

The tests of usefulness and applicability to which Ivanov referred were being prepared during the time that *The Magic Flute* was in rehearsal on the Maryinsky stage. Another examination of the system was concluded on 14 April 1893:

Upon his return to Petersburg at the end of last year, Mr Stepanov was allowed by the direction of the Imperial theatres, as an experiment, to teach choreographic stenography to students of the theatre school. On Wednesday, 14 April, an examination was given in Mr Stepanov's class in the presence of the Director of Imperial Theatres, Mr I. A. Vsevolozhsky, the Supervisor of the Bureau, Mr Pogozhev, the Head of the School, I. I. Ryumin, the balletmaster A. [*sic*] Ivanov, teachers of dance Ch. P. Johanson and A. A. Oblakov, Mr Gerdt and the ballet régisseur Mr Langhammer. The result proved most brilliant: some of the female students easily notated in Stepanov's system some dance themes given to them, and others sorted out and danced themes given to them. At the wish of someone present an attempt at notating character dances was made, and this was also successful. After such successful results achieved in a short time, the teaching of choreographic stenography will surely be introduced in an obligatory ballet course at the theatre school.[16]

On 22 April, at the examination performance of the theatre school, Stepanov revived Perrot's *An Artist's Dream* (*Le Rêve d'un peintre*) with notations of dances he had worked up after consulting Christian Johanson, who in 1848 had danced the leading male role of Alvarez, the painter, opposite Fanny Elssler as Florida. This was the last test of the practical utility of

---

vospominaniya, stat'i [Marius Petipa. Materials Recollections, Articles], ed. Yu. Slonimskii *et al.* (Leningrad: 'Iskusstvo', 1971) [hereafter: *MarPet*], 121–2; it is translated in part in *Two Essays on Stepanov Dance Notation by Alexander Gorsky*, trans. Wiley, pp. xii–xiii. Petipa's original reads, in part: 'Ma conviction est . . . que les maîtres de ballet d'un haut mérite, ne se serviront pas de cette méthode dont Monsieur Stépanow n'est pas le premier en tête.' And to close: 'Mr Stépanow a le mérite de travailler afin de pouvoir progresser dans cette méthode. Je le félicite et lui désire pour l'avenir un succès complet.'

[16] *Peterburgskaya gazeta*, 16 Apr. 1893, p. 4.

his system. Stepanov went on to become a teacher in the theatre school. After his death, in 1896 at the age of 30, his system was taken up by Alexandre Gorsky and then by Nikolay Sergeyev, who supervised a notation project, the products of which provide insights about the Petersburg repertoire to this day.[17]

The Offerings to Cupid

Petipa's illness was a continuing cause for concern as the spring season of 1893 ended, to which the critic of *The New Time* added:

The ballet season ended yesterday. *The Nutcracker* and *The Magic Flute* were given. What will next season bring? As yet we know only that two foreign ballerinas are engaged. Besides Miss Gorshenkova, who is leaving the stage, Petersburg balletomanes are losing yet another Russian ballerina, who is abandoning her artistic career in the full flower of her likeable gift. We are speaking of Miss Nikitina, who is leaving the stage. During her service on the ballet stage Miss Nikitina with complete justification enjoyed the love of the public and great success, here and also in Berlin, where she was invited on tour. The distinctive features of this ballerina are unusual lightness of movements, notable *ballon*, and precision in the execution of classical *pas*. The ballerina was offered a benefit, which she refused.[18]

The 1893/4 season would be difficult for Ivanov. A hyperbole of woe began in July with an announcement that the ballet orchestra would be abolished, and the opera orchestra would now play ballet performances.[19] The departures of Gorshenkova and Nikitina sparked complaints in the press about the treatment and status of Russian dancers. Professionally, Petipa was barely functioning: he reputedly did not stage a single dance the entire season. Nor for a time was the outlook bright for visiting celebrities. Palmyra Pollini, who replaced Carlotta Brianza in October, had a middling success. Later that month a tragedy occurred which, if the outpouring of grief is any indication, had no less impact than the passing of an emperor: the death of Pyotr Ilyich Tchaikovsky.

For all this, the circumstances were not unremittingly bleak. The hiring of Enrico Cecchetti was vindicated as he now began to shoulder his share of the work, contributing to *Zolushka*, the only scheduled novelty of the season, and reviving Perrot's *Caterina* and Saint-Léon's *Coppélia*. Two débuts also warrant mention. Lydia Pashkova, a writer slighted in the Russian press, wrote the scenario for *Zolushka* 'by "special commission" of the theatre direction. Why this "special commission" was necessary is still an un-

---

[17] Concerning the surviving Stepanov notations, see Roland John Wiley, 'Dances from Russia: An Introduction to the Sergejev Collection', *Harvard Library Bulletin*, 24 (1976), 94–112.

[18] *Novoe vremya*, 8 May 1893, p. 3.   [19] *Novoe vremya*, 16 July 1893, p. 3.

answered question.'[20] A Parisian bohemian and occasional correspondent for *Le Figaro* who (as rumour had it) was related to Vsevolozhsky, Pashkova wrote two more libretti for St Petersburg, one of which— *Raymonda*—brought her such recognition as she enjoys in the history of ballet. The bright light of the season was a rising star recently appearing in a garden theatre in Moscow who went on to enjoy the longest tenure of any Italian ballerina on the Petersburg stage. The historical coincidence by which Pierina Legnani crossed paths with Lev Ivanov opened the way for an eloquent response to Tchaikovsky's death.

The shortage of new repertoire persisted, and the direction again called on Ivanov to revive one of Petipa's earlier ballets: *The Offerings to Cupid, or The Joys of Love* on 26 September 1893, which the elder balletmaster had staged for Evgenia Sokolova in 1886. It was a bagatelle in one act, reminiscent of *Cupid's Pranks* in its flirtations and pastoral setting.

The stage represents a forest with a statue of Cupid on a pedestal, at which shepherds and shepherdesses leave gifts and pray. Hylas appears, beloved of the beautiful Lise, and places a wreath of roses at the foot of the altar. Lise enters; jealous, she thinks that Hylas has come for some other shepherdess. She reproaches him, but after vows and hesitation Lise forgets all and both swear eternal love. Happy at the reconciliation, the shepherds and shepherdesses dance and withdraw into the copse.

Paris rushes in, looking for Chloë. She appears and listens to the birds, though she hears not a bird but Paris imitating a nightingale. Chloë runs from tree to tree, trying to catch the nightingale. Finding Paris at last, she rushes to him; a scene of jealousy ends in peace and a passionate kiss.

Presently Venus appears from inside the altar. Chloë tears herself away from Paris and wants to run into the forest, but Venus promises to protect the lovers. Cupid arrives with a brilliant cortège. Considering the sacrifices left at the altar unworthy, he puts out the light and would destroy the temple. Venus reproaches him; the shepherds and shepherdesses fall at her feet; forgiven, Cupid rushes to his mother, who unites the loving couples. Hymen appears, assuring them that true happiness resides in love; the lovers' enthusiasm is expressed in dances.

The Offerings to Cupid invoked the awkward arrangement, unremarkable to Ivanov by now, whereby he made new dances to a scenario by Petipa. That Sokolova was teaching in the theatre school at the time and was available for consultation must have relieved the pressure on Ivanov's memory, for *The Offerings to Cupid* had been performed only twice in its original production, once privately before the imperial family and once for Sokolova's farewell benefit.

It is clear from press reports that the division of labour in *The Offerings*

---

[20] *Peterburgskaya gazeta*, 6 Dec. 1893, p. 3.

to Cupid was recognized in the revival, and the result well received. Olga Preobrazhenskaya as Chloë was praised in all quarters. 'Miss Preobrazhenskaya was the heroine of yesterday's performance,' wrote Nikolay Bezobrazov in *The Petersburg Gazette*,

She put a wealth of coquetry and natural gracefulness into her role and dances, which recalled in this respect the charming former ballerina E. P. Sokolova, and besides, in her yellow-blue costume and white wig Miss Preobrazhenskaya made a most charming shepherdess. Of her dances let us note the *entrée* and *adagio* with Mr Litavkin. Miss Preobrazhenskaya's first experience in a responsible role was wholly successful, and rewarded by the public according to its merit.[21]

That the revival was part of a multiple bill limited the space allotted to it in reviews, all of which touched upon similar issues. The reviewer for *The Saint Petersburg News* stressed the young ballerina's strong impression as well, and remarked on the sense of changing of the guard that the revival prompted:

The palm of excellence must be given to Miss Preobrazhenskaya, who had a special success. She appeared in *The Sacrifices to Cupid*, the dances of which were newly and successfully staged by Mr Ivanov, who substituted the previous performers of the principal roles, Miss Sokolova, Miss Gorshenkova, and Mr Gerdt, with Miss Preobrazhenskaya, Miss Rykhlyakova, and Mr Litavkin. The role of the shepherdess Chloë brought memories of E. P. Sokolova, with her grace and art. In a beautiful costume and a powdered wig Miss Preobrazhenskaya was a most charming Chloë, [and] recalled, not to her detriment, her predecessor, having justified by her dancing and success the gift of flowers with a gathering of light blue silk material attached. It remains to wish that all further appearances of the likeable dancer in responsible roles would be as successful as her first, yesterday.[22]

The Offerings to Cupid was given twenty times in the next two seasons in a variety of mixed bills. Its reception speaks to a new interest in short pastoral ballets after the middling success of *Cupid's Pranks* three years earlier.

Zolushka

Making the story of Cinderella (*Zolushka* in Russian) into a ballet was a second attempt to capitalize on the success of *The Sleeping Beauty*. The basis of the scenario was the familiar tale by Charles Perrault, enriched in the following description by details of costume and staging quoted from a notice of the first performance.[23]

In search of Cinderella, her sisters Aloisa and Odette interrupt the danc-

[21] *Peterburgskaya gazeta*, 27 Sept.1893, p. 3.
[22] *Sanktpeterburgskie vedomosti*, 28 Sept.1893, p. 3.
[23] *Novosti i birzhevaya gazeta*, 7 Dec. 1893, p. 3.

ing scullery maids, 'dressed in cooks' jackets and caps of white satin with
kitchen knives at the waist and saucepans in their hands'. Cinderella enters,
and grudgingly helps her sisters prepare for the ball; she begs to go along.
Left at home, she dreams of going. Living sparks fly out of the hearth and
dance a *pas des étincelles* 'dressed in grey, smoke-coloured costumes . . . in
the background of the multicoloured flames'. The good fairy appears and
agrees to send Cinderella to the ball, provided she remain no later than midnight. Cinderella agrees, and with a wave of her wand the good fairy produces a brilliant retinue who make Cinderella ready. 'At the fairy's gesture
the rear wall of the kitchen vanishes and opens out into a delightful nocturnal landscape with a river, silver moon, and a castle gleaming in the distance
with rows of illuminated windows.'

In the throne-room of a castle the royal couple enter with Prince Charming and take their places. Fanfares announce guests from Moscow and
Poland, and then an unknown princess. Prince Charming lavishes his attention on the unexpected guest, dancing only with her, arousing the envy of
the others. The clock begins to strike midnight, but Cinderella forgets the
good fairy's condition until the last stroke, then rushes out. When a slipper
she lost is recovered, the Prince announces a search throughout the land for
the woman it fits, who will be his bride.

In a garden at the Prince's castle, 'among the terraces and the palace peri-
styles', the Prince enquires if the beautiful stranger is present. She is, but
furtively, hunting for her slipper, not as a guest. The good fairy scolds her
for disobeying, but agrees to help again. The invited women try on
Cinderella's slipper. It fits none. The herald announces Cinderella, the good
fairy, the princessses of the night, and the Fairy of the Sun, 'dressed in dark
blue ballet skirts with spangles and with metal stars in their hands'. The
slipper fits Cinderella, and she is proclaimed the Prince's bride. The special
guests perform a divertissement in which night-time on the Nile, in
Grenada, and in Paris is depicted 'in groupings appearing from beneath
the earth', followed by a *grand pas* of the four elements: 'Earth—in grey
costumes with flowers . . . Air—pale blue with butterflies . . . Water—pale
green with scarves . . . and Fire—in bright red and gold costumes, with
metal, fiery swords'.

We first learn of *Zolushka* while critics were expressing their displeasure
with *The Nutcracker*. 'Stories for ballet scenarios are whatever you please,
but fairy-tales, especially French ones, are especially liked by the present
direction: this is already the second new ballet staged to such a scenario, and
next year *Cinderella* will be produced, especially commissioned from Miss
Lydie Paschkoff, as if there were no stories in Russian tales.'[24] Assigned to

---

[24] *Peterburgskaya gazeta*, 7 Dec. 1892, p. 3.

Pierina Legnani as early as July 1893,[25] *Zolushka* was to be Petipa's production, to another score by Boris Fitinhof-Schell. But as the season got underway, events took a familiar turn: Petipa's continuing infirmity shifted the task onto Ivanov and Cecchetti. The libretto attributes the production and the dances to all three balletmasters, but Skalkovsky recalled: 'Three balletmasters staged *Zolushka*, or to be more exact, Mr Cecchetti produced Acts I and III, and Mr Ivanov Act II, but Mr Petipa, barely recovered from a serious illness, supervised the overall ensemble.'[26]

As a story *Zolushka* may have had a happy ending, but its beginning as a stage work, on 5 December 1893, came at a time of tension and sadness. A few weeks before the first performance, the decision had been taken to produce a Tchaikovsky memorial concert, for which Ivanov would stage Act II of *Swan Lake*. In light of this prospect, the ironic if random parallels between that work and *Zolushka* could not have been lost on him: an important character named Odette, an enchanted princess played by Pierina Legnani who arrives unexpectedly at a ball after *entrées* from various countries. Nor could it have been comforting that Legnani, new to the company, arrived in St Petersburg in mid-November, barely three weeks before the première. Finally, the fairy-tale atmosphere of the ballet was darkened by a terrible accident at rehearsal. On 3 December Maria Anderson, who had recently been dancing Ilka in Ivanov's *The Enchanted Forest* and the White Cat in the divertissement of *The Sleeping Beauty*, was in her dressing-room preparing to come on stage for *Zolushka*. She bent down to tie the ribbons on her ballet shoes, and as she did, her costume touched a small spirit lamp used for heating curling irons. Her dress burst into flame and she was seriously burned.[27] For a time it seemed she would not survive, and though she lived for another fifty years, her exceptional stage career had ended at the age of 23. The libretto of *Zolushka* passed the censor that day, and went to press before Anderson's name could be replaced by that of her replacement, Claudia Kulichevskaya.

As for the ballet, such a motley collaboration precludes cogent assessment. The innocuous scenario is representative of the entire work. The story was considered dull, and criticized for what was by now an old complaint—the undue emphasis on spectacle. Reviewers noted the likeness of the ballet to *féeries* produced at the Châtelet in Paris and the Cirque Ciniselli in St Petersburg. Lydia Pashkova was dubbed 'without taste',[28] and was

---

[25] *Peterburgskaya gazeta*, 28 July 1893, p. 3; *Novoe vremya*, 31 July 1893, p. 3.
[26] *Skalkovsky*, 209. Most other sources agree, such as the reviewers in *Peterburgskaya gazeta* and *Novoe vremya* on 7 Dec. 1893, *Krasovskaya*, 375, *MarPet*, 384. But compare the slight nuance in *Pleshcheyev*, 379: 'Three balletmasters, Mr Petipa, Mr Ivanov, and Mr Cecchetti laboured on the production of *Zolushka* and on the composition of the dances of this ballet.'
[27] *Peterburgskaya gazeta*, 4 Dec. 1893, p. 3.
[28] *Novosti i birzhevaya gazeta*, 7 Dec. 1893, p. 3.

found lacking imagination, as she 'took little advantage of the worthwhile material of the story and limited herself to the well-known scenes . . .'.[29]

These complaints would be just if they were true. A manuscript libretto of the ballet, unsigned but probably Pashkova's submission copy to the direction,[30] presents the story in a much more extravagant way. The ballet opens in the sisters' dressing-room, and in the next scene the good fairy, here called the Snowflake Fairy, makes her appearance in a blizzard. The ambassadors in Act II are from Gaul, Elsinore, Byzantium, and the realm of the Amazons (altered in Petipa's hand to come from Moscow and Poland), and the Fairy of the Snowflakes comes to the ball in disguise as the enigmatic Ambassadress of the Amazons of Kerassund, with a retinue of fairies: sapphire, ruby, rose, and rainbow. Act III is divided into two scenes, the first at Cinderella's house, where she is discovered without much ado to be the owner of the lost slipper, and the second, which is the royal wedding. Act II is quite different: Cinderella makes her appearance after the presentation of the ambassadors, and performs with each a dance from his country; this is followed by the arrival of the Fairy of the Snowflakes in disguise (though Cinderella recognizes her), who dances a *pas guerrier*. The Prince waited for a *Grand cotillon* for the opportunity to dance with Cinderella, which is interrupted by the tolling of midnight. At Cinderella's distress and the subsequent confusion, the Snowflake Fairy smiles maliciously. In a second version of the scenario from the same collection,[31] in Vsevolozhsky's hand, this variant is omitted, and the action agrees with the published libretto.

The spectacular night tableaux in Act III do not appear in the first scenario, and seem to have been the invention of officials in St Petersburg. 'If you believe the evidence of ballet,' according to one notice,

then in Egypt nights pass in the embraces of Egyptian men and women, after which inevitably follows the poisoning of the Egyptian man who has partaken from cups presented to him by his beloved. Miss Kshesinskaya I was a very effective and typical charmer and poisoner. In Granada at night, with brio and fiery grace, Miss Kshesinskaya II dances a cachucha amidst young girl students, dressed in characteristic costumes of an *estudianta*, with guitars and with spoons on their hats. Finally, in the Parisian night comic scenes are played out between *Leander*—Miss Kulichevskaya, a *neighbour*—Miss Fonaryova, and Pierrot—Mr Gorsky.[32]

The faintly derisive tone sounded here is echoed in another review:

When the opportunity arises, one could omit from [Act III] without detriment the tableaux 'La nuit du Nil' and 'La nuit parisienne'. In these tableaux, which appear out of the water at the wave of the fairy's wand, the producer wanted to present

    [29] *Birzhevye vedomosti*, 7 Dec. 1893, p. 3.   [30] *TMB 205*, no. 176.
    [31] *TMB 205*, no. 177.   [32] *Novosti i birzhevaya gazeta*, 7 Dec. 1893, p. 3.

some kind of pantomime; the idea could be original, but nothing came of it. In the 'Egyptian night' Cleopatra poisons somebody; such a scene is utterly inappropriate for a wedding celebration.[33]

Nikolay Bezobrazov complained of the staging: 'Columns were placed in the second act without the least need, which constrained the dances; in the third act the trees also hindered the dances.' Of the costumes the Russian and Polish were best, he continued, but 'the kitchen was too dark, and at the end of the act a failure spoiled the final effect. The back curtain did not rise and the view of the castle was completely lost.'[34]

These problems counted for little because the new ballerina swept all before her. Encomiums addressed to Pierina Legnani were exceptional even in this age of hyperbole. 'An absolute sensation',[35] who 'executes the most dizzying difficulties of ballet technique with absolute ease, without the least tension and fatigue'.[36] 'The glory of Zucchi and Limido pales before Miss Legnani's phenomenal art.'[37] 'Miss Legnani must unquestionably be counted among the greatest virtuosas of choreography which Petersburg has ever seen,' wrote another,

With her first appearance on stage the ballerina revealed such perfection of technique and such strength as are difficult to imagine. With each new variation the public was convinced that it was dealing with an *artiste* who had taken the technique of dance to a completely unprecedented perfection. . . . One must observe in this connection that one does not see at all in her dances that sharpness of movement which usually distinguishes Italian ballerinas. All her poses and movements are plastic and graceful.[38]

Even Skalkovsky, normally worldly and sanguine about artists, was humbled:

Legnani turned out to be a magnificent dancer. No renown had preceded her. In strength of technique she did not yield to the best dancers which Petersburg had just seen. Assurance in movements and complete balance she observed to perfection, she performed pirouettes and fouettés with astonishing exactitude. She stopped after turns with assurance, thanks to her astonishing aplomb, such that the general line of her torso, arms, and legs was always true. She is auburn haired, of medium height, with a pleasant expression, lively facial features, and merry eyes. The ballerina was lithe, her movements smooth, but she did not have enough lightness.

In the first act Legnani danced three variations; in them, so to speak, she only prepared the public for the furore which she created in the second act in the *pas d'action*. In the variation here she positively stunned [the audience] with her tech-

[33] *Novoe vremya*, 7 Dec. 1893, p. 3.   [34] *Peterburgskaya gazeta*, 6 Dec. 1893, p. 3.
[35] *Peterburgskii listok*, 6 Dec. 1893, p. 4.   [36] *Peterburgskii listok*, 7 Dec. 1893, p. 3.
[37] *Russkie vedomosti*, 12 Dec. 1893, p. 2.   [38] *Birzhevye vedomosti*, 7 Dec. 1893, p. 3.

nique. Double turns on pointe are not a rarity now, but what this ballerina did we had not yet seen. On pointe, Legnani made one turn three times and then two turns, repeating this four times. Despite the amazing difficulty of the variation, Legnani repeated her *pas* without the slightest sign of fatigue.

In the last act Legnani positively outdid herself. Bessone in *The Tulip of Haarlem* did fourteen fouettés. Legnani made thirty-two of them without stopping, and without travelling one inch! The public delightedly applauded the ballerina and compelled her to repeat this variation as well. On the repetition she nevertheless did twenty-eight fouettés. To count them became the favourite occupation of the public.

Legnani clearly had a huge success; for a long time we had not had such ovations in the ballet. There was a kind of hum in the air from the applause when the ballerina finished the last act. In the wings the entire ballet troupe gave Legnani an ovation as well. . . .[39]

One critic gave a detailed account of Act II, which Ivanov had set:

In the second act Mr Shishkov's magnificent decoration represents the grand hall of a royal palace, all white, with a multitude of columns and statues and an infinite perspective [Plate 22]. Crowds of courtiers are dressed in costumes striking for their richness and taste. Here all historical styles merge with completely fairy-tale fantasy, which suits the style of the story better than anything else. The king (Mr Aistov) and queen (Miss Ogoleit I) arrive with their son, Prince Charming (Mr Gerdt). The master of ceremonies introduces the ambassadors, Russian and Polish. The Russians are wearing green velvet boyars' and boyarinyas' costumes, stitched in gold, and the Poles similarly sewn Polish costumes, orange with sky-blue. After the ambassadors, Cinderella appears with her magnificent retinue, unexpectedly and unannounced, and immediately captures the prince's heart.

The celebration begins with a Russian Dance, smoothly and characteristically executed by Miss Petipa II, Mr Lukyanov, and the corps de ballet. Next a Polish mazurka is led by the beautiful Miss Petipa I and Mr Bekefy. At the conclusion a *grand pas d'action* is performed by ballerinas Miss Kshesinskaya II and Miss Kulichevskaya, Mr Gerdt, and the others taking part. The adagio of this *pas* is beautifully staged and danced, where the young dancers honourably sustain the reputation of our glorious ballet, and Miss Legnani displays much gracefulness and such flexibility of body that she might have no bones. The variations of Miss Kulichevskaya and Miss Kshesinskaya are brilliantly staged and magnificently executed. Each of them displayed the characteristic qualities of the dance with full clarity: Miss Kulichevskaya's precision and lightness in classical dances, and the talented Miss Kshesinskaya II's strength, energy and fire.[40]

Other reviewers joined the chorus of praise in similar accents. 'As the most successful numbers one can point to the *grand pas d'action* and the mazurka in the second act.'[41] 'The ball in the fairy-tale hall is magnificent,' wrote the Petersburg correspondent for *The Russian News* of Moscow,

[39] *Skalkovsky*, 209–10.   [40] *Novosti i birzhevaya gazeta*, 7 Dec. 1893, p. 3.
[41] *Novoe vremya*, 7 Dec. 1893, p. 3.

At the ball is a kaleidoscopic riot of colours of rich, bright costumes in all historical styles. Each costume is a self-sufficient picture, overflowing with great talent and taste. The celebration opens with a 'Russian' dance; a fiery-rakish ensemble mazurka follows it.[42]

When *Zolushka* was performed the following autumn, the impression made by these two dances was sustained:

In the devil-may-care mazurka in the second act Miss Petipa I distinguished herself, and here Miss Legat attracted attention for her Russian Dance. In a rich brocade sarafan, with flowing graceful gestures, Miss Legat was a typical Russian beauty. The Russian Dance was repeated.[43]

Skalkovsky found the costumes too elaborate and heavy, which 'hinder the dancers in dancing, in doing those *pas* and groupings which succeed beautifully in rehearsal in light tunics. The more they give up dances for splendid costumes, the more they encumber the stage with decorations to the detriment of dances.'[44] Some idea of this problem may be inferred from a cast list for *Zolushka* dated 4 November 1893, a month and a day before the first performance. The characters listed are identified by the name of the artist performing a role and by reference to the *figurine*, or costume drawing, prepared for each character. There are fifty-four costumes cited in this document for Act II, at least fifty-three accessories to go with them, and the assignment of fifty-one understudies among 114 artists.[45] In addition to creating the dances, Ivanov had to approve these costumes and co-ordinate the assignment of artists and substitutes with the other two acts.

Ivanov's contribution to *Zolushka* was less important as a milestone in his own career than as a footnote to Legnani's. So delighted was the direction with her dancing, Skalkovsky noted, that she was immediately invited for the next two seasons.[46] For the next two seasons, and the two after that, and the two after that, and the two after that. Five years earlier, Virginia Zucchi had refused to dance in Petipa's *The Vestal*, and Vsevolozhsky had not renewed her contract. If the director took this step because he had a vision for the Petersburg ballet of the 1890s—of extraordinary production and virtuoso ballerinas—that vision was being realized. It had been realized in a near-ideal collaboration in *The Sleeping Beauty*, and now in *Zolushka* the components were in place again. Even with Petipa reduced to a supervisor and without Tchaikovsky, the combination worked. Ticket prices for *Zolushka* had been raised by the second performance, and the ballet went on to twenty-four complete performances between 5 December 1893 and 29 December 1897. In 1898 it was dropped from the repertoire in St Petersburg because the production was being sent to Moscow, where Lev

[42] *Russkie vedomosti*, 12 Dec. 1893, p. 2.
[43] *Novoe vremya*, 18 Oct. 1894, p. 3.   [44] *Skalkovsky*, 209.
[45] St Petersburg, Historical Archive, 497.10.888, fos. 4–5.   [46] *Skalkovsky*, 210.

Ivanov staged it.[47] On three other occasions after that, one act of *Zolushka* was given separately in St Petersburg: once in a mixed bill, once in a benefit for the Russian Theatrical Society, and finally on 23 January 1900 for Pierina Legnani's farewell benefit performance. On all three occasions, Ivanov's act—Act II—was chosen.

Flora's Awakening

On 6 April 1894 there was an announcement in *The New Time*: 'In June at New Peterhof Mr Drigo's new ballet, *Le Bal champêtre*, will be produced.'[48] In the May issue of *The Artist* it was mentioned again:

In the course of the summer the studios of the theatre direction will seethe with the most frenetic activity in the preparation of new stagings and revivals for next season. Now the decorations are being drafted and the costumes sewn for Mr Petipa's new ballet *Le Bal champêtre*, already being rehearsed in the theatre school earmarked for production in the summer. Mr Drigo composed the music for this ballet.[49]

After this *Le Bal champêtre* disappears from view, but on 26 April we read:

On Saturday, 23 April, in the rehearsal hall of the theatre school a rehearsal took place of the new ballet *Flora's Awakening*, the first performance of which will take place in the summer at Peterhof. Our balletmaster M. I. Petipa is in charge of the production of the ballet.[50]

From these data it would seem that what started as *Le Bal champêtre* was reformulated as *Flora's Awakening*, perhaps when it was decided to produce a ballet for a royal wedding. Already by 12 April a detailed cast list of *Flora's Awakening* had been submitted to the direction by ballet régisseur Konstantin Efimov, though it makes no reference to a choreographer.[51]

The wedding of Grand Duchess Xenia Alexandrovna and Grand Duke Alexandre Mikhailovich took place on 25 July 1894. Three days later *Flora's Awakening* was given in the imperial theatre at Peterhof, after Act II of Gounod's *Romeo and Juliet*. The performance was not reviewed by the press, while official chroniclers disdained evaluation in favour of describing the pomp of the occasion and the beauty of the setting:

For the present gala performance the entire auditorium of the theatre was newly renovated. The middle, Imperial box is now significantly widened and occupies the

---

[47] *Peterburgskaya gazeta*, 28 Feb. 1898, p. 3.   [48] *Novoe vremya*, 6 Apr. 1894, p. 4.
[49] 'Chronicle', *Artist. Zhurnal izyashchnykh iskusstv i literatury* [The Artist: Journal of the Elegant Arts and Literature], no. 37 [Year 6, Book 5, May 1894], 234.
[50] *Novoe vremya*, 25 Apr. 1894, p. 3.
[51] St Petersburg, Historical Archive, 497.8/2.443, fos. 6–7.

place of the former box and two neighbouring boxes of the *bel étage* on either side; its aspect is of a magnificent tent, topped off by the Imperial crown, from beneath which falls, in beautiful folds, luxurious red draperies edged in gold velvet, supported by spiral gold beams. The curtain between the auditorium and the stage was newly drawn by the decorator Mr Levogt. The theatre was illuminated on this occasion by electricity, specially installed for this day. All rooms adjacent to the Imperial boxes, and the interior galleries and corridors of the theatre, were beautifully decorated with tropical plants.

At 9 o'clock in the evening the Imperial entrance into the Imperial box took place; the Most August Newly-weds entered first, followed by Their Imperial Majesties the Sovereign Emperor and the Sovereign Empress, His Imperial Highness the Tsarevich Heir, Most August foreign Guests and other Members of the Imperial Family. At the appearance of Their Imperial Majesties all stood, and the orchestra played 'God Save the Tsar'.

[A detailed list of persons in attendance follows.]

. . . On this evening the entire square in front of the theatre was luxuriously illuminated by electric sunlamps. Located opposite the front façade of the theatre was a series of Ionic columns entwined with garlands of greenery, and blazing altars at the tops; along both sides of the square illuminated arches and shields in the style of Louis XV were constructed. In addition, the entire way from Alexandria to the Great Palace of Peterhof was illuminated, along which, at the end of the performance, Their Imperial Majesties and the Most August Newly-weds deigned to pass.[52]

The scenario of *Flora's Awakening* is an appropriate metaphor for a wedding—the dawning of a day. The ballet begins at night-time; Diana is protecting Flora and her nymphs. Aquilon rushes through, chilling Flora, who begs help from Aurora. Aurora arrives, followed by Apollo, who brings warmth and animation. Others arrive in his wake: Zephyr, Ganymede and Hébé, Bacchus and Ariadne. An apotheosis depicts Olympus, with Jupiter and other gods and goddesses.

The roles of Flora and Apollo were taken by Mathilde Kshesinskaya and Pavel Gerdt; Anna Johanson was Aurora, Nikolay Legat was Mercury, Alexandre Gorsky was Aquilon, and Vera Trefilova was Cupid.

Petipa's part in the production of *Flora's Awakening* is not as clear as the initial announcements suggest. Perhaps being in charge of the production meant making the dances. Perhaps it meant that the dances would be entrusted to Lev Ivanov. Without differentiating their contributions, the published score, *The Yearbook of the Imperial Theatres*, printed programmes,[53] and the press all attribute *Flora's Awakening* to both Ivanov and Petipa, as does this report of the dress rehearsal:

---

[52] *Ezhegodnik Imperatorskikh Teatrov*, 1893/4, 422, 430.

[53] A manuscript cast list cites the ballet as 'com[posed] by M. Petipa and L. Ivanov' (Harvard Theatre Collection, bMS Thr 245 (45)), and programmes for later performances of *Flora's Awakening*, on 26 Oct. 1903, 7 Feb. 1904 and 24 Oct. 1904 (Harvard Theatre Collection, bMS Thr 245 (247)),

The programme of the ballet is composed by the balletmaster L. I. Ivanov, the production of the dances belongs to him as well, but chiefly to M. I. Petipa. The beauties of the picturesque groupings and general ensembles, the consistent classical character of the dances, the stamp of fine taste which lies on all this, show again on this occasion the inexhaustible talent and diverse imagination of our first balletmaster M. I. Petipa, found here in full strength.[54]

Petipa accepted the compliment but took issue with the division of labour. In a letter to the editor of *The Petersburg Gazette* two days later, he made the following claim:

In No. 201 of your much-respected newspaper, a not fully accurate communication was reported about the production of the ballet *Flora's Awakening* (*Le Réveil de Flore*). The programme of this ballet was created by Mr L. I. Ivanov and *me* together, [and] the production of the dances and the *mise-en-scène* belong exclusively to me; Mr L. I. Ivanov had no part in them.[55]

The burden of the evidence suggests that Petipa was right, and that *Flora's Awakening* is more properly his legacy than Ivanov's. In the scenario and choreography there is no natural division, as there will be in *Swan Lake*, which would make reasonable the assignment of particular dances to Ivanov; nor is the work in more than one act or scene, which would suggest shared labours along structural lines. Moreover, all official attributions to Ivanov are as author of the scenario, in the same relationship to choreography that Petipa's name is connected to *The Nutcracker* and Ivanov's revival of *The Offerings to Cupid*. Such production documents as testify to the point also favour an attribution to Petipa. A manuscript cast list for the ballet among Petipa's papers,[56] less detailed and probably earlier than those régisseur Efimov submitted to the direction, suggests Petipa's advanced stage of planning for the ballet by its list of principal dancers, which is coordinated with costume drawings.

Flora's Awakening was staged in the Maryinsky Theatre on 8 January 1895, for the farewell benefit performance of Maria Anderson after her recovery from burn injuries. The new ballet was somewhat lost in the sentiment of the occasion, placed on a programme which also included parts of *The Sleeping Beauty* and Perrot's *Caterina*, and the appearance of the benefit artist in a revival of Petipa's *The Parisian Market*, first produced in 1859. Such reviewers as made an issue of choreography on this occasion gave precedence to Petipa.

state the attribution clearly: 'Anacreontic ballet in one act, com[posed] and staged by the Soloist of HIS MAJESTY Marius Petipa and merited artist of the IMPERIAL Theatres L. Ivanov'.

[54] *Peterburgskaya gazeta*, 25 July 1894, p. 3.
[55] *Peterburgskaya gazeta*, 27 July 1894, p. 3.   [56] *TMB 205*, no. 448.

Flora's Awakening produced a most pleasant impression. It is one of those master-pieces with which Marius Petipa has made a gift to the ballet stage. And there are no few of those . . . In *Flora's Awakening* the balletmaster's talent [and] elegant taste were manifest in all their brilliance.

The groupings are both picturesque and original, and there is much variety in the dances . . . Each time a new work of Marius Petipa appears on stage one must note that without question, another balletmaster like Petipa does not exist anywhere at the present time.[57]

Although not mentioned by name, Petipa is clearly being referred to in another critic's remarks: 'The groupings are effective, the dances less so, but in them the experienced hand of a great master of his art is evident; the inexhaustible creative imagination of the master choreographer speaks here.'[58] And again: 'In this ballet, as in all his other choreographic compositions, the balletmaster M. Petipa displayed much taste.'[59]

Petipa's claim of authorship accords with criticisms of his high-handed treatment of colleagues, but may also signal that he was back on the job, ready to assume control, to relieve Ivanov of the choreographic duties which illness had forced the elder man to yield up since *The Nutcracker*. Knowing what Petipa went on to accomplish from 1894 onwards, that he had put his illness behind him in the spring of that year is eminently credible. *Flora's Awakening* was Petipa's awakening as well, the dawning of the last great flowering of his art. For Ivanov this meant fewer opportunities to compose, but more autonomy when they came. With one important exception, his days of collaborating with Petipa were over.

[57] *Peterburgskaya gazeta*, 9 Jan. 1895, p. 3.   [58] *Novosti i birzhevaya gazeta*, 10 Jan. 1895, p. 3.
[59] *Novoe vremya*, 10 Jan. 1895, p. 3.

9

Swan Lake

The Concert in Memory of Tchaikovsky

At the time of Tchaikovsky's death, preparations for *Zolushka* were under way. The new ballet, with the Christmas season to follow, meant that 17 and 22 February 1894 were the earliest feasible dates to give a Tchaikovsky memorial concert, considering that all its numbers were to be staged, some for the first time. There are hints that the initial steps to mount *Swan Lake* in St Petersburg were taken while Tchaikovsky was still alive. Costume drawings by Ponomaryov for Odile and for a swan maiden survive from 1892. A sketch of the first lakeside scene in Petipa's hand suggests that he had begun to work out the initial appearance of the swans before Ivanov was assigned that scene for the memorial concert.[1] And music orchestrated by Drigo from Tchaikovsky's piano pieces for use in the revival was published with the indication that the composer himself approved the choice.[2]

Within a month of Tchaikovsky's death Vsevolozhsky had organized a memorial performance and requested permission from the Minister of the Imperial Court to make it so.[3] On the same day—19 November 1893—we read of the performance in the press: 'In January in the Maryinsky Theatre a performance will be given of works by the late P. I. Tchaikovsky, the proceeds from which will be put towards a monument to the composer.'[4]

The first performance of *Swan Lake* Scene 2 as we presently know it was not considered momentous when it happened. Various problems dampened

---

[1] For a reproduction of this sketch, see *MarPet*, 216. Petipa's text, which suggests a naturalistic transition from swan to maiden, is divided into two paragraphs separated by a simple drawing of a figure: 'Lorsque les Cygnes tombent dans | l'eau, il faut 6 figurantes | qui se montrent sur l'eau. Celles | qui viennent sur la scène ne peuvent | pas venir sur l'eau. [drawing] puis à genou[x?], corps en arrière | les deux bras en l'air puis | [diagram] bras descendus et tout le | monde arrabesque [*sic*] puis à genoux | très en arrière'.

[2] For details, see *Tchaikovsky's Ballets*, 243–5.

[3] Ibid., 245–6.   [4] *Novoe vremya*, 19 Nov. 1893, p. 4.

enthusiasm for the memorial concert. First, the direction miscalculated by setting ticket prices much too high. Notice after notice complained of this, citing as the cause of a poor turn-out prices higher than those for Italian opera. The hall was half empty, and at 5,000 roubles the receipts were about half what was projected.[5] Second, the programme was mixed: *Swan Lake* was the only ballet on the bill, competing with excerpts from three of Tchaikovsky's operas and a patriotic cantata sung with chorus and soloists dressed in boyars' costumes in front of a decoration which represented a hall in the Kremlin. Third, little was known about *Swan Lake* except that it had previously been staged in Moscow. The scenario of Scene 2 was not provided, but had to be inferred from the stage action. 'The story of the whole ballet is unknown to me,' one critic wrote,

the stage represents a forest glade, in the depth of which extends a picturesque lake with willows hanging over it. To the right are the ruins of a castle or something of the kind, with a high, sloping staircase. The decoration was drawn by Mr Bocharov with great taste and elegance; the lighting is very fine. To this place come, on a hunt, Prince Siegfried (Mr Gerdt) with his friend Benno and with several knights. Siegfried falls in love with Odette, the queen of the swans (Miss Legnani), and when the swans fly in to the shore and are turned into women, Siegfried at her request orders the hunters not to fire at them. In place of the hunt dances are begun, at the end of which the enchanted beauties rush out, and in the form of real swans, swim along the lake. Above the flock of swans hovers some kind of predatory black bird with fiery eyes. By these eyes I divined that the black bird plays an important role in the piece, but this role is probably explained in those acts which were not presented.[6]

These problems apart, Legnani again dominated the performance. 'Miss Legnani, the ballerina, dazzled as always,' one critic wrote.[7] 'In *Swan Lake* the ballerina Miss Legnani (in the role of Odette) won loud [applause] and deserved laurels,' another reviewer commented, 'she astonished our balletomanes with the amazing lightness of her aeriel technique, the gracefulness and plasticity of her dances.'[8] Nikolay Bezobrazov indulged in hyperbole:

In *Swan Lake* the incomparable ballerina Pierina Legnani dances the first role. We do not hesitate to call Legnani incomparable—someone more graceful, elegant, and plastic than her is impossible to imagine. In the act of *Swan Lake* they gave yesterday, Miss Legnani has exclusively classical dances. She performs a *pas de deux à trois* . . . with Mr Gerdt and Mr Oblakov. The adagio of this *pas* [the duet for violin and cello] is a complete choreographic poem, and the ballerina's performance of it is above art. The smoothness of her movements, the elasticity of her body, the elegance of her poses arouse spontaneous delight. In the variation Legnani performed

[5] *Journal de Saint-Pétersbourg*, 19 Feb. 1894, p. 3.   [6] *Novoe vremya*, 19 Feb. 1894, p. 3.
[7] *Journal de Saint-Pétersbourg*, 19 Feb. 1894, p. 3.
[8] *Peterburgskii listok*, 19 Feb. 1894, p. 3.

many difficulties, such as only she is able to do, that is, not allowing one to notice there are difficulties. The ballerina had a magnificent success.[9]

After voicing an objection to a passage in the score, the German-language critic was even more expansive:

What turned out, however, to be an altogether extraordinary pleasure in the performance of one act of *Swan Lake* yesterday was the magnificent, enchanting performance, to unanimous approval, that Miss Pierina Legnani offered as the queen of the swans. Someone who displays more charm, attractiveness and *plastique* than Miss Legnani in the purely classical dances of this act is simply unthinkable. In Miss Legnani a power has been won for our ballet which may again unleash enthusiasm for the choreographic art in its classical perfection to the height of olden times. In the variation of the adagio, in itself a complete dance poem, Miss Legnani, on the other hand, amasses bewildering difficulty to overcome, likewise surprising, with sovereign ease. Our public, usually so quick to demand an encore, contented itself yesterday with stormy donations of applause and thereby displayed a genuine respect for the classical dancer's achievement, so that not a single call for a repetition was heard.[10]

After Legnani, no one else warranted more than honourable mention, though Ivanov was among them. One critic found the swans' waltz especially elegant, 'excellently staged by the balletmaster Mr Ivanov'.[11] Bezobrazov remarked:

The staging of dances in *Swan Lake* is the work of the balletmaster L. I. Ivanov and does him great honour. Mr Ivanov revealed a great deal of the finest, most elegant taste. To all the dances the balletmaster imparted a noble stamp, a consistent style.[12]

The next day he continued with a mention of the *pas de quatre* of the four little swans:

Supplementing yesterday's notice of the first performance of *Swan Lake*, we must say that besides the dances of the ballerina and the corps de ballet, the balletmaster L. I. Ivanov staged a pizzicato very nicely and excellently performed (Rykhlyakova, Noskova, Ivanova, etc.). The act of *Swan Lake* we saw yesterday, successful in all respects, that is, in music and dance, compels us to wonder why this ballet, given in the Bolshoy Theatre in Moscow, was not successful there.[13]

The reviewer for *The New Time* gave details about the dance suite at the heart of the act:

The *Grand pas des cygnes* consists of four numbers—waltz, adagio, variation, and coda. The first three balletmaster Mr L. Ivanov composed and staged with great

[9] *Peterburgskaya gazeta*, 18 Feb. 1894, p. 3.   [10] *Sanktpeterburger Zeitung*, 19 Feb. 1894, p. 3.
[11] *Novosti i birzhevaya gazeta*, 18 Feb. 1894, p. 3.
[12] *Peterburgskaya gazeta*, 18 Feb. 1894, p. 3.   [13] *Peterburgskaya gazeta*, 19 Feb. 1894, p. 3.

taste: there is much *plastique* and feeling in them. The coda turned out rather weaker, perhaps because of certain sluggish tempi in the music. Against the background of the beautiful decoration, the adagio produces an enchanting impression. The balletmaster cleverly introduced into the dance imitations of the movements of a swimming swan. The *pas* which Miss Legnani dances in this part is very poetical, as regards artistically conceived poses and the smooth, natural transitions from one position to another. In certain poses, very effective though very risky, Mr Gerdt supports the ballerina magnificently, and indeed with such a cavalier an adagio like the one with which Miss Legnani astonished us yesterday is possible. The gifted ballerina performed it with rare power, flexibility, and grace. Her variations were equally pleasing and graceful.[14]

The second scene of *Swan Lake* in 1894 was a prelude to the revival of the complete work. While Ivanov's choreography of the lakeside scenes has become the basis of virtually all later revivals of *Swan Lake*, it was, to all appearances at the time, no more than another assignment in an already busy season. By the time the last curtain rang down in the spring, Ivanov's involvement in the 1893/4 season had been considerable: of fifteen ballets presented (eight large, three small, and four separate acts or scenes), he was responsible, in whole or in part, for seven.

The Revival of *Swan Lake*

The death of Alexandre III, and the mourning which followed, brought ballet performances to a close for the year on 19 October 1894. This respite made time available to prepare *Swan Lake* as the next novelty on the Petersburg ballet stage. Petipa was comparatively healthy, and Ivanov, if the absence of entries in his service record is any indication, was relieved for the moment from requesting loans from the direction. Because the original libretto of *Swan Lake* was found wanting, Modest Tchaikovsky, the composer's brother and a dramatist in his own right, was called upon to make the now familiar version.

There is much carousing at Prince Siegfried's coming-of-age celebration when the prince's mother arrives to tell her son that he must select a bride from young women to be invited to her castle the next day. As night begins to fall, swans fly overhead. Seeing them, the youths decide to end the day with a hunt.

In a wooded locale next to a chapel at the shore of a lake, Siegfried meets Odette, the swan queen. She explains the spell cast over her, which will only be broken with a pledge of eternal love. Siegfried pledges this.

[14] *Novoe vremya*, 19 Feb. 1894, p. 3.

At the princess's ball a number of prospective brides are presented to Siegfried, whom he rejects. Unexpected guests arrive: von Rothbart and his daughter Odile, who exactly resembles Odette. Deceived by this Siegfried swears his love to her, breaking his vow to Odette.

At a deserted place near the lakeside ruins, the swan maidens await Odette. She returns and tells them of Siegfried's betrayal. Siegfried arrives and begs forgiveness; the lovers resolve to die together. As they perish in the lake, the evil genie falls dead.

At first glance, the assignment of dances to choreographers in *Swan Lake* is neater than in *The Nutcracker*: Pleshcheyev and Skalkovsky cite Ivanov as the creator of the lakeside scenes (Act I, Scene 2, and Act III), and Petipa of the worldly scenes (Act I, Scene 1, and Act II). Ivanov shared the duties of making the divertissement in Act II, taking the Venetian and Hungarian Dances, while Petipa set the Spanish Dance and the mazurka.

A closer look at Petipa's sketches indicates that this attribution was not so clear-cut. While Petipa noted that 'Le second tableau est composé',[15] his return to health permitted him a substantial hand in the collaboration. The sketches suggest that, for a time at least, he planned to set everything in *Swan Lake* except the scene that Ivanov had choreographed for the Tchaikovsky memorial concert. Unlike his preliminary sketch for the first lakeside scene (above, n. 1), those for the last act are more involved. He has identified the dancers of various numbers; he has pondered the colour scheme of the costumes, deciding first on groups of swan maidens dressed in white, black, and rose, but then deleting the latter. In his commentary on the sketches, Fyodor Lopukhov wrote, 'It is well known that Petipa did not compose *Swan Lake* alone: L. Ivanov staged the second scene—the swan lake—and then (I know this from A. Shiryaev's own words) Petipa assigned to Ivanov the last act as well.'[16]

Maintaining stylistic consistency would be sufficient warrant for this decision. Since *The Sleeping Beauty* Petipa's works had taken on a commanding exterior brilliance which tended to formalize expressions of personal emotion. These qualities would make Petipa the ideal producer of the first and third scenes. One can imagine the problems he faced before giving Ivanov Act III—not just in shifting worlds between the ballroom and the lakeside, but in making the final scene effective and sustaining the atmosphere of mystery and intimacy Ivanov had established in Scene 2. Perhaps for once he resisted the temptation to better his assistant. *Swan Lake* was also unusual in its tragic ending, mitigated only by the image of Odette and Siegfried rising to a better world in the last bars of the score. Petipa's strength was the joyful or triumphant apotheosis.

¹⁵ *TMB 205*, no. 231.   ¹⁶ *MarPet*, 210.

Another factor affecting the collaboration was the music. What influence did the new libretto or the balletmasters have on Riccardo Drigo's musical redaction, which deleted about a quarter of Tchaikovsky's original score, reshaped certain numbers, relocated others, and rearranged the order of still others? Did Tchaikovsky really select the piano pieces from his Op. 72 which were interpolated, in Drigo's orchestrations, into Acts II and III, as their title-pages indicate? These questions affect the evaluation of Petipa's and Ivanov's joint effort, usually found to be superior, in relation to a musical revision which could easily be seen as a mutilation.

If the press response is any measure the collaboration worked, especially Ivanov's contribution to it. 'What a poetical ballet *Swan Lake* is, what decorations, which create the impression of something mysterious and lovely, what swans, which glided across the lake, and especially what a charming white swan, Miss Legnani!' wrote one critic to open his notice.[17] Another observed that 'the attention and interest of the spectator were drawn by the ballet itself, with its poetic story and music, which compels us to listen and take delight, making *Swan Lake* a pleasure not only for the eye but also for the ear'.[18]

Most reviewers dispensed praise or censure on particular dances or artists. This was true of the national dances in Act II, especially the mazurka in which Felix Kshesinsky, 'the king of the mazurka', appeared as partner to his daughter Julia, and with his son dancing among the additional couples. As for Ivanov's Hungarian Dance, it was 'produced simply and nicely; the corps de ballet would profit a great deal if only one pair danced, as was done in Moscow. In group dances, beautiful figures and precise execution are essential. Miss Petipa and Mr Bekefy danced in masterful fashion. Miss Petipa's costume went especially well on her; the men's costumes rather recall boyars than Hungarians.'[19] A colleague added:

In the Venetian Dance the costumes are quite beautiful; the corps de ballet danced this *pas* with great fire. This *pas*, which had success, would undoubtedly profit still more if some soloist danced at the head of it. In the czardas the beautiful M[arie] Petipa and Mr [Alfred] Bekefy produced a furore. Here also the women's costumes were beautiful, but Miss Petipa supplemented her costume with diamonds worth several tens of thousands of roubles.[20]

Act III elicited general impressions, no richer in detail than the libretto but interspersed with the artists' names:

The third act: the stage represents a deserted locale next to the swan lake; the enchanted chapel; cliffs; it is night. The swans are waiting for their queen; in order to

---

[17] *Novoe vremya*, 16 Jan. 1895, p. 3.   [18] *Sanktpeterburgskie vedomosti*, 17 Jan. 1895, p. 3.
[19] *Novosti i birzhevaya gazeta*, 17 Jan. 1895, p. 3.
[20] *Peterburgskaya gazeta*, 16 Jan. 1895, p. 3.

shorten the time of their frightening wait, they dance. The *Valse des cygnes* (Miss Johanson, Miss Kulichevskaya, and others). Odette appears and explains that Siegfried has abandoned her and now all of them, having fallen under the power of the evil genie, must perish. Siegfried enters; all shun him; A *scène dansante* takes place. Miss Johanson dances in a charming manner, Miss Kulichevskaya diligently and nicely. Miss Legnani's adagio is very effective; here too the unbeautiful position of the arms merits reproach [which the reviewer had observed in connection with her dances in Act II] when she, supported by Mr Gerdt, flies up high and with amazing lightness and purity performs *grands rondes de jambe en l'air*, the elbows of her outstretched arms are drawn out downwards, her wrists lower than her shoulders.

The evil genie appears (Mr Bulgakov) and interrupts the dances, declaring to Siegfried that he must part with Odette, having vowed his love to another. A stormy scene ensues. Odette, not wishing to become a swan again, throws herself into the water, and Siegfried follows her. An apotheosis: Siegfried and Odette appear in the clouds, seated on enormous swans.[21]

The Petersburg correspondent for *The Russian News* in Moscow reported an unusual scenic effect at the end of Act III:

Quite correctly fixed in the illumination of a summer dawn is the battle between the expiring night and the first glimmers of morning. The entire decoration is held in the blue-gold hue of a Kuindzhi.[22] Splendidly the clouds grow and give way before the evil tempest which coincides with the dramatic finale of the tale. The music here clearly reveals Tchaikovsky; in it are many feelings, lyricism, freshness, and the clash of powers.[23]

Ivanov's undisputed success came in Scene 2, composed the year before. As one critic succinctly put it, 'The second scene is full of poetry; it is the best in the entire ballet. It was produced by L. Ivanov, with a decoration by Mr Bocharov.'[24] Another gave us a sense of how the stage looked:

The tableau of *Swan Lake* in the second scene was planned with great talent and permeated with true poetry, gloomy and expressive. Among the craggy rocks in the far distance a mysterious and deathly quiet lake is seen. The entire stage is filled with soft, quivering moonlight[25] (Plate 25).

As part of his lengthy description and critique, the reviewer who signed himself 'Veteran' observed various details of the dances of this scene:

Entrée des cygnes. To melodious sounds, lightly and beautifully, like the music, a flock of swans floats out. Benno [Siegfried's friend] wants to shoot at them, but they

[21] *Novosti i birzhevaya gazeta*, 17 Jan. 1895, p. 3.

[22] Arkhip Ivanovich Kuindzhi (1842–1910) studied at the Academy of Fine Arts in St Petersburg from 1868 to 1870 and joined the 'Itinerants' group in 1874; in 1894–7 he was head of the studio of landscape painting at the Academy. His work is mostly landscape painting, distinguished by striking luminous effects.

[23] *Russkie vedomosti*, 29 Jan. 1895, p. 2.

[24] *Novosti i birzhevaya gazeta*, 17 Jan. 1895, p. 3.   [25] *Russkie vedomosti*, 29 Jan. 1895, p. 2.

surround him. Feeling faint, he calls his comrades, but Siegfried prevents them from shooting. Odette thanks him.

The waltz of the swans is simple and beautiful. The adagio (Miss Legnani and Mr Gerdt) is the ballerina's masterpiece, in the performance of which she revealed brilliant technique, lightness of movement, and plasticity of pose. Clearly, she has taken to heart the excellent aspects of school she acquired here; borrowing them, she was very successful in perfecting herself. The *en deux sur la pointe* she performs is remarkable in its purity of finish and precise choreographic transmission. If at times in her dances there breaks through, especially in allegro (in the various *jetés en tournant en l'air*) the sharp devices of the Italian school, one must believe that with her continued perfection they will be smoothed out. Mr Gerdt was an excellent partner for her.

The variation of Rykhlyakova, Voronova, and others [that is, the so-called 'Dance of the Little Swans'] is original in composition; the variation following it for Miss Ofitserova, Miss Obukhova, and others is not bad as regards music and execution, and is watched with interest. Miss Legnani's variation, consisting of a series of turns, primarily of *rondes de jambes et pas de bourrées en tournant*, is irreproachably performed; one could not ask for more correctness and purity.[26]

When *Swan Lake* came to be recorded in Stepanov notation—probably in the first decade of the twentieth century—other details of the staging, not mentioned by critics of the first performance, were preserved.[27] Two sections of the manuscript, for example, are devoted to dances for children, a dozen of whom first came on stage as Odette's retinue in Scene 2.[28] They stay to participate in the waltz of the swans.

The affiche of the first performance also indicates that the hunters, absent in modern productions, remained on stage and took part in the *Grand pas des cygnes*, and possibly also in the *Coda et finale*.[29] Modest's libretto makes no mention of the hunters leaving the stage, and it would be reasonable for them to stay, providing a contrast with the second lakeside scene, where Siegfried encounters Odette and the swan maidens by himself.

Like most ballets of the period, *Swan Lake* was a showpiece for the ballerina, and the success of the work in 1895, as now, in large part rested with her.

Yesterday's performance was, of course, an uninterrupted ovation directed at Miss Legnani from a brilliant public which literally overflowed the Maryinsky Theatre; the benefit artist surpassed herself. . . . In the second scene Miss Legnani reigns completely and indivisibly among the various *pas* of the swans. Her solo is the height of perfection and grace; further than this, it seems, is impossible for the

---

[26] *Novosti i birzhevaya gazeta*, 17 Jan. 1895, p. 3.

[27] Harvard Theatre Collection, fMS Thr 186 (11–13).

[28] See *Tchaikovsky's Ballets*, plate 18; earlier in the manuscript, another setting of the dance, probably later in origin, calls for eight small students (not twelve) to enter with Odette.

[29] *SlonChai*, plate between pp. 96–7.

choreographic art to go. Before Legnani all the talk was of the pernicious influence of the Italian school, with its *tours de force*, on our classical school; but Miss Legnani came and showed that it was quite possible to unite amazing, striking technique with gracefulness, beauty, and *plastique* in demands for a pure, elevated choreographic art.[30]

Many other critics concurred. 'In *Swan Lake* broad rein was given to Miss Legnani's rich talent,' wrote Bezobrazov:

In classical dances Legnani displayed gracefulness, *plastique* of pose and virtuosity in full brilliance. The *grand pas des cygnes*, which we saw last year in the performance in memory of Tchaikovsky, now also had the greatest success. In it the ballerina's *attitudes* were one more plastic, more beautiful than the last. In the *pas d'action* of the second act there are several remarkably bold and beautiful groupings, and there too Miss Legnani flaunted her astonishing technique. Especially effective are those *renversées* which the ballerina performed in the variation of this *pas*. Miss Legnani created a veritable furore with her miraculous dances. With every new ballet the public sympathy and number of admirers of this immense choreographic talent increase.

The benefit artist received from the public, by subscription, a magnificent bracelet with diamonds and a sapphire, a large porcelain swan with flowers, a laurel wreath and several baskets of flowers. After each act, of course, were many calls, and an ovation at the end of the ballet.[31]

Although dwarfed by the praise, complaints were raised about the new production. One critic was cautious about Legnani:

Classical dances, however, have first place in this choreographic work, and in them Miss Legnani deploys a cleanness, vigour, and an audacity that could not be surpassed. Still, the acrobatic element trespasses a little too much on grace and lightness.[32]

The Moscow correspondent took a similar line:

Miss Legnani performs miracles in the sphere of choreographic technique and gymnastics. This brilliant representative of the latest balletic school amazes with the precision, speed and smoothness of her movements, the strength of her 'steel' pointes and the steadiness of her balance. The dances here veer close to plastic gymnastics. Solo dances are bereft of ethereality and gracefulness, but have been made very difficult and complex. At the least slip the ballerina risks breaking her arm or leg.[33]

The critic of *The Petersburg Leaflet* was not alone in finding fault with the scenario of *Swan Lake*, but he also took strong objection to the music:

The ballet's principal defect is its music, and one simply cannot believe that it was written by such a great master as the late P. I. Tchaikovsky.

[30] *Sanktpeterburgskie vedomosti*, 17 Jan. 1895, p. 3.
[31] *Peterburgskaya gazeta*, 16 Jan. 1895, p. 3.
[32] *Journal de Saint-Pétersbourg*, 24 Jan. 1895, p. 3.   [33] *Russkie vedomosti*, 29 Jan. 1895, p. 2.

The composer himself was probably very dissatisfied with his work, and therefore during his life it was not performed.

In places the music of *Swan Lake* completely hinders the ballet and does not at all correspond to the dances produced by Petipa and Ivanov.[34]

Swan Lake did not dominate the repertoire as *The Sleeping Beauty* had in its initial season. It was given sixteen performances between the first, on 15 January 1895, and 14 November 1896, three of these in Moscow during the coronation festivities for Nicholas II. In 1897 it was not performed at all, and was given only four times in 1898 and 1899. It remained Legnani's ballet as long as she danced in the imperial theatres, and then passed to Mathilde Kshesinskaya in the spring of 1901.

Kshesinskaya's début as Odette marked a burst of fresh enthusiasm for *Swan Lake* and was important for other reasons. It ensured that the ballet would not be lost with Legnani's departure. In its praise of Kshesinskaya, the press made judgements about Legnani which are difficult to assess. These complaints may have been true, but coming after the ballerina had left St Petersburg, and in light of Kshesinskaya's reputed jealousy of her Italian colleague, they hint at balletic politics. By now Ivanov's contribution was lost in fawning over the new ballerina:

The elegant ballet *Swan Lake*, with Tchaikovsky's unfading music, especially suited Miss Legnani's gift. In this ballet there is no complex drama, no or almost no complicated mimed scenes, in which the Italian ballerina was not wholly successful, but rather the utmost opportunity to reveal technique broadly and to astonish the public with brilliant dances. Miss Legnani took full advantage of this aspect of the role, and in *Swan Lake* enjoyed a constantly huge, outstanding success.

Miss Legnani, who has forsaken our Neva's banks, as we all know had a numerous party of ardent supporters, who, attracted by her outstanding technique, closed their eyes to her defects and this ballerina's inherent weak side. These 'adherents' were utterly foreign to impartial criticism, and of course will still for a long time respond in hostile fashion to any ballerina who tries to replace their idol who, truth be told, had nevertheless put on weight. It is clear that Miss Kshesinskaya, appearing under such circumstances in *Swan Lake*, performed a genuine feat, showing yet again our ballerina's agile and varied talent and her self-assurance. She emerged victorious from a difficult assignment.

To pause in detail on the ballerina's dances is hardly necessary. They were all performed with Miss Kshesinskaya's inherent brilliance, they were all plastic and graceful and not without ethereality, and in the variations one noticed something new. Let us note the double pirouettes in the first act, which the artist performed irreproachably. The ballerina was very effective in the second act, in her elegant black dress, which went so well on her, and danced the famous *pas d'action* with aplomb and great artistic finish.[35]

---

[34] *Peterburgskii listok*, 17 Jan. 1895, p. 3.
[35] *Novosti i birzhevaya gazeta*, 6 Apr. 1901, p. 3.

The changing of the guard in 1901 was also the point of departure for several important tendencies in the history of *Swan Lake*. Detached from its first cast, the choreography began to adapt to the talents of new performers. When Nikolay Legat took the role of Siegfried, for example, he was able to partner the ballerina without the assistance of a second cavalier, and so the famous love duet, which Ivanov had staged as a *pas de deux à trois* for Odette, Siegfried, and Benno, passed into history until the first revivals by Nikolay Sergeyev in the West after the Revolution. Referring to this innovation, our reviewer continued, Legat, 'not sparing his strength, took it upon himself to partner the ballerina in all dances. Gerdt never did this, and in the *pas d'action* in the second act [*sic*] the ballerina always danced with another cavalier.'

The lakeside scenes of *Swan Lake*, especially the first, are the only examples of Lev Ivanov's choreography still performed today much as he created them. This circumstance has prompted extensive commentary about *Swan Lake* at the same time that Ivanov's other ballets are viewed simply as artefacts.[36] The commentary, in turn, has brought *Swan Lake* into the history of ideas with interpretations which leave the details of its stage action far behind. Certain issues raised in this literature are relevant to Ivanov in his lifetime, while the literature itself is notable for having originated in reviews of Kshesinskaya as Odette. Whatever explanations, rooted in exalted patronage, account for the unstinting praise lavished upon Kshesinskaya by the press, there is no question that a divide separates the critical response to her as distinct from that to Legnani. On one side are technical feats and their nomenclature, the focus of Legnani's art; on the other is a view of the dances and the narrative for their symbolic meanings, a transformation and elevation of Legnani's balletic lexicography. In brief, a change occurred at the turn of the century from the denotative to the connotative.

It cannot be our purpose here to reprise this substantial literature in detail, but rather to sample issues within it pertinent to Lev Ivanov and his work. In December 1902 we see the first hints of a shift to the symbolic in a notice of Kshesinskaya:

The ballerina succeeded first of all in the general character of the role. In the course of all three acts, a symbolic image was before the public, full of an elusive, magical, poetic quality. The dances, which in *Swan Lake* are so numerous as could suffice for two ballets, were performed with the same artistic perfection, with the same bril-

---

[36] The longevity of *Swan Lake* in Ivanov's version has been a particular boon to Soviet interpretation (as distinct from historiography). See especially, among recent studies: V[adim Moiseevich] Gaevskii, *Divertisment* [Divertissement] (Moscow: 'Iskusstvo', 1981) [hereafter: *Gaevsky*]; and A[leksandr Pavlovich] Demidov, *Lebedinoe ozero* [Swan Lake]. Masterpieces of the Ballet (Moscow: 'Iskusstvo', 1985) [hereafter: *Demidov*].

liance and animation, not accessible to many except fully finished, powerful talents.[37]

These points were reprised a month later:

Our prima ballerina M. F. Kshesinskaya in the role of Odette was dazzling in all respects. Not only did she easily deal with the immense technical difficulties of this role, but also produced before the spectators an unusually poetical, symbolic image. The artist's beautiful acting to a large degree contributed to that mood which Tchaikovsky obviously had in mind when composing the divine, melodious music for this ballet. All the enchanting charm of *Swan Lake* is contained, in fact, in the moments of mood, which ought to possess the spectators but which, unfortunately, in prior stagings was not achieved at all.[38]

The shift from denotative to connotative in reviews of *Swan Lake* before the Revolution was the point of departure for decades of Soviet criticism which seeks to ally the binary contrasts of the story—Odette/Odile, swan/human, lakeside/castle, night/day, black/white—with a vast array of implications which probably never crossed Ivanov's mind. While many such interpretations have been specific to conditions of Soviet life and may strike Western readers as eccentric or over-meditated, the effort as a whole has advanced the goals of ballet analysis, which continues primitive in the literature of any language. Part of Soviet interpretation has focused on structural symmetries within *Swan Lake* which appear to be unrelated on the surface, but which in fact reveal a sense of formal pattern not immediately evident from the libretto. While *Swan Lake* has been changed in a series of Soviet productions since 1895, some of these parallels may reasonably be assumed to originate with Ivanov himself.

Ivanov's treatment of white and black in Act III is pointed by the introduction of eight swan maidens dressed in black costumes into a white corps de ballet. At first there are only white swans, as there had been in Scene 2. Then the black swan maidens appear and braid their way in a serpentine pattern through a line of white swan maidens posed in the middle of the stage, front to back.

Their entrance creates a structural parallel with Scene 2, where Ivanov had formed the swan maidens' entire entrance on a serpentine pattern which spanned the whole stage. Danger had been present there, in the hunters's threat, to which the swan maidens responded by forming protective groupings, such as a triangle and oblique lines. When the danger was earthly and alarming the swan maidens were all in white. In Act III there is no alarm; the unexpected intrusion of the colour of Odile's costume by the

---

[37] *Novosti i birzhevaya gazeta*, 17 Dec. 1902, p. 3.
[38] *Novosti i birzhevaya gazeta*, 28 Jan. 1903, p. 3.

cygnets forecasts the fateful outcome of the narrative even before Odette explains Siegfried's betrayal. Pattern forms the structural symmetry between the scenes; colour intimates the dread of Odette's message.

In discussing Scene 2, Alexandre Demidov develops another structural parallel within that scene, between the pantomime of the lovers' first meeting and the adagio. Discounting the difference that the first gives exposition to Odette's plight and the second is a love duet, he proposes a parallel between them in the element of the lovers' revelation of each other, the first in mime, the second in dance.[39]

Vadim Gaevsky finds a symmetry between the first lakeside scene and the ballroom, with its otherwise distinctive contrasts. The element common to both is the hunt. Ivanov's literal hunt, replete with arquebuses and mime, is a foil for Petipa's metaphorical hunt at the ball, where everything is danced, the gender roles are reversed, and the huntress Odile prevails over defenceless Siegfried.[40] This reading places the two passages in the same relationship as Ivanov's love scene in *The Tulip of Haarlem* to Petipa's vision scene in *The Sleeping Beauty*: it is as if Petipa were glossing or answering Ivanov. To Gaevsky, these differences also illustrate the nature of the relationship between Ivanov and Petipa as collaborators. By giving fullest rein to his poetical impulses in a narrative framework that was ostensibly simple and naturalistic, Ivanov stimulated Petipa's inspiration while avoiding any breach of professional protocol.

Without citing critics of the 1895 production who found Tchaikovsky's music wanting, Demidov offers an explanation of why such a criticism might actually have been reasonable. It is the ever-present liability, when placing pre-existent music into a new narrative context, that the two will not completely match. In the case of *Swan Lake* the difficulty lay in using music composed for the Moscow production of 1877 in the St Petersburg revival. It is a problem pointed by Modest Tchaikovsky's revision of the scenario, Riccardo Drigo's radical revision of the score, and Lev Ivanov's approach to music.

In the lakeside scenes of 1877, Demidov points out, Odette is protected by a benevolent grandfather from a hateful stepmother. Odette's situation, indulgent in girlish amusements, is not especially threatening as long as she wears the crown her grandfather gave her. Her freedom will come simply with marriage. Modest Tchaikovsky, Demidov argues, transformed Odette with world-weariness: she is banished from the external world, which is marked by betrayal and suspicion.[41] This is why Modest has her impose the condition that the man who swears his love to her must never have sworn it

---

[39] *Demidov*, 189.   [40] *Gaevsky*, 65–6.   [41] *Demidov*, 185–6.

to anyone else, and why Siegfried's innocence of heart does not mitigate the fact of his betrayal.

Taking into account the cliché that Ivanov interpreted music in his dance images, some tension would be inevitable between his perception of lightheartedness in Tchaikovsky's music for the first lakeside scene and having to portray the swan maidens as sorrowful captives. This tension, not a defective musical ear, could have been responsible for objections to the music when the revival was new, objections impossible to explain in the immediacy of impression at the time and in ignorance of the Moscow production. Ivanov's perfect choreographic rendering of the quartet of little swans also accords with an interpretation of Tchaikovsky's dance music as carefree and childlike: the cygnets do not seem to be suffering from the woes of the world.

Demidov senses similar artistic consequences in the last act, in Drigo's omission of the lovely 'Dances of the Little Swans' (No. 27 in Tchaikovsky's original sequence) and the interpolation of two of Tchaikovsky's piano pieces from Op. 72. The first of these was used as a waltz for the corps de ballet, balancing the presence of a waltz in every preceding scene. Yet Tchaikovsky's omission of a waltz in the last act of the original score was no accident. By the last act catastrophe had struck, the hero and heroine were doomed. The composer wanted to signal this by avoiding music whose images were celebratory and vital; when they included a waltz, Demidov alleges, Tchaikovsky's redactors committed an offence against this conception.[42]

The history of *Swan Lake* may be seen in two stages. The first is the work as Ivanov made it, in the context of his other ballets. In this perspective it is a perfect reflection of his relationship with Petipa—the intensely lyrical juxtaposed with the intensely formal—expressed in lasting dance images. To the extent it is typical of his entire choreographic output, *Swan Lake* (together with the classical *pas* in *The Nutcracker*, where his choreography may also survive) can only inspire in us the desire to see what else Ivanov created.

The second stage is the history of the work's interpretation. Here it is subject to extraordinary scrutiny which may cast some light on Ivanov, but more readily speaks to the concerns and world-view of the interpreter. In this respect, *Swan Lake* has become the balletic counterpart of *Hamlet* or *Macbeth*.

[42] Ibid., 196–7.

10

Ivanov's Last Ballets

In the six years remaining to Ivanov after *Swan Lake*, he was involved in the production of three new ballets, one revival, and a substantial addition to a classic of the repertoire. Of the three new ballets, one was a brief pastoral (*Acis and Galatea*), one was a major enterprise on which much state money was spent (*The Mikado's Daughter*), and one—not brought to the stage during his lifetime—was for a private imperial staging (*An Egyptian Night*). The revival was of Delibes's *Sylvia*, which Ivanov began but Pavel Gerdt finished during Ivanov's final illness; the substantial addition was a setting of Liszt's Second Hungarian Rhapsody performed as a czardas in Saint-Léon's *The Little Humpbacked Horse*.

Acis and Galatea

Acis and Galatea was produced for the twenty-fifth anniversary of Marie Petipa's official service, and performed for the first time at her benefit on 21 January 1896. Her father's works rounded out the programme: a new ballet, *The Halt of the Cavalry*; the second act of the grand ballet of 1889, *The Talisman*, and a divertissement.

Acis and Galatea was set to a libretto by the ballet régisseur Vladimir Ivanovich Langhammer (formerly of the German drama troupe) and to music by Andrey Kadlets (1859–1928), a violin soloist in the Maryinsky orchestra.

The enamoured Polyphemus espies Galatea, and prays to Hymen for the reciprocation of his love; Hymen counsels gentleness and patience, yet must restrain the Cyclops when Acis sounds his fife in the distance. Nereids entwine the enraged Polyphemus with garlands and lead him away. Upon noticing the gift that he has brought, Galatea accepts it courteously, and the giant waxes fulsome in his protestations of love. She finally persuades him to leave. Acis arrives and the lovers learn that Polyphemus will not be deterred in his wish to marry Galatea. Hymen summons Cupid, who promises to protect the lovers; the cyclops sees Galatea with his rival, and swears a cruel revenge.

He invites the lovers to a celebration, whence to kidnap Galatea. Acis swears his love to Galatea, whereupon Polyphemus, in a rage, hurls a huge stone at Acis which crushes him. Galatea vanishes into the lake. Polyphemus sits by the shore, awaiting her return. The nearby river first runs blood red, then returns to its lucid stream. An apotheosis depicts Acis, Galatea, Hymen, and Cupid.

The antiquated genre of *Acis and Galatea* put it at a disadvantage. In no sense *chic*, made exclusively of classical dances, it offered no competition to Petipa's vivacious *The Halt of the Cavalry*, which nicely balanced classical dance with character. The benefit artist, moreover, did not appear in *Acis and Galatea*, and even worse, the ballerina for whom it was created did not appear in it either. Mathilde Kshesinskaya was to have taken the role of Galatea (balancing the appearances of Marie Petipa and Pierina Legnani as rival soubrettes in *The Halt of the Cavalry*), but she withdrew, claiming illness, to be replaced late in rehearsals by Lyubov Roslavleva, a rising star from Moscow.

These circumstances, together with the celebration of a public favourite, tended to diffuse the critical response to *Acis and Galatea*, which was impressionistic and widely variable. Langhammer's début as a librettist passed with no more than ritual compliment. 'Mr Langhammer's present libretto is put together in an interesting way,' remarked the critic of *The Petersburg Gazette*.[1]

Attention focused on the principals. Roslavleva won the affection of the Petersburg audience for being a good trouper, and only then for being a good dancer. She had to learn the part of Galatea in three days, 'and rose to the occasion brilliantly'.

This young ballerina conquers the sympathy of the Petersburg public more and more each time, and, one must give credit where it is due, she is winning it very deservedly.

. . . In her Galatea there is so much life, she is so right in the representation of the beloved, that it is most difficult not to be drawn to this kind of acting. Besides mime, fully suitable gestures, very soft as appropriate, Miss Roslavleva dances beautifully; she brings together the difficulties of the Italian school with the gracefulness and *plastique* of the French. In our opinion, Miss Legnani has a serious rival in Petersburg in Miss Roslavleva.[2]

[1] *Peterburgskaya gazeta*, 22 Jan. 1896, p. 3.
[2] *Peterburgskii listok*, 23 Jan. 1896, p. 3.

'She is a very fine ballerina with strong legs who performs difficult *pas* in fast tempi with quite enough assurance; she is rich in a kind of soft gracefulness,' wrote the critic for *The New Time*, 'She had a great success, and a fully deserved one.'[3] Another claimed that she danced without assurance, due to lack of preparation,[4] and a third that Roslavleva 'in her mime was utterly weak; in dances requiring speed, and movements distinguished by smartness, beauty, and elegance—these were lacking'.[5]

Roslavleva's partner Sergey Legat, in contrast, won consistently flattering notice. 'Mr Legat proved to be a superb cavalier,' wrote one critic, 'One can predict an excellent future for the young artist.'[6] 'Mr Legat III, a young and handsome artist,' wrote another, 'dealt beautifully with the role of the cavalier in this ballet.'[7] A third reported that 'the young dancer Legat III positively dazzled', but then commented on the need for him to eliminate 'defects, such as the ungraceful raising of the arms, the bending of the spine, etc., which spoil his impression at times and from which it is not difficult to break away'.[8] Perhaps Legat's greatest compliment was paid by the critic of *The Petersburg Gazette*:

Mr Legat III, who appeared for the first time in a responsible role, produced a most pleasant impression as a *jeune noble* by his acting, comportment on stage, and his dances. With time and favourable circumstances, he can turn into Mr Gerdt's successor.[9]

For Olga Preobrazhenskaya, the role of Hymen in *Acis and Galatea* was another step on the road to stardom. 'Miss Preobrazhenskaya shared the ballerina's success,' *The Petersburg Gazette* continued, 'In Miss Preobrazhenskaya's variation she performed, precisely and beautifully along the diagonal of the stage, *entrechats cinq* many times in succession. This variation was encored.' The dimensions of Preobrazhenskaya's part also sparked comment:

For the number of dances assigned to her, we are surprised that the ballet is not called 'Hymen, Galatea, and Acis'. In every ballet story there should be two central characters on which the audience's attention is concentrated; a third character given too prominent a place only slows the action and wearies the public, and then wearies it more. In the staging of Hymen's dances the balletmaster was clearly guided by some extraneous consideration.[10]

Ritual compliments to Kadlets's music were perfunctory, detailed observations critical.

[3] *Novoe vremya*, 23 Jan. 1896, p. 3.   [4] *Syn otechestva*, 23 Jan. 1896, p. 3.
[5] *Sanktpeterburgskie vedomosti*, 23 Jan. 1896, p. 4.
[6] *Novosti i birzhevaya gazeta*, 23 Jan. 1896, p. 3.
[7] *Novoe vremya*, 23 Jan. 1896, p. 3.
[8] *Sanktpeterburgskie vedomosti*, 23 Jan. 1896, p. 4.
[9] *Peterburgskaya gazeta*, 23 Jan. 1896, p. 3.   [10] *Peterburgskii listok*, 23 Jan. 1896, p. 3.

[O]ne does not find in it a single likeable melody—it is very drawn out, dry, insuffer-ably boring and completely uncoordinated with the story. In this respect it is strange: one encounters places where Polyphemus's wrath is expressed in music of a *piano* dynamic, at the same time when in Acis and Galatea's declarations of love, where the music should express the lovers' tender feelings, it goes on at a *forte*.[11]

On balance, Ivanov came out the worse for staging *Acis and Galatea*. He received polite mention, but there was much carping about the new work. '*Acis and Galatea* had a fine success, but would profit still more if several cuts were made in it,' one critic commented.[12] 'There is no denying Mr Ivanov his talent,' wrote another,

manifest in flashes thrown off during the composition of several dances, which pro-duce a quite good impression separately, but in general, thanks to the length of the work, the endless number of times the same movements are repeated, his ballet, which has pretentions to attractiveness, wearies the spectator.[13]

'In our opinion,' wrote a third in somewhat stronger terms,

the balletmaster was not able to distribute masses; there were no beautiful group-ings, the dances were insipid, repetitious, and above all, so numerous that towards the end of the ballet it was getting very long and the audience was nodding off.[14]

In the autumn of 1898, we read again of the effects of length: 'Despite the harmonious performance of this ballet, towards the end it wearies the spec-tators. The impression is weakened by the length of the dances, in which cuts are necessary.'[15]

After the first performance there were few direct comparisons between Petipa's new work and Ivanov's. At the end of one review a little dialogue was published:

'What an event! Two new ballets in one evening!'

'Yes, and both quite good, especially *Acis and Galatea*; its music and story are very original, but in *The Halt of the Cavalry*, alas, the story is weak and at the very least naïve.'[16]

Translation blunts the edge of sarcasm here, in reference to the story of *Acis and Galatea* being new. Apart from the sheer silliness, a balletomane of 1896 would have realized that anything published in *The Petersburg Gazette* at this time would favour Petipa, and that *The Halt of the Cavalry* was much more enthusiastically received than *Acis and Galatea*. The reader's leg is being pulled; despite the literal meaning of the words, an insult is being directed here at Ivanov.

---

[11] Ibid.   [12] *Peterburgskaya gazeta*, 23 Jan. 1896, p. 3.
[13] *Sanktpeterburgskie vedomosti*, 23 Jan. 1896, p. 4.
[14] *Peterburgskii listok*, 23 Jan. 1896, p. 3.
[15] *Peterburgskaya gazeta*, 5 Oct. 1898, p. 3.   [16] *Peterburgskaya gazeta*, 22 Jan. 1896, p. 3.

Acis and Galatea was performed eight times between 21 January 1896 and 29 September 1899. It was dropped from the repertoire after that, except for a revival for students of the theatre school on 20 April 1905.

The Mikado's Daughter

The summer of 1896 was taken up with coronation festivities for which Marius Petipa created *The Pearl*, to Drigo's music. Not until the autumn of 1897 was another new ballet staged in St Petersburg; this was *The Mikado's Daughter*.

There is no indication that Petipa suffered any relapse of his illness during this period. He prepared four gala performances in 1897, including *Thetis and Peleus*, a new staging of one act of his ballet of 1876, *The Adventures of Peleus*, on Olga Island at Peterhof in the presence of the Emperor of Germany. And as the autumn proceeded, he began work on a new masterpiece, *Raymonda*, to be performed in the first days of 1898.

At that, the autumn of 1897 was not an especially happy period for the Petersburg ballet. One writer outlined its troubles: two new productions were in the offing at a time when important soloists were leaving the stage without proper replacements; stage illumination in the Maryinsky Theatre was faulty and had to be improved; Legnani was ill, and as a consequence Kshesinskaya had to dance every ballet. The article ends with remarks about new productions:

Mikado will be staged with unusual splendour in its costumes (some 600 new ones), but the story, taken from Japanese life, is very unsuitable for ballet, and since the music is very poor, Mr Petipa declined the production, and second balletmaster Mr Ivanov will stage the work.[17]

It is a testament to the accuracy of balletic gossip that this assessment of *The Mikado's Daughter*, made three weeks before the first performance, is so accurate. Why such an elaborate production went forward after the chief balletmaster declined to stage it is but one of the questions which hint at curious decision-making in the imperial theatres and feed into a larger riddle: why was this ballet produced at all? Let us look first at the scenario of *The Mikado's Daughter*, the point of departure for the production.

O-gen-mi, daughter of one of the Mikado's retainers, loves Ioritomo, who is about to wed Gotaru-Hime, the Mikado's daughter. In her despair, O-gen-mi swears vengeance on Gotaru-Hime, and invokes a ferocious dragon, which appears in a whirlwind and flies off with the young bride.

The shipwrecked Ioritomo swims ashore onto the dragon's desolate island, finds and frees Gotaru-Hime. She explains that the dragon turns

[17] *Novoe vremya*, 17 Oct. 1897, p. 3.

into a sorcerer every night, and if he were defeated, the sprinkling of his blood over the rocks would bring back to life the women he has kidnapped and the heroes who fell in the attempt to rescue them.

The dragon arrives in another whirlwind, and Ioritomo vanquishes it, letting fall its blood, whereupon the earth comes alive. Led by the fisherman Urashima, the reanimated men and women construct a raft on which Gotaru-Hime and Ioritomo depart.

A grand divertissement marks a day of national celebration. In simple dress, Ioritomo and Gotaru-Hime wait among the crowd for the Mikado. They are recognized. The Mikado is deeply moved by his daughter's safe return.

Of all Ivanov's ballets, this is the most curious. *Japonaiserie* itself is not at issue, for it was in the air, and would soon produce a monument in Puccini's *Madama Butterfly*. A reviewer commented, 'Japanese life was reproduced on the stage for the first time in operetta (*The Mikado*), then last year at the Bolshoy Theatre in Moscow a ballet was staged based on Japanese mores (*Daita*), which had no success despite its magnificent production.'[18] Was *The Mikado's Daughter* perhaps prompted by the memory of Gilbert and Sullivan, whose operetta had been staged in a Petersburg garden theatre ten years earlier under the title *The Mikado's Son*, where we find Ko-Ko the tailor and his bride Yum-Yum, with whom the Mikado's son Nanki-Pu falls in love? Was the direction again transforming the popular into the spectacular, as it had in *The Sleeping Beauty*? Was *The Mikado's Daughter* the furthest point that Vsevolozhsky carried his mission to outdo the West in the *ballet-féerie*? Could its extravagance have contributed to his downfall as Director? In less than two years he would be retired to another post. Was Vladimir Langhammer, raised on German drama, a Japanist of such attainments as to command the ethnic lore described in the libretto? What purpose do its details serve, offered up in such profusion, if they are merely ornament set adrift from some deeper parable?[19]

Two points about *The Mikado's Daughter* focus study and critique.

[18]   *Vsemirnaya illyustratsiya*, 58 (issue for 22 Nov. 1897), p. 522. *Daita*, it will be noted, had been produced in Paris not long before its Moscow staging.

[19]   There is a deeper parable linked to Langhammer's scenario, but he made little of it. The fisherman Urashima, a secondary character here, is the subject of a Japanese legend approximate to the American tale of Rip van Winkle. One day while fishing Urashima catches a tortoise, a sacred creature, and returns it to the sea. The tortoise was the daughter in disguise of the Dragon God of the Sea; she reappeared to Urashima in human form and invited him to live with her in her father's castle. He accepted her invitation, and lived in blissful happiness for several centuries. In what he thought to be only three years, Urashima longed to return to his parents, and his wish was granted. He went back to discover the changes wrought by epochs; wishing now to be reunited with the Princess, Urashima realized he did not know how to find her again. A talisman given him fails, he withers into a 400-year-old man and dies. The grafting of a central character from an external source onto a ballet libretto where that character is secondary recalls the adaptation of the Moscow libretto of *Swan Lake* from Johann Karl August Musäus's tale, 'The Pond of Swans'. In Musäus Benno is the hero drawn to the pond of swans; in the ballet he is merely a friend of Prince Siegfried.

First, it lacks a dramatic point. Yet it extends opulence of staging to the limits of size. One waggish poem compared librettist Langhammer to a hippopotamus:

BALLET (A TALE OF THE NILE)

Not a drunkard, not a spendthrift,
But a good lad, very businesslike,
Once a hippopotamus
Ventured an aimless labour.
  Having abandoned the Nile,
He composed a ballet
And not without system and not without rules
  He staged it!
  The people gaze,
  Their mouths drop,
And say with an awkward smile:
  'Ah, hippopotamus!
You might take a job trampling things down!'[20]

Some of the '600 new costumes' remarked in our newspaper report are described in a massive cast list for *The Mikado's Daughter*,[21] unprecedented in its reference to ethnic terminology and extremity of detail. It appears to be authentic in some respects (as in the first five entries in the following list), and exotic in others (the Western hunting horns in no. 10, the 'Turkish' boots and beards in no. 12*c* would be exotic in a Japanese context). The following sample comprises half of one number, namely the first of two groups of entrants in the March of the Festive Procession of Act III:

THE DAUGHTER OF THE MIKADO
Festive Procession of the Third Act

Before the entrance

2 extras appear before the cortège with brooms and sweep away the tiniest stones. from the street, or remove obstacles from the road.

1 extra: a water pedlar wets the roadway alley by means of perforated buckets hanging on both ends of a bamboo yoke, which he balances on his shoulders.

MARCH
First Section

1. *2 extras* (*Ikunin*-police): there are no other distinctive signs of their office except a round and sharply pointed cap of varnished cardboard, and two sabres

---

[20] *Peterburgskaya gazeta*, 13 Nov. 1897, p. 3.
[21] St Petersburg, Historical Archive 497.8/2.467, 'Ballet 1897', fos. 46ᵛ–48ᵛ.

hanging at the waist—from the left side one large sabre, the handle of which is so long that one must grasp it with both hands, and the other small, in the manner of a sword, which serves for one-to-one combat. They announce the fearsome *Staniero* [Shita ni ero?], and the people kneel.

2. *1 extra*: a huge, luxurious canopy (umbrella), and beneath it a shield with the name of a certain street on a bamboo pole. Of the person being carried only the feet are visible; the canopy is embroidered, the upper part covered with emblematic figures which recall the simplicity and virtues of the ancient Japanese; others represent celebrated men and women, or birds and animals, which recall well-known locales. Finally, others point at trades which are honoured in Japan.

3. *Ivanov 2*: *Otona* (the principal civic official) in a silk gown, a low lacquered hat, with two sabres.

4. *9 extras*: musicians walk in masks, sing, accompanying themselves on drums, native flutes, bells, and cymbals.

5. *10 extras*: soldiers (hunters) with firearms on their shoulders (right) in low, varnished caps, in green, knee-length gowns with coats of arms embroidered on the chest, and belts of dark green ribbon; in wide trousers, in sandals, and with sabres.

6. *5 extras*: (imperial soldiers) have silk *haori* in black with white stripes on the flaps and on the back.

7. *Sosnovsky and Voronin 2* [i.e. the surnames of dancers]: *Otona*, described in no. 3.

8. *1 extra*: a banner with an inscription embroidered in gold on a white background. A short robe called a *haori*, above his gown, worn open. Light blue *haori* with a white circle on the spine.

9. *1 Extra*: an attendant carries a lance on a long pole. The same costume as above, only black with white on the back of the 4-corner.

10. *4 extras*: hunters with horns (musical instruments); very rich, it consists of wide trousers and a short frock, similar to a long mantilla, which is made of rich silk material and embroidered in gold, silver and silks. These gowns are in various colours.

11. *1 extra*: like the preceding, with a large lacquered and gilt drum, decorated with silk tassles.

12a. *1 extra* (a soldier): carries an adornment, in the form of a Japanese broom, with magnificent feathers and a large banner on which a gold monogram is embroidered.

12b. *Terpilovsky* (but not on horseback): the governor. His gown is luxurious, of silver canvas with a helmet lacquered in gold, edged in silver; his gold coat of arms. At his waist two sabres, and at the back, also on the waist, a symbol of his power; in his hand, a fan.

12c. *2 extras*: attendants with standards (in red costumes). The persons in this group wear beards, a pointed cap with plumage, high boots, a long robe with a belt (waistband).

13. *10 extras*: Tatar music, with flutes, gong, drums, cymbals, tambourines.

14. *White elephant*: an animal out of cardboard is moved by the legs of his carriers, who are hardly glimpsed from beneath the steps of the colossus.

15. *5 extras*: Soldiers carry in their hands unfurling Chinese banners, covered with representations of dragons.

16. *2 monsters*: two frightening monsters with the snout of a tiger (Korean) and ox horns. Their immense croup is raised high above the helmets of the surrounding arms-bearers. In this grouping are also carried ancient weapons—spears, halberds, two-headed sabres, bows, arrows, military fans, and distinctive marks of command.

[16*a*.] *6 extras*: arms-bearers.

16*b*. *2 extras*: with flat fans on long bamboo poles.

17. *A huge sea crab* on a two-wheeled chariot; people pull the chariot; on top of the crab sits 1 extra, priest of the cult of Kama; a crowd of Negroes, 9 extras, make up this grouping. The sea crab plays an important role during the distribution of festival gifts. It is preserved in each family from one year to the next, in the event of the need for crushing it and taking it as a proper medicine. The crab, by its crooked back, represents old age, long life.

18*a*. *Dorina, Urakova, Kil, and Nikolaidis*: 4 beautiful women, to whom the whole country renders honour, in gala costume. Behind each follows a housemaid (4 female extras) and a *koskeis* (4 extras holding in their hands a high and full silk umbrella shielding from the sun). On the head of each principal rises up a coiffure in the shape of a two- or three-tiered building, held in place by wide combs, wound round by crêpe, and fortified with a halo of gigantic pins of white tortoiseshell. Her face is luminous from the most complicated cosmetic preparations. Their dress permits consideration of a number of garments, thanks to the 5–6 collars, if not more, displayed across the chest. They are all covered with a wide kimono, the train of which would sweep the ground if not raised to form gathers around the waist, with the help of a huge waistband of silk or velvet. The beautiful woman has not forgotten to don elevated footwear, which adds centimetres to her majestic height. These courtesans are well known to the people; in addition, their names are embroidered on their luxurious gala costumes:

(1) *Woman of the Military Fan*: she holds the fan, displaying it on a broad velvet waistband and joins thereto four cockerels with varied feathers, of which two are white, embroidered in high relief on the hem and on the broad sleeves of her kimono, the silk feathers of the cockerels' tails, gracefully fluttering with each of the beauty's steps.

(2) *Woman of the Golden Fishes*. These fish, one on each side of her dress, are embroidered with beaten silver in the background which represents waves and foam: the secondary embroidery represents children playing with multicoloured ribbons which are fluttering freely around her kimono;

(3) *Woman of the Skulls* and (4) *Woman of the Golden Flowers*, etc., adorned in accordance with their names.

18*b*. *4 Porters* (extras) with an expensive *Norimono* (in which no one is sitting). *Norimonos* are a type of wheeled basket made of thin planks and bamboo canes, with windows at the front and along both sides over the doors. Inside, the *norimono* is upholstered with fine silk and velvet. In the back of it is a velvet mattress, covered with a velvet bedspread. One's back and elbows rest on cushions, but one actually sits on a round cushion in which an opening has been made. In the forward part are little shelves where one may place an inkwell, books, and similar items. The window above the doors lowers if one wants to let in air, or is closed with little curtains and bamboo shades. From the outside, the body of the carriage is covered with varnish and is picturesquely decorated. Above the body extends a staff which the porters grasp, no fewer than 4 and no more than 10. Half will be prepared to relieve the others carrying the *norimono*. *Norimonos* are carried on the shoulders; if either a prince or the ruler of a province is being carried, the porter holds the staff in his hands. All porters are dressed in their master's livery.

19. *8 extras*, serving persons with lanterns on long bamboo poles.

A host of dances supplements the story line of *The Mikado's Daughter*, which justifies the presence of many of these ornate characters. Even if Langhammer had managed to design some powerful catharsis into the drama, it risked being engulfed in extraneous dance and staging, so rich is the ballet in effects without causes.

The question persists: what was driving the collaborators? Why would Ivanov, criticized in *Acis and Galatea* for being too generous with dances, repeat this fault in a much larger work? Was he being asked to stage *The Mikado's Daughter* without regard for its liabilities? Why was such advance publicity lavished on the ballet, including the publication not simply of synopses but of its complete libretto in a daily newspaper?[22] Perhaps most curious of all, why were no cuts made in *The Mikado's Daughter*, as they had been in *The Vestal* and *The Sleeping Beauty*, when in rehearsal the scenario was found to be too diffuse and the dances too numerous? If Sergey Khudekov permitted cuts in *The Vestal* and Vsevolozhsky in *The Sleeping Beauty*, surely Langhammer could not stand by his authorial rights.

The conclusion implicit in these circumstances is that the collaborators were being overruled by higher authority, possibly Vsevolozhsky himself. As Director of Imperial Theatres, he had to make the controversial decisions. This possibility accords to some degree with Petipa's declining the project for its unsuitable libretto and poor music (though staging both *The Mikado's Daughter* and *Raymonda* in the same season would strain the 79-year-old Petipa's workload). Under normal circumstances a balletmaster could demand changes in the story or the music. Was Petipa denied this? Was there still or again some friction between him and Vsevolozhsky, as there had been with *The Nutcracker*, similarly flawed in its libretto and over-extended in its production? Was Ivanov being called in because Vsevolozhsky insisted on standing by a project even though his chief balletmaster had refused it?

It is possible to view *The Mikado's Daughter* as an ending, as a late example of *féerie*, coupled with display so extravagant and production so over-

---

[22] *Novosti i birzhevaya gazeta*, 9 Nov. 1897, p. 3.

whelming of the narrative as to signal the grand apotheosis and the death knell of that genre. Certain critics came to this conclusion. But the ballet may also represent a beginning, a new stage in Vsevolozhsky's developing aesthetic. The richness of ethnic detail in *The Mikado's Daughter* links it with Petipa's *The Vestal* of 1888.[23] The identification and appreciation of such detail, however, would give new importance to the libretto, which must now explain to a spectator such particulars of costume and mores as could never be assimilated without it. The emphasis on production here, hardly unusual for a costume designer (Vsevolozhsky's métier as an artist), was raised to the level of competing with the dancing. We now realize how important this shift in focus would become, expressed in Sergey Diaghilev's ever-greater involvement of important painters in balletic collaborations—Diaghilev, who within a year of this production would join the staff of the imperial theatres. Might *The Mikado's Daughter* have represented an emergent *genre nouveau* to the eyes of 1897, compared to the *vieux genre* of Petipa's steadfastly classical dance variations? Ivanov's ballet takes on a new significance in this light, with *Raymonda* to follow two months later, as new style to old, as the still imperfect realization of a balletic spectacle which was to dominate the early twentieth century. Nor is it irrelevant that after the first Diaghilev masterworks—*The Firebird* and *Petrushka*—the element of parable lost importance in favour of the exotic and the decorative. If Vsevolozhsky was experimenting once again, Ivanov's place in *The Mikado's Daughter* is ironic, the retrospective artist who becomes an agency of innovation.

Petipa's declining also raises questions of what choreographic guidance Baron Vasily Georgievich Wrangell received in advance of composing, and from whom. While he was not untried as a ballet composer (having written scores for the privately performed *The Princess of the Sea* and *Le Mariage interrompu*) was his music inviolate, protected from change by his social position? That Wrangell sent an elaborate gift to Kshesinskaya—a fan with vignettes by the artist Bogdanov—delivered on stage after the first performance, hints more at the relationship of aristocratic admirer (or astute courtier) than specialist composer.

Whatever the circumstances, *The Mikado's Daughter* was given its first performance on 9 November 1897. On the surface, it was a success. A first-night audience cheered and presented gifts. Several dances were encored—a curiosity in light of the number performed. There were persistent complaints about the heaviness of the costumes and the dancers' black wigs, and the typical rebukes when an effect did not materialize as the libretto led one to expect. The dragon in Act I did not fly onto the stage, but

---

[23] The libretto of Petipa's *The Vestal* is translated in *Wiley*, 324–49.

slowly crawled out from a wing at the side, and the people reborn from the rocks and the crags were not exclusively Japanese, but of other Asian nationalities, so as to justify the variegated divertissement in Act III. In general the reception was lively and favourable. Ivanov was presented with two wreaths, one of laurel, one of silver.

Yet this impression is misleading. Virtually the first point made in press accounts of the ballet is about factional disputes which arose over the ballet well before it was staged. These support the possibility that Petipa withdrew from the project in irritation. 'Long before the beginning of rehearsals a rumour was circulating in the public, but mostly in certain parts of the press, that the ballet would be very bad,' one critic wrote, adding the next day that 'an inveterate balletomane initiated the rumour that M. I. Petipa *refused* to take on the production'.[24] 'Quite a few varied and contradictory rumours hampered the first performance of *The Mikado's Daughter*,' wrote a colleague, pointing out that the true motives for Petipa's refusal remained unknown to the public.[25] A fresh critical voice, who signed articles with the Russian possessive adjective *Svoi* (possibly an abbreviation for *Svoi chelovek*, or 'habitué'), put the matter in perspective. For several months before the première,

one followed the wicked hissing of its adversaries' impotent rage, who bellicosely took up arms against it in advance, and the immoderate praise of its adherents, who at times lapsed into servile obsequiousness. Being equally premature and inappropriate, both understandably cast an unseemly shadow over what they were doing, the gentlemen spoilers who so obligingly spiced their escapades with doses of insinuation, the gentlemen panegyrists who observed no limits in the zeal of their praise. . . . In such a scheme of things it is difficult to expect that in evaluating the new ballet the hoped-for role would be allotted to *fairness*.

. . . Most of the prophets and savants of the choreographic art got that way not by calling or by right, but simply by accident—'whoever took up the staff was made the corporal'. This circumstance can hardly prove a salutary influence on the fate of the ballet.[26]

Petipa's adherents used *The Petersburg Gazette* as their voice. In the formal review of *The Mikado's Daughter* in that newspaper the war of rumours is not mentioned, but the public was well supplied with derisive poetry from its pages, beginning with a *post mortem* in doggerel entitled 'A Balletic Burial', printed two days after the first performance:

> Peacefully the curtain fell . . .
> Sadly the farewell breath died down . . .
> Langhammer wounded the poor thing,

---

[24] *Peterburgskii listok*, 10 Nov. 1897, p. 3; 11 Nov. 1897, p. 3.
[25] *Novosti i birzhevaya gazeta*, 11 Nov. 1897, p. 3.   [26] *Birzhevye vedomosti*, 13 Nov. 1897, p. 3.

Wrangell began to cry . . .
The strings weep . . . The trumpets wail . . .
The drums sound the alarm . . .
Forty thousand—they say
Is what the burial cost . . .[27]

The Librettist, Langhammer, having stated his views about ballet in an interview (thought pretentious given his background in spoken theatre), was the target of jibes. 'Mr Langhammer . . . finds that choreography is declining, that *féeries* are now called for, and that he himself is writing a ballet libretto that imitates Pushkin: Pushkin composed *Ruslan and Lyudmila* and Mr Langhammer *The Mikado's Daughter*. In Pushkin Chernomor abducts Lyudmila, and here a dragon the Mikado's daughter,' we read in *The New Time*. 'In general Mr Langhammer displayed such knowledge of Japan as would require the spectator to take Reclus's weighty volume of geography with him to the theatre for information.'[28] The critic of *The Petersburg Gazette* was more acrid:

Mr Langhammer's thoughts, as far as we can recall, came down to this: that in our time ballet has fallen into deep decline everywhere, here and abroad, that there are neither dancers nor balletmasters nor professors of dance any more . . . Mr Langhammer's ideals regarding the choreographic art apparently come down to a type of ballet in the *balagan-like* manner, which in the London 'Alhambra' and 'Empire' Theatres expels genuine ballet under the pressure of the London crowd's coarse tastes. In these theatres the spectators, sitting at little tables and having a drink of *soda and whisky* and *pale ale* [words in English], or strolling about the *promenoir*, take pleasure in spectacles where clowns and jugglers alternate with performing dogs, and ballets in 10–15 scenes are given without the curtain coming down. In London ballets are appropriate when performed by extras and backstage hands, where lighting effects, marches involving great numbers of people and properties are of the greatest importance. Here, at least for the present, different demands are made of ballet. Our public values its artistic side, seeks aesthetic pleasure in it, and lo, precisely nothing of this does Mr Langhammer, consistent with his views on contemporary ballet, provide us in programme of *The Mikado's Daughter*, which they gave yesterday on the Maryinsky stage for the first time.[29]

Sarcasm aside, one finds hints in the press of an awareness of a new aesthetic. 'One can guess that the librettist Mr Langhammer was trying to invent a new type of *ballet-féerie*, something midway between classical ballet and *féerie*, but absolutely nothing came of this attempt.'[30] Another critic sensed the tension between choreography and naturalistic *mise-en-scène*: 'The extreme striving for realism ought not to have a place in ballet, since

[27] *Peterburgskaya gazeta*, 11 Nov. 1897, p. 3.   [28] *Novoe vremya*, 11 Nov. 1897, p. 3.
[29] *Peterburgskaya gazeta*, 10 Nov. 1897, p. 3.
[30] *Vsemirnaya illyustratsiya*, 58 (issue for 22 Nov. 1897), p. 522.

choreography is the most conventional of all the arts. In ballet everything is conventional, and for that reason there is no need to achieve a particularly realistic truth in costumes.'[31] *Svoi* may have been alluding to a new aesthetic in the remark, 'Mr Langhammer made his début as creator of the programme and prospector of sources, not excluding secret ones intended to serve the purposes of the new ballet,' adding that

The lion's share of the work fell to the author of the programme, Mr Langhammer, thanks to whose data the production was lifelike down to the last detail. This successful photography in colour, soft in tone and interesting in the highest degree as regards ethnographic data, replaces the whim of idle imagination in normal ballets. In the new work, it is true, 'don't wait in vain for a sign from the heavens' which creates the *art*, for in places it merrily rambles along; [it] isn't strong enough to blend into one general, clear, powerful flame, but it does have its excellent side, which has been missing for some time now—to give free rein to intelligent, deliberate thought. This is a good sign.[32]

If the ballet's creators were bad, its performers were excellent. Mathilde Kshesinskaya as Gotaru-Hime was given much to do, and she did it well:

Not every ballerina can sustain three *pas de deux* in one ballet. We very much liked Miss Kshesinskaya II's variation in the first act. It is lively, fast, and in her virtuoso execution produced a great effect. Also magnificently performed was Miss Kshesinskaya's adagio with Mr Gerdt and Mr Kyaksht in the grotto scene. The flight Miss Kshesinskaya makes from one cavalier to the other was very effective. She has a charming pizzicato in the last act, which created a furore. It was encored. Our ballerina's talent and art were featured in this ballet in full brilliance and strength.[33]

The second act *pas d'action* was a show-piece for the ballerina:

Here Miss Kshesinskaya was given breadth to display her full brilliance and virtuosity, and her technique is *hors-ligne*. In the double turns *en dedans* and [poses within] groupings which fill the adagio of this dance, each bolder than the last, the ballerina produced a great effect. Miss Kshesinskaya's characteristic *chic* and speed in dances, without detriment to gracefulness—were brought out in high relief. . . .[34]

Another critic gave Kshesinskaya the palm of excellence. In the 'difficult and wearying' role of Gotaru-Hime she displayed her 'dazzling choreographic gift', emerging the 'total victrix in her difficult assignment'.

Our ballerina managed especially well the beautiful but difficult variations of the first and third acts, with a multitude of double turns and effective pirouettes. In them our ballerina's rare gracefulness was revealed. Her 'pizzicato' on pointe in the third act was elegant in the highest degree. It was encored. M. F. Kshesinskaya had

[31] *Novosti i birzhevaya gazeta*, 11 Nov. 1897, p. 3.   [32] *Birzhevye vedomosti*, 13 Nov. 1897, p. 3.
[33] *Peterburgskaya gazeta*, 10 Nov. 1897, p. 3.
[34] *Vsemirnaya illyustratsiya*, 58 (issue for 22 Nov. 1897), p. 523.

a complete success. The audience applauded her with rare unanimity. One hardly needs add that her success was fully deserved. Mr Gerdt and Mr Kyaksht were Miss Kshesinskaya's partners. The latter had two solos, which as ever called forth a burst of noisy plaudits.[35]

Among the other soloists, Olga Preobrazhenskaya won consistent honourable mention, dancing 'with great brilliance, a finished virtuosity and genuine animation'.[36] She performed the steps of her Act I variation precisely, 'as if minting every movement, and finished it after several *entrechats six* with a series of turns on one leg. This variation, difficult because it was staged in such a slow tempo, produced a great effect.'[37]

In the spring of 1898, Preobrazhenskaya took over the role of Gotaru-Hime.

Wrangell's score met with mixed responses. Some were expediently balletomanic: 'The virtue of Baron Wrangell's music is that it is *dansante* and rhythmic, but its weak side is its lack of melody and poverty of orchestration.'[38] The *dansante* element was seconded by others: 'The composer Baron Wrangell was also called repeatedly, whose indisputable merits consist of giving back to our ballet, after a rather prolonged interval, music to which one can actually dance.'[39] The more literate critic found much to praise:

Baron Wrangell's music is original, very melodious, and in places preserves oriental coloration. In the entrance of the Mikado, for example, the theme with the original cadenzas played by the flute is genuinely Japanese, as is the *cortège nuptial*. The *pas d'action* and adagio performed by Mr Auer, Loganovsky, and Zabel, are positively magnificent, both in harmony, and instrumentation. The introduction to the second act, in which the poetical theme of a quartet is built on an orchestral background of flageolets, warrants complete approbation. The introduction moves to the *danse de feux de St Elme* by imitating the sounds of an Aeolian harp, which drift out from the stage. This passage is very melodious and offers indisputable artistic interest. The sound of Japanese instruments on which young girls play is transmitted in characteristic fashion by four mandolins.[40]

Apart from the widespread complaint that the ballet contained too many dances, and slights directed at him in the exchange of rumours before the première, Ivanov emerged from his labours on *The Mikado's Daughter* covered with praise. 'In general the dances are staged very well, especially the classical ones,' wrote the critic of the pro-Petipa faction. 'It's just that L. I. Ivanov somewhat overuses double turns, stuffing them into the *pas* of all dancers who can perform this newest balletic innovation.'[41] Yet to his

[35] *Novosti i birzhevaya gazeta*, 11 Nov. 1897, p. 3.
[36] *Novosti i birzhevaya gazeta*, 11 Nov. 1897, p. 3.
[37] *Peterburgskaya gazeta*, 10 Nov. 1897, p. 3.   [38] Ibid.
[39] *Novosti i birzhevaya gazeta*, 11 Nov. 1897, p. 3.   [40] *Peterburgskii listok*, 11 Nov. 1897, p. 3.
[41] *Peterburgskaya gazeta*, 10 Nov. 1897, p. 3.

honour, Ivanov 'strictly maintained the traditions of the old classical ballets'.

Of the classical dances, Ivanov staged especially well the ballerina's two *pas de deux*; in one of them he reintroduced the long since abandoned flight of the ballerina from one cavalier to another, achieving a complete and dazzling effect. Also extremely beautiful and often original are the variations the balletmaster composed for the women soloists, thereby giving our artists work which, it seems, they were long since unused to.[42]

To the extent the libretto constrained him, Ivanov was excused if his staging was not entirely effective. 'Mr Langhammer is a great lover of processions and of transforming the corps de ballet into extras; it was therefore difficult for Mr Ivanov to let his imagination run free.'[43] 'The massive *entrées* are wearying,' another notice reports, 'In the first place they are numerous, and in the second, they move very slowly. . . .'[44]

In character dance Ivanov was weaker, but here the array of exotic locales which he was called upon to represent was an extenuating factor. He probably knew no more about authentic Javanese or Filipino dance in *The Mikado's Daughter* than he did of ancient Slavic dances in *Mlada*. In any event, his illusion was not persuasive enough for his critics. 'The character dances were not especially successful, probably because they were all created in Petersburg, not Asia,' one critic remarked wryly.[45]

In the production of the ballet Mr Ivanov exceeded expectations. The classical dances are full of taste and elegance, and the character dances are variously typical. If they at times lack specificity, he is less to blame than the direction, which makes immense outlays on production without spending to bring in outstanding talents from abroad and from around Russia to collect and study materials suitable for choreography.[46]

Ivanov's inability to realize the exhaustive ethnographic detail of libretto and costume again raises the possibility of a clash of new aesthetic with old. The critic of *The Petersburg Leaflet* noticed the strain the new ethnicity was placing on character dance:

Balletmaster and composer must be considered from two standpoints not easily compared, (1) from the ethnographic side, the mores on which the subject is based, and (2) from the standpoint of European taste. Managing these considerations, Mr Ivanov attempted while staging the dances to divide the ballet into two, that is, to give a more or less exact representation of Japanese life and also to satisfy the demands of choreography. As a result the ensemble, all the purely Japanese pro-

[42] *Novosti i birzhevaya gazeta*, 11 Nov. 1897, p. 3.
[43] *Novoe vremya*, 11 Nov. 1897, p. 3.
[44] *Peterburgskii listok*, 11 Nov. 1897, p. 3.
[45] *Novoe vremya*, 11 Nov. 1897, p. 3.
[46] *Birzhevye vedomosti*, 13 Nov. 1897, p. 3.

cessions and groupings, are free of any 'spice' (forgive this word), whereas the variations and the *pas d'action* accord with European tastes.[47]

The treatment of *The Mikado's Daughter* in these reviews is not harsh given the norms of the day. Its reception, and the preferential programming it was given (seven performances between 9 November 1897 and 4 January 1898), permit the conclusion that the new ballet was more a success than a failure. At the same time, critics did not shrink from unflattering observations and advice:

There are so many dances that much of the audience got up and left before the end of the performance. In our opinion, all the dances for the men of the corps de ballet—the *jeu de balle* and the military dance—could be cut for the good of the ballet. Such a fate, one hopes, would also befall the children's dance with pantomime, in which young boys reproduce, *simulacre*, the ripping apart of an animal. This is not just unaesthetic, it is outright inartistic.[48]

The third performance of *The Mikado's Daughter* was for Claudia Kulichevskaya's benefit, at which Marius Petipa made an appearance, presented her with a gift, and 'said several heartfelt words apropos her diligent and talented stage activity and good relations with her colleagues'. By that time attention had been paid to the surfeit of dances. 'The first step towards abbreviation was taken,' reports *Svoi* with a certain regret, '. . . in the last act the children's pantomime is omitted, which quite truly characterized one of the particulars of the country's mores'.[49] Even this fair-minded critic could not resist offering suggestions for 'not-unuseful abbreviations'. *The Mikado's Daughter* was making its way without disaster, but its ponderous structure was very delicately poised.

The ballet struck a reef after the first performance of *Raymonda*. The harsh ridicule of *The Mikado's Daughter* in the wake of *Raymonda*'s first performance, which exceeded anything in the reviews just quoted, surely reflected continuing factional rivalries. Once again *The Petersburg Gazette* expressed its views in silly verse. Two days after the first performance, we read 'A Fable' by 'Not Krylov' [the Russian equivalent of 'not Aesop']:

'RAYMONDA' AND 'THE MIKADO'S DAUGHTER' (A FABLE)

> *The Mikado's Daughter* is angry, she rants and raves.
> Yet it is not her place to rant and rave
> When the little she-devil has to die—
> Although Langhammer (a German!) is providing treatment.
> 'What illness does she have?' they asked
> The doctor, and he, giving it up as a bad job,

---

[47] *Peterburgskii listok*, 11 Nov. 1897, p. 3.   [48] *Peterburgskaya gazeta*, 10 Nov. 1897, p. 3.
[49] *Birzhevye vedomosti*, 18 Nov. 1897, p. 3.

Said: 'Such a stream of feebleness,
That's simply the wolf's howl
Of the theatrical beau monde
The Mikado's Daughter will tire straightaway,
Point her to the door, alas, *Raymonda* is
Petipa's daughter![50]

A second poem, published about six weeks later, was in the manner of an epitaph:

The Mikado's Daughter came as guest,
And while awaiting the marriage, vanished.
Raymonda appeared in her place, and charmed
All, from the gallery to the stalls![51]

It is as if the poet already knows that subsequent performances of *The Mikado's Daughter* were to be limited to Act I (the entire work having 'vanished'), which was given eight times between 19 April 1898 and 19 April 1900. An exceptional revival was mounted on 14 December 1902, to celebrate the centenary of the founding of His Majesty's Pages' Corps.

An Egyptian Night

For most of the next three years Ivanov created no new ballet, but rather busied himself at Krasnoe Selo, with revivals, official trips to Moscow and Warsaw to stage ballets, writing his memoirs, and jury duty. During this time his health deteriorated seriously; there are many requests for him and his family to live outside St Petersburg. It would hardly have been surprising, after serving Russian ballet for half a century, if Ivanov had ceased composition. But he persisted, showing the same stubborn dedication now with respect to choreography that kept him on the stage as a dancer through the 1880s.

We first become aware of *An Egyptian Night* in a sprinkling of newspaper reports in the spring of 1900. As early as 11 April it was announced in *The Petersburg Gazette* that

The production of the new ballet, *An Egyptian Night*, scheduled for a gala performance in the summer of this year, and in which Miss Kshesinskaya will perform the role of Cleopatra, has been entrusted to balletmaster L. I. Ivanov. Rehearsals of this ballet will begin by 20 April.[52]

On 19 June *The New Time* reported:

---

[50] *Peterburgskaya gazeta*, 9 Jan. 1898, p. 3. [51] *Peterburgskaya gazeta*, 21 Feb. 1898, p. 3.
[52] *Peterburgskaya gazeta*, 11 Apr. 1900, p. 4.

At the present time rehearsals are under way of the new ballet *An Egyptian Night*, the programme of which was written by Mr Lopukhin, author of the pantomime *De la lune au Japon*, and the music by Mr Arensky. Production of the ballet is assigned to the balletmaster L. I. Ivanov. The new ballet will be given at Peterhof on Olga Island in a performance proposed for the visit of the Shah of Persia.[53]

From this point the picture gets confused. On 28 June the new ballet is reported as 'completely finished', but as a result of unspecified causes, rehearsals had been stopped. Music critic Herman Laroche nevertheless reports hearing the score in rehearsal at Peterhof on 12 August, and mentions that the new ballet, not to be staged that summer 'due to circumstances', will probably not be given at the Maryinsky either, because the staging is designed for a garden.[54] Yet a week before this, *An Egyptian Night* was announced for the forthcoming winter season, and on 20 August once again postponed, to Peterhof the following summer; on 20 March and 27 April of 1901, announcements of the new work persisted.[55] As late as 25 May 1901 we read:

At Peterhof a gala performance is proposed for which a new small ballet, *An Egyptian Night*, with music by Arensky, is being prepared. This ballet was to have been given last year, but its production was put off. The ballerina Miss Kshesinskaya will perform the principal role.[56]

Daily rehearsals are still being reported as late as 8 July 1901, though *An Egyptian Night* will be given only with the proviso that the weather is fine.[57] After this the ballet disappears from view until Fokine revived the project in 1909.

Lopukhin's scenario for *An Egyptian Night* has not come to light, and may differ from the Pushkin tale upon which Fokine based his staging, which centres around Cleopatra's provocative question:

Speak! Who among you will pay for
A night with me with his life?

One wonders how Fokine's lascivious tale of Cleopatra taking the slave Amoun as her lover for a night, for which he gives his life, might fit the imperial gala honouring a Mediterranean head of state for which Ivanov was preparing. Perhaps the disjunction between topic and occasion prompted cancellations. Nevertheless, Fokine used Arensky's music for his version, and the published score, which Ivanov presumably used as well, contains a *Scène d'empoisonnement* which links the two productions.

That *An Egyptian Night* was completely cast (or recast) by 3 March 1901

[53] *Novoe vremya*, 19 June 1900, p. 3.   [54] *Moskovskie vedomosti*, 16 Aug. 1900, p. 4.
[55] Reported in *Krasovskaya*, 397.
[56] *Novoe vremya*, 25 May 1901, p. 4.   [57] *Novoe vremya*, 8 July 1901, p. 4.

is affirmed by an official cast list submitted on that date. The principal parts were distributed as follows:

Cleopatra	Petipa I
Verenice	Kshesinskaya II
Anthony	Gerdt
Amoun	Legat III
High Priest	Gillert
Arsinoe, a slave	Trefilova

The additional women personnel included:

  6 Egyptians
  6 Jewesses
  8 Greeks
  9 Philistines
  4 women of Cleopatra's retinue
12 women of the people

The additional men personnel included:

  4 guards of Cleopatra
18 Roman soldiers
  8 gladiators
  8 patricians[58]

Uncertainties of the imperial calendar, which had kept Ivanov's new ballet from the stage for more than a year, ultimately consigned it to oblivion. *An Egyptian Night* is the only production Ivanov mounted that was never shown to an audience outside rehearsal.

The Second Hungarian Rhapsody of Liszt

In the autumn of 1900, possibly in response to the successful divertissement on Hungarian motifs that Petipa had created in Act III of *Raymonda*, Ivanov choreographed this celebrated Liszt work, which was interpolated into a performance of Saint-Léon's *The Little Humpbacked Horse* on 11 October. Alexandre Shiryaev remembered it (in about 1940?) as an example of Ivanov's talent as a maker of character dances: 'The Second Hungarian Rhapsody of Liszt can serve as a remarkable example of his character compositions, one which is still being performed (true, in a somewhat reworked form) in the last act of *The Little Humpbacked Horse*.'[59] At the time it was introduced, the reviewer for *The Petersburg Leaflet* gave a sense of the dance:

[58] St Petersburg, Historical Archive, 497.18.611, fos. 59–60.   [59] *Shiryaev*, 63.

In *The Little Humpbacked Horse* there is something new and interesting for the lovers of ballet. In the last act is a czardas produced by the balletmaster L. I. Ivanov to the marvellous sounds of Liszt's rhapsody. Such a successful staging, such a wonderful grouping of masses we have long not had the occasion to see. Such life, such vast temperament, and how picturesquely this czardas is produced! Twenty-eight persons dance it, headed by Miss Preobrazhenskaya with Mr Shiryaev, and Miss Obukhova with Mr Bekefy. The names of these performers speak for themselves, and it is hardly necessary to add that the czardas came off with extraordinary success. The general ensemble in this wonderful dance is supported in a friendly way by Miss Borkhardt, Vaganova, Fonaryova, and others.[60]

In *The Petersburg Gazette* we learn of the principal rhythmic novelty (and the greatest liability for performers) of the new dance, namely its frequent change of tempo, requiring substantial rehearsal and careful co-ordination between dancers and conductor.

The *Kapellmeister* Drigo masterfully went through this music. The czardas has been staged by the balletmaster L. I. Ivanov, whose name they forgot to put on the *affiche*. The staging of this dance is original and beautiful. The balletmaster tastefully fitted the dances and the various figures to the tempi, which shift unexpectedly from slow to fast. This czardas can be considered one of the most beautiful character dances and had an immense success yesterday. Its execution harmonized with its staging. The numerous entourage of artists danced with verve. Among them Miss Borkhardt stood out. The czardas was encored.[61]

The difficulty of co-ordinating music and dance when the tempo changed frequently was complicated by the number of dancers:

For the balletmaster this was a kind of *tour de force*. It seems to us that the ballet owed much of its success to Liszt's magnificent orchestration and its effective modulations. We did not like the dances at all: amidst the extremely fast tempi and, moreover, their constant changing, it is difficult to devise something for dancing; this would be possible if the Lisztian czardas were performed by two [or] three pairs of first artists, but for the entire corps de ballet it is difficult to perform.[62]

Six months after Ivanov's czardas was introduced into *The Little Humpbacked Horse*, one critic, probably Pleshcheyev, challenged the dramatic propriety of the interpolation, a complaint that rings a little odd given the far-flung fantasy of the ballet's story. More important is the offhand observation about the origin of the dance, which throws light indirectly on the history of *An Egyptian Night*:

Whence this czardas? If Saint-Léon rose from the grave he would be most astonished at the sight of a czardas in his ballet. This was done for a gala performance in honour of the Shah of Persia, and accidentally survived. A czardas here is the same as ordering a trepak to be danced in *Giselle*, but much is permitted in ballet. This is

---

[60]　*Peterburgskii listok*, 12 Oct. 1900, p. 4.　　　[61]　*Peterburgskaya gazeta*, 12 Oct. 1900, p. 4.
[62]　*Novoe vremya*, 13 Oct. 1900, p. 4.

what is funny: on the *affiche* it says, 'Dances of the various peoples who inhabit Russia'. And suddenly Hungarians![63]

From this statement it would appear that the direction reconsidered *An Egyptian Night* as inappropriate to perform before the Shah of Persia, and Ivanov composed his czardas as a substitute.

In general, however, Ivanov's new dance and its performers were widely praised. Olga Preobrazhenskaya had a great success, performing it 'with brio and attractiveness'.[64] 'The czardas . . . came off magnificently, eliciting loud applause on behalf of the performers.'[65] 'The czardas is very effectively staged by our balletmaster L. I. Ivanov.'[66] 'This dance, to the eternally youthful sounds of Liszt's Rhapsody, provided great aesthetic pleasure to the public.'[67]

Vera Krasovskaya has described the dance, presumably in the 'somewhat reworked form' to which Shiryaev alluded:

Twelve pairs of the corps de ballet began the first, slow part of the rhapsody. Each girl made as if to allow her partner, who was holding her by the waist, to lead her, putting both hands on his shoulder and leaning her head on them. In the triumphant, smooth, proud path of movement, the step just hesitating as, softly but clearly, the leg was thrown forward, the couples came down from the far upper wing, encompassing the stage. Compact at first, the chain of dancers thins out, the space between the couples gradually widening; towards the end of the first path of movement the entire stage filled with dancers. Each pair danced only for each other, and yet the unifying theme, vivid and growing intensely, sounded in the capricious play of turns, in the uninterrupted flowing outline of the arm movements which highlight the syncopations of the crossing pathways. The couples now came together, now dispersed, forming ever more fantastic groupings in ceaseless movement.

In a new upsurge of the music four pairs of coryphées flowed into the dance, then two pairs of soloists. They descended, transmitting in their gliding path the flying outline of the melody, while the mass of dancers which had made way for them, standing in place, accompanied them with rhythmic stamping, underscored by waving the hands on welcoming, upraised arms. Accelerating with the music, the dance filled the stage in proportion to the force of the mass of sound from the orchestra, reproducing all its melodic ornaments and figures. Here the most precise technique of sharp movement and synchronization was required. Each man, holding his partner's hand, now led her around him in a staccato, jumping rhythm, now twirled her on the spot in furious turns, which mirrored the upward flights of the violin glissandi. An image of elemental dance, the image which conveys the character of the Hungarian people, was clearly affirmed in the devices of traditional theatricalization for the first time.[68]

---

[63] *Novoe vremya*, 13 Apr. 1901, p. 4.   [64] *Novosti i birzhevaya gazeta*, 13 Oct. 1900, p. 3.
[65] *Peterburgskii listok*, 30 Oct. 1900, p. 3.
[66] *Novosti i birzhevaya gazeta*, 21 Dec. 1900, p. 3.
[67] *Novosti i birzhevaya gazeta*, 20 Nov. 1901, p. 3.   [68] *Krasovskaya*, pp. 396–7.

As the seasons passed *The Little Humpbacked Horse* came to be 'crowded throughout with interpolated numbers'.[69] With dances introduced into it from Saint-Léon's *Météora*, Petipa's *Calcabrino*, *The Halt of the Cavalry*, Perrot's *The Naiad and the Fisherman*, and *Faust*, the ballet was in danger of losing its identity. Alexandre Gorsky mounted a new production of it in St Petersburg in 1912, in which Ivanov's czardas was retained. Of this staging Andrey Levinson wrote:

In general, the repetition of *The Humpbacked Horse* confirmed my original impression about the gifted Mr Gorsky's production: the charm of the old production, pitiful and decrepit, is that it recalled to us so much that is dear; it recalled to me personally the picturesque figures in ancient dress with whom I played in childhood; exactly thus was the yellow field with the fence, the peasants were the same. The new production is by outstanding artists and stages, but is not infused with naïve dream; it is a talented but inessential experiment: it's a toy, but all the same, the fairy-tale spirit of the ballet has flown away.[70]

Gorsky's production survived into the Soviet era.

Sylvia

This ballet, to a scenario by Jules Barbier and music by Leo Delibes, was not produced in the Russian imperial ballet until 1901, although by then it had been performed by a number of famous ballerinas in Russia. On 2 August 1886 Antonietta Dell'Era had fashioned dances from *Sylvia* into a divertissement at the Arcadia Theatre; in the 1891/2 season an Italian company with Adelina Rossi and Virginia Zucchi performed a complete version in the Maly Theatre; and in the summer of 1892 Carlotta Brianza appeared in *Sylvia* at the Fantasia Theatre in Moscow.

From sources relating to the work of Sergey Diaghilev and Alexandre Benois we know that these men were contemplating a production of *Sylvia* during the time that Diaghilev was employed by the direction of the imperial theatres. It was to be a model staging, supervised by Diaghilev as intermediary between the direction and the gifted young artists of his acquaintance. But in January 1901 this project came to nothing after Diaghilev quarrelled with the Director of Theatres, Prince Sergey Mikhailovich Volkonsky; in July 1901, after another contretemps, Volkonsky was replaced as Director. At that time, however disabled by the loss of inspired collaborators, *Sylvia* was still on the schedule for the 1901/2 season.

Benois wrote that Olga Preobrazhenskaya had been chosen as the bal-

[69] *Rech'*, 28 Oct. 1908, p. 5.   [70] *Rech'*, 1 Jan. 1913, p. 7.

lerina for the model production of *Sylvia*, and indeed she ended up with the role, but the choreographers, he claimed, were to have been Nikolay and Sergey Legat.[71] Ivanov was called in after the dispute in order to stage a ballet which the direction had already scheduled.

His was a many-sided burden. *Sylvia* was passed to him as a rejected collaboration of outsiders who had been promised optimum conditions. The demeaning implications of becoming the trustee of a discarded project, together with his own poor health that autumn, augured ill for the project. We know from notes appended to Ivanov's memoirs what happened next: he began to stage *Sylvia* on 1 October, and on 14 and 15 October Act I was almost completed.

When Ivanov could no longer function because of his final illness, the production of *Sylvia* passed to Pavel Gerdt, who, wrote Alexander Shiryaev,

conducted himself in a most disorganized way in the work which he took upon himself after Ivanov's death [*sic*] in 1901—to finish the production begun by Ivanov of Delibes's ballet *Sylvia*. Gerdt could not manage mass dances at all, changed them endlessly, and from this lost his authority with the company, got upset, and finally, having strained himself to breaking-point, asked me to finish the production of these scenes and dances for him.[72]

It is hardly a surprise that the new production was a rather sorrowful affair, and we are left to wonder if the Benois-Diaghilev circle could have made it any better. The general lines of criticism in 1901 were the same as they had been when the Italian troupe had performed *Sylvia* a decade earlier: the music was beautiful, but the story was too slight, which made monotony in the dances almost inevitable.

The shepherd Aminta loves Sylvia, a nymph of Diana, and is punished for overlooking her gambols in the forest. Cupid takes his part and fires his arrow at the nymph, causing her to love the shepherd. The hunter Orion kidnaps Sylvia, but she makes him drunk and escapes with Cupid's help. The ballet ends with celebrations.

'Many claim that this ballet is boring because of the genre, which is too antiquated,' we read after the third performance,

Sylvia is rich in purely classical dances (if one does not count the little Ethiopian character dance in the second act), which are very consistent and suit the antiquated story as no other, but at the same time, thanks to this the indisputably lovely *Sylvia* suffers a certain dryness and slightly wearies spectators accustomed to a more contemporary story.[73]

---

[71] Alexandre Benois, *Reminiscences of the Russian Ballet*, trans. Mary Britnieva (London: Putnam, 1941), 211–12.

[72] *Shiryaev*, 64.   [73] *Novosti i birzhevaya gazeta*, 21 Dec. 1901, p. 3.

The performers were highly praised, but *Sylvia* languished in a mediocre production. '*Sylvia* has been produced on our stage quite negligently,' we read in one notice, 'This speaks to the benefit of economy, but little guarantees the success of the ballet.'[74] 'It is unfortunate that for a ballet like *Sylvia* they have not troubled to make new decorations,' another critic remarked, 'The old and worn-out production quite mars the general impression.'[75]

The response to choreography confirmed Shiryaev's remembrance: 'Unfortunately, the choreographic aspect of *Sylvia* also leaves much to be desired. The dances are pale and monotonous; they lack novelty and originality. Most of the public, and we ourselves liked the music much more than the ballet.'[76]

The reviewer for *The New Time* found the production pleasant but lacking in energy:

In the first act the entrance of the huntress-nymphs is not lively and energetic enough; the representation of a floating gallery in the third scene is too long; Cupid is not merry and mischievous enough, the bacchic scene in the cave does not produce the desired impression.[77]

Another critic pointed out a limitation of the pastoral ballet, remarking that Ivanov and Gerdt could not produce effective classical choreography with the dancers in long Greek tunics.[78]

The Petersburg Leaflet was the least charitable. The production was unsatisfactory because 'The balletmasters Mr Ivanov and Mr Gerdt did not take pains to enliven it, but provided several classical *pas* staged in a trite manner, as if extinguished. . . . Everything was as if dead, as a result of which the ballet produces a soporific effect.'[79]

The terminology of death was sadly appropriate. After five performances between 2 December 1901 and 3 February 1902, *Sylvia* was dropped from the repertoire. Act I was revived for five more performances in the depth of the war, between 24 April and 11 September 1916.

Lev Ivanov never took a farewell benefit, and never retired. He worked the year around, during the regular season, the summertimes, and for special occasions, making it likely that his death, whenever it came, would interrupt a work in progress. The financial burdens of his last years may have precluded retirement, or the choice may have been voluntary—Ivanov, like Timofei Stukolkin and others before him—may have wanted to depart this earth still in harness. The exuberant Stukolkin went out like a

---

[74] *Novosti i birzhevaya gazeta*, 4 Dec. 1901, p. 3.
[75] *Novosti i birzhevaya gazeta*, 21 Dec. 1901, p. 3.
[76] *Novosti i birzhevaya gazeta*, 4 Dec. 1901, p. 3.
[77] *Novoe vremya*, 4 Dec. 1901, p. 4.
[78] *Peterburgskaya gazeta*, 3 Dec. 1901; quoted in *Krasovskaya*, 399.
[79] *Peterburgskii listok*, 3 Dec. 1901, p. 3.

trouper—in costume, on the spot, dramatically, having just come off the stage. Ivanov also died as he had lived: nondescript, subordinate, flowing with rather than commanding the events of which he was a part. For that reason one looks at *Sylvia*, as the critics of *The Mikado's Daughter* looked at that work, and finding fault place it at someone else's doorstep. Ivanov, though an essential collaborator, maintained too low a profile to engage in other than the politest criticism once the obligations of his service were discounted. This time, when fault with *Sylvia* was to be found, he was no longer there.

Conclusion

———

To learn more about Lev Ivanov's art, it would be helpful to know more of the workings of the theatre administration, how it came to make decisions to go forward with particular projects, and how questions were decided of who was assigned what task. It would be a blessing to have more of Ivanov's preliminary materials—sketches and notes—assuming that he made them.

Yet most of the abiding questions about Ivanov have to do with Ivanov the man. We know he was capable of emotion and zeal, but all evidence of these qualities is in the private arena, within the community of artists. While it may be proper for creative artists not to respond to criticism publicly, it is striking that we have so little sense of how Ivanov reacted to events which affected him. Was he so private a person as to conceal distress when critics faulted his works? Petipa, who for the most part maintained his composure in this regard, was known occasionally to grant an interview or to write a letter to the editor venting his spleen. But not Ivanov. Or was Ivanov simply oblivious to critics and his audience? This seems unlikely, though it is possible that he lived so much within his own reveries as a creator that he answered only to himself.

Equally distressing is that we know so little of Ivanov's response to the circumstances of his employment. Did he, like Petipa, object when faced with projects he did not like, but object within, unable to wield his rank successfully against his administrative seniors? Or was he guided by the language of his contract, to do what he was assigned, and was perhaps content, casting an eye back to his humble artistic beginnings, with being as much in the swing of things as he was? Ivanov described himself as having risen from a private to a general, a journey on which subordination and duty count for something.

The source of ambiguity about Ivanov lies here, in our ignorance of his motivations and feelings. One thing is certain: until we can establish more of what Ivanov thought about himself and his situation, there will be a danger of distorting who and what he was. We must continue to hold in abeyance the contention that he was a victim, and that in some socialist utopia he would have produced masterwork after masterwork of the calibre of *Swan Lake*. On the basis of the evidence we have, it is just as plausible that in relation to the other graduates of the theatre school in 1852, Ivanov counted himself lucky for the long stage career he enjoyed and the opportunities it put in his way. This contention remains valid regardless of any clash of artistic temperament, which would have been inevitable wherever Ivanov worked, and despite the onset of infirmity, which under different circumstances may or may not have developed as it did.

The principal issue in Ivanov's personality, to which all evidence points, is that he was loyal—to his fellow artists, to his institution, to his art. This quality implies a willingness to compromise or neutralize one's personal ambitions, and may also nurture an indifference to critical assault from without. Ivanov may not have chaffed at the prospect of staging *The Mikado's Daughter* after Petipa rejected it. He may sincerely have believed that it was his duty to accept the project and to give it his best for the sake of his company, however unpromising the work's prospects.

As a stylist, Ivanov appears to have been indebted, as his contemporaries claimed, to Marius Petipa. This was to be expected not only because Ivanov took over so many projects from Petipa, but also because Petipa was Ivanov's administrative and artistic senior for over fifty years. The sources also suggest that a Saint-Léonic element was present in Ivanov's thinking. Ivanov, like Saint-Léon, was perfectly content with ballet scenarios of minimal coherence and drama, which provided much opportunity for dance. From *The Tulip of Haarlem* to *The Mikado's Daughter*, critics complained about the insipid stories of Ivanov's ballets while stressing the *amount* of dancing, the *number* of dances, implicitly affirming that for Ivanov, dance held sway over drama. Choreographed movement, more than mime, more than the clash of hero and villain or of rival lovers, was for Ivanov the point of a ballet. Ivanov, moreover, like Saint-Léon, could fashion a dazzling solo variation for the ballerina. In this regard it was fortuitous that Ivanov's work as a balletmaster coincided exactly with the tenure of Italian virtuosas in Russia: he was appointed balletmaster when Virginia Zucchi was invited to the imperial theatres and he died the year Pierina Legnani left Russia. From performances of Emma Bessone to those of Legnani, critics remarked on the technical difficulties of the solo variations. To be sure, Ivanov learned the latest forays of technique from the Italian visitors, but he assimilated them quickly and turned them from near-acrobatics into art. Little wonder that the wreath Legnani sent to Ivanov's half-century benefit was signed, 'de la part d'Odette'. For taming raw virtuosity, tempering it with gentler artistic nuances, Ivanov deserves to share credit with Petipa for reconciling the Italian and French schools, and (to state the cliché) forging from this reconciliation a characteristic Russian school with such dissimilar exponents as Mathilde Kshesinskaya and Anna Pavlova.

In the ensemble dance, by contrast, especially classical dances for the women of the corps de ballet, Ivanov charted an individual course. Perhaps the easiest way to demonstrate this would be to set his work and that of Petipa, his point of departure, within the formulas of the grand ballet. For this purpose let us take two snowscapes: Ivanov's Waltz of the Snowflakes and from *La Bayadère*, Petipa's Kingdom of the Shades. The latter takes place in an seasonally neutral 'enchanted locale', which in the apotheosis is nevertheless within sight of the 'peaks of the Himalayas' as Nikia and Solor are wafted towards them.

The formulaic element of such ensembles calls for the women of the corps de ballet to be deployed in various geometric designs which articulate the structure of the dance. The entrance of the corps is typically additive or cumulative. In *La Bayadère* the famous downward-angled ramp (a stylized Himalaya) on which the dancers appear singly in a sequence of arabesques, adds an element of peril to this already precarious pose. In his revival of 1900 Petipa called upon forty-eight of the bayadère Nikia's sister shades to come on stage in this way, gradually amassing, in number and in the ritualistic effect of precisely executed unisons, an imposing effect of weight and expressive gravity. Once all the dancers were on stage, the arabesque was featured in the geometric designs which made up the rest of the dance. In every such design, Petipa in effect invited his audience to admire the perfection of a particular dancer's arabesque among the others all doing the same; the fact that the group were arranged in simple rank and file was incidental, so powerful was the effect of mass and the almost Hellenic severity of line. Only the appearance of Solor and Nikia's shade reminded the audience that the scene represented a paradise. The importance of snowscape, however understated in the libretto, is also as distant from the spectator's consciousness as one might expect of a Hellenic muse, or of a balletmaster born in Marseilles.

Ivanov produced a totally different effect in the Waltz of the Snowflakes by ringing changes on the formula. He too brought the snowflakes on stage additively, but rapidly in groups of three from each side, each trio, upon reaching centre stage, swirling off to the back as if carried there by the wind, to be succeeded by the next entrants. If Petipa's *entrée* was based on hypnotic repetition and cumulative effect, Ivanov's, while symmetrical, imparts a much greater sense of volatility. This volatility, in turn, mimicking a winter breeze, was the first of many style features of the Waltz that linked it graphically with its topic in the libretto. Throughout the dance Ivanov's imagery was more openly and easily relatable to a real snowstorm than Petipa's was to a paradise of India.

Where Petipa in the Kingdom of the Shades insisted on poses that were difficult to sustain and tested the abilities of an ensemble by requiring them to be held in unison, Ivanov shifted the focus away from pose towards individual steps so simple as to discourage appreciation solely for their technique. These would be repeated *ad infinitum*, and remarked accordingly by critics—when observing the Waltz of the Snowflakes, or the dances of *The Magic Flute* ('quite simplified, [and] do not go further than the *ballonné* and *balancé*') or *Acis* and *Galatea* ('the endless number of times the same movement is repeated'). It is clear that to Ivanov, little steps with soft articulations, inconsequential individually, were effective when performed by many dancers. To focus on any single dancer in the Waltz would little repay the spectator: the individual snowflake is not a vehicle of particular aesthetic pleasure; to admire just one would be missing the forest for the trees.

Instead, they are the means by which floor patterns were formed and sustained. At important structural points Ivanov again put forward naïve if pleasing analogies to his topic in the geometrical designs he chose: stars and circulating crosses and whirlwinds, important symbols of a snowstorm. Like Petipa, Ivanov invited the spectator to perceive the whole figure of a floor plan, with the difference that Ivanov's dancers were not set in a pose, but constantly in motion. (Many of the oblique lines and circles, serpentines and triangles in the lakeside dances in *Swan Lake* are similarly outlined in constantly hovering or undulating movement of simple, repeated steps.) The incessant motion almost defies focus on a single point or dancer in favour of the totality.

All of these properties, to say nothing of a lyrical quality that owes little or nothing to Petipa, make us conscious of snow in Ivanov's Waltz as a concept in nature he chose to emulate. It is the art of a Petersburger, a man from northern climes, for whom winter could be poeticized.

Ivanov's ensemble dances are another proof of the contention that for him choreography was the point of a dance. Unambiguous denotation in floor plan or mimetic gesture might be extremely rare in his dances, if present at all. Connoisseurs of Ivanov's time would have had no difficulty appreciating the stylization of his creations, but in the perspective of Russian ballet at the time, the clash of his aesthetic with developing trends towards literal and highly dramatic dance was certainly a liability. In his dogged attachment, so often remarked by critics, to 'our ballet's traditions'—the canons of the *danse d'école*—Ivanov may have exceeded Petipa in his zeal, or perhaps in his indifference to the new. On this point questions of art, personality, and institution converge. Petipa went on record as opposing the *danse libre* of Isadora Duncan and the modernizing tendencies of

Alexandre Gorsky. Because we know so little of Ivanov's personal views, it is impossible to determine whether his retrospective tendency was a function of wilful detachment or lack of adaptability, his early training, or his institutional outlook. In any case, his lack of response to the new, whatever Petipa's intrigues and the foibles of bureaucracy, was a brake on Ivanov's progress to celebrity.

In the end, what is the basis of that celebrity? The personal testimony that survives from his contemporaries identifies Ivanov as sturdy, talented, and unexceptional. Even granting the currents which seemed to swirl around the theatre direction, would not one of Ivanov's contemporaries have come forward to proclaim his genius if that were to any degree the perception of him? Was he unjustly neglected by all his contemporaries? If so, to what end? And why, after his death, or even after Petipa's, when no liability would be incurred for doing so, was no steadfast voice raised on Ivanov's behalf?

Yet we should not rush too hastily to judgement. Shortly after Ivanov's death came the great disruptions in Russian society—of 1905 and later—and in ballet, the Diaghilev era with its devotion to *chic*. Either factor could readily diminish the memory of so modest an artist so little dedicated to *réclame*. Yet Ivanov left a legacy—for posterity directly in *Swan Lake*, and for generations near him in other ways. While nothing is ever said of it, there is a distinctive if not invariable tendency to cluster Ivanov's works on multiple bills, as if in recognition of his identity as a creator during his life, and in acknowledgement of his legacy afterwards. His *Acis and Galatea*, it will be recalled, was given its first performance on the same evening as a première by Petipa, *The Halt of the Cavalry*. But in five of the subsequent eight performances of *Acis* in the regular season, it is given either with another of Ivanov's ballets to fill the bill, or in the case of triple bills, with another of his and a third ballet by Petipa, so that two of three works of an evening would be Ivanov's. *The Offerings to Cupid*, Ivanov's rechoreographing of Petipa's ballet, was variously coupled in the first two years of its three-year run. But in its last year, 1895, it is programmed exclusively with a variety of Ivanov's other ballets in seven of eight showings. In the spring of 1893, after *The Magic Flute* was on the boards, *The Nutcracker* was detached from *Iolanthe*, its companion opera, and in the nine performances of it from 11 April 1893 to 10 September 1895, it was inevitably paired with *The Magic Flute* or *The Enchanted Forest*. Subtle tendencies like these deserve consideration when accusations are made that the direction discriminated against Ivanov, or that Petipa maltreated him.

But there is more. Ivanov's ballets are part of a direct transition from the Russian ballet of the nineteenth century to that of the twentieth, as expressed in the works of Mikhail Fokine. In one of his more self-aggrandizing claims, Fokine wrote in his memoirs of having had little exposure to Ivanov and his methods. The passage in question follows the description, already quoted, of Fokine's participation as a student in *The Magic Flute*:

This was the only ballet of Ivanov which was produced during my time. I know that he assisted M. I. Petipa in many productions, that he staged several ballets independently, never thereafter did I have occasion to see him at his creative work. For that reason I recall what astonished my child's mind at the time in L. I. Ivanov's work.

R. E. Drigo wrote the music for this ballet. He wrote in accordance with the production of the ballet. In the morning he played at the piano in rehearsal what he had composed the night before, and in the evening composed for rehearsal the next day. L[ev] I[vanovich], composing dances, would ask him for 16 bars. Having set them, he would ask for the next 16 bars to be played, etc. I recall, during the staging of the grand final waltz, L[ev] I[vanovich] said: 'Now, then, further.' 'Further isn't written,' Drigo answered. The continuation of the staging was put off until the next rehearsal. And so, the ballet was mounted not only without any conception of the whole or even of a separate number, but it was completely obvious that L[ev] I[vanovich] had not even listened through what the composer brought him in advance of the staging. I do not recall what I thought at the time, of what to make of this unusual system, but from the fact that I remembered this incident my entire life I conclude that it seemed strange to me at the time.[1]

The implications of this anecdote, which on the surface is amusing, are manifestly slanted. *The Magic Flute* the only Ivanov ballet of Fokine's time to be produced? Fokine, who played the Nutcracker in 1895, Adonis in *Cupid's Pranks* in 1897, the Genie of the Forest in *The Enchanted Forest* in 1901, and performed a *pas de deux* in *The Tulip of Haarlem* in 1903? Fokine, creator of *The Dying Swan*, was not influenced by *Swan Lake*, which was first produced the year after *The Magic Flute*, while he was still a student? Fokine, who staged *Acis and Galatea* to Kadlets's music in 1905 for the theatre school, had no idea of Ivanov's production? Fokine, who later in the year that he danced in *The Magic Flute*, did not notice 'La Nuit de Nil' in *Zolushka*, where Cleopatra poisoned her lover, or Ivanov's *An Egyptian Night* to Arensky's music, and conceived his version of the work in 1909 wholly on his own? While it is true that staff composers in the imperial theatres were known to have composed in units, by phrase and period, there are few alternatives to setting steps consecutively, as Fokine describes Ivanov doing, and it would be a surprise if he did not work that way himself.

Fokine's dismissal of Ivanov strains credibility, and may be explained by the cult of originality which infused the Diaghilev enterprise and declared anathema anything which seemed old-fashioned. In fact, Fokine's roots go well back into the works and world of his teachers, Ivanov and Petipa, and

---

[1] M. Fokin, *Protiv techeniya* [Against the Current] (Leningrad: 'Iskusstvo', 1981), 47.

some of his celebrated works, ballets in which his originality was hymned in the first Diaghilev years, are simply updated reworkings of borrowed ideas. In this regard it may be significant that Ivanov had set a dance to Schumann's music as early as 1886 at Krasnoe Selo, and that Nikolay Legat had choreographed an orchestration of that composer's *Carnaval* for Marie Petipa and Olga Preobrazhenskaya as early as 1902 (for a performance at the Petersburg Conservatoire), three years before Fokine's first acknowledged choreography and eight before his own setting of Schumann's music. Fokine's setting of the Polovtsian Dances from *Prince Igor*, which won him great celebrity in the West, was, according to Alexandre Shiryaev, clearly indebted to Ivanov:

We are accustomed to think that the entire credit for the composition of these dances belonged to Fokine. In point of fact he only strengthened, vivified, sharpened, and embellished various details of the motifs of the dances composed by L. Ivanov for the old production of *Prince Igor* in 1890. The latter I remember very well, as I took part in them, performing the solo with the bow.[2]

It is logical that Fokine would distance himself from the old, but to do so at the expense of a choreographer from whom he borrowed so liberally is manifestly ungracious. In doing this, he contributed to the obscurity of Ivanov's rightful place in history. More gracious was the critic for *The Petersburg Gazette*, who wrote on 1 January 1900 that the ballet of the nineteenth century had ended the night before with a performance of *Swan Lake*. In fact *The Little Humpbacked Horse* had been given on New Year's Eve, but the point was well taken nevertheless: the critic was paying tribute to Petipa and Ivanov and to one of the century's lasting balletic statements. Little could he have known how important this work would be in the century just begun.

---

[2] *Shiryaev*, 91.

Appendix A

WORKS IN WHICH
LEV IVANOV DANCED

The following data reflect the scarcity of information about Lev Ivanov the dancer, in that he doubtless performed in many more works than listed here. The sources are indicated: standard histories or the press (either a review with a date and page, or the ballet programme announced for a given date, indicated by the word 'news' followed by the source and date). Dates about which there is some question are so indicated. Nor is precedence certain: the first indication listed here of an Ivanov performance is no assurance that he had not performed it before.

1850

The Millers (Jean-Baptiste Blache/Aug. Poirot), a *pas de deux* (composed by Jean Petipa), 7 June (*Krasovskaya*, 340).
A polka-schottishe (by Alexandre Nikolaevich Picheau, a dancer) (*Krasovskaya*, 340).

1851

A *pas de deux*, 15 Jan. (*Krasovskaya*, 340).
A Peasant Wedding (Steffani), the mazurka, 27 Apr. (*Krasovskaya*, 340).

1852

A *pas de deux*, 19 Aug. (*Krasovskaya*, 340).
A *pas de trois*, 8 Sept. (*Krasovskaya*, 340).
A *polka demi-caractère*, 10 Sept. (*Krasovskaya*, 340).

1853

The Hungarian Hut (Didelot; new music by K. A. Lyadov), the role of Ulrich, 22 Feb. (*Krasovskaya*, 341).
La Fille mal gardée (Dauberval), *grand pas de deux*, 3 Nov. (*Krasovskaya*, 341).

1854

The Millers (Blache/Poirot), the role of Luki, mid-Sept. (*Krasovskaya*, 341–2).

1856

A *pas de deux* at the coronation of Emperor Alexandre II (Memoirs).

1857

La Muette de Portici (Auber), a bolero (by Ivanov), 3 Dec. (*Krasovskaya*, 342).

1858

A *pas de mazurka*, 21 Jan. (*Pleshcheyev*, 180).
'The Scotsman and the Sylphide' (*tableau vivant* by Ivanov), 17 Feb. (*Krasovskaya*, 343).
'Giselle' (*tableau vivant* by Ivanov), 20 Feb. (*Krasovskaya*, 343).
   (Later in the paragraph Krasovskaya assigns these *tableaux vivants* to 1857.)
A new Spanish *pas de quatre* (Bogdanov), 1 Apr. (*Teatral'nyi i muzykal'nyi vestnik*, 30 Mar. 1858, p. 137).
Robert and Bertram (François Augué/Felix Kshesinsky), a waltz in Scene 6, 29 Apr. (*Krasovskaya*, 343).
A Neapolitan Dance (Ivanov), 29 July (*Krasovskaya*, 343).
La Vivandière (Saint-Léon), the role of Hans, 18 Nov. (*Krasovskaya*, 344).
La Fille mal gardée (Dauberval), the role of Colin (*Krasovskaya*, 344), 14 Oct.?
Armide (Perrot), the role of Adrast (*Krasovskaya*, 344), from 2 Oct.?
Marcobomba (Perrot), the role of Verra (*Krasovskaya*, 344).
A Regency Marriage (Petipa), the role of Marquis Bierneff (*Krasovskaya*, 344); a tarantella (*Pleshcheyev*, 183), 18 Dec.

1859

The Parisian Market (Petipa), role of Brighella, 3 May (*Krasovskaya*, 344).
Jovita, ou les Boucaniers mexicains (Saint-Léon, after Mazilier), role of Don Alvaro, 13 Sept. (*Krasovskaya*, 344).
Saltarello (Saint-Léon), Pipers' Dance, 8 Oct. (*Krasovskaya*, 344).
Gazelda (Perrot), role of Karl, 29 Nov. (*Krasovskaya*, 344).

1860

Pâquerette (Saint-Léon), part unspecified, 20 Jan. (*Pleshcheyev*, 190).
The Blue Dahlia (Petipa), part unspecified, 12 Apr. (*Pleshcheyev*, 190).

1862

Météora (Saint-Léon), part unspecified, 19 Aug. (news *Severnaya pchela*, 19 Aug.).
Faust (Perrot), part unspecified, 16 Sept. (news *Severnaya pchela*, 16 Sept.).
The Pearl of Seville (Saint-Léon), leader of the gypsy band (*Pleshcheyev*, 194), 27 Sept. (news *Severnaya pchela*, 27 Sept.).

1864

Fiammetta (Saint-Léon), the role of Sternholdt (*Krasovskaya*, 347), 13 Feb. (*Pleshcheyev*, 197).
An Artist's Dream (Perrot), role of Alvarez (*Pleshcheyev*, 197), 29 Feb. (St Petersburg, Historical Archive 497.18.648).

The Pharaoh's Daughter (Petipa), role of Taor, 11 Oct. (*Pleshcheyev*, 197).
The Little Humpbacked Horse (Saint-Léon), Russian Dance (Act I), Urals Dance (Act III), 3 Dec. (*Krasovskaya*, 346).

1865

Fiammetta (Saint-Léon), 'new scene with dances', 28 Sept. (*Pleshcheyev*, 199).

1866

Théolinde (Saint-Léon), *grand pas mixte* (*Pleshcheyev*, 200), 16 Jan. (news *Golos*, 16 Jan.).
Florida (Petipa), the role of Ernest (*Krasovskaya*, 347), 20 Jan.? (news *Golos*, 22 Jan.).
Le Carnaval de Venise (*Pleshcheyev*, 201), 24 Apr.? (news *Golos*, 24 Apr.).
Esmeralda (Perrot), Act I, part unspecified, 24 Apr. (news *Golos*, 24 Apr.).
La Péri (Coralli), Act I, part unspecified, 21 Aug. (news *Golos*, 21 Aug.).
Satanilla [Le Diable amoureux] (Mazilier), the role of Fabio (*Krasovskaya*, 348), 18 Oct. (*Pleshcheyev*, 202).
The Golden Fish (Saint-Léon), 1st part, role of Petro, 8 Nov. (*Pleshcheyev*, 202).
A divertissement, an American fantasia, 17 Nov. (*Krasovskaya*, 346).

1867

Faust (Petipa), the role of Faust (*Krasovskaya*, 347), 8 Jan.?
Météora (Saint-Léon), the role of John Barker (*Krasovskaya*, 347), 17 Jan.?
La Péri (Coralli), the role of Akhmeta (*Krasovskaya*, 348), 22 Jan.
The Wilful Wife [Le Diable à quatre] (Perrot, after Mazilier), the role of the Count (*Krasovskaya*, 348), 9 Feb.
Esmeralda (Perrot), a new part?, 20 Apr. (news *Golos*, 20 Apr.).
The Naiad and the Fisherman (Perrot), part unspecified, 10 Sept. (news *Golos*, 10 Sept.).
The Golden Fish (Saint-Léon), the role of Petro (*Krasovskaya*, 347), 26 Sept.

1868

Corsaire (Mazilier), part unspecified, 25 Jan. (news *Golos*, 25 Jan.).
Giselle (Coralli), part unspecified, 5 Apr. (news *Golos*, 5 Apr.).
The Slave (Petipa), part unspecified (this work was apparently a *pas de quatre*, an entry in a larger divertissement), 27 Apr. (Moscow, Central State Archive of Literature and Art, *fond* 1945.1.1, fo. 3).
Le Roi Candaule (Petipa), the role of Gyges (*Krasovskaya*, 347), 17 Oct.

1869

The Lily (Saint-Léon), son of the Chinese gardener (*Golos*, 23 Oct. 1869, pp. 1–2), *grand pas* (*Pleshcheyev*, 213–14), 21 Oct.

1871

The Two Stars (Petipa), the role of Endymion (*Krasovskaya*, 348), 31 Jan.
Don Quixote (Petipa), the role of Basilio (*Krasovskaya*, 348), 9 Nov.

1872

Hamlet, opera by Ambroise Thomas (Petipa), a hunter in the divertissement, 'Fête du printemps' (*TMB 205*, no. 628), 14 Oct.? (*MarPet*, 386).
Camargo (Petipa), the role of Count de Melenne (*Krasovskaya*, 348), 17 Dec.

1874

The Butterfly (Petipa), the role of Prince Jalma, 6 Jan. (libretto).
Tannhäuser, opera by Richard Wagner (Petipa), a shepherd in the bacchanale (*TMB 205*, no. 673), 13 Dec.? (*MarPet*, 386).

1875

The Bandits (Petipa), the role of Señor Flaminio Mendoza, 26 Jan. (libretto).

1876

The Adventures of Peleus (Petipa), the role of King Acastus, the role of the Genie of the Darkness (*Krasovskaya*, 348), the role of Satan (in the scene of Act III, 'The Divinities of Hell') (*TMB 205*, no. 423), 11 Jan.

1877

La Bayadère (Petipa), the role of Solor (*Krasovskaya*, 347), 23 Jan.

1878

Roxana (Petipa), the role of Yanko, 'friend of the hero Marko' (*Krasovskaya*, 348), 29 Jan. NB: the libretto lists Yanko as the hero, and Marko as one of four of his friends.

1879

The Daughter of the Snows (Petipa), Norwegian Wedding Dance, 7 Jan. (*Pleshcheyev*, 238–9).
Frizak the Barber (Petipa), the Polka musketeer (Moscow, Central State Archive of Literature and Art, *fond* 1657.3.132), 11 Mar. (*MarPet*, 381).
Mlada (Petipa), Gypsy Dance, 2 Dec. (*Peterburgskaya gazeta*, 4 Dec. 1897, p. 3).

1880

Graziella (Saint-Léon), 'La Sicilienne', 2 Nov. (*Pleshcheyev*, 244).
Corsaire (Mazilier), the role of Conrad (*Krasovskaya*, 349), 30 Nov.

1881

Zoraya (Petipa), the role of Ali-ben-Tamarat (*Krasovskaya*, 348), 1 Feb.

1882

Pâquerette (Saint-Léon), the role of Bridoux (*Krasovskaya*, 348), 10 Jan.

1883

Night and Day (Petipa), Little Russian Dance, 18 May (*TMB 205*, no. 316).

1884

La Bayadère (Petipa), the role of the Rajah, 16 Sept. (*Novosti i birzhevaya gazeta*, 18 Sept. 1884, p. 3).

1885

The Pharaoh's Daughter (Petipa), the role of the Pharaoh, 10 Nov. (*Peterburgskaya gazeta*, 12 Nov. 1885, p. 3).

1886

The Wilful Wife [Le Diable à quatre], the role of the husband, 26 Jan. (*Peterburgskaya gazeta*, 28 Jan. 1886, p. 3).
The King's Command (Petipa), the role of Milon (*Krasovskaya*, 348), 14 Feb.

1888

Caterina (Perrot), the role of the duke (*Krasovskaya*, 348), 25 Sept.?

1891

'Una chica andalusa', 30 July (*Novoe vremya*, 1 Aug. 1891, p. 3).

1893

A divertissement, Spanish Dance, 3 Jan. (*Krasovskaya*, 350).

1899

The *polka champêtre* in Jean Petipa's *Marcobomba* (*Ezhegodnik Imperatorskikh Teatrov*, 1899/1900, 99–100).

1900

The Students of Dupré (Petipa), the role of Comte de Montagnac, 14 Feb. (*Peterburgskaya gazeta*, 16 Feb. 1900, p. 3).

In addition, Ivanov mentions in his memoirs, without citing a date, that he performed the parts of Claude Frollo in *Esmeralda*, Valentine in *Faust*, and Coppélius in *Coppélia*.

Appendix B

THE COMPOSITIONS OF LEV IVANOV

(Sources of information are provided for the more obscure works.)

I Ballets (including joint projects)

The Enchanted Forest, 24 Mar. 1887, Imperial Theatre School, St Petersburg.
—— Maryinsky Theatre, 3 May 1887.
The Tulip of Haarlem, 4 Nov. 1887, Maryinsky Theatre.
The Beauty of Seville, 29 July 1888, Krasnoe Selo.
Cupid's Pranks, 24 July 1890, Krasnoe Selo.
—— Maryinsky Theatre, 11 Nov. 1890.
The Boatmen's Festival, 26 July 1891, Krasnoe Selo.
The Nutcracker, 6 Dec. 1892, Maryinsky Theatre.
The Magic Flute, 10 Mar. 1893, Imperial Theatre School, St Petersburg.
—— Maryinsky Theatre, 11 Apr. 1893.
Zolushka (Cinderella) Act II, 5 Dec. 1893, Maryinsky Theatre.
Swan Lake Act I, Scene 2, 17 Feb. 1894, Maryinsky Theatre.
Flora's Awakening, 28 July 1894, Peterhof (Ivanov assisted with the scenario).
—— Maryinsky Theatre, 8 Jan. 1895.
Swan Lake Act I, Scene 2 and Act III, 15 Jan. 1895, Maryinsky Theatre.
Acis and Galatea, 21 Jan. 1896, Maryinsky Theatre.
The Mikado's Daughter, 9 Nov. 1897, Maryinsky Theatre.
An Egyptian Night, 1901, Peterhof (produced but not performed).
Sylvia (with Pavel Gerdt), 2 Dec. 1901, Maryinsky Theatre.

II Revivals (of Complete Ballets)

The Nymphs and the Satyr (Saint-Léon), 8 July 1887 (?), Krasnoe Selo (*Peterburgskii listok*, 22 June 1887, p. 3).
Fiammetta (Saint-Léon), 6 Dec. 1887, Maryinsky Theatre (with Petipa and

Cecchetti) (*MarPet*, 383; *Peterburgskii listok*, 6 Dec. 1887, p. 4, attributes the revival to Petipa alone).

Graziella (Saint-Léon), 27 July 1890, Krasnoe Selo (*Peterburgskii listok*, 26 July 1890, p. 3).

The Parisian Market (Petipa), 6 July 1892, Krasnoe Selo (*Novoe vremya*, 8 July 1892, p. 4).

Fiammetta (Saint-Léon), 27 Dec. 1892, Moscow, Bolshoy Theatre (benefit performance of Lydia Geiten).

The Travelling Dancer (Paul Taglioni/Petipa), 23 July 1893, Krasnoe Selo (*Novoe vremya*, 26 July 1893, p. 3).

The Offerings to Cupid [Les Offrandes à l'Amour] (Petipa), 26 Sept. 1893, Maryinsky Theatre.

La Fille mal gardée (Dauberval), 25 Sept. 1894, Alexandrinsky Theatre.

The Parisian Market (Petipa), Warsaw, 1897 (Memoirs).

The Magic Flute (Ivanov), Warsaw, 1897 (Memoirs).

The Halt of the Cavalry (Petipa), Warsaw, 1897 (Memoirs).

Zolushka (Petipa/Ivanov/Cecchetti), 1 Sept. 1898, Moscow, Bolshoy Theatre.

Marcobomba (Jean Petipa), 5 Dec. 1899, Maryinsky Theatre.

Zolushka Act II (Petipa and Ivanov), 23 Jan. 1900, Maryinsky Theatre.

Graziella (Saint-Léon), 12 Apr. 1900, Maryinsky Theatre.

Camargo (Petipa), 28 Jan. 1901 (farewell benefit of Pierina Legnani), Maryinsky Theatre.

Markitanka [La Vivandière] (Saint-Léon), 4 Feb. 1901, Maryinsky Theatre (25th anniversary benefit of Marie Petipa).

La Fille mal gardée (Dauberval), 8 Apr. 1901 (attributed to Petipa and Ivanov in *Ezhegodnik Imperatorskikh Teatrov*, 1900/1, 193).

III Separate Dances

A Neapolitan Dance, 29 July 1858, St Petersburg, Kamenny Ostrov Theatre (*Krasovskaya*, 343).

A classical *pas de deux* (to music by Schumann), 9 July 1886, Krasnoe Selo (*Pleshcheyev*, 287).

Grand ballabile classique, 5 July 1889, Krasnoe Selo (*Novoe vremya*, 7 July 1889, p. 3).

Czardas (*Chardache*), for five couples, to music by Drigo, 28 July 1889, Krasnoe Selo (*Novoe vremya*, 26 July 1889, p. 3).

Grand pas des voiles to music by Pugni, 6 Aug. 1889, Krasnoe Selo (*Peterburgskaya gazeta*, 6 Aug. 1889, p. 3).

Polonaise, *pas hongroise*, and '*La danse des heures*', 4 July 1900, Krasnoe Selo (*Novosti i birzhevaya gazeta*, 6 July 1900, p. 3).

Pas des voiles, '*Nymphes et Satyre, scène dansante*', 17 July 1900, Krasnoe Selo (*Novosti i birzhevaya gazeta*, 19 July 1900, p. 3).

Czardas to Liszt's Second Hungarian Rhapsody, added to Saint-Léon's *The Little Humpbacked Horse*, 11 Oct. 1900, Maryinsky Theatre (various newspaper reports).

iv Dances in Operas

La Muette de Portici (Auber), the bolero, 3 Dec. 1857, St Petersburg Bolshoy Theatre (*Krasovskaya*, 343).

La Juive (Halévy), 1859 (*Krasovskaya*, 55).

Mazepa (Tchaikovsky), 1884 (*Krasovskaya*, 57).

Evgenii Onegin (Tchaikovsky), 1884 (*Krasovskaya*, 56).

Der Freischütz (Weber), 1885 (*Krasovskaya*, 55).

The Merchant Kalashnikov (Rubinstein), 1889 (*Krasovskaya*, 55).

La Traviata (Verdi), 1884 (*Krasovskaya*, 55).

The Enchantress (Tchaikovsky), 1887 (*Krasovskaya*, 55).

Guillaume Tell (Rossini), 1888 (*Krasovskaya*, 55).

Goryusha (Rubinstein), 1889, Dance of the Serf Peasants (*Krasovskaya*, 56).

Judith (Serov), 1889 (*Krasovskaya*, 55).

L'Africaine (Meyerbeer), 1890 (*Krasovskaya*, 55).

Prince Igor (Borodin), 23 Oct. 1890, Maryinsky Theatre.

Romeo and Juliet (Gounod), 11 Feb. 1891, Maryinsky Theatre.

The Queen of Spades (Tchaikovsky), 4 Nov. 1891, Moscow Bolshoy Theatre ('The dances composed by the chief balletmaster of the St Petersburg ballet troupe M. I. Petipa were staged by the Petersburg second balletmaster L. I. Ivanov, who was specially dispatched to Moscow for this purpose' (*Ezhegodnik Imperatorskikh Teatrov*, 1891/2, 225)).

Mlada (Rimsky-Korsakov), 20 Oct. 1892 (with Enrico Cecchetti), Maryinsky Theatre.

Evgenii Onegin (Tchaikovsky), Russian Dance in Act I, 27 Oct. 1892, Maryinsky Theatre.

Tannhäuser (Wagner), 15 Oct. 1893, Maryinsky Theatre ('Groupings and dances of Act I of the opera, composed by the chief balletmaster M. I. Petipa, were newly staged by the second balletmaster L. Ivanov' (*Ezhegodnik Imperatorskikh Teatrov*, 1893/4, 204)).

Djamileh (Bizet), 23 Nov. 1893, Maryinsky Theatre.

May Night (Rimsky-Korsakov), 28 Sept. 1894, Maryinsky Theatre.

Dubrovsky (Nápravník), Russian Dance, 3 Jan. 1895, Maryinsky Theatre.

Christmas Eve (Rimsky-Korsakov), 28 Nov. 1895, Maryinsky Theatre.

Samson and Delilah (Saint-Saëns), 19 Nov. 1896, Maryinsky Theatre.

The Merry Wives of Windsor (Nicolai), 3 Feb. 1897, Maryinsky Theatre.

Esclarmonde (Massenet), for a special performance by Sybil Sanderson, 21 Feb. 1897, Maryinsky Theatre.

The Oprichnik (Tchaikovsky), 2 Sept. 1897, Maryinsky Theatre.

The Demon (Rubinstein), Warsaw, 1897 (Memoirs).
The Tales of Hoffmann (Offenbach), 1899 (*Krasovskaya*, 55).
Carmen (Bizet), 1901 (*Krasovskaya*, 55).

v Dances in Other Theatre Works

Dances for a masquerade (with Marie Mariusovna Petipa), Feb. 1891? (*Peterburgskaya gazeta*, 24 Feb. 1891, p. 4).
Interpolated ballet and other dances in Shakhovskoy's play 'Batyushkin's Daughter, or He Has Met His Match', 27 Jan. 1894, benefit of the actress Maria Gavrilovna Savina (*Ezhegodnik Imperatorskikh Teatrov*, 1893/4, 17).
Dances in Shakespeare's *A Midsummer Night's Dream*, Moscow, Bolshoy Theatre, 27 Oct. 1889 (Service Record, affiche).

vi Music

1. Mazurka, 'Pétulance'. Performed 8 Apr. 1858 at the Théâtre-Cirque in St Petersburg by Vera Lyadova and Alexey Bogdanov (*Krasovskaya*, 343).
2. Hymn in honour of King Otto I of Greece (orchestrated by E. A. Klamrot). Performed [summer] 1867 in the Theatre at Krasnoe Selo (*Krasovskaya*, 347).
3. 'Persian March' for orchestra. Performed at the benefit performance of Pavel Gerdt on 12 Jan. 1875 (which was also the début of Marie Mariusovna Petipa): 'In one of the intervals the orchestra will perform the "Persian March" by the dancer L. Ivanov for the first time' (*Novoe vremya*, 11 Jan. 1875, p. 2).
4. Variation for Evgenia Sokolova for the ballet *The Little Humpbacked Horse*. Performed at the ballerina's benefit performance, Bolshoy Theatre, St Petersburg, 10 Dec. 1878 (*Peterburgskaya gazeta*, 8 Dec. 1878, reported in *Krasovskaya*, 348).

('Affiches of the official theatres also named separate dances to the music of Lev Ivanov. More often these were mazurkas and czardases, but sometimes also classical dances' (*Krasovskaya*, 347–8).)

Appendix C

THE LIBRETTI OF
LEV IVANOV'S BALLETS

—————

A note on translation: to readers a century after their publication, these libretti in the original are florid and redundant in their style, rich in idioms which seem stilted and formal. They been translated below into idiomatic English without detriment to essential meaning.

I *The Enchanted Forest*

The libretto seems never to have been published separately. *Borisoglebsky* (i. 296) provides a synopsis:

THE ENCHANTED FOREST
Fantastic ballet in One Act

The action takes place in Hungary

Valeria, walking with her girlfriends in the forest, caught unawares by a storm, has lost sight of them, and cannot get out of the forest. The storm continues; Valeria falls in a faint.

Little genies and dryads appear on the stage; seeing the sleeping girl, they admire and take delight in her. Valeria awakes, and finding herself surrounded by unusual creatures, takes fright. They calm her and she begs them to lead her out of the forest, but they cannot agree; she weeps in despair.

The genie of the forest appears. He is also delighted with Valeria's beauty, declares his love to her and proposes that she be sovereigness in his realm. She declines, explaining that she has a fiancé whom she loves. The genie, angered by her refusal, declares that she will never see her fiancé again, and will die here; then he makes a gesture, as if to mesmerize her. Valeria steps back and faints.

One of the small genies announces to his sovereign that several mortals are approaching. The genies, dryads, and little genies withdraw.

Several peasant men and women enter, searching for Valeria. Seeing her they call Petrus, who runs on stage and rushes headlong to her. Finding her motionless, he takes fright; but putting his hand to her heart and assuring himself that she is alive, he thanks God. Valeria opens her eyes at Petrus's touch, but still under the spell of what has happened to her, jumps up in fright and runs away, not recognizing Petrus. 'Come to your senses! What's the matter with you? You see it is I, your fiancé!' Only then does Valeria, recognizing him, rush into his embrace. Then she explains what happened to her. After her story, Petrus thinks that everything that happened to her was a dream. Valeria does not believe it. 'You ought to have died— and did not; consequently this was all a dream.' Convinced of the truth of her fiancé's words, Valeria calms down. Rejoicing, all dance a 'czardas'.

THE TULIP OF HAARLEM

Fantastic Ballet in 3 acts and 4 scenes

Composed by L. Ivanov
Performed for the first time on the stage of the Maryinsky
Theatre in St Petersburg on 4 October 1887

St Petersburg
Publication of Eduard Hoppe,
Typographer of the Imperial SPb. Theatres
Voznesensky Prospect, No. 53
1887

Permitted by the censor. SPB, 28 September 1887

Typographer of the Imperial SPb. Theatres
(Eduard Hoppe), Voznes. Pr., No. 53

LIST OF CHARACTERS

Mr Vandersmit, *a former sailor*	Mr Kshesinsky I
Mrs Vandersmit, *his wife*	Miss Legat I
Pieters, *their son, a maritime officer*	Mr Gerdt
Emma, *a young peasant girl, an orphan*	Miss Bessone
Janson, *an old peasant who is giving refuge to Emma*	Mr Stukolkin
Friedland, *a tax farmer, an ominous man*	Mr Geltser
Mariana, *his daughter*	Miss Zhukova
Anders, *son of a rich farmer*	Mr Bekefy
A Gypsy Woman, *with a reputation among the people as a witch*	Miss Zest
Cityfolk, peasant men and women, merchants, servants, etc.	

FANTASTIC CHARACTERS (second act)

The Fairy of the Enchanted Field	Miss Zest
Queen of the Tulips	Miss Bessone
The Living Tulips	Miss Petrova and Miss Vinogradova
A Butterfly	Miss Frolova
Moths	Students of the Imperial Theatre School

The persons listed above took part in the first performance.

In Place of a Foreword

In the seventeenth century, in Holland, not far from the city of Haarlem, there was a small field sown with beautiful tulips. From ancient stories about this field comes a legend. Rumour had it that on nights with a full moon mysterious things happened there. The field would be lit by a bright, unusual light, young women not of this earth would appear; they danced and made merry until the first ray of the rising sun, when everything was instantly quiet and disappeared. The collective mind of the folk added to this that the beautiful women were none other than the tulips sown in the field, and that if some mortal were bold enough to appear among these unearthly visions and abduct one of them as his wife (she would bring wealth and happiness into his house), he must embrace and kiss her, since with this contact all spells would vanish and the unearthly being would become an ordinary mortal.

And in fact, it once happened that a man kidnapped one of the women and lived with her his entire life in wealth and happiness, but as a result the enchantment of the tulip field was lost.

In one of the suburbs of Amsterdam, a retired captain in the maritime service, Vandersmit, lives quietly with his wife. They have won their neighbours' general love and esteem for their goodness and tolerance. They have a son, also a sailor, who has been away four years on a round-the-world journey.

Among the Vandersmits' neighbours is a beautiful young orphan, Emma, who has taken refuge with an old peasant whom she loves's as a father. The peasant men and women of the suburb do not like Emma very much, the men because she is very proud, the women because she is more beautiful than them; this enmity arose still in her childhood. The captain's son, as it were, when as children they played together, often defended her from attacks from the other boys and girls. As a result, a powerful love grew in her young heart for her defender. But it pleased fate to separate them for a long time; despite this, the young orphan's love has grown stronger, although she sometimes thinks that the captain's son might have forgotten her in their separation.

On the outskirts of the city, near a tulip field, a gypsy whom the people think is a witch lives in a run-down cottage. She loves Emma very much, protects her, and often defends her from being pursued by other youth. She knows that Emma loves the old sailor's son, since Emma quite often drops in on her to chat.

Captain Vandersmit lives a solitary life, but sometimes has visitors from the city: his friend and fellow farmer Friedland, Friedland's young daughter Marianna, and Anders, a comrade of his son, himself the son of a rich farmer. The captain and the farmer have decided to become related by the marriage of their children as soon as the young sailor returns from his journey.

Finally the day comes with news of his return. The action of the ballet commences on this day.

ACT I

The stage represents a suburb of Amsterdam. To the spectator's left is Vandersmit's house; to the right a cottage—the dwelling of the orphan Emma; a canal flows in the depth of the stage; in the distance the city itself is seen.

Scene 1

At the rise of the curtain peasant men and women, preparing for a celebration, are decorating the captain's house with flowers and garlands. The captain's wife comes out of the house, admires their work, is pleased with it and invites all to have fun at the celebration. The peasant men are delighted with the invitation, thank her and gradually disperse.

Scene 2

Emma appears with her benefactor Janson; she is carrying a basket; they are returning from the market. Emma suggests that the old man go into the cottage and have a rest while she prepares breakfast; he exits.

Seeing Emma, several peasant girls run up to her with the news of the captain's son's imminent return. Emma gets flustered and blushes. Noticing this, the peasant girls begin to tease her; their mocking drives the poor orphan to tears.

Scene 3

Hearing the girls hurting Emma's feelings, Janson comes out of the cottage, brandishes his crutch at them and drives them away. Laughing, they disperse. When they are gone he calms Emma; she seats him on a bench by the cottage, where the old man, warmed by the sun, soon falls asleep, leaning on his crutch.

Alone, Emma yields to her favourite dream. She will soon see her beloved! Her heart pounds with joy, then sorrowful thoughts spread over her like a cloud: what if he has quite forgotten her and does not pay her the least attention? she asks herself. This thought torments her ever more obsessively. Sobbing, she falls to the ground.

Scene 4

Just then her protector, the gypsy, enters. Emma throws her arms around the gypsy's neck, and sobbing, tells of her woe. The gypsy consoles her and gives her a tulip, explaining that it is a talisman whereby she will win the young sailor's heart, a task made all the easier in that she has grown into a truly beautiful woman during his absence. Emma becomes completely calm. She embraces the gypsy joyfully and thanks her, then runs over to Janson, who has been asleep the whole time, helps him up, and leads him into the cottage. The gypsy follows them.

Scene 5

The tax farmer, his daughter, and the young Anders come on stage, walk up to the captain's house, call him and report that the boat bringing Pieters is close at hand.

Everyone in the house comes out, excited.

Scene 6

The stage gradually fills with guests, and peasants dressed for the celebration, with bouquets and various gifts.

The boat is in sight, and everyone looks to the side of the canal whence it appears. It finally makes the shore, and Pieters jumps onto the bank. A touching scene ensues. His father and mother, tears of joy in their eyes, incessantly embrace and kiss their beloved son. After such a long separation they cannot gaze at him enough. The peasant men wave their hats, the women their kerchiefs. General rejoicing. When the first ardour of reunion has somewhat cooled, the young sailor makes his way through the crowd, shaking hands with some, though others he barely recognizes, and walking up to Emma stops, smitten by her beauty. Blushing, she curtsies to him. 'Who is this beautiful woman?' Pieters asks his father. 'What, you really do not recognize the friend you played with as a child?', the captain responds. 'Emma, is it really you?' Pieters cries, taking her by the hand, leading her to the front of the stage, and continuing, 'How you have grown, Emma! How pretty you have become! . . . You have become a beautiful woman!' . . . Meanwhile the captain tends to the celebration, and arranges the peasant men and women who have gathered to present gifts to his son.

Scene 7

Dances begin: a *pas des offrandes* and a *pas d'action*.

The latter begins when Emma presents Pieters not a gift, but the tulip. Pieters accepts it joyfully. During the dances he whispers to Emma of his ardent, passionate love. She seems to respond coolly, but in her heart she harbours endless delight. Anders and Marianna also take part in the dances. They are satisfied and happy that, unnoticed by the others, they can express their love for one another with a glance, the press of a hand, and even a fleeting stolen kiss. The old people, sitting at the table, are talking at this time, drinking wine and watching the youth make merry. Evening comes, and the dances cease.

Scene 8

The captain, noticing Pieters's strong interest in Emma and fearing that this could spoil his coveted goal, announces, in order to break off his son's attraction immediately, his decision to marry his son to Marianna. The guests are overjoyed at this news, and congratulate the captain. But into what despair the announcement casts the plans of Pieters, Anders, and Marianna! Emma is astounded most of all: she pales, and her body trembles. The gypsy rushes to her help. 'Be calm, dear friend,' she says, 'I promised to settle your fate, and you will be happy. Pieters will be yours forever; run to my cottage and wait for me there!' Emma obeys, and rushes out, still despairing. Pieters, meanwhile, asks his father not to force him to marry, for he does not love Marianna. His father insists, and says that they can consider the question later; now they must bring the feasting to an end. He invites his honoured guests into his house. The peasant men and women thank their host and disperse to their homes. The guests follow Vandersmit into the house, including Marianna and Anders—who are sad. Pieters remains alone on stage.

Scene 9

Despairing, Pieters does not know where events will lead. He sits down, ponders his situation, then takes the little flower, kisses it and says, 'O my dear Emma! You and no other will be my wife! I swear it on this tulip! . . .' He cannot remain calm. He wants to see her—without fail, immediately. He goes to the orphan's cottage, but as he approaches it the gypsy comes out.

Scene 10

Pieters stops in amazement and asks who she is. 'I protect the one you love!' she answers. 'I ask you,' Pieters entreats, 'to tell her that I want to see her and to speak to her!' 'That is impossible!' 'Why?' 'Because she is not here, she has gone far away!' 'Has she really run away?!' exclaims Pieters, despairing. It is quiet for a time. 'Are you really bold and courageous enough', the gypsy finally asks him, 'to do what I suggest?' 'Yes,' declares the young sailor. 'Then hear me well! You know the enchanted tulip field where marvellous girls not of this earth come at night? Your beloved is one of those girls! If you really want to possess her, you must go there at once; night is falling, she is there. I will help you abduct her. But you must seize her and press a kiss on her shoulder. Only then will the spell disappear, and she will become a mortal such as yourself; only then can she be your wife!' 'I am prepared for anything, only let Emma be mine!' Pieters exclaims, with pathos. 'Then let us go quickly!' the gypsy says. They run out.

The curtain falls.

ACT II

The stage represents a field sown with beautiful tulips. To the left the gypsy's dwelling—a cottage half in ruins. It is night. The moon now hides in the clouds, now glances out.

Scene 1

The fog which covers the stage gradually begins to disperse. In the distance two shadows are seen: the gypsy leading Pieters to meet his beloved. At last the fog disperses, the heavens are clear, and the moon emits a magic light. 'Stop, we have arrived!' the gypsy declares. 'Here you will see Emma, but have patience, you must hide in my cottage so as not to frighten the fairies!' 'No, I will not leave until I see my beloved,' Pieters answers fervently, 'You want to deceive me, but you will not succeed!' At these words the gypsy is transformed into an enchanting woman—her true form as the fairy protectress of the field—and waving her magic wand, forces Pieters to withdraw into the cottage. He would resist, but a supernatural force compels him. He falls onto a rock near the cottage.

The fairy proceeds through the field, magic wand in hand; as she waves it, beautiful women in the guise of tulips emerge from the field. Moths circle around them. Illuminated by an unusually bright light, they give themselves over to games and dances. Among them Emma appears as the most beautiful tulip—she is their queen. Seeing Pieters lying on a stone, she delightedly thanks the fairy, then rushes to him and taps him on the shoulder. He jumps up in astonishment, as if coming to his senses, and looks around. The girls rush off in a fright. The queen of the flowers remains alone with Pieters.

Scene 2

A love scene and dances ensue. Pieters declares that he is happy to see her again, that he loves her passionately, and that she must be his. The queen of the flowers answers that she also loves him, but cannot be his because she is not a mortal, and because he will belong to another. Pieters assures her that no one but her is to be his wife; he would embrace her to press his kiss, but his attempts are in vain. The queen of the flowers runs off and vanishes behind a tree. Pieters searches for her. Suddenly she appears among the trees. Pieters rushes to her but several moths bar his way. Repulsing them, he is near exhaustion. At the fairy's command, the butterflies disperse. The enchanted girls appear again and form various groupings (*grand pas des fleurs*). During the dances Pieters tries to find the right moment for a kiss, but the enchanted maidens prevent him.

Scene 3

Finally, Pieters manages to catch the queen of the flowers and kiss her. The spell instantly falls away; in his embrace he finds not a beautiful magic flower but Emma herself, his beloved. The maidens retreat in horror. Just then the first ray of the rising sun comes over the horizon. The maidens, sad and weeping over the loss of their girlfriend, hide in the bowers. With an imperious gesture the fairy of the field commands Pieters to flee this place with his beloved.

The curtain falls.

ACT III
Tableau I

The stage represents a room in Vandersmit's house, with a large window in the middle and two doors along the sides.

Scene 1

At the rise of the curtain Anders and Marianna enter from different sides. Seizing the moment, they discuss how to convince her father to change his plan with the captain, and be permitted to marry each other.

Marianna is sad, and to Anders's question, 'What has happened?' responds that she can never belong to him because her father and Vandersmit have decided to marry her to Pieters at all costs. She weeps. Consoling her, Anders says that they were hoping for a happy outcome, since Pieters does not love her and will not agree to the marriage. Marianna, somewhat calmed by Anders's words, extends her hand to him; Anders kisses it. But the noise of opening doors forces them to rush off to the sides.

Scene 2

Vandersmit enters with his wife and Friedland.

The captain calls for Pieters, to announce his firm decision that he be wed to Marianna. With her glances his wife entreats the captain not to do this, but he is inflexible; gnashing her teeth, she goes to find Pieters.

Scene 3

'Why are you so pale? What is the matter?' father asks son. 'Nothing, father!'

Pieters responds. 'I called you to declare my absolute wish that you marry Marianna, the daughter of my esteemed friend Friedland, as soon as possible!' 'Forgive me, father, but I cannot! . . .' 'But I wish it! . . . and it shall be!' the captain exclaims angrily. 'Have mercy on me, father!' Pieters begs. 'I cannot marry Marianna because I already love another!' 'What? Who is this other?' 'You will recognize her immediately!' Pieters runs to the door on the right side, and leads in Emma. Behind them old Janson appears; he has followed everything that has taken place. Emma, agitated, stops at the front of the stage.

Vandersmit gets even angrier with the poor orphan standing before him. 'No, no! Never will I agree to such an uneven match!' he cries. At that point Emma, lifting her head proudly, turns to him: 'O captain, how callous you are! You are rending our loving hearts with your cruelty! I have loved Pieters since childhood, and I love him now even more! I prefer death to eternal separation with him! You will answer for me to God!' . . . 'Yes, death is better!' Pieters exclaims, 'and we shall die together!' They rush into each other's embrace, then to the window and are about to throw themselves out of it. All are horrified. The captain's wife and Marianna are flustered to the point of helplessness. In fright they cover their faces with their hands. But the others come to their senses and rush to stop the unfortunates from carrying out their plan. Emma falls unconscious into her beloved's arms. Janson rushes to the captain, kneels, and begs him to show mercy to his only treasure.

The catastrophe has hardly struck Vandersmit before he agrees to the marriage of Pieters and Emma. All regain their composure, and fright gives way to joy and contentment. Only Friedland looks perplexed and morose. Anders, taking advantage of the moment, tells him of his profound love for Marianna and asks for her hand. Marianna casts entreating looks at her father.

The latter agrees.

'So, isn't that beautiful!' exclaims the captain, slapping his old friend on the shoulder, 'We shall celebrate two weddings in one day! Isn't that so, old chap?' 'Of course it's so!' the latter answers, 'But today, in order to celebrate this fine day, I am inviting you to my place—a fair is just beginning!'

All are happy and are having a good time.

Tableau II

The stage represents a square in Amsterdam during the fair.

To the right of the public, Friedland's house, with a terrace coming out onto the square.

Around the stage several tents and little wooden stalls are scattered with various kinds of wares.

Scene 1

The fair is in full swing. People crowd around the stalls. Some are buying, others only looking. Activity and noise.

Scene 2

Then two carriages appear, bringing Friedland with his daughter and Anders, and the Vandersmits with Pieters and Emma. They make their way to the house, where servants await them. Finally they reach it, go out on the terrace, and admire the dances of the merry crowd. A divertissement of national dances.

THE END

III *Cupid's Prank*

CUPID'S PRANK

Anacreontic ballet, in one act

By L. Ivanov

Music by A. Friedmann

Presented for the 1st time 11 November 1890

St Petersburg

Publication of the Typographer of the IMPERIAL SPB. Theatres
(Department of Crown Domains)

1890

Permitted by the censor. St Petersburg, 8 November 1890

Typogr. of the Imper. SPB Theatr. (Dept. of Crown Domains),
Mokhovaya, 40

DRAMATIS PERSONAE:

Diana	Miss Johanson
Venus	Miss Petipa
Cupid	Miss Anderson
A nymph, *favourite of Diana*	Miss Nikitina
Endymion	Mr Gerdt
Morpheus	Mr Belov

Nymphs and serving women of Diana.

DANCES AND MIMED SCENES:

1. The Return from the hunt. *Nymphs*: Nikitina, Johanson, Kulichevskaya, Rykhlyakova, Kshesinskaya II, Preobrazhenskaya, Noskova, Ogoleit III, Labunskaya, Slantsova, Andreyeva, Nikolaeva, Ogoleit II, Savitskaya, Kuskova, Egorova II, Vishnevskaya II, Skorsyuk, Lits, Shchedrina, Kshesinskaya I, Rubtsov, Aistova, Sheberg, Onegina II, Ryabova, Dorina, Stepanova III, Radina, Stepanova IV.

Servants of Diana: Vsevolodskaya, Pavlova, Legat III, Alexandrova, Levenson II, Golubina, Kunitskaya, Levenson I, Kasatkina, Golovkina, Verzhinskaya, and Kuzmina II.

2. The Appearance of Venus and Cupid: Miss Petipa and Miss Anderson.

3. Cupid's Amusements: Miss Anderson.

4. Endymion's passion: Miss Nikitina, Miss Johanson, Miss Anderson, and Mr Gerdt.

5. Scene of seduction: Miss Nikitina, Miss Anderson, and Mr Gerdt.

6. Diana's jealousy and Cupid's punishment: Miss Nikitina, Miss Petipa, Miss Johanson, Miss Anderson, and Mr Gerdt.

7. Dances of the nymphs.
8. Variations: Miss Kulichevskaya, Johanson, Petipa, Anderson, and Nikitina.
9. Finale: All participants.

Conductor: Mr Kannegisser

The stage represents a forest of palm trees. Before the curtain rises horns are heard in the distance announcing Diana's return from the hunt, her favourite amusement.

Scene 1

Several nymphs of Diana's retinue enter, returning from the hunt to their favourite resting place. They were ordered to build two couches—one for Diana, one for her favourite—and to grace them with flowers and garlands.

Scene 2

Diana appears with her friend, a nymph. Fatigued from the hunt, she commands that cooling drinks be served and then gives herself up to repose, as do the others, arranging themselves in various groupings. Weariness after the hunt, dances and games forces the nymphs quickly to sleep. Morpheus appears, and wafting sleep over them, withdraws.

Scene 3

Venus approaches, leading mischievous Cupid by the hand; the grouping of charming, sleeping nymphs compels her to stop and admire them. Cupid also takes delight in the slumbering beauties. Wishing not to disturb the goddess's dreams, Venus explains to Cupid that Diana and her nymphs are sleeping after the hunt, and leads Cupid away, But Cupid begins to act capriciously and to resist, begging to be left there for a time, that he might admire them. At first Venus refuses, then yielding to his affectionate and pressing entreaties, she finally agrees but warns him against staying too long, and most of all against playing tricks, as he always does. Delighted that his request is granted, Cupid remains with the sleeping nymphs; but hardly a moment passes before his mischievous habit overcomes him, and he pinches one of the nymphs, runs up to another and pricks her lightly with an arrow, hiding each time, amused, so as not to be noticed. Suddenly it occurs to him to play a trick on Diana herself, and he is about to do so when he hears hastening footsteps in the distance, runs towards them, and sees Endymion walking towards his beloved Diana. 'Ah! I'll play a trick on him!' thinks Cupid in delight, and hides behind a tree, anxious to amuse himself with a prank he has just conceived.

Scene 4

Endymion strides in, but not knowing where Diana is resting among the sleeping women, stops in bewilderment. He walks from nymph to nymph, hunting for his beloved. Just as he approaches Diana's favourite, Cupid from behind a tree shoots an arrow that strikes him in the heart. Endymion is instantly enamoured of the nymph, takes her by the hand and begins to declare his passionate love, then kneels. The nymph, awakened, at first takes fright, is indignant at Endymion and aston-

ished at his instant love, but then mischievous Cupid, running up to the nymph unnoticed, pricks her lightly in the heart with an arrow, compelling her to fall in love
with Endymion. Unable to control herself, aroused by passion, the nymph is about
to rush to Endymion's embrace. Noticing Diana, who has just awakened, she stops.
Perceiving her beloved, Diana greets him with delight and at the same moment
orders her favourite to awaken the sleeping nymphs. Having noticed Endymion's
coolness towards her, Diana tries to attract him with caresses and tenderness. Fail-
ing in this, she would choose a suitable moment to talk to him alone, and hoping to
find an appropriate place she invites all into the glade, where one can walk and sport
a bit. Endymion is forced to follow.

Scene 5

Cupid remains in the forest hidden behind a tree, as too the nymph in frightful woe,
possessed by a love she does not understand towards the beloved of Diana, her
protectress and friend. Jealousy and gratitude are battling within her, and she resolves to conquer her love, to flee. Observing her intention, Cupid approaches her,
counsels her to stay, and promises his patronage in a new and happy love. Uncertain, the nymph stops. Cupid, noticing Endymion walking in the distance, hides
behind a tree.

Scene 6

Having seized the moment to abandon Diana, Endymion is returning to the nymph
he loves, to explain and declare his passion, and to assure her that he has fallen out of
love with Diana and will not return to her. At first the nymph wavers, choosing not
to respond to his love, but Cupid perforce compels her, and unable to restrain her
passion any longer, she rushes into Endymion's embrace.

Scene 7

Just then Diana, having observed during games her beloved's absence, quickly
exits with the nymphs. Seeing Endymion holding her girlfriend in his arms, she
reproaches the nymph in a burst of jealousy, repulsing her angrily. Suddenly Diana,
noticing Cupid glancing out from his ambush, understands what has happened and
commands the nymphs to bring him to her. Knowing that he is to blame for her unhappiness, of which Endymion persuades her still more when he relates how love
was awakened in him, Diana orders the nymphs to punish Cupid. The latter, sobbing, rushes to Diana, kneels and begs her to forgive him just this once; Diana is im-
placable and repeats the order to her nymphs.

Scene 8

Venus, astonished at Cupid's long absence and hunting for him, comes back to
where she left him. Having watched the latest scene and realizing that Cupid's serious prank had forced Diana to punish him without mercy, she hastens to his rescue.
Seeing Venus, Diana goes to meet her and relates Cupid's prank, impossible to forgive. Venus calls Cupid, takes away his bow and arrow, and commands him to unite
Diana with Endymion again. Cupid obeys. The nymph, recognizing that Cupid's

prank nearly forced her to commit an imprudent deed, kneels, begging Diana's forgiveness; the latter, delighted that Endymion is returned to her, joyfully forgives her.

THE NUTCRACKER
(Casse-Noisette)

Ballet-féerie in two acts and three scenes

Scenario by the balletmaseter M. Petipa

Story borrowed from the stories of E. Hoffmann

Dances and production by the balletmaster L. Ivanov
Music by P. I. Tchaikovsky

Decorations: 1st and 3rd scenes by K. M. Ivanov; 2nd scene by the academician M. I. Bocharov. Machinist N. A. Berger

Men's costumes by I. Caffi, women's by E. M. Ofitserova and A. T. Ivanov; women's headwear by A. A. Terman, men's by L. Bruneau. Wigs and coiffures by G. Pedder. Flowers and feathers by E. P. Simonova. Accessories by the sculptor P. P. Kamensky. Metal decorations by M. Inginen. Footwear by A. Levstedt.

Presented for the 1st time: 6 December 1892.
St Petersburg
Typographer of the Imperial Spb. Theatres, Mokhovoaya, No. 40
1892

Permitted by the censor, Spb. 1 December 1892

ACT I
CHARACTERS:

President Silberhaus	Mr Kshesinsky I
His wife	Miss Ogoleit I
Clara, *their daughter*	Student Belinskaya
Fritz, *their son*	Student Stukolkin
Mariana, *the president's niece*	Miss Rubtsova
Drosselmeyer, *Clara's godfather*	Mr Stukolkin
First of the president's relatives	Miss Onegina I
Second of the president's relatives	Miss Onegina II
The Nutcracker	Student Legat
A Footman in the president's house	Mr Lozhkin

Guests of the president and their children; servants of the president.

TO DANCE IN THE FIRST SCENE:

1. *Marche et petit galop des enfants*: boy and girl students of the Imperial Theatre School.

2. *Danse des Incroyables et Merveilleuses*: Petipa I, Petipa II, Tatarinova, Vishnevskaya I, Noskova, Kshesinskaya I, Kuskova, Legat I, Oblakova and Pavlova; Lukyanov, Gillert, Shiryaev, Voronkov I, Solyannikov I, Kshesinsky II, Gorsky, Voronkov II, Tatarinov and Yakovlev.

3. *Danses des poupées mécaniques*: (*a*) A Sutler—Miss Anderson, A Recruit—Mr Litavkin; (*b*) Colombine—Miss Kshesinskaya II [*sic*], Harlequin—Mr Kyaksht.

4. *Polka et la berceuse*: Student Belinskaya and Student Stukolkin.

5. *Danse 'Grossvater'*: Ogoleit I, Tatarinova, Vishnevskaya I, Legat I, Onegina I, Kshesinskaya I, Oblakova, Noskova, Lits, Kuskova, Rubtsova and Pavlova; Kshesinsky I, Stukolkin, Shiryaev, Tatarinov, Solyannikov I, Voronkov I, Kshesinsky II, Voronkov II, Gorsky, Legat II, Yakovlev, Voronkov II, boy and girl students of the Imperial Theatre School.

6. *Bataille des souris avec les soldats de pain d'épice et les soldats de plomb.*

King of the Mice: Student Vasiliev. His retinue: boy students of the Imperial Theatre School. The Mouse King's guard of honour and mouse soldiers: students of the Life Guards Finnish Regiment.

Gingerbread, tin soldiers, dolls, dancers, sentries by their booth, and little rabbits: boy and girl students of the Imperial Theatre School.

TO DANCE IN THE SECOND SCENE:

Valse des flocons de neige: Andreyeva, Ogoleit III, Slantsova, Nikolaeva, Matveyeva I, Parfentieva, Isaeva, Sheberg, Fyodorova III, Rosh, Levenson II, Matveyeva II, Gorskaya, Kasatkina, Niman, Egorova II, Semyonova II, Rykhlyakova II, Tsalison, Peters, Belikhova, Vsevolodskaya, Ryabova, Stepanova II, Fyodorova I, Peshkova, Davydova, Dorina, Picheau I, Stepanova I, Picheau II, Mikhailova II, Golubina, Golovkina, Lobanova, Davydova, Vertinskaya, Urakova, Yakovleva, Natarova II, Serebrovskaya II, Fyodorova III, Erler, Ilyina I, Sadovskaya II, Tivolskaya, Kurbanova, Egorova I, Kunitskaya, Kil, Stepanova III, Ilyina II, Alexandrova II, Sitnikova, Ermolaeva, Kuzmina II, Lavrentieva, Golubeva, and Postolenko.

ACT II

Miss Dell'Era will perform the role of the 'Sugar Plum Fairy'.

CHARACTERS:

Sugar Plum Fairy	Miss Dell'Era
Prince Coqueluche	Mr Gerdt
Clara	Student Belinskaya
Prince Nutcracker	Student Legat
Major-Domo	Student Ivanov

Fairies: of *melodies, flowers, pictures, fruit, dolls, nights, dancers* and *dreams*: girl students of the Imperial Theatre School.

The sisters of Prince Nutcracker, silver soldiers, etc.

The action takes place in the land of sweets.

CONFECTIONS AND SWEETS:

Caramels: Egorova I, Semyonova II and Erler; Biscuits: Artemieva and

Bogdanova; Barley sugar: Serebrovskaya II and Ilyina I; Chocolate: Tivolskaya and Smirnova; Petits-four: Alexeyeva I, Zasedateleva and Onegina I; Nougat: Natarova I and Kil; Peppermints: Kusterer and Matveyeva II; Dragées: Maslova and Mikhailova II; Brioches: Sitnikova and Svirskaya; Pistachios: Savelieva and Zhikhoreva; Macaron: Fyodorova IV and Alexandrova II.

Emerald pages, ruby pages, and moors: boy and girl students of the Imperial Theatre School.

TO DANCE IN THE DIVERTISSEMENT:

1. *Chocolat (Danse espagnole)*: Petipa I, Vertinskaya, Golovkina, Lobanova, Golubeva, Rosh and Golubina; Lukyanov, Voronkov III, Bershadsky, Novikov, Pashchenko I, Trudov and Ivanov.

2. *Café (Danse arabe)*: Petipa II, Picheau II, Urakova, Davydova, Yakovleva, Kuzmina II, Postolenko; Voronin, Kunitsky, Sosnovsky, Solyannikov II, Plessyuk and Chernikov.

3. *Thé (Danse chinoise)*: Kshesinskaya II, Niman, Gorskaya, Ermolaeva, Levenson II; Gorsky, Legat II, Solntsev, Fyodorov II and Tikhomirov II.

4. *Danse des Bouffons*: Mr Shiryaev and boy students of the Imperial Theatre School.

5. *Danse des mirlitons*: Zhukova, Fyodorova II, Gruzdovskaya, Tatarinova, Ivanova, Noskova, Parfentieva and Obukhova.

6. *La mère Gigogne et les polichinelles*: Mr Yakovlev, and boy and girl students of the Imperial Theatre School.

7. *Grand Ballabile*: Johanson, Kulichevskaya, Anderson, Preobrazhenskaya, Rykhlyakova I, Voronova, Petrova, Tistrova, Ogoleit III, Andreyeva, Slantsova, Matveyeva I, Isaeva, Sheberg, Lits, Kuskova, Pavlova, Tsalison, Ogoleit II, Kunitskaya, Onegina II, Lavrentieva, Rykhlyakova II, Prokofieva, Kasatkina, Shchedrina, Aistova, Radina, Rubtsova, Egorova II, Ryabova, Stepanova III; Baltser, Dorofeyev, Fomichyov, Voronkov II, Solyannikov I, Usachyov, Fyodorov I, Alexandrov, Pashchenko II, Bykov, Balashev, Oblakov II, Marzhetsky, Panteleyev, Nikitin, Titov, Andreyev II, Gavlikovsky, Petrov, Ponomaryov, Rakhmanov, Fedulov, Tikhomirov I and Smirnov.

8. *Pas de deux*: Miss Dell'Era and Mr Gerdt.

9. *Coda générale*: all participants.

APOTHEOSIS

Conductor: R. Drigo

The harp solo will be played by the Soloist of the Court of His Imperial Majesty Mr Zabel.

ACT I

Scene 1

The stage represents a room in Silberhaus's home.

First Tableau

A Christmas party in Silberhaus's home; his relatives are busy decorating the tree;

the guests are chatting merrily, servants are distributing drinks and refreshments; guests are arriving. Finally the Christmas tree is decorated and lit. Mr Silberhaus asks his niece Marianna to bring in the children.

Second Tableau

The door opens and Marianna leads in the children, arranged in pairs. At the sight of the tree, they rush over to it and delightedly admire the gold and silver apples, nuts, confections, and other delicacies that are hanging from its branches. Silberhaus's children thank their parents. Pleased with the celebration, the guests, smiling, watch the children's pleasure. Silberhaus distributes gifts to the children, to their delight; they dance while one of the host's relatives plays the piano.

Third Tableau

New guests arrive, whom the company greets merrily; dances begin; in order to keep clear of the dancing, the children sit around the Christmas tree.

Fourth Tableau

The wall clock begins to chime; an owl peeps out from it and flaps its wings; at the last stroke Drosselmeyer appears in the doorway. At the sight of him the children run off to the sides. After standing for a moment in the doorway he comes into the room, and greets Silberhaus and his wife cheerfully. Excusing himself for being late, Drosselmeyer requests to see Silberhaus's children forthwith, especially his god-daughter Clara. After greeting the children, he orders their gifts to be brought in, and footmen roll in two large dolls wrapped in paper. The company is somewhat astonished at this, and makes fun of his conceits; Drosselmeyer unwraps the paper, and out come two dolls, one a sutler, the other a recruit in the French army. He winds them with a key and they dance. Children and guests admire the dolls. Out of other papers Drosselmeyer takes a Harlequin and a Columbine. The children are delighted; they thank their godfather and cannot part with their enchanting toys. But Silberhaus, fearing for the safety of the expensive gifts, orders the footmen to put them in the study. Clara and Fritz cry. As a consolation, Drosselmeyer takes the cleverest doll out of his pocket—a nutcracker—and makes it crack nuts. The children forget their tempers and rejoice in the new toy.

Clara and Fritz quarrel over it; Drosselmeyer announces that the nutcracker is everyone's and must crack nuts for all. Clara reluctantly gives the nutcracker to Fritz, who forces it to crack the largest nuts and finally breaks its jaws. Vexed, Fritz throws down the toy; Clara runs to the nutcracker, takes it into her arms, and begins to rock it as she would a sick child. Meanwhile Fritz and the other children form an orchestra and make a frightful noise. Clara begs the mischievous children to be quiet, and to give the injured nutcracker a chance to go to sleep. At first the children obey, but soon take up again as before; Clara puts the nutcracker in the bed of her favourite doll, and wraps him in a blanket. Silberhaus proposes a dance for his guests, and orders the furniture moved to make a space for the dancers. When the dances are over Mrs Silberhaus reminds her husband that it is time for the children to go to bed. Clara wants to take the nutcracker with her, but her father will not permit it. Marianna leads the Silberhaus children out. The guests thank host and hostess, then gradually disperse. Their guests departed, host and hostess go to their rooms. Soon the hall is empty, lit only by the moonlight through the window.

Fifth Tableau

Worried about the nutcracker, Clara cannot sleep, and convinced that everyone has gone to bed, decides to have a look at her injured beloved. She goes to the bed and looks at the nutcracker tenderly. Suddenly, from behind the chairs and the cupboard, she hears the quiet rustle, bustle, and scratching of mice. Frightened, she wants to run, but at that moment the clock begins to strike, and in its face she sees not an owl but godfather Drosselmeyer himself, looking down at her with a sardonic smile and waving the flaps of his caftan as an owl waves its wings. The rustle and bustle increase on all sides; from the cracks, from under the ledges a host of bright little eyes peep out—the room is filled with mice. Scared, Clara runs to the nutcracker's bed, seeking protection there.

Sixth Tableau

The moon, hidden by the clouds for a time, begins to shine through the window again, illuminating Clara. The Christmas tree grows to huge dimensions; the dolls begin to stir. Toy rabbits diligently sound the alarm, the sentry in his booth salutes with his rifle, and then fires. The dolls run about frightened, waving their arms and trying to get away. A detachment of gingerbread soldiers appears and forms into ranks. There is a special enthusiasm in the enemy detachment of mice. The battle begins and the army of mice, driving back the gingerbread soldiers, is victorious. In triumph the mice return with pieces of the gingerbread soldiers, which they devour on the spot.

Seventh Tableau

Observing the failure of the gingerbread army, the Nutcracker rises quickly from his bed despite his wound, and orders the little rabbits to sound the alarm again. In the capacity of army doctors, dancers appear and order soldiers to pick up the wounded on stretchers, and the dolls diligently bandage the injured. Responding to the alarm, boxes of tin soldiers open, whence emerge the Nutcracker's army, which forms a square. At this moment the Mouse King appears with his guard of honour and boldly orders an attack. Sensing the presence of their king and wishing to excel, the mice repeatedly attack the square but fall back with many casualties.

Eighth Tableau

The Mouse King and the Nutcracker enter into single combat. The Mouse King is about to kill his foe when Clara, seeing her beloved in danger, instinctively takes off her slipper and throws it with all her might at the Mouse King's back. The latter quickly whirls about, at which moment the Nutcracker, taking advantage of his foe's blunder, wounds him. The Mouse King retreats with his army. The Nutcracker, bloodstained sword in hand, goes up to Clara, kneels, is transformed into a beautiful prince, and asks her to follow him. Happy to see the Nutcracker alive and well, she gives him her hand; they walk to the Christmas tree, and are lost in its branches.

Scene 2

The stage is transformed into a forest of fir trees in winter. Large flakes of snow begin to fall; a whirlwind and blizzard arise. Gradually the storm quietens and the winter landscape is illuminated by soft moonlight, in which the snow sparkles like diamonds.

ACT II

The Palace of Sweets: Confitürembourg

First Tableau

The Sugar Plum Fairy and Prince Coqueluche are standing in a sugar kiosk adorned by dolphins from whose mouths pour fountains of currant syrup, orgeat, lemonade, and other sweet, refreshing drinks. The sovereign awaits Clara and Prince Nutcracker. All is prepared for their reception. The Sugar Plum Fairy and her Prince step down from the kiosk. Fairies and confections, picturesquely grouped, bow before her, and silver soldiers salute her. She asks them to entertain the clever and dutiful Clara, who is worthy of the most joyful reception; all happily express the desire to oblige.

Second Tableau

The major-domo, at the approach of the guests, arranges the little moors and pages; the heads of the latter are made of pearl, their bodies of rubies and emeralds, their legs of pure gold; they are holding flaming torches. Clara and the Nutcracker are sailing calmly along the river in a gilded nut-shell. When they come ashore the silver soldiers salute, and the little moors, in costumes made of iridescent hummingbird feathers, take Clara's hand and help her disembark. The sugar kiosk on the rose-coloured river begins to melt from the scorching sun, the fountains stop gushing, and the kiosk disappears. The Sugar Plum Fairy and Prince Coqueluche greet Clara and the Nutcracker amiably, while all around them bow with profound esteem. The major-domo respectfully greets Prince Nutcracker on his safe return to the palace of Confitürembourg. Astonished and delighted, Clara admires the magnificence of the city which stretches out before her. The princesses, the Nutcracker's sisters, at the sight of him run and embrace him tenderly. The Nutcracker, touched by this reception, takes Clara by the hand and presents her to his sisters, adding that she is the one to whom he is obliged for his miraculous rescue. The Sugar Plum Fairy, hugging Clara, praises her heroic deed, and the princesses, deeply moved, express their gratitude to Clara, embracing her tenderly. Meanwhile the Sugar Plum Fairy gives the major-domo a sign to begin the celebration; the latter gives a sign and the moors carry in a table covered with various confections and fruits. The Sugar Plum Fairy, Prince Coqueluche, and their retinue withdraw, not to interfere with the merriment of the newly-arrived. The major-domo seeks to entertain the guests with a beautiful divertissement, made up of dances the Sugar Plum Fairy had chosen earlier.

Tableau 3

The Sugar Plum Fairy appears again with her retinue and Prince Coqueluche. See-ing her wishes being carried out by the efficient major-domo, she wants to take part in the celebration. Clara is dazzled by the enchanting spectacle; she thinks she is see-ing all this in a dream, and that it would be awful to wake up now. Prince Nut-cracker, overjoyed that he was able to please his pretty young rescuer, tells her of the fairy-tale wonders and unusual customs of the kingdom of the sweets.

APOTHEOSIS

The apotheosis represents a large beehive with flying bees closely guarding their riches.

v *The Magic Flute*

The libretto of this work was never published. The following account of the action is taken from a choreographic notation, made sometime before May 1902, of the first two and the beginning of the third numbers of the eleven which comprise the music (Harvard Theatre Collection, bMS Thr 245 (58)), a *répétiteur* (St Petersburg, Central Music Library, I4 D74(Re Vol), and a printed piano reduction of the score (*La flûte magique (Die Zauberflöte)*. Ballet comique en 1 acte de Léon Ivanoff; musique de Richard Drigo. Leipzig, St Petersburg, Moscow, Riga, and London: Jul. Heinr. Zimmermann, 1912).

The stage represents a pretty French village among the hills. At the right the house of a judge; at the left that of a farmer. In the distance the outlines of peasants' homes.

At the beginning of the opening scene the farmer comes on stage, and gestures for others to follow. Men and women peasants come in, returning from work in the fields. The farmer's wife and Lise come out, moving to the front of the stage, and then the corps de ballet enters in pairs. The farmer expresses satisfaction with their work, and gestures to them, 'You and you work well there and I here am asking you to have some wine.' According to the printed score beer, not wine, is served, which domestics bring out and which the peasants accept with pleasure.

Luc appears in the distance on a hill. He tries to make Lise notice him. She does, and rushes to meet him so as not to arouse her parents' suspicion. A peasant man asks permission to dance, to which the farmer replies, 'But you should feel tired after your work.' 'We do not feel any effects of fatigue,' answers the peasant, 'It is with pleasure that we dance.' The farmer grants his request, then sits down with his wife to a beer near their house during a figured ensemble dance.

Unnoticed by her parents, Lise joins the dance, taking several turns with Luc. It is about to come to a rousing conclusion when Lise's mother notices her daughter and Luc together and rushes to separate them.

The farmer's wife addresses Luc in mime: 'Ah, it is you here again, what are you going to do here? I have forbidden you from courting my daughter, go away.' Luc begs her consent to marry Lise. 'What, you want to marry my daughter? Don't even dream of it!' Then she chases Luc away. Lise would follow, but her mother, furious, restrains her and orders her into the house. All in tears, Lise obeys. The peasant men and women encircle the farmer's wife and try to calm her, while the farmer rushes off after Luc, shaking his fists.

The Marquis's courier appears on a hill with a message for the farmer. At the sight of him the peasants break out laughing: Drigo creates a grotesque effect with a musette-like bass and downbeat dissonances. The courier delivers a letter, then exits.

The farmer opens the letter with much ceremony, taking up his spectacles, while his wife, burning with curiosity, begins to press him. She tears the letter from his hands and hurries to the other side of the stage. The crowd follows; but the farmer follows too and takes back the letter, rushing back to his side. The farmer's wife repeats the manœuvre and finally succeeds in reading the latter, explaining that the Marquis is about to arrive, and will choose a fiancée from among their women. This no sooner happens than the courier returns, announcing the Marquis. Flustered, the peasant women hurry on stage and arrange their dresses, the better to please the Marquis. Then they line up along the sides of the stage.

In a *pas d'action* the Marquis makes his entrance. He stops at the top of the hill and surveys the landscape through his pince-nez. Then he descends, greets the peasants, and makes gracious gestures towards the women, bestowing some attention on each one. Caressing a head, patting a chin, blowing a kiss, the Marquis tries to appear young and risqué, but his gout takes its vengeance each time, making him constantly grab his leg.

The farmer greets him with a low bow and asks to present Lise. The farmer's wife goes to find her, but she resists, and her parents drag her forcibly. Smitten by her beauty, the Marquis chooses her for his bride. At the height of happiness, he would take her by the hand, but Lise, drawing out her curtsy, turns her back to him and runs to the other side of the stage. The Marquis insists that she give him her hand. At every attempt Lise turns away. Then her parents place her hand in the Marquis's. The latter makes a turn with her and goes to the middle of the stage. Lise plods along at his side.

Luc arrives. The Marquis declares his love for Lise, and promises her a merry, happy existence; she will reign in his magnificent castle, where he will shower her with gifts. Luc prowls about, thinking to put an end to the Marquis's kind attentions, and the peasants mock the old man. The Marquis kneels and requests to kiss Lise's hand. Suddenly Luc, standing behind Lise, offers *his* hand upon which the Marquis, suspecting nothing, places a kiss.

Lise steals away, and the Marquis sees he has been tricked. He is annoyed, but cannot get up. Several peasants rush to help him. The Marquis asks Lise if she dances the minuet. She says no, and he offers to demonstrate, performing with ridiculous gestures and becoming exhausted after eight bars. She then takes a fan and shows how they dance in her native village. Lise's example inspires the peasant women, who dance a Farandole. The men join, and then Lise and Luc, unnoticed by her parents. At the end the Marquis wants to embrace Lise, rushing in pursuit of her, but inadvertently falls into Luc's arms. Witness to this contempt, Lise's parents chase Luc away.

The farmer's wife invites the Marquis to their home. He takes Lise's hand, who indulges him with ill humour and glances over to Luc, standing on the hillock. The crowd leaves the stage, saluting the Marquis.

Utterly miserable, Luc returns. He makes a last attempt to sway Lise's parents, entering the farmer's house just to be thrown out by the Marquis's courier. Dejected, he crosses the stage and collapses by the judge's house. A hermit enters, exhausted and starving, walks to the farmer's house, knocks and knocks again. The farmer's wife answers, and pushes him away so rudely that he falls down. Witness to this scene, Luc assists the hermit. He takes his only money from his pocket and gives it to the old man. The hermit enquires why Luc is dejected. Weeping, Luc recounts his story; during this recital, the hermit disappears. Luc is amazed, and looks for him.

Luc finds instead a flute hanging from a rock, above which is inscribed, in large letters: 'Take this flute and play, all will begin to dance against their will, which will bring you happiness.' Luc seizes the flute and runs to his seat near the judge's house. He tries to play the flute, but cannot produce a melody. Hearing the flute, Lise comes on stage and runs over to Luc. As she approaches Luc begins to draw a melody from the instrument. This melody, labelled *ancien air de ballet d'auteur inconnu*, is repeated whenever Luc plays. Charmed by the flute, Lise is compelled to dance. At the end of the melody her dance also ends, and she falls, exhausted.

Seeing Lise exhausted, Luc rushes to help her up. Lise describes the strange feeling which took possession of her and forced her to dance. During this testimony to the power of his flute, Luc tells Lise of the appearance of the hermit, and declares his resolve to take vengeance on her parents. Lise opposes vengeance; Luc accuses her of not really loving him and is about to leave, but Lise begs him to stay. A love scene ensues, at the end of which the lovers embrace.

The farmer's wife comes out, sees the lovers, throws herself between them, pushes Luc away and chases Lise into the house. Enraged, she calls the farmer, the Marquis, and his courier. The farmer's wife explains what happened, and that it is up to the Marquis, as his daughter's fiancé, to punish Luc.

The Marquis takes his sword, the farmer his cane, the farmer's wife her broom, the courier his sceptre, and all rush at Luc. Unperturbed, he begins to play his flute. As if compelled by an invisible power, his assailants begin to dance, jump, and turn. The Marquis does his best to run Luc through, but each attempt is repelled by a mysterious hand. The courier circles around Luc, trying to deliver a blow, but he is rejected from above and from the side. Nor can the farmer and his wife reach Luc. The unbridled dance continues as long as the melody. At the last note, the farmer and his wife sink down, and the Marquis falls into his courier's arms, who himself can barely stand.

Coming around, the Marquis accuses Luc of sorcery and orders his courier to fetch the police. The courier returns with a superintendent and four soldiers. A crowd gathers. The superintendent asks the cause of alarm, then tries to have his soldiers seize Luc. He continues his melody, and the dance recommences until he stops.

Fatigued and annoyed, the superintendent insists that Luc hand over his flute. Luc refuses and tries to flee, but the soldiers seize him. The superintendent wrests the flute from his hands, and sends a soldier to fetch the judge. The lazy judge, after several exchanges between the soldiers and his clerk, enters malcontent and yawning. The superintendent explains what has happened. 'But I see nothing wrong in that,' the judge responds. 'One dances, one becomes merry, and that is all.' 'But everyone was forced to dance unwilled by a mysterious power.' 'Is such a thing possible!' exclaims the judge. 'Give him back the flute, I want to convince myself of a power which would force a judge to dance.' He and his clerk take a seat.

Luc plays the tune with the same effect. The judge and his clerk jump up above their seats; the judge clings to the table but to no avail; he continues to jump with his chair as long as the melody sounds. Choking with an indescribable fury, the judge declares to Luc: 'Ah, I see now that you are a sorcerer, I shall punish you.' Luc kneels, begging for a pardon. 'No,' replies the judge, 'there is no hope for you. Prepare to die; you will be hanged.' He orders Luc to be seized and led to the tribunal.

Oberon, on a rock, plays Luc's melody on his hunting horn. Those present begin to dance again, but softly. Uneasy, they turn to see Oberon on the rock in all his splendour. Surprised and frightened, they prostrate themselves before him. Luc rushes to Oberon to ask for mercy.

Oberon promises him protection. He comes down from the rock to the front of the stage, and addresses the judge: 'Do not dare to judge or to condemn this man; he has a heart of gold and he is under my protection.' Then he calls the farmer's wife, who prostrates herself. 'You are an evil woman,' Oberon tells her. 'Today you rejected a poor old man who asked alms of you. I was that old man.' Seeing who it was, the farmer and his wife beg Oberon for pardon. 'You shall obtain my pardon only when you have joined these two loving hearts.' He points to Lise and Luc.

The farmer and his wife happily consent. The Marquis, seeing that he is being mocked, makes off quietly with his courier. Oberon remounts the rock, and disappears.

A wedding celebration, in the form of a divertissement of four dances and a final *ballabile*, ends the ballet.

VI *Zolushka* (*Cinderella*)

ZOLUSHKA

Fantastic ballet in 3 acts by L. Pashkova
Music by B. Schell
Production and dances by the balletmasters:
M. Petipa, E. Cecchetti and L. Ivanov

New decorations: of Act I—Mr Levogt; of Act II by Professor M. Shishkov; of Act III by Academician M. Bocharov. The machinist is Mr Berger. New costumes: women's—Miss Ofitserova and Miss Ivanova, and men's—Mr Caffi and Pipar. Headwear: women's—Miss Termen and men's—Mr Bruneau. Flowers and feathers—Miss Simonova; metal accessories—Mr Inginen; other accessories—Mr Kamensky; wigs—Mr Pedder, footwear—Miss Levstedt.

Presented for the first time 5 December 1893

St-Petersburg
Printer of the Imperial Spb. Theatres, Mokhovaya, 10
1893

Permitted by the censor, St-Petersburg, 3 December 1893

ZOLUSHKA

DRAMATIS PERSONNAE:

King	Mr Aistov
Queen	Miss Ogoleit I
Prince Charming	Mr Gerdt
Chamberlain	Mr Bulgakov
Master of Ceremonies	Mr Voronkov I
Cavalier Pignarole	Mr Stukolkin
Henrietta, *his wife*	Mme Cecchetti
Cinderella	Miss Legnani
Odette, *his daughter*	Miss Kshesinskaya II
Aloisa, *his daughter*	Miss Anderson
The good fairy	Miss Johanson
Gianna, *a cook*	Miss Zhukova

Courtly ladies and cavaliers, pages, the king's guard, heralds, servants; the princesses of the night, sparks, servants, pages, messenger-fairies, scullery maids, etc.

TO DANCE IN ACT I:

1. *Jeu dansant des marmitons*: Miss Zhukova and students of the Imperial Theatre School.

2. *Scène dansante*: Miss Legnani, Miss Kshesinskaya II and Miss Anderson.

3. *Scène mimique*: Miss Legnani.

4. *Pas des étincelles*: Miss Legnani, Preobrazhenskaya, Rykhlyakova I, Slantsova, Matveyeva I, Nikolaeva, Andreyeva, Isaeva, Kasatkina, Stepanova III, Matveyeva III, Matveyeva II, Vasilieva, Lavrentieva, Rykhlyakova II, Lobanova, Vertinskaya, Golubina, Gorskaya, Niman.

5. *Leçon de maintien*: Miss Legnani and Miss Johanson.

6. *Cortège et départ de Cendrillon pour le bal*: Miss Legnani and Miss Johanson, boy and girl students of the Imperial Theatre School.

TO DANCE IN ACT II:

1. *L'arrivée des invités*: Efimova, Zasedateleva, Natarova I, Savelieva, Bastman, Mikhailova I, Smirnova, Tivolskaya, Kurbanova, Akhmakova, Svirskaya, Bogdanova; Bogdanov, Balashev, Tikhomirov I, Konstantinov, Andreyev I, Tikhomirov II, Picheau and others.

2. *Entrée du roi et de la reine*: Miss Ogoleit I; Mr Aistov and Mr Gerdt.

3. *Réception des ambassadeurs*: Mr Bekefy and Mr Lukyanov; Miss Petipa I and Miss Petipa II.

4. *Apparition de Cendrillon*: Miss Legnani.

5. *Danse russe*: Miss Petipa II, Legat I, Kuzmina, Vishnevskaya II, Urakova, Gorshenkova, Semyonova I, Onegina I, Alexandrova I; Mr Lukyanov, Tatarinov, Voronin, Titov, Legat II, Alexandrov, Kunitsky, Panteleyev, Bykov.

6. *Danse polonaise*: Miss Petipa I, Andreyeva, Troitskaya, Ogoleit III, Kshesinskaya I, Aistova, Slantsova, Korsak, Tsalison, Onegina II, Lits, Ogoleit II, Rubtsova, Vsevolodskaya, Ryabova, Picheau II, Ilyina II; Mr Bekefy, Yakovlev, Voronkov II, Usachyov, Fedulov, Baltser, Pashchenko I, Marzhetsky, Levenson, Fyodorov I, Voronkov III, Andreyev II, Petrov, Smirnov, Rykhlyakov, Romanov, Rakhmanov.

7. *Grand pas d'action*: Miss Legnani, Cecchetti, Anderson, Kshesinskaya II, Petrova, Tistrova, Nikolaeva, Pavlova, Lavrentieva, Konetskaya, Dorina, Golubeva II, Levina, Shtikhling; Mr Gerdt, Stukolkin, Litavkin, Oblakov I, Gavlikovsky, Ivanov, Bershadsky, Fyodorov II, Pashchenko II, Ponomaryov, Fomichyov, Martyanov.

8. *Fuite de Cendrillon*: Miss Legnani and all participants.

TO DANCE IN ACT III:

1. *Scène mimique de Cendrillon et la fée bienfaisante*: Miss Legnani and Miss Johanson.

2. *Marche et entrée des invités*: Miss Cecchetti, Ogoleit I, Kshesinskaya II, Anderson, Efimova, Zasedateleva, Natarova I, Savelieva, Bastman, Mikhailova I, Smirnova, Tivolskaya, Kurbanova, Akhmakova, Svirskaya, Bogdanova; Mr Gerdt, Aistov, Stukolkin, Bogdanov, Balashev, Tikhomirov I, Konstantinov, Andreyev I, Tikhomirov II, Picheau and others. *Demoiselles d'honneur*: Miss Nikolaeva, Lavrentieva, Pavlova, Konetskaya, Dorina, Golubeva II, Levina, Shtikhling; *Chevaliers d'honneur*: Mr Gavlikovsky, Bershadsky, Ivanov, Martyanov, Pashchenko II, Fomichyov, Ponomaryov, Fyodorov II. *Garde du roi*:

Mr Chernikov, Plessyuk, Lozhkin, Voskresensky, Solyannikov II, Sosnovsky, Oblakov II and Pugni. *Pages*: students of the Imperial Theatre School.

3. *Apparitions de Cendrillon, la fée bienfaisante et les princesses de la nuit*: Miss Legnani, Johanson, Sheberg, Savitskaya, Ilyina I, Kurochkina, Fyodorova III, Kunitskaya, Vsevolodskaya, Lobanova, Sitnikova, Slantsova, Tselikhova, Vishnevskaya II, Legat II, Lits, Rubtsova, Starostina, Onegina II, Urakova, Aistova, Tsalison, Radina, Korsak, Gorshenkova, Oblakova.

4. *Pas des princesses de la nuit et de la fée du soleil*: Miss Johanson; *Stars*: Lits, Oblakova, Rubtsova, Urakova, Onegina II, Legat II, Radina, Tsalison, Korsak, Slantsova, Starostina, Aistova, Gorshenkova, Sheberg, Ilyina I, Kurochkina, Vsevolodskaya, Lobanova, Sitnikova, Savitskaya, Fyodorova III, Kunitskaya, Tselikhova, Vishnevskaya II.

5. *La nuit du Nil*: Miss Kshesinskaya I and Mr Solyannikov I; Antonova, Davydova, Golubeva I, Onegina I, Alexandrova II, Kil, Potaikova, Emelyanova; Voronin, Kunitsky, Rykhlyakov, Marzhetsky, Bykov, Fedulov, Panteleyev.

6. *La nuit de Grenade*: Miss Kshesinskaya II; *Students*: students of the Imperial Theatre School: Yakovleva, Makhotina, Astafieva, Isaeva, Rikhartova, Goryacheva, Sazonova, Rakhmanova.

7. *La nuit parisienne*: *Leander*: Miss Anderson. *Neighbour*: Student Fonaryova; *Pierrot*: Mr Kyaksht. *Amour*: Student Petropavlovskaya.

8. *Danse de quatre éléments*: *Earth*: Miss Preobrazhenskaya, girl students of the Imperial Theatre School: Trefilova, Ilyina, Borkhardt and Chumakova. *Water*: Miss Kulichevskaya, Obukhova, Vasilieva, Rykhlyakova II, Parfentieva. *Air*: Miss Rykhlyakova I, Andreyeva, Isaeva, Matveyeva I, Kasatkina. *Fire*: Miss Skorsyuk, Golubina, Golovkina, Stepanova III, Rosh and others.

9. *Grand pas*: Miss Legnani, Miss Kshesinskaya II, Miss Anderson and Mr Gerdt.

10. *Coda générale*: all participants.

APOTHEOSIS

Conductor: Mr Drigo

Solos performed by: Soloists of the Court of His Imperial Majesty: on the violin, Mr Auer, on the harp, Mr Zabel.

Solos also performed by: Mr Galkin on the viola, and Mr Loganovsky on the cello.

ACT I

The stage represents a large kitchen

Scene 1

At the rise of the curtain Gianna and her scullery maids are busy preparing dinner; but Gianna no sooner leaves the kitchen than the scullery maids abandon their duties and begin to dance and play with saucepans and skillets.

Gianna returns, sees their mischief, and sternly orders them back to business; they pay her no heed and Gianna, drawn into their merriment, begins to dance with them. A bell is heard. Gianna now emphatically orders her helpers to calm down; in confusion they rush back to their places.

Scene 2

Aloisa and Odette enter hurriedly, hunting for their little sister to help them dress for the ball. Seeing that Cinderella is not there, they order the scullery maids to find her at once. The sisters are in a frightful worry. The hour of their departure for the royal celebration is approaching, and their *toilettes* are not yet finished; they begin to smarten themselves up, angry and astonished at Cinderella's absence.

Scene 3

Cinderella runs in holding a sheaf of straw; her sisters rush over to push and pinch her, and make their poor sister suffer, then order her to set right their *toilettes*, which Cinderella willingly tries to do. The sisters, now content, begin to dream and boast to one another of their successes at the ball. Making fun of Cinderella, they dance and force her to dance as well. Their parents enter and press their daughters to get ready to leave. In vain Cinderella begs her parents and sisters to take her along. Her sisters laugh, and her father orders her sternly to stay at home and tend to her chores.

Scene 4

Alone and sad, Cinderella dreams about the pleasures of the ball, imagining the dances, but realizing that she cannot go, and hurries about her work. The hearth flares up; Cinderella watches astonished as living sparks fly out of the fireplace. They surround her; delighted, she admires them and dances with them.

Scene 5

The good fairy appears, Cinderella's godmother and protector. Amazed by the goodwill and patience with which Cinderella bears her undeserved debasement, she promises to grant her any wish. Cinderella asks to go to the royal ball. With pleasure the fairy agrees, but on the condition that she stay no later than midnight: with the last stroke of twelve o'clock, all the luxuries granted her will disappear. Cinderella happily thanks the good fairy, at a wave of whose hand a brilliant cortège appears. Servant-fairies assist Cinderella in completing her *toilette* for the ball and putting on magnificent slippers. The fairy, when Cinderella is properly dressed, gives her a lesson in deportment and hurries her off, reminding her of the condition she set.

ACT II

The throne room of a castle

Scene 1

Courtiers have gathered to greet the king, and promenade in expectation of his arrival; a few make lively conversation about the celebration. The master of ceremonies announces the royal family; the courtiers hurry to their places.

Scene 2

The royal couple enter and take their places, Prince Charming standing next to them. The guests, including the Pignarole family, pay their profound respects to the queen and king. The king, enraptured by the prettiness of Cavalier Pignarole's daughters, invites them to take a place next to the throne.

Scene 3

Just then the heralds' trumpets sound, announcing guests from Moscow and Poland, who, charmed by their welcome, pay their respects to the king and take their places. The chamberlain rushes in and announces the arrival of an unknown princess, accompanied by a brilliant retinue. General excitement; the prince hastens to meet the stranger.

Scene 4

Cinderella enters; Prince Charming, respectfully offering his arm, presents her to the king, queen, and court. The onlookers are struck by the unknown princess's beauty and brilliant *toilette*. The Pignaroles are amazed at the stranger's striking likeness to their youngest daughter, who was left at home. The prince lavishes his attentions on the newly arrived princess, and the king and queen invite her to take a place next to them; this causes Aloisa and Odette to bear her malice and to envy the unknown guest. The prince orders the master of ceremonies to begin the ball; the prince takes part, dancing only with the princess, delighted by her beauty. Odette and Aloisa also take part in the dances and try to attract the prince's attention; but he is charmed by Cinderella's beauty.

Scene 5

The clock begins to strike midnight. Cinderella, enchanted by the prince's attentions, completely forgets the good fairy's condition. With the last stroke of twelve she suddenly remembers, and quickly retires at the moment her mother walks up to the prince and engages him in conversation. Cinderella, whose rich attire has turned simple, tries to leave the royal palace unnoticed. The prince, observing the beautiful stranger's disappearance, orders his chamberlain to follow her, but just then a page enters and gives the prince the slipper which the princess lost. The prince, admiring the slipper, orders it to be announced throughout the land that he will choose for his bride the woman whose foot the slipper fits.

ACT III

A fantastic garden in the prince's castle

Scene 1

Servants and pages, preparing for the prince's celebration, walk through the garden from time to time. The prince enters with his retinue, wanting to know if his wishes have been met and if the beautiful stranger has turned up. The chamberlain calms the prince, adding that the princess is probably there. Contented with the chamberlain's assurances, the prince invites the king and queen into the ball.

Scene 2

On the day after the ball Cinderella, wishing to see the prince again and to look for her lost slipper, comes to the royal garden. Hearing footsteps, she hides in the bushes, frightened, falls to her knees in despair, and prays for her godmother to help her.

Scene 3

The good fairy appears, and wishing to help her favourite again, still reproaches her for disobeying and not coming home in time. Cinderella begs the good fairy's forgiveness and asks her to help. Trumpets sound; the herald announces that Prince Charming will choose as his bride the woman whose foot fits the slipper which was found. Cinderella wants to be at the celebration to see him again, and begs the fairy to let her go to this ball. The fairy gladly agrees; they withdraw.

Scene 4

The king and queen enter with the prince and the others invited to the celebration. The prince asks the assembled beauties to try on the slipper, but their efforts are in vain; the slipper does not fit any of them. The herald now announces the good fairy with Cinderella. The prince suggests that Cinderella also try the slipper, and, to the astonishment of all, the slipper fits and stays on her foot. The onlookers are struck by Cinderella's beauty, and the prince, delighted, declares his love to her; her sisters beg forgiveness for treating her badly. She forgives them, and the heralds announce Cinderella as the prince's bride. The entire court congratulates them.

VII *Flora's Awakening*

In the absence of a separately published libretto, this account of the scenario is taken from 'Celebration at Peterhof', *Ezhegodnik Imperatorskikh Teatrov*, 1893/4, 426–9.

Scene 1. It is night. Flora and her nymphs are deep asleep; Diana, the goddess of night, guards their peace. With the approach of dawn a freshness is felt in the air. Diana hides in the clouds.

Scene 2. Aquilon rushes stormily over the locale; his cold breath of wind awakens the sleepers and forces them to seek refuge in the foliage. The appearance of chilling dew brings Flora to despair, and she implores Aurora to help them.

Scene 3. Aurora consoles Flora with tender caresses and announces that the god of day, Apollo, who will end their sufferings, is following behind her.

Scene 4. With the appearance of resplendent Apollo everything becomes animated. Smitten with the beauty of the goddess of flowers, he kisses her. At the call of the god of day, the light and tender breeze, Zephyr, flies to his beloved Flora's embrace. 'You must be his helpmate,' Apollo tells her, 'It is the gods' will.' Everyone is delighted; Cupid, amours, and nymphs rejoice over the lovers' happiness.

Scene 5. Mercury, messenger of the gods, announces Ganymede and Hebé, who present Flora and Zephyr a cup of nectar and proclaim that Jupiter has given them eternal youth.

Scene 6. A procession. The chariot of Bacchus and Ariadne is accompanied by bacchantes, satyrs, fauns, sylvans, and others.

Apotheosis. Olympus is revealed; Jupiter appears, Juno, Neptune, Vulcan, Minerva, Ceres, Mars, Pluto, Proserpina, Venus, and others.

The following artists appeared as performers in the ballet: Miss Kshesinskaya II—Flora, Miss Johanson—Aurora, Miss Leonova—Diana, Mr Gerdt—Apollo, Mr Legat I—Zephyr, Mr Gorsky—Aquilon, Miss Trefilova—Cupid, Mr Legat III—Mercury, Mr Litavkin—Ganymede, Miss Kulichevskaya—Hebé, and others.

In the apotheosis the following artists appeared: Jupiter—Mr Aistov, Juno—Miss Ogoleit I, Neptune—Mr Voronkov I, Vulcan—Mr Bulgakov, Minerva—Miss Bastman, Ceres—Miss Goryacheva, Mars—Mr Yakovlev, Pluto—Mr Gillert, Proserpina—Miss Khomyakova, Venus—Miss Davydova, Psyché—Miss Mikhailova, and others.

In the dances, which followed this order, these artists took part: (1) 'Danse de Diane'—Miss Leonova. (2) 'Entrée d'Aquilon'—Mr Gorsky. (3) 'La rosée'—Miss Voronova, Fyodorova II, Parfentieva, Tatarinova, Kasatkina, Fonaryova, Ofitserova, and Borkhardt. (4) 'Arrivée d'Aurore'—Miss Johanson. (5) 'Valse'—Miss Kshesinskaya II, Johanson, Noskova, Ryklyakova I, Obukhova, Ivanov,

Lits, Korsak, Legat I, Nikolaeva, Ogoleit II, Troitskaya, Vasilieva and Slantsova. (6) 'Entrée d'Apollon, Zéphyre, Cupidon et des Amours'—Mr Gerdt, Mr Legat I, Miss Trefilova, and girl students of the Imperial Theatre School. (7) 'Pas d'action'— Miss Kshesinskaya II, Trefilova, Noskova, Rykhlyakova I, Ivanova, Obukhova, Lits, Korsak, Legat I, Nikolaeva, Ogoleit II, Troitskaya, Vasilieva, Slantsova, Mr Gerdt and Legat I. (8) 'Arrivée de Mercure, Ganymède et Hébé—Miss Kulichevskaya, Mr Legat III and Litavkin. (9) 'Cortège': Ariadne—Miss Kshesinskaya I; Bacchus—Mr Solyannikov I; satyrs—Mr Martyanov, Novikov and Trudov; fauns—Mr Levenson and Marzhetsky; Silvains—Mr Gavlikovsky, Ivanov and Fyodorov I; bacchantes—Miss Alexandrova II, Kil, Pakhomova, Erler I, Vertinskaya, Golubeva I, Rykhlyakova II, Ilyina III, Kunitskaya, Gorskaya, Lavrentieva, Fyodorova III, Aistova, Ryabova, Levina, Stepanova III, Tsalison, Ilyina II, Konetskaya, Tselikhova, Dorina, Golubeva II, Yakovleva II and Stepanova II; bacchants—Mr Baltser, Fedulov, Vasiliev, Usachyov, Tatarinov, Alexandrov, Titov, Romanov, Volkov, Voronkov III, Rykhlyakov and Panteleyev. (10) 'Grand pas'—Miss Kshesinskaya II and all participants.

SWAN LAKE

Fantastic ballet in 3 acts and 4 scenes

Music by P. I. Tchaikovsky

Production and dances by the balletmasters M. Petipa and L. Ivanov

Decoration of Act I, Scene 1 by Mr Andreyev; of Act I, Scene 2, Act III and the apotheosis by academician M. Bocharov; of Act II by Mr Levogt. Machinist—Mr Berger. Costumes after drawings by Mr Ponomaryov: women's by Miss Ofitserova, men's by Mr Caffi. Headwear: men's—by Mr Bruneau, women's—by Miss Termen. Accessories by the sculptor Mr Kamensky. Footwear—by Miss Levstedt. Wigs by Mr Pedder.

Given for the first time [1]5 January 1895

St Petersburg
Typographer of the Imperial SPb Theatres, Mokhovaya No. 40
1895

Permitted by the censor, St Petersburg, 11 January 1895

ACT I
CHARACTERS:

A Sovereign Princess	Mme Cecchetti
Prince Siegfried, her son	Mr Gerdt
Benno, his friend	Mr Oblakov I
Wolfgang, the prince's tutor	Mr Gillert
Odette (queen of the swans)	Miss Legnani
Evil genie	Mr Bulgakov

Friends of the prince, courtly gentlemen, footmen, courtly women and pages in the retinue of the princess, guests, peasant men and women, swans, little swans.

The action takes place in fairy-tale times, in Germany.

TO DANCE IN ACT I, SCENE 1:

1. *Pas de trois*: Miss Preobrazhenskaya, Miss Rykhlyakova I and Mr Kyaksht.

2. *Valse champêtre*: Trefilova, Borkharkht, Fonaryova, Parfentieva, Kasatkina, Korsak, Onegina II, Pavlova, Stepanova II, Niman, Yakovleva I, Lobanova, Kunitskaya, Ilyina III, Levina, Yakovleva II, Golubeva II, Rikhartova, Gorskaya and Isaeva II; Gorsky, Legat III, Voronkov II, Kusov, Fyodorov I, Pashchenko I, Trudov, Novikov, Tikhomirov II, Martyanov, Levinson, Rakhmanov, Ivanov, Gavlikovsky, Nikitin, Smirnov, Fyodorov II, Vasiliev, Ponomaryov, and Sergeyev.

3. *Danse au cliquetis de verres*: all participants.

IN SCENE 2:

1. *Scène dansante*: Miss Legnani and Mr Gerdt.

2. *Entrée des cygnes*: Ivanova, Rykhlyakova I, Noskova, Ofitserova, Voronova, Fyodorova II, Obukhova, Slantsova, Tatarinova, Ogoleit II, Legat I, Matveyeva I, Troitskaya, Nikolaeva, Andreyeva, Matveyeva III, Kshesinskaya I, Aistova, Rykhlyakova II, Vsevolodskaya, Radina, Ryabova, Vasilieva, Tsalison, Konetskaya, Lavrentieva, Fyodorova III, Stepanova III, Tselikhova, Dorina, and Kuzmina II.

3. *Grand pas des cygnes*: Legnani, Rykhlyakova I, Ivanova, Noskova, Voronova, Rykhlyakova II, Fyodorova II, Obukhova; Gerdt, Oblakov I; men and women dancers, and female students of the Theatre School.

(a) *Valse*.

(b) *Adagio*.

(c) *Variation*: Rykhlyakova I, Voronova, Ivanova, Noskova. Ofitserova, Obukhova, Fyodorova II and Rykhlyakova II. Miss Legnani.

(d) *Coda et Final*: Miss Legnani, Mr Gerdt, and all participants.

ACT II

CHARACTERS

A Sovereign Princess	Mme Cecchetti
Siegfried	Mr Gerdt
Von Rothbart, *the evil genie in the guise of a guest*	Mr Bulgakov
Odile, *his daughter, who resembles Odette*	Miss Legnani
Master of Ceremonies	Mr Voronkov I
A herald	Mr Sosnovsky

Men and women courtiers, guests, masks, pages, footmen.

TO DANCE:

1. *Valse des fiancées*: Miss Ivanova, Leonova, Petipa II, Noskova, Lits, Kuskova, and Mr Gerdt.

2. *Pas Espagnol*: Miss Skorsyuk and Miss Obukhova, Mr Shiryaev and Mr Litavkin.

3. *Danse Vénitienne*: Miss Savitskaya, Isaeva I, Kunitskaya, Lavrentieva, Rikhartova, Ryabova, Dorina, Levina, Matveyeva III, Pavlova, Matveyeva I, Stepanova II, Tselikhova, Radina, Aistova and Konetskaya; Mr Ivanov, Martyanov, Fyodorov II, Alexeyev, Marzhetsky, Levinson, Ponomaryov, Oblakov II, Gavlikovsky, Trudov, Fyodorov I, Sergeyev, Pashchenko I, Smirnov, Rykhlyakov, and Panteleyev.

4. *Pas Hongrois*: Miss Petipa I and Mr Bekefy; Miss Andreyeva, Ogoleit III, Nikolaeva, Troitskaya, Ogoleit II, Tsalison, Vasilieva and Onegina II; Mr Alexandrov, Baltser, Yakovlev, Voronkov III, Voronin, Usachyov, Titov and Fedulov.

5. *Mazurka*: Miss Legat I, Tatarinova, Kshesinskaya I and Slantsova; Mr Kshesinsky I, Lukyanov, Oblakov I and Kshesinsky II.

6. *Pas d'action*: Miss Legnani; Mr Gerdt, Mr Gorsky, and Mr Bulgakov.

ACT III

CHARACTERS:

Odette	Miss Legnani
Siegfried	Mr Gerdt
Evil genie	Mr Bulgakov
	Swans.

TO DANCE:

1. *Valse des cygnes*: Miss Johanson, Kulichevskaya, Ivanova, Leonova, Noskova, Obukhova, Legat I, Tatarinova, Nikolaeva, Isaeva I, Matveyeva I, Slantsova, Troitskaya, Savitskaya, Kshesinskaya I, Ogoleit II, Vasilieva, Matveyeva III, Aistova, Tsalison, Ryabova, Stepanova III. Black swans: Miss Fonaryova, Kasatkina, Borgkhardt, Trefilova, Rykhlyakova II, Ofitserova, Lavrentieva, Kunitskaya.

2. *Scène dansante*: Miss Legnani; Mr Gerdt, Mr Bulgakov, and all participants.

APOTHEOSIS

Conductor R. Drigo

Solos performed by soloists of the Court of His Imperial Majesty:
on the violin—by Mr Auer, on the harp—by Mr Zabel.
In addition, the solo on violincello is performed by Mr Loganovsky.

SWAN LAKE

ACT I

Tableau I

A park in front of a castle.

Scene 1

Benno and his comrades are waiting for Prince Siegfried in order to celebrate his coming of age. Prince Siegfried enters with Wolfgang. The feast begins. Peasant men and women arrive to congratulate the Prince, who invites the men to wine and gives ribbons to the women. The tipsy Wolfgang sees to Siegfried's wishes. Dances of the peasants.

Scene 2

Servants announce the arrival of the Princess, Siegfried's mother, which throws the party into disarray. The dances stop, servants hurriedly take away the tables and conceal the traces of celebration. Wolfgang and the young men feign abstinence. The Princess enters, preceded by her retinue; Siegfried greets her respectfully. She gently reproaches him for trying to deceive her, for she knows he has been celebrating, and she has come not to keep him from that, but to remind him that his last day of bachelorhood has dawned, and that tomorrow he must be married. To the question, 'Who will be the bride?' the Princess answers that this will be decided at a ball the next day to which she has invited all the young women worthy of becoming her daughter and his wife. He shall select the one that pleases him most.

Wishing to let the party continue, the Princess departs.

Scene 3

The Prince is pensive over parting with his free and easy bachelor's life. Benno persuades him not to spoil an agreeable present by his concern for the future. Siegfried signals for the party to continue, and the feast and dancing are renewed. Wolfgang, completely drunk, amuses everybody with his dancing.

Scene 4

Night is falling. A farewell dance and it will be time to disperse. A dance with cups.

Scene 5

A band of swans flies overhead. At the sight the young men, still wide awake, decide to end the day with a hunt. Benno knows where the swans fly for the night. Leaving the drunken Wolfgang behind, the youth depart.

Tableau II

A rocky, wild locale. In the depth of the stage, a lake. At the right, on the shore, the ruins of a chapel. A moonlit night.

Scene 1

A band of white swans swims around the lake. In front, a swan with a crown on its head.

Scene 2

Benno and several of the Prince's other friends rush in. Noticing the swans, they take aim, but the swans swim away. Benno, having sent the others to inform the Prince, is left alone. Swans transformed into beautiful young women surround him; he is staggered by the magical phenomenon and is powerless against their spells. The Prince's comrades return, and the swans fall back. The young men are about to shoot; the Prince arrives and also takes aim, but the ruins are illuminated by a magic light and Odette appears, pleading for mercy.

Scene 3

Siegfried, struck by her beauty, forbids his comrades to shoot. She thanks him, and explains that she, Princess Odette, and the other young women are the unhappy victims of an evil genie who has bewitched them. They are fated by day to take the form of swans and only at night, near these ruins, can they regain their human form. Their master, in the form of an owl, stands guard over them. His terrible spell will continue until someone falls truly in love with her, for life; only a person who has never sworn his love to another woman can be her rescuer and return her to her previous state. Siegfried listens, enchanted. The owl flies in, and transformed into an evil genie appears amidst the ruins, overhears them, and disappears. Horror possesses Siegfried at the thought that he might have killed Odette when she was still a swan. He breaks his bow and indignantly throws it away. Odette consoles him.

Scene 4

Odette summons her friends and with them tries to divert him with dances. Siegfried is ever more captivated by Princess Odette's beauty and offers to be her rescuer. He has yet to swear his love to anyone, and can therefore free her from the evil genie. He will kill it and so free Odette. She responds that this is impossible: the evil genie's end will come only when some madman sacrifices himself to Odette's love. Siegfried is prepared to do this; for her sake he would gladly die. Odette believes in his love, and that he has never sworn it before. But tomorrow a number of beautiful women will come to his mother's court, and he must choose one of them as his spouse. Siegfried says that he will be a bridegroom only when she, Odette, appears at the ball. Odette responds that she cannot because at that time she can only fly around the castle as a swan. The Prince swears that he will not betray her. Touched by his love, Odette accepts his vow, but warns that the evil genie will do everything to make him swear it to another woman. Siegfried still promises that no spell will take Odette from him.

Scene 5

Dawn is breaking. Odette takes leave of her beloved, and disappears with her friends into the ruins. The dawn brightens. A flock of swans swims out on the lake, and above them flies a large owl, waving its wings heavily.

ACT II

A magnificent hall.
Everything is ready for a celebration.

Scene 1

The master of ceremonies gives last-minute orders to the servants. He meets and places the arriving guests. The Princess and Siegfried enter in the vanguard of the court. A procession of the prospective brides and their parents. A general dance. Waltz of the brides.

Scene 2

The Princess asks her son which of the young women pleases him most. Siegfried finds them all charming, but to none could he swear eternal love.

Scene 3

Trumpets announce new guests: Von Rothbart and his daughter Odile. Siegfried is struck by her likeness to Odette and greets her enthusiastically. Odette, in the form of a swan, appears in the window, warning her beloved of the evil genie's spell. But attracted to the beauty of the new guest, he sees only her. The dances begin again.

Scene 4

Siegfried's choice is made. Convinced that Odile and Odette are the same, he chooses Odile as his bride. Von Rothbart triumphantly takes his daughter's hand and gives it to the young man, who vows his eternal love.

Siegfried then sees Odette in the window. He realizes he has been deceived, but it is too late: the vow is spoken, Rothbart and Odile disappear. Odette must remain forever in the evil genie's power; as an owl it appears above Odette in the window. The Prince runs out in a burst of despair. General confusion.

ACT III

A deserted place near the swan lake.
The magic ruins are in the distance. Cliffs. Night.

Scene 1

The swan maidens anxiously await Odette's return. To shorten their time of anguish, they try to divert themselves by dancing.

Scene 2

Odette runs in. The swans greet her joyfully, but despair when they learn of Siegfried's betrayal. All is finished; the evil genie has triumphed and there is no rescue for Odette: the evil spell will last forever. It would be better, while she is still a woman, to perish in the waves of the lake than to live without Siegfried. In vain her friends try to console her.

Scene 3

Siegfried runs in. He is searching for Odette so that he can beg forgiveness at her feet for his unintended betrayal. He loves her alone and swore fidelity to Odile because he thought she was Odette. At the sight of her beloved, Odette forgets her grief, and both give themselves over to the joy of meeting.

Scene 4

The evil genie interrupts this momentary enchantment. Siegfried must fulfil his vow and marry Odile; with the coming of dawn Odette will change into a swan forever. It is better for her to die while there is time. Siegfried swears to die with her. The evil genie vanishes in terror: death for the sake of Odette's love is his end. The unfortunate girl embraces Siegfried one last time, and runs to the cliff to jump from its height. The evil genie as an owl hovers over her, trying to change her into a swan. Siegfried rushes to her assistance, and with her throws himself into the lake. The owl falls, dead.

APOTHEOSIS

IX *Acis and Galatea*

ACIS AND GALATEA

Mythological ballet in one act by V. Langhammer

Music by A. V. Kadlets

Dances and production by the balletmaster L. Ivanov

Decoration—Mr Perminov. Fountain—Mr Berger. Costumes after drawings by Mr Ponomaryov, men's—Mr Caffi, women's—Miss Ofitserova. Flowers—Miss Simonova. Wigs—Mr Pedder. Footwear—Mr Levshtedt. Tricot—Miss Dobrovolskaya.

The role of 'Galatea' will be performed by Miss L. A. Roslavleva, artist of the Imperial Moscow Theatres.

Presented for the first time for the benefit of Miss M. Petipa, 21 January 1896.

St Petersburg
Typographer of the Imperial SPB. Theatres, Mokhovaya, 40
1896

Permitted by the censor. St Petersburg, 19 January 1896

DRAMATIS PERSONAE:

Polyphemus, a Cyclops	Mr Aistov
Galatea	Miss Roslavleva
Acis	Mr Legat III
Hymen	Miss Preobrazhenskaya
Cupid	Miss Trefilova
Thetis	Miss Levinson II
Ether	Miss Rosh
Nyx	Miss Urakova

Limnaeae, nereids, fauns and cupids.

TO DANCE:

1. *Les espiègleries des Limniades*: Miss Borkhardt, Ofitserova, Kasatkina, Chumakova, Vasilieva, Fonaryova, Pavlova, Matveyeva II, and Mr Aistov.

2. *Grand pas des guirlandes*:

(a) *Adagio et groupes*: Miss Roslavleva and Miss Preobrazhenskaya; *Limoniades*: Miss Borkhardt, Ofitserova, Kasatkina, Fonaryova, Matveyeva III, Vasilieva, Pavlova, and Chumakova. *Nereids*: Miss Andreyeva, Rubtsova, Ogoleit II, Kunitskaya, Korsak, Matveyeva I, Messarosh, Isaeva I, Vsevolodskaya, Sheberg, Dorina, Tsalison, Tselikova, Ilyina III, Radina, Ryabova, Konetskaya, Vertinskaya, Golubeva II, Yakovleva II, Shtikhling, Lobanova, Sazonova, and Kuzmina.

(*b*)   *Variations*: Miss Roslavleva and Miss Preobrazhenskaya.

(*c*)   *Grand coda*: Miss Roslavleva, Miss Preobrazhenskaya, and other women dancers.

3. *Pas de deux scènique*: Miss Roslavleva and Mr Legat III.

4. *Danse et marche nuptiale*: Miss Roslavleva, Miss Preobrazhenskaya, Miss Trefilova, Mr Legat III. *Limniades and nereids*: Miss Borkhardt, Ofitserova, Pavlova, Kasatkina, Fonaryova, Matveyeva III, Vasilieva, Chumakova, Andreyeva, Rubtsova, Ogoleit II, Kunitskaya, Korsak, Matveyeva I, Messarosh, Isaeva I, Vsevolodskaya, Sheberg, Dorina, Tsalison, Tselikhova, Ilyina III, Radina, Ryabova, Konetskaya, Vertinskaya, Golubeva II, Yakovleva II, Shtikhling, Lobanova, Sazonova, and Kuzmina. *Cupids*: girl students of the Imperial Theatre School.

5. *Scène et danse des faunes*: Mr Aistov and boy students of the Imperial Theatre School.

6. *Final*: Miss Roslavleva, Miss Preobrazhenskaya, Miss Trefilova, Mr Legat III, and all other participants.

APOTHEOSIS

Conductor R. Drigo

Solos performed by: soloists of the Court of His Imperial Majesty:

On the violin—Mr Auer

On the harp—Mr Zabel

ACIS AND GALATEA

(The Metamorphoses of Ovid, XIII. 750–897)

The stage represents a picturesque ravine, surrounded by a cliff, with beautiful vegetation. It is late at night.

Scene 1

Galatea, with her girlfriend-nereids, protected by the gods, is resting sweetly on the soft grass. Aether, the cool breeze and herald of morning, glides lightly along the ravine. Thetis hastens to open the gates of Helios, the chariot which has already departed the bright mansions of the sun and begins to gild the surroundings with its approach. The giant cyclops Polyphemus enters cautiously, pursuing the beautiful Galatea in his unbounded love; seeing her asleep among the nereids, he can hardly contain his passion, admiring her, yet cannot bring himself to disturb her sweet reverie. The coarse, scorned son of the celestials has come to know love, with its anxiety and feelings of jealousy. His passion for Galatea utterly possesses him. A bright flame glows in his heart, and the wild cyclops has forgotten his flock and his cave. A desire to please has come over him, and with it a concern for the beauty of his person. His natural wildness and bloodthirstiness have vanished; he has begun to curb his raging outbursts, and foreign ships steam past him safely. Having abundantly admired the sleeping Galatea, the cyclops hastens to withdraw, to bring her fragrant honey and succulent fruits when she awakes.

Scene 2

On his way he encounters Hymen; overjoyed by this meeting, he prays to Hymen to persuade Galatea to love him and be united in the bonds of matrimony, and promises to fulfil all her wishes. Wishing not to anger the fierce cyclops, Hymen advises him to continue his tenderness and courtesy, and then his love will succeed and Galatea, perhaps, might quickly forget about Acis. In the distance the melodious fife of Galatea's beloved is heard; Polyphemus, in a fury, would rush to the place whence the sounds are coming and tear Acis to pieces. Hymen calms and restrains him, advising him to second Acis's playing on his own fife, which is made of long and coarse pipes. Polyphemus blows on it so hard that its harsh sounds reach beyond the sea and the mountains to awaken the sleeping nereids.

Scene 3

Seeing Hymen with the frightful cyclops, Galatea and the nereids want to escape; in jest they entwine him with garlands, and dancing, persuade him to retire. At the sight of Galatea, Polyphemus patiently bears their jests and promises them honey and fruit; the nereids hurry him along and leave with him despite his resistance. Galatea, who has not seen Acis for a long time, becomes sad and aggrieved. Seeing her thus, Hymen asks the reason. The reason is Acis's long absence, responds Galatea, his delay worries her a great deal. Hymen assures her that Acis must be near, since his fife was just sounding. Galatea is nevertheless dissatisfied, pouts her lips and threatens not to forgive her beloved, though he knows that she can be happy and content only with him. The nereids return and report that they have managed to send the cyclops on his way. Hymen orders the nereids to lighten Galatea's woe with dances; they summon their girlfriends and urge her to forget her unfounded sorrow in the belief that Acis will soon appear. They invite Galatea and Hymen to go to the lake and adorn themselves with flowers for the meeting with Acis. Galatea refuses, and plans to wait for him at the agreed-upon place.

Scene 4

Galatea, accustomed to meeting Acis at sunrise in their chosen place in a picturesque valley, and who the day before agreed to meet him there, again begins to worry about his long absence. The fear that misfortune has befallen him forces her into a deep reverie, and she does not hear the cyclops bringing her honey and fruit. Seeing him she trembles, but hiding her agitation, courteously receives his gifts. Tempted by this reception he declares his love, promising to give her all the blessings in the world, asks not to be rejected and despised, adding that his father, the all-powerful Poseidon, sovereign of the sea, will be her father-in-law. Galatea, knowing that Acis might arrive any minute and worried about him, makes various pretences to send Polyphemus away, but the latter, who has lost his sense from the hope of love, swears to obey her in everything, and having understood her wish—to be left alone—promises more gifts for her and to return soon. Then he leaves.

Scene 5

After Polyphemus's exit, Hymen leads in Acis and withdraws; the youth walks joyfully up to Galatea, who is overjoyed at his arrival but wants to punish him for his delay. She tries to hide her joy and assume a dissatisfied look. Acis tries to calm his capricious lover, and after long exhortations, they are gradually reconciled. Hymen returns to see if Galatea has made up, and pleased with the reconciliation expresses his sympathy for them. Just then the nereids run in, adorned with water lilies; they are agitated, and explain that fauns with Polyphemus at his cave told them that the cyclops had promised to return to Galatea soon to be united with her, and had threatened to kill Acis if he stood in the way. Hearing of Polyphemus's threats and fearing for Acis, Galatea begs Hymen to defend them; the latter calms them, and decides to call Cupid.

Scene 6

Cupid appears, and protected by the almighty Zeus, promises to defend them always. The onlookers hail his promise, express their delight to Cupid and Hymen, and at Hymen's insistence dance and form picturesque groupings in honour of Venus, the goddess of love. When the dances are over Polyphemus appears; seeing his rival with Galatea, in despair and vexation he swears a cruel revenge, and leaves in wrath. With the coming of evening, all wish to take Galatea to her cottage on the neighbouring lake, and the whole cortège sets out on its way.

Scene 7

The moon appears from behind the clouds and illuminates the canyon with its tender, silvery light. With an extinguished torch the goddess of night, Nyx, slips over the environs, which fall into slumber. The cyclops, looking around carefully, appears in the valley. From all sides he summons his friends, the fauns, and invites their assistance in the abduction of Galatea. Burning with impatience, and having not seen the beautiful Galatea with her beloved Acis for some time, he begins to worry. Wishing to hide his vexation and anger, he asks the fauns to withdraw, that he might invite the nereids—and with them Galatea and Acis—to dance and make merry, and during the merriment to accomplish his revenge. When they have gone, unable to hide his sorrow and suppress the thought that his dream might not be realized, he kneels and implores Poseidon to help him gain the love of the beautiful nereid, then sadly withdraws.

Scene 8

The fauns and the nereids, Galatea, Acis, Cupid, and Hymen run in merrily and begin to dance; when the dances are finished Acis tenderly embraces Galatea and vows eternal love. The cyclops enters. Seeing them, Polyphemus swears that they have caressed for the last time, and in a frightful rage rushes at Acis, who frightened runs to a cliff and begs Zeus to save him. The wild cyclops pursues him, tears a huge stone away from the cliff and aims it at the youth; the stone covers and crushes him. In terrible fright and woe Galatea begs her parents to save Acis, who is transformed, with fate's permission, into a river. Praying for Acis's rescue, Galatea runs to the lake and vanishes in it. The cyclops, pursuing her and seeing her disappear in the water, sits down by the lake in terrible anxiety, awaiting her return. Scarlet blood flows from beneath the cliff, but presently this colour vanishes and the river takes on the colour of water dulled by the rain. Soon this colour also disappears, and lucid water begins to flow from beneath the cracked rock face.

APOTHEOSIS

From the depths rises up a new river god. Acis, and with him, besides Galatea, Cupid and Hymen.

The Daughter of the Mikado
Ballet
Permitted by the censor. St Petersburg, 29 October 1897

The Daughter of the Mikado
Fantastic ballet in three acts
by V. I. Langammer
Music by Baron V. G. Wrangell

Act I The Abduction

Act II The Vanquished Dragon

Act III The People's Festival

Dances and Production by the Balletmaster L. I. Ivanov

The role of 'Gotaru-Hime' is performed by Miss M. Kshesinskaya II.

New decorations: for Act I by Mr Allegri; for Acts II and III by Mr Levogt.
Machines by Mr Berger.

Costumes after drawings by the artist E. P. Ponomaryov: women's by Miss Ofitserova, men's by Mr Caffi. Headwear: women's by Miss Termen, men's by Mr Bruneau. Accessories by P. P. Kamensky. Wigs and coiffures by Mr Pedder. Footwear by Miss Levstedt. Metalwork by Mr Inginen. Flowers by Miss Revenskaya.

Produced for the first time on the stage of the Imperial Maryinsky Theatre, 9 November 1897

ST PETERSBURG
Publication of the Typographer of the Imperial SPb Theatres
(Chief of Crown Domains)
1897

PERSONNAGES:

Go-Ikhi-io-Tenno, Mikado	Mr Aistov
Gotaru-Hime, *his daughter*	Miss Kshesinskaya II
Yuesugi-Sama, *daimyo*	Mr Bulgakov
Ioritomo, *his son*	Mr Gerdt
Iazum Ippeida, *retainer of the Mikado*	Mr Cecchetti
O-Gen-mi ⎫	Miss Skorsyuk
O-Ioshi ⎬ *his daughters*	Miss Preobrazhenskaya
O-Tama ⎭	Miss Kulichevskaya
Matsudiera-Satsuma-no-kami, *son of*	

the shogun	Mr Kyaksht
Sen-Nin ⎱ *girlfriends of Gotaru-Hime*	Miss Obukhova
Kai-riu ⎰	Miss Trefilova
Ka-ke-ki-go, *commander*	Mr Oblakov I
Vataneo, *secretary of Ippeida*	Mr Tatarinov
Urashima, *fisherman*	Mr Gillert

The action takes place in Japan, in the city of Miyako (Kyoto) and its environs.

IN THE FIRST ACT:

1. *Scène de désespoir*: Miss Skorsyuk and Mr Cecchetti.

2. *Danse Ta-tao (Le passage des nuages)*: Geishas: Miss Ofitserova, Borkhardt, Vaganova, Chumakova, Kshesinskaya I, Pavlova, Bakerkina, Kunitskaya, Ogoleit II, Kasatkina, Leonova II, Vasilieva; Manzais: Mr Loboiko, Nikitin, Pashchenko I, Fyodorov I, Kristerson, Baltser, Usachyov, Aslin. Girl and boy students of the Imperial Theatre School.

3. *Entrée du Mikado*: Mr Aistov, Mr Oblakov I; *Gobaniozi*: Mr Marzhetsky; Officers: Mr Balashev, Ivanov I; *Kizaki*: Miss Solyannikova. Wives of the Mikado: Miss Egorova I, Natarova, Kusterer, Niman, Pakhomova, Maslova, and others. Retinue: Mr Alexeyev, Maslov, Mikhailov, Smirnov, Martyanov, Tikhomirov and others.

4. *Cortège nuptial*: Miss Kshesinskaya II, Kulichevskaya, Preobrazhenskaya, Obukhova, Trefilova; Mr Gerdt, Kyaksht, Bulgakov. Relatives and friends of Ioritomo: Miss Svirskaya, Timireva, Semyonova II, Frank, Sitnikova and others. Mr Andreyev, Navatsky, Dmitriev, Romanov, Zelenov, Fyodorov II and others. Bonzes: Mr Solyannkov II, Kunitsky, Plessyuk, Chernikov.

5. *Sakadzouki (La cérémonie du mariage)*: Miss Trefilova, Obukhova, Ofitserova, Borkhardt, Chumakova, Vaganova, Pavlova, Kshesinskaya I, Ogoleit II, Bakerkina, Kunitskaya, Kasatkina, Vasilieva, Leonova II.

6. *Entrée des ambassadeurs*—from the island of Liu-chu: Mr Bykov; Timor: Mr Vasiliev; Mongolia: Mr Ponomaryov; China: Mr Chekrygin; Korea: Mr Sosnovsky; Tibet: Mr Terpilovsky; India: Mr Voskresensky; Borneo: Mr Voronin, and others.

7. *Variations*: Miss Kulichevskaya, Miss Preobrazhenskaya, Miss Skorsyuk.

8. *Pas d'action*: Miss M. Kshesinskaya II, Kulichevskaya, Preobrazhenskaya, Skorsyuk, Obukhova, Trefilova; Mr Gerdt, Kyaksht, Cecchetti, Oblakov I, and others.

9. *Apparition du dragon et scène finale*.

IN THE SECOND ACT:

1. *Danse des feux de St Elme*: girl students of the Imperial Theatre School.

2. *Scène de délivrance*: Miss Kshesinskaya II and Mr Gerdt.

3. *Ballabile orientale*: Himalayas: Miss Ogoleit II, Slantsova, Pavlova, Goncharova; Javanese: Miss Kasatkina, Bakerkina, Vasilieva, Kunitskaya; Tahiti: Miss Levina, Dorina, Tsalison, Nikolaidis; from the island of Lyusom [Luzon?]: Miss Chernyavskaya, Sazonova; Mr Vasiliev and Presnyakov; Cambodia: Miss Konetskaya and Mr Legat II; Siam: Miss Peters and Mr Ivanov II; Sumatra: Miss Urakova and Mr Panteleyev; Chinese: Miss Leonova II and Mr

Kristerson; Hawaii: Miss Kil and Mr Voronin; Korea: Miss Stepanova III and Mr Pashchenko II; Inhabitants of Timor (warriors): Mr Alexandrov, Titov, Gavlikovsky, Levinson, Pashchenko I, Rykhlyakov, Fedulov, Fyodorov I; Annam: Mr Loboiko and Aslin; New Zealand: Mr Voronkov III and Bykov; Japanese men and women: Miss Niman, Lobanova, Dyuzhikova and Ilyina III; Mr Medalinsky, Ponomaryov, Pechatnikov, Oblakov II and others.

4. *Bakemono azuma (Les fantômes d'Orient)*: Miss Rykhlyakova I, Geltser, Obukhova, Leonova I, Mosolova, Trefilova.

(a) *Adagio*: Miss Kshesinskaya II, Mr Gerdt, Mr Kyaksht, and all participants.

(b) *Allegro*: Miss Obukhova, Leonova I, Trefilova, Mosolova.

(c) *Danse de Java*: Miss Skorsyuk and Mr Lukyanov.

(d) *Danse Lente*: Miss Geltser, Rykhlyakova I.

(e) *Danse de Marama*: Miss Tatarinova and Mr Kshesinsky II and with them: Miss Pavlova, Bakerkina, Slantsova, Kasatkina.

(f) *Danse de Formosa*: Mr Kyaksht.

(g) *Danse de l'Hindoustan*: Miss Petipa I and Mr Bekefy.

(h) *Variation*: Miss Kshesinskaya II.

5. *Grande Valse*: all participants.

IN THE THIRD ACT:

1. *Fête nationale*: (Peuple, marchandes, gjoghi, heki, enfants, jongleurs etc). Marchandes de patisserie: Miss Ogoleit III, Miss Pakhomova and others.

2. *Danse des Iammabosses*: Mr Alexandrov, Voronkov II, Rakhmanov, Rykhlyakov, Voronkov III, Panteleyev, Titov, Vasiliev.

3. *Grande marche*. During the march, a pantomime: Chiu-Shingoura. (La fidélité des vassaux), performed by boy students of the Imperial Theatre School.

4. *Danse*: Komainu (*Le lion de Corèe*). Mr Gorsky, girl and boy students of the Imperial Theatre School.

5. *Danse*: Kiogetsubo (*L'admiration folle de la lune*): Miss Obukhova and girl students.

6. *Danse*: Ake-no-haru (*Le nouveau printemps*):

(a) *L'été*: Miss Mosolova; Les papillons: Miss Ofitserova, Fonaryova, and Chumakova.

(b) *L'automne*: Miss Geltser, Konetskaya, and Shchedrina.

(c) *L'hiver*: Miss Skorsyuk, Slantsova, and Vaganova.

(d) *Le printemps*: Miss M. Kshesinskaya II, Matveyeva III, Repina, Sevina, and Tsalison.

7. *Danse Jeu de papillon*: Miss Preobrazhenskaya and Mr Legat III.

8. *Divertissements des éventails et des parasoles*: Miss Pavlova, Kshesinskaya I, Bakerkina, Kunitskaya, Vasilieva, Kasatkina, Ogoleit II, Leonova II, Golubeva I, Matyatina, Golubeva II, Przhbeletskaya, Rosh, Stepanova III, Shtikhling, Yakovleva II; Mr Loboiko, Nikitin, Pashchenko I, Fyodorov I, Baltser, Kristerson, Usachyov, Aslin and others. Girl and boy students of the Imperial Theatre School.

(a) *Danse Ko-Suzume (Le petit moineau)*: girl student Baldina and Miss Postolenko.

(b)   *Danse Goi-kan-go (Jeu de balle)*: Mr Kusov and boy students of the Imperial Theatre School.

(c)   *Danse Sous le parasol*: Miss Rykhlyakova I and Mr Legat I.

(d)   *Danse avec serpent*: Miss Kulichevskaya.

(e)   *Andante*: Miss M. Kshesinskaya II and Mr Gerdt.

9.   *Coda finale*: all participants.

Soloists of the Court of His Imperial Majesty perform solos:
on the violin—Mr Auer, on the harp—Mr Zabel.

Also to perform solos: on the violoncello—Mr Loganovsky, on the flute—
Mr E. Keller; and the mandolins will be played by: Messrs Paris, Shroeder,
Sergeyev, and Vasiliev.

The conductor: R. Drigo

ACT I

The Abduction

The ceremonial hall in the Mikado's palace

Scene 1

Ippeida, the Mikado's retainer, enters quickly, with little steps, to inspect the preparations for the wedding feast and the reception of the newly-weds, who any minute now should arrive from the temple. His elder daughter, O-Gen-mi, follows persistently; she loves Ioritomo, the happy groom of the Mikado's daughter, and she alone, on some specious excuse, declines participation in the wedding ceremony.

In frightful sorrow, all in tears, O-Gen-mi mourns her bitter fate. Trying to console her, her father begs her not to dream of an impossible happiness; the very thought that she might become a rival of the 'divine' Mikado's daughter fills him with superstitious horror. Checking timorously to make sure nobody has overheard, he silences her and asks her never to repeat this dangerous conversation. O-Gen-mi despairs, and disregarding her father's admonition swears vengeance on the newly-weds, calling down upon them the anger of the ferocious Dragon. The frightened Ippeida tries forcibly to lead his daughter from the hall, explaining that the wrath of the Mikado could destroy her and all her family; he advises her to try, according to custom, to be merry and rejoice with the others in the happiness of the great Mikado's daughter.

O-Gen-mi exits. Ippeida follows her, and then, with strokes of a fan on his palm, summons Vataneo, whom he orders to invite the musicians and dancers. At Vataneo's exit, Ippeida falls into a deep reverie over whether his sovereign's commands have been fulfilled precisely.

Dancers enter. Ippeida, satisfied with their stateliness and beautiful attire, orders them to demonstrate their art.

Scene 2

A loud stroke on the gong announces the Mikado and the procession of the newly-weds; the dances stop; the dancers assume proper poses; Ippeida, frightened and perplexed, nervously bows low to the side whence his sovereign should appear.

The Mikado's guard of honour enters, followed by the *daimyo* Yuesugi-Sama with his retinue and finally the Mikado himself, who walks majestically to his place. At his entrance all fall down low. The Mikado gives a sign, and all decorously rise slightly; then he permits the newly-weds to enter, and the others invited to the marriage ceremony.

The wedding procession appears, and making its way around the hall stops at the places which the *gobanyoji* point out. The newly-weds, approaching the Mikado, kneel and thank him for his gracious consent to their union. The Mikado, very contented, smiles condescendingly, commands them to stand and to strengthen their union by performing their forebears' ancient custom—draining 'the newly-weds' cup'.

The girlfriends of the happy bride, Sen-Nin and Kai-riu, entertain the guests, fluttering from one group to another. As the newly-weds kneel, a middle-aged women presents to them the wedding cup, which they drink to the bottom.

The Mikado, having heard Ippeida's report of the arrival of ambassadors with gifts, commands them to be brought into the hall.

Scene 3

Graciously accepting the gifts, the Mikado orders the wedding celebration to begin, and dancers open it with the performance of 'The honouring of the Newly-weds'; servants offer *sake* to the guests.

With the Mikado's permission, Ippeida orders his daughters to perform a dance prepared for this occasion, during which their father, noticing the Mikado's satisfaction, casts ingratiating glances at his daughters. A large ensemble dance follows, in which Ioritomo, delighted by his wife, enchanted by her alone, declares his love for her. Gotaru-Hime smiles at him cordially.

Yuesugi-Sama looks at his son proudly and receives congratulations from the guests.

Ippeida's other two daughters, pleased with Ioritomo's wedding, dance merrily and with animation, while the young son of the *shogun* Matsudiera-Satsuma-no-kami pays court to them both; O-Gen-mi tries constantly to be close to her rival's husband, to serve as a living reproach for his betrayal. The guests do not notice O-Gen-mi's evil intention, and take part in the festival.

Seeing Ioritomo's passionate love for his young bride, Ippeida's elder daughter, the wicked O-Gen-mi, seethes with indignation and revenge. She invokes the Dragon to disrupt the newly-weds' happiness.

Scene 4

A frightful whirlwind arises, with powerful thunderclaps, darkness falls, and the Dragon the vengeful O-Gen-mi has summoned appears in the hall. The company are horrified, the women fall to their knees hiding their faces in their hands, the men prostrate themselves, burying their faces in the floor; the Mikado remains seated, as if petrified.

Gotaru-Hime runs from the hall seeking help, but Ioritomo, defending his young bride, seizes a lance from a soldier and tries to strike the horrible monster. Flames spewing from its mouth, the Dragon singes the daring man, who falls unconscious to the floor. The monster pursues Gotaru-Hime; appearing with her for a moment in the hall, the Dragon flies off, holding her in its claws.

Scene 5

The darkness dissipates, the whirlwind and thunder become quiet; everything takes on its former appearance, the company gradually come to their senses and try to bring Ioritomo around. Regaining consciousness, he asks permission to pursue the Dragon and free his wife from its claws. The Mikado agrees; he triumphantly gives the order to fit out a ship and make ready a voyage to free his beloved daughter.

Ippeida, in despair because the Dragon disturbed the 'divine' Mikado and disrupted the well-planned celebration, has decided to disembowel himself, but the bold chieftain Ka-ke-ki-go restrains him and swears to avenge him; he promises to kill the monster by any necessary means. The grieving Ippeida cannot be calmed; he glances timorously at his sovereign, who tries to conceal his frightful woe over the loss of his beloved daughter. Ka-ke-ki-go, consoling Ippeida and giving various orders to fulfil the Mikado's wish, invites those present to set out at once to find the lovely Gotaru-Hime; they hasten to comply.

O-Gen-mi, triumphing, laughs spitefully, content with her revenge and the destruction of her rival's happiness.

ACT II

The Vanquished Dragon

A rocky locale by a seashore. The cliffs are covered with sparse and stunted vegetation. Fumes rise up from the sea, enveloping the landscape in a bluish fog. Above the water wills-o-the-wisp flare up and die out; the tender sounds of an Aeolian harp are heard. The entire scene is gloomy and despondent.

Scene 1

Ioritomo is swimming through the sea, expending his last energies; finally, in exhaustion, he makes the shore.

In his search for his young wife he has suffered a terrible shipwreck; he managed to save himself with several sailors in a boat, but a storm smashed the boat on a cliff and carried off most of his surviving comrades; by some miracle he has reached dry land.

Having rested, Ioritomo timidly looks around; gloomy nature, the dark, low-hanging storm-clouds frighten him. He finds his way cautiously among the crags without encountering one living being, but only skeletons and weapons left near them.

Approaching a cave Ioritomo suddenly sees Gotaru-Hime; joyously he rushes to her; she makes a violent movement towards him, but the chains restraining her rattle. Seeing his wife in such a horrible situation and wishing to free her immediately,

Ioritomo takes the first sword he sees at the roadside, breaks the fetters, frees his beloved, and embraces her in delight.

After a tender reunion, the lovers take stock of their situation. Gotaru-Hime tells her husband how the Dragon carried her beyond the clouds with dizzying speed, and put down with her on this enchanted island. Here, transformed every sunset into an evil sorcerer, he tried to force her to be his wife, threatening to change her into stone if she did not agree. He pointed to the cliffs and explained that all the women who had refused his proposal he had turned into cold stone. The skeletons along the roadside were those of courageous warriors who had come to free their brides and wives. They had not killed the Dragon, and had perished ingloriously. If, however, one of them had destroyed the monster and sprinkled the nearby cliffs with its blood, it would have restored to life the women transformed into stone and the corpses, and nature would have lost its gloom. Pointing at the cave, Gotaru-Hime explains that the Dragon will soon fly into it, and woe to Ioritomo if the monster finds him there; she begs him to flee with her from the island without losing another minute.

Ioritomo despairs; he cannot conceive a solution to the hopeless situation; it is impossible to throw together a raft so quickly, to set out, danger or no, and make their way over the ocean. Dejected, he seizes his sword and resolves to fight the monster, to give all to save his lovely wife and himself. Gotaru-Hime again begs him to abandon this plan, and proposes that he deceive the sorcerer by guile, and then flee the island.

Scene 2

The sea grows wildly agitated, the heavens are filled with threatening clouds; lightning flashes, thunder sounds, the wind whistles, a storm comes up. The dragon produces a mighty whirlwind with its wings; cutting through the air like a hurricane, the monster flies into its cave.

Ioritomo would rush at it immediately with his sword and kill it. Gotaru-Hime, dreadfully frightened, restrains him and advises hiding from the monster's fierce anger, avoiding obvious mortal danger; but the young hero breaks away from her embrace and rushes headlong into the cave, whence flames issue forth. But even this cannot deter Ioritomo's resolve.

After a short struggle, during which Gotaru-Hime falls to the ground in a swoon, Ioritomo strikes down the dragon and carries its head out from the cave. Along the way, blood dripping from the monster's head begins magically to transform nature: trees, flowers, and bushes appear. Ioritomo rushes triumphantly to his beloved; Gotaru-Hime regains consciousness, and seeing her husband alive, joyfully embraces him. Giving thanks to the gods for the miraculous victory, they set out to find their way from the enchanted island. Gotaru-Hime, recalling the evil sorceress's words about the bewitched cliffs, asks her husband to sprinkle them with the Dragon's blood; Ioritomo seizes the monster's head and fulfils his wife's request.

Scene 3

Women coming to life appear on the cliffs and rocks; in the distance a fantastic castle is outlined; skeletons are transformed into warriors, stone sculptures come alive, trees and bushes flower, birds awaken and begin to chirp. The women find their husbands and suitors, embrace joyfully after a long separation and vie with one another in thanking Ioritomo and Gotaru-Hime.

Among those returned to life is the fisherman Urashima, cast onto the island by a storm and killed by the Dragon; On Ioritomo's advice, he gathers sword-hewn trunks of trees. Others help him, pulling the unfinished logs together and lashing up a raft. A sail is constructed of veils and cloaks, and the raft is put into the water. The newly-weds exult, joyfully anticipating imminent rescue. When the work is finished they embark on the raft, inviting Urashima to join them. The fisherman impales the Dragon's head on a spear, stands next to them, and the raft sails away with a following wind. The moon illumines them brightly. Those left on the island ask that help be sent back to them quickly, and joyfully see their rescuers off.

ACT III
The People's Festival

An open locale with luxurious vegetation; in the distance, on an eminence, a broad staircase leading to a temple. A bright, sunlit day.

Scene 1

Traders on the day of a national festival have opened their booths; people scurry about, trading and selling various items anticipating the grand procession, headed by the 'divine' Mikado, which should pass by the temple. Water carriers pour water onto the dry street; traders in fish and other foods walk by, offering their wares. In the city a *norimono* is carrying a rich Japanese woman, who takes a suitable place on one of the terraces, for the best view of the celebration. *Jugi* walk around among the people, begging alms, and jugglers vie with one another; sword swallowers, holding on their waists a staff on which little boys perform various unusual gymnastic exercises, draw paper ribbons from their mouths and twirl plates. Native apothecaries grind ointment in mortars and sell bear's fat, which cures all illnesses; traders offer fans, rosaries, and various knick-knacks; one of them dispenses fire for the lighting of pipes. *Yamabushi* offer their services to pattern-makers promising to acquaint people with the miracles of the temples; others, honouring the festival, perform a military dance. Acquaintances meeting one another bow with customary ceremony.

Scene 2

A gong sounds, and music signals the approach of the brilliant ceremonial procession, preceded by guards who announce the powerful *staniero*. The people kneel reverently as the procession nears. It stops in the square, as on other main squares of the city, to give a representation of heroic content. The people rise and await the beginning of the performance impatiently, following the actors with intense attention and pleasure. *Kurambo* is being prepared, in order to be placed 'during the acting' of the chief characters, and the *todori* announces the beginning of the play with strokes of wood blocks; having briefly explained the story of the 'tragedy', he invites the actors to commence.

'Legends of the fidelity of *ronin*'

The important dignitary Asano-Takumi-no-kami was being plagued by petty insults from one of his colleagues, Kara-Katsuke-no-Suke; for a long time he bore these insults submissively, but the latest offences were so great that Asano-Takumi-no-kami was forced to leave his lord's court.

Unable to endure the latest blood insult, he prepares a will, and invites over his relatives and friends according to custom, having decided to commit *hara-kiri*, that is, to take his own life triumphantly in their presence.

In despair his friends weep and vow to avenge the insult. In order to undermine their enemy's vigilance, they change clothes to begin life in the guise of various artisans, and for the time being are not to meet with one another. To achieve their vengeance more certainly, they choose the *samurai* Oishi-Kurano-Suke as their leader. Devoting himself completely to the well-conceived plan, the *samurai* decides to sacrifice his passionately beloved wife and part with her forever. But wishing not to apprise her of his plan, which should remain secret, he begins to drink and lead a debauched life, to inspire revulsion towards him in his wife. The people reject him scornfully; many inflict blows and spit on him. In tears, his wife and son implore him to regain his former life. He summons great effort to subdue his feelings, and explains to his beloved wife that he is leaving her forever, and abandoning his son.

As all her efforts to bring him to reason are coming to nought, his wife, in tears and despair, withdraws from her unworthy husband, followed by her sorrowful son.

Alone, crying bitterly and regretting the separation, the *samurai* puts the plan for vengeance into effect. He summons his faithful comrades, orders them to climb into the enemy castle and to kidnap him by force. They execute the *samurai*'s order, lead in Kara-Kadzuke-no-Suke, punish him then and there, and put his body into another's grave. They sing praises to the deceased around this grave, then take their own lives one after the other. There you have faithful *ronin*!

When the pantomime is over, the procession proceeds on its way, and the people await the continuation of the celebration.

Scene 3

Having learned along the road to the capital of a celebration at which the Mikado would be present, Ioritomo and Gotaru-Hime, simply dressed, hasten to the city. They come to the square before the temple, and the young hero thirsts to report to the Mikado his daughter's miraculous rescue and his victory over the frightful Dragon. Awaiting the Mikado's exit from the temple, the newly-weds take part in the 'Festival of Spring'.

Scene 4

Exhausted, Urashima appears bearing the Dragon's head on a spear and seeking Ioritomo, whom he lost in the crowd. Frightened, the people recoil at the sight of the monster's head, but several, somewhat braver, ask the fisherman how such an extraordinary deed was accomplished. Urashima points to Ioritomo, explains that he, the son of a *daimyo*, is the victor over the Dragon, and that Ioritomo's companion is the 'divine' Mikado's daughter, whom the Dragon, 'the Horror of Good People', abducted on her wedding day. The people greet them with enthusiasm and respect. Urashima and one of the warriors hasten into the temple to ask that important news be announced to the sovereign: that his children, whose loss was long lamented by the country, have returned. Jugglers and *keiki* continue to divert the crowd, performing the dance, 'The Butterfly and the Fan'.

Scene 5

The doors of the temple burst open and the people, seeing their ruler, fall on their knees, admiring in delight the unusual luxury of the temple's interior and the brilliant retinue and clergy present inside. Ioritomo and Gotaru-Hime proceed up the stairs of the temple and stop, kneeling. The Mikado, maintaining his dignity before the people, tries to appear composed, but a joyful and touching smile appears on his lips at the sight of his beloved daughter. The people exult at their monarch's contentment. Ioritomo asks the Mikado to allow him and Gotaru-Hime to take part in the remainder of the festival. The Mikado graciously agrees, and looks indulgently at the merrymaking crowd from within the temple.

Appendix D

EVGENIA PAVLOVNA SOKOLOVA'S NOTES ON THE PART OF LISE IN *LA FILLE MAL GARDÉE*

Translated from Yu[rii Iosifovich] Slonimskii, *Tshchetnaya predostorozhnost'* [The Vain Precaution] (Leningrad: State Music Publishers, 1961), 20–6. Slonimsky notes on p. 23: 'For some reason the scene of the forced matchmaking is omitted, in which a role of considerable importance belongs to Lise . . . Unfortunately, a description of Lise's behaviour in the second scene of the first act is also lacking.'

FIRST ACT

Lise, quietly running out (from the right side) of her door, says: 'My mama has fallen asleep there, I have come here to see a certain handsome lad whom I love!' She looks around (to the left), and seeing the henhouse, says lovingly: 'Ah, my little hens! Poor things, they need feeding.' From the top of the henhouse she takes a basket with oats, and, dancing, throws oats to the hens. Then she hearkens: 'Someone is coming—probably HE!' She quickly takes a ribbon from the pocket of her apron (or from her corsage), hangs the little ribbon on a tack on the door, and runs into the house.

Colin enters. Presently Lise appears in the doorway, signals to him with her hand, wants to come out, but just then her mother, from the balcony, throws various objects, even the bonnet from her head. Colin hides to the left behind the house. Lise picks up the bonnet, runs to her house, but meets her mother at the threshold.

She hides the bonnet behind her (both arms to the back) and with a frightened look, on pointe, moves backwards (with the music). Her mother threatens her, shaking her finger in front of Lise's nose. Lise makes a pleading face when her mother wants to beat her. Lise says: 'Mama dear, look at your head. Where's your bonnet?' The mother: 'Well, it seems I don't have a bonnet!' She looks around on the ground, as does Lise (still holding the bonnet behind her), but when she accidentally turns her back to her mother, the latter notices it, wrests the bonnet from Lise's hands, and gets angry. Lise begs forgiveness; her mother asks for a pin. Lise searches in her corsage, finds one and gives it to her mother, who fastens her bonnet, and pricking her finger, gets terribly angry at Lise for laughing at her, and threatens her, but Lise evades her reach and points out that people are coming.

Village girls enter to find work as reapers. Lise meets them, greets them, and enquires what they want. They answer that they want approximately 4 francs (4 fingers: 1, 2, 3, 4). Lise tells her mother, who does not agree; she will give only 3 francs. The village girls are about to leave when Lise stops them, and goes back to ask her mother to add [to the amount]: 'Mama! It's only one franc—agree!' Her mother agrees and gives her a little purse, with which Lise dances, giving money to each girl (they stand on an oblique line to the tsar's box). Then she returns the purse to her mother. The village girls also stand on an oblique line by twos; Lise dances between them, and, passing next to all of them, begins to spin, bumping against her mother. The mother angers and says: 'You've gone mad, don't you see where you are flying?' 'Ah forgive me, mama, don't be angry!' The mother passes out sickles, then brings baskets; Lise takes them one by one from her mother and hands them to the village girls.

As she passes out the last one and the village girls are heading towards the gate, Lise wants to slip away behind them, but her mother catches her and turns her around. She tries to steal away again the same way, her mother catches her again, pushes her on the left shoulder, then on the right, pinches her right and left arms, gives her a slap on the back of the head (head down) and on the chin (head up).

Just then Colin peeps out from his hiding-place (behind the house), and sends a loud kiss; Lise, hearing it, says 'Mama, look up, some bird is flying up there very high!' While her mother stands gaping at the sky, Lise very quietly runs to Colin, leads him to the right (where the henhouse is), then takes a bucket with milk there and reluctantly carries it to the middle of the stage, puts [it down] and makes lazy poses. Her mother approaches and orders her to go churn butter; she does not want to. The mother insists, Lise behaves capriciously, the mother drags her by the hands, and to the music pushes her into a chair. While the mother collects the bucket standing in the middle of the stage, Lise sits, finger to her cheek, looking at one point, deep in thought, rocking gently back and forth. Her mother brings the bucket, sees Lise, mimics her (to herself), and slaps her on the shoulder; Lise makes it appear she is terribly frightened. Her mother tells her to hold the lid of the butter churn and begins to pour in the milk, while Lise, seeing Colin by the henhouse, waves to him, and thus lets fall the lid. Her mother gets angry. Lise asks forgiveness and holds the lid again while trying to see Colin, and winks at him. The mother, suspecting something, looks her in the eye; Lise makes an innocent face. The mother exits, ordering her to churn the butter.

Colin enters. 'May I approach?' Lise: 'As you wish.' He walks up to her. 'Hello! You are angry with me, why?' 'Yes, I was here alone, and you weren't here!' [she says] continuing to churn the butter. He interrupts her, putting his hand (twice) on her hands. She does not want to stop, whereupon he wants to leave; she tears the little ribbon from his staff. Colin: 'You took my ribbon, why?' Lise: 'This little ribbon ought not to be on your staff, it ought to be there, next to your heart.' (Absolutely to the music): Colin: 'Tie it on.' Lise begins to tie [the ribbon]; he takes her by the hands, prevents her from doing this (twice); she, getting angry (but not very much, *there must be no spite*), throws the ribbon on the floor. At that point he says: 'Well then, I will stand at attention, tie it on.' Lise: 'Swear to it!' Colin vows, puts his hands behind his back; she finishes, he peers around—is there no one here?—and kisses her on the neck. Lise, playfully, cunningly: 'I see then, one kiss is nothing!' She runs to work again, he says: 'You are getting tired, let me churn the butter!' Tenderly bumping her from her chair with his shoulder, he begins to work. She, going around him from the right side, interrupts him just the same as he had interrupted her, putting her hand on his hands (twice); the second time he takes her by the hand, draws [her] to him a little onto his lap and kisses her shoulder. Lise: 'Two! . . . So, nothing! Go, look, is there anyone there? We shall dance together.' *Pas de ruban*. After the *Pas de ruban* they hear someone coming. Lise rushes to the chair to churn the butter; seeing Colin's hat, she calls him back, hastily giving it to him, continues working, sees his walking-stick, calls him back and gives him his walking-stick; she [then] churns the butter energetically, looking at one spot with a frightened mien.

Villagers arrive. Seeing her they go up to her; she takes no notice, but continues to churn the butter as one possessed; the village girls shake her. Lise, coming to herself, says: 'Ah, it is you—praise the Lord—I thought it was Mama, she'd be angry!' She is about to dance with her girlfriends. Her mother enters and tries to catch her, but her girlfriends defend her. Finally she slips away from her mother and runs into the house, slamming the door almost in her mother's face.

[ACT TWO]
A Little Room after a Rain

It is essential to be in the same costume in which they came in from the field.

Lise enters with her mother, Lise with a sheaf of straw on her head. Wearily, she puts the straw on the floor to the left, shakes off her apron, brushes off the straw, dries the rain off her neck and arms, goes to her mother and tries to put her in order as well. Noticing that her mother's kerchief is wet, she takes it off, shakes it, goes to the chest of drawers (at the right) and opens a drawer. While she is getting a kerchief for her mother, she notices a pretty neck scarf. The thought strikes her to beg it from her mother . . . She brings a kerchief to her mother, puts it on her carefully, and says, tenderly: 'Wait a moment, Mama, I'll bring you a mirror.' She brings a mirror from the chest of drawers. The mother looks; Lise takes the mirror back. Returning to her mother she says, embracing her tenderly beforehand: 'Mama, I beg you, I would like a neck scarf just like yours.' The mother says: 'What? Look at you, aren't you a clever girl! But then, fine, so be it.' She goes to the chest of drawers and gets the scarf. Lise is overjoyed, and puts it on. She takes care that her mother forgets to lock the door of the room. With a naïve look she tries to hide the door with her body, but her mother leads her away by the hand, locks the door, and puts the key in her left pocket. Lise is vexed, then turns to her mother: 'Mama, tell me, you and I, what will we do here?' The mother: 'You will weave flax, and I will spin.' Lise: 'How boring, I don't want to do it, and I won't!' The mother goes for the spindle, puts it into her hands, and orders her to work. Lise takes the spindle unwillingly, and when her mother turns away, drags it along the floor behind her, as if carting some kind of toy; the mother stamps her foot, orders her to sit on the straw and work. Lise sits down unwillingly, her mother does not look to her side. Lise leads the spindle around herself; her mother turns; Lise takes fright, as if setting to work, and then begins to play with the spindle again: she draws wisps of flax from the tow, lets them fly into the air, blowing them in various directions. (This is done three times.) During this time she does not sit erect, but her body follows the direction that the flax is flying—that is, the flax flies to the right, and her torso almost lies down to the right as well; and in turn, when to the left, also to the left; sometimes one can lean with the arms. Her mother threatens again, then calms a little again; Lise next wraps and rocks the spindle, as if it were a child. During the following music, noticing that her mother has fallen asleep, ever so quietly and carefully stands on tiptoe, goes up to the mother, and walks around her chair, wheeling to the left; she sees Colin in the door above, and ever so quietly goes to the door. Colin: 'Let me in, let me into the room!' Lise: 'I can't, it's locked, and the key is in her pocket.' Colin: 'Get the key!' Lise: 'Wait a moment, I'll try!' Quietly, on tiptoe, she goes back to her mother, and with great fright and care is about to draw the key from her pocket, when her mother awakens and asks: 'What are you doing?' Lise: 'You were sleeping, and a fly was hovering about, and I caught it. (She says all this in great confusion.) Mama! I beg you, let me dance!' The mother agrees, Lise gives her a tambourine and asks her to play. She dances, the first eight bars from centre above [down] a little on an oblique line, heading towards her mother's chair, the second eight bars on an oblique line above, turning now towards her mother cunningly-tenderly, and now towards Colin with the gesture, 'careful', that her mother not notice him; then eight bars to the left, then in a circle: during a transition of the music she notices that her mother is falling asleep; on tiptoe, she carefully tries to reach into her pocket. But every time the old woman makes some movement [Lise] starts, and makes an innocent face; during the quickening music she makes, *comically*, with a perplexed look, a *pas de bourrée* around her mother; then, seeing that she has dozed off again, makes two or three gestures in front of her face, and convinced that she is not waking up, tries to take the key from her pocket. But alas, her mother has just put her hand in her pocket. All is lost; she says with vexation: 'I can't do it!' Turning to Colin, pointing out the situation with the sleeping woman, then carefully on tiptoe stealing her way to the door again, quietly takes a chair and stands on it. Colin takes one hand, kisses the other, then kisses both. With the music the old woman awakens. Like someone besotted, Lise jumps down from the chair and rushes to dance, not knowing exactly what to do, *as comically as possible*—her arms in the air, two jumps to the right, two jumps to the left (this done twice), then in a circle and ends by her mother with a terribly frightened look, weakly, out of breath from her improvised dances, saying in her mind: 'Really, Mama, I was dancing, dancing the whole time . . .' (and can even show this hastily).

Villagers bringing straw knock; Lise asks for the key to open [the door]; her mother does not give it to her but goes herself, and is surprised that a chair is standing by the door, moving it aside. Lise is a little anxious at her mother's surprise at the chair next to the door, and when everything turns out well, calms down and rejoices. Lise thinks that Colin will come in with the villagers, but she does not see him and is vexed. Her mother exits with the villagers, and despite Lise's most tender entreaties, leaves her alone in the room and locks the door in front of her nose.

In despair Lise pounds the door, and pounds it again, cries, stamps her feet, misbehaves, gets angry. 'I am alone here, and what am I to do?' She rushes to a chair (to the right of the door), cries, acts capriciously, turns on the chair to the right, to the left, again to the right, saying: 'Ah! Poor me!' She stamps her foot; then it occurs to her to imagine her future life. She says: 'Ah, when I am married, I will have children.' On the left side show one child of about 3, another of about 5, and a third of about 7; on the right side the smallest—about a year and a half. To the left, turning towards the 7-year-old: 'I ask you, have you studied the lesson in your book?' 'No.' 'Then you wait a moment, I'll give it to you (shakes her finger), I'll turn up your shirt and spank you!' To the right—she hears the small child crying; she carefully and tenderly picks it up, kisses, cradles, and caresses it, saying 'Ah, you, my poor little one' (not concealing her face from the public). She walks towards the straw, somewhat above, trying not to stand, when Colin enters, forward of the straw and not on one line with it but rather behind, so that only her face is visible to the public. When the straw breaks up she has a terrible fright, arms immobile, in one pose, all trembly, chest heaving the whole time, as if sobbing. Lise: 'You don't love me!' Colin: 'How I adore you, I love you to distraction!' He wants to embrace her, she stops bashfully. Quietly, shyly, both place their hands on the spindle, calmly lift it up, three steps forward to the right, three to the back, one step forward, one back. Colin quietly attempts to touch her hands, she lets fall the spindle, runs across from it to the left side, makes a bashful gesture (arms in front). Colin: 'You don't love me! In that case farewell, I am leaving!' He heads for the door. Lise: 'You can't leave here.' Colin: 'Why not?' Lise: 'My mother locked the door.' Colin: 'What joyful news! It means we are here together, I can embrace you and kiss you!' He rushes to her, she stops him, he obeys, saying: 'Does it mean that you want me to leave, you don't want to love me?' He sobs and goes to the right, [and] sits down in a chair. Lise: 'Poor thing, he is crying, but you see I love him, I feel sorry for him! I love you!' Colin is delighted, hearing that Lise loves him, and runs up to her; he would embrace her (in the middle of the stage); she slips away from him again and runs to the right (to the tsar's box); he takes her by the hand and tenderly, slowly draws her to the straw. Both sit on it calmly, both are bashful; Lise takes the scarf from her neck, Colin takes another from his pocket; they exchange scarves, Lise quietly waves her scarf one time, Colin does the same immediately after her, and then both together put the scarves around their necks; all this is tender, calm, bashful (according to the music). Then Colin draws Lise to his shoulder, and she nestles up to him. Suddenly steps; both are terribly frightened. Lise says, 'Ah, this is surely Mama! Where will you hide?' Both run, hunting for somewhere he could hide, rush to the straw; he tries to hide, she helps him, but nothing succeeds. Then she remembers the little storeroom above, shoves him into it, and rushes to the chair at the right. Fearfully, without picking up the spindle, she spins flax, nervously, hastily, frightened, her eyes focused on one point. (It is necessary to make this very comical.)

As her mother taps her on the shoulder she asks, 'What is it with you? Have you lost your wits? Where is the spindle?' At this point Lise realizes that she is caught, and holds her head in her hands [as if in despair]: what will happen now? She runs across to the straw; the mother sees the disorder there, the straw being strewn all about: 'What does this mean?', the mother asks, and then notices a different scarf on [Lise's] neck. 'Ah, something is not right here. You wait here!' The mother takes the spindle, seizes Lise by the arm and beats her. Lise begs for mercy; she is very sore, and then the mother drags her to the storehouse to lock her in there. In horror and fright Lise says: 'I beg you, Mama, just not there, not there!' The mother locks her in [the storeroom] nevertheless.

When the door of the storeroom is opened, both—Lise and Colin—stand guilty, *dos à dos*; Lise is very embarrassed, comes down the stairs very quietly, very quietly, flustered, asks her mother to forgive her, begs on her knees, sobs, tries to avoid looking at the others. Finally, when her mother agrees to her marriage, endless rejoicing. She kisses her mother and asks when her wedding will be. The whole time is occupied with Colin and the mother.

The ending must be done with all the others.

Select Bibliography

I Published Works

Artist. Zhurnal izyashchnykh iskusstv i literatury [The Artist: Journal of the Elegant Arts and Literature] (Moscow, 1889–95).

Benois, Alexandre, *Reminiscences of the Russian Ballet*, trans. Mary Britnieva (London: Putnam, 1941).

Borisoglebskii, M., *Proshloe baletnogo otdeleniya Peterburgskogo teatral'nogo uchilishcha, nyne Leningradskogo Gosudarstvennogo Khoregrafisheskogo uchilishcha. Materialy po istorii russkogo baleta* [The Past of the Ballet Division of the Petersburg Theatre School, now the Leningrad State Choreographic School. Materials Relating to the History of Russian Ballet], 2 vols. (Leningrad: Leningrad State Choreographic School, 1938–9). [*Borisoglebsky*]

Bryanskii, V. A., 'V. A. Lyadova (1870—March—1920)', *Zhizn' iskusstva* [Life of Art], nos. 419–21 (1920).

[Chaikovskii, Petr Il'ich, and Yurgenson, Petr Ivanovich], *P. I. Chaikovskii, Perepiska s P. I. Yurgensonom* [P. I. Tchaikovsky: Correspondence with P. I. Jurgenson], 2 vols. (Moscow and Leningrad: State Music Publishers, 1938, 1952).

Demidov, A[leksandr Pavlovich], *Lebedinoe ozero* [Swan Lake], Masterpieces of the Ballet (Moscow: 'Iskusstvo', 1985). [*Demidov*]

[Drigo, Riccardo], 'Memoirs of R. E. Drigo', trans. Roland John Wiley, *Dancing Times*, 72 (1981–2): 577–8, 661–2 (issues for May and June 1982).

Ezhegodnik Imperatorskikh Teatrov [Yearbook of the Imperial Theatres], St Petersburg/Petrograd, 1890–1915.

La Fille mal Gardée, Famous Ballets, No. 1, ed. Ivor Guest (London: The Dancing Times, 1960). [*Fille*]

Fokin [Fokine], M[ikhail Mikhailovich], *Protiv techeniya. Vospominaniya baletmeistera. Stsenarii i zamysly baletov. Stat'i, interv'yu i pis'ma* [Against the Current. Recollections of a Balletmaster. Scenarios and Projects of Ballets. Articles, Interviews, Letters] (Leningrad: 'Iskusstvo', 1981).

——*Fokine: Memoirs of a Ballet Master*, trans. Vitale Fokine, ed. Anatole Chujoy (London: Constable, 1961).

Gaevskii, Vadim Moiseevich, *Divertisment* [Divertissement] (Moscow: 'Iskusstvo', 1981). [*Gaevsky*]

Garafola, Lynn, ed. and trans., *The Diaries of Marius Petipa*, Studies in Dance History, 3/1 (Spring 1992).

Guest, Ann Hutchinson, *Dance Notation: The Process of Recording Movement on Paper* (London: Dance Books, 1984).

Guest, Ivor, *The Divine Virginia: A Biography of Virginia Zucchi* (New York: Marcel Dekker, 1977).

Ivanov, Lev [Ivanovich], 'My Reminiscences . . .', *Sovetskii balet* [Soviet Ballet], 32 (Jan.–Feb. 1987), 37–43.

—— 'The Autobiography of L. I. Ivanov (My Little Reminiscences)', *Peterburgskaya gazeta* [Petersburg Gazette], 13 Dec. 1901, no. 342, p. 5.

[Kartsev, E. E.], *Nashi artistki. Vypusk III. M. F. Kshesinskaya. Kritiko-biograficheskii etyud E. E. Kartseva* [Our Artistes. 3rd issue. M. F. Kshesinskaya. Critico-biographical Study by E. E. Kartsev]. Publication of the St Petersburg Association of Printing and Publishing Affairs, 'Labour' (St Petersburg, 1900).

Khudekov, S[ergei] N[ikolaevich], *Istoriya tantsev* [The History of Dances], vol. iv (Petrograd, 1918). [*Khudekov*]

—— 'The Petersburg Ballet during the Production of *The Little Humpbacked Horse* (Recollections)', *Peterburgskaya gazeta* [Petersburg Gazette], 14 Jan. 1896, no. 13, p. 5; 21 Jan. 1896, no. 20, p. 5.

[Kondrat'ev, Gennady Petrovich], 'The Diaries of G. P. Kondratiev', in *Muzykal'noe nasledstvo* [Musical Legacy], vol. iii, ed. M. P. Alekseev *et al.* (Moscow: 'Muzyka', 1970), 347–[352].

Krasovskaya, Vera [Mikhailovna], 'Marius Petipa and "The Sleeping Beauty"', trans. Cynthia Read, *Dance Perspectives*, 49 (Spring 1972).

—— *Russkii baletnyi teatr vtoroi poloviny XIX veka* [Russian Ballet Theatre of the Second Half of the XIX Century] (Moscow and Leningrad: 'Iskusstvo', 1963). [*Krasovskaya*]

Kshesinskaya, Matil'da [Feliksovna], *Vospominaniya* [Recollections] (Moscow: 'Artist, Régisseur, Theatre', 1992). [*Kshesinskaya*]

—— See also under Romanovsky-Krassinsky.

Larosh [Laroche], [German Avgustovich], 'P. I. Tchaikovsky as a Dramatic Composer', *Ezhegodnik Imperatorskikh Teatrov* [Yearbook of the Imperial Theatres], 1893/4, Supplement 1, 81–182.

Medv., P., 'Vera Alexandrovna Lyadova: Biographical Essay', *Vsemirnaya illyustratsiya* [World Illustration], 1870, 3/66 (issue for 4 Apr.), 247–8, 250.

Muzykal'noe nasledie Chaikovskogo. Iz istorii ego proizvedenii [Tchaikovsky's Musical Heritage: From the History of his Works], ed. Karl Yul'evich Davydov, Vladimir Vasil'evich Protopopov, and Nadezhda Vasil'evna Tumanina (Moscow: Academy of Sciences of the USSR, 1958).

Natarova, A[nna] P[etrovna], 'From the Recollections of the Artiste A. P. Natarova', *Istoricheskii vestnik* [The Historical Messenger], 94 (1903), 25–44, 420–42, 778–803.

[Petipa, Marius Ivanovich], *Russian Ballet Master: The Memoirs of Marius Petipa*, ed. Lillian Moore, trans. Helen Whittaker (London: A. & C. Black, 1958).

——*Marius Petipa. Materialy, vospominaniya, stat'i* [Marius Petipa. Materials, Recollections, Articles], ed. Yu[rii Iosifovich] Slonimskii *et al.* (Leningrad: 'Iskusstvo', 1971). [*MarPet*]

——*Marius Petipa. Meister des klassischen Balletts. Selbstzeugnisse, Dokumente, Erinnerungen* (A German translation of *MarPet*), ed. Eberhard Rebling (Berlin: Henschelverlag, 1975).

Pleshcheev, Aleksandr [Alekseevich], *Nash balet* [Our Ballet], 2nd, supplemented edn. with a foreword by K. A. Skal'kovskii (St Petersburg: Th. A. Pereyaslavtsev and A. A. Pleshcheyev, 1899). [*Pleshcheyev*]

Rimskii-Korsakov, N[ikolai Andreyevich]. *Letopis' moei muzykal'noi zhizni* [Chronicle of my Musical Life], 8th edn. (Moscow: 'Muzyka', 1980).

Romanovsky-Krassinsky, HSH the Princess [Mathilde Felixovna Kshesinskaya], *Dancing in Petersburg: The Memoirs of Kschessinska*, trans. Arnold Haskell (London: Victor Gollancz, 1960).

Rozanova, Yu[lia Andreevna], *Simfonicheskie printsipy baletov Chaikovskogo* [Symphonic Principles of Tchaikovsky's Ballets] (Moscow: 'Muzyka', 1976).

Shpilevskii, P., 'The Theatre at Krasnoe Selo', *Teatral'nyi i muzykal'nyi vestnik* [Theatrical and Musical Messenger], 1858, no. 24 (issue for 22 June), 286–7.

Skal'kovskii, K[onstantin] A[pollonovich], *V teatral'nom mire; nablyudeniya, vospominaniya i rassuzhdeniya* [In the Theatre World: Observations, Recollections, Discourses] (St Petersburg: A. S. Suvorin, 1899). [*Skalkovsky*]

Slonimskii, Yu[rii Iosifovich], *'Lebedinoe ozero' P. Chaikovskogo* ['Swan Lake' by P. Tchaikovsky] (Leningrad: State Music Publishers, 1962).

——*Mastera baleta* [Masters of the Ballet] (Leningrad: 'Iskusstvo', 1937). [*SlonMasters*]

——*P. I. Chaikovskii i baletnyi teatr ego vremeni* [P. I. Tchaikovsky and the Ballet Theatre of his Time] (Moscow: State Music Publishers, 1956). [*SlonChai*]

——*Tshchetnaya predostorozhnost'* [The Vain Precaution] (Leningrad: State Music Publishers, 1961).

——'Writings on Lev Ivanov . . . with a biography of Ivanov in excerpts from M. Borisoglebsky', trans. and ed. Anatole Chujoy, *Dance Perspectives*, 2 (Spring 1959).

[Stepanov, Vladimir Ivanovich, and Aleksandr Alekseevich Gorsky], *Two Essays on Stepanov Dance Notation by Alexander Gorsky*, trans. Roland John Wiley (New York: Congress on Research in Dance, 1978).

Stukolkin, T[imofei] A[lekseevich]. 'Recollections of T. A. Stukolkin, Artist of the Imperial Theatres, copied from his account by A. Valberg', *Artist* [The Artist], no. 45 (Jan. 1895), 126–33; no. 46 (Feb. 1895), 117–25.

Tchaikovsky. See Chaikovskii.

[Vaganova, Agrippina Yakovlevna], *Agrippina Yakovlevna Vaganova. Stat'i, vospominaniya, materialy* [Agrippina Yakovlevna Vaganova. Articles, Recollections, Materials] (Leningrad and Moscow: 'Iskusstvo', 1958). [*Vaganova*]

Vazem, Ekaterina Ottovna, *Zapiski baleriny Sankt-Peterburgskogo Bol'shogo teatra*,

1867–1884 (Memoirs of a Ballerina of the St Petersburg Bolshoy Theatre, 1867–1884] (Moscow and Leningrad: 'Iskusstvo', 1937). [*Vazem*]

Volynskii, A[kim L'vovich], 'A Wretched Housepainter', *Zhizn' iskusstva* [The Life of Art], 1923, no. 7 (20 Feb.), 4–5.

Wiley, Roland John, 'Dances from Russia: An Introduction to the Sergejev Collection', *Harvard Library Bulletin*, 24 (1976), 94–112.

——'On Meaning in *Nutcracker*', *Dance Research*, 3/1 (Autumn 1984), 3–28.

——*Tchaikovsky's Ballets* (Oxford: Clarendon Press, 1985). [*Tchaikovsky's Ballets*]

——trans., *A Century of Russian Ballet: Documents and Eyewitness Accounts 1810–1910* (Oxford: Clarendon Press, 1990). [*Wiley*]

——'The Imperial Theatre at Krasnoe Selo', *Dancing Times*, 988 (Jan. 1993), 352–4.

II Unpublished Sources

Cambridge, Massachusetts, Harvard Theatre Collection, bMS Thr 245 (16) and (27) (choreographic notation for the dances in Alexandre Borodin's opera *Prince Igor*).

——bMS Thr 245 (58) (choreographic notation of *The Magic Flute*).

——bMS Thr 245 (197) (choreographic notation of *The Nutcracker*).

——fMS Thr 186 (11–13) (choreographic notation of *Swan Lake*).

Ivanov, Lev [Ivanovich], 'My Recollections. Manuscript', St Petersburg, St Petersburg Museum of Theatrical and Musical Art, KP 7154/76.

Kshesinskii, Ios[if] Fel[iksovich], 'Several extracts from my memoirs touching on reminiscences of Marius Iv[anovich] Petipa', 2 vols., Moscow, Theatre Museum named after A. A. Bakhrushin, *fond* 134, no. 2. [*Kshesinsky*]

Moscow, Theatre Museum named after A. A. Bakhrushin, *fond* 205, archive of documents pertaining to the work of Marius Petipa. [*TMB 205*]

St Petersburg, Central Music Library, I4 D74/*Re Vol* (*répétiteur* of Drigo's *The Magic Flute*).

St Petersburg, Historical Archive, Record 497.5.2106, 'On the Service of the Chief Régisseur of the Ballet Troupe Lev *Ivanov*, 10/II/50 to 11/XII/01'. [Ivanov Service Record]

——497.6.4102, 'About the commanding of the artist of the ballet troupe Vladimir Stepanov abroad for the perfection of the system, invented by him, of graphic representation of balletic bodily movements and dances . . .'.

——497.8/2.443, 'Ballet 1894'.

——497.8/2.467, 'Ballet 1897'.

——497.10.388, 'Ballet 1893'.

——497.18.611, 'The Production of the Ballets: Caterina, Camargo, The Fairy of the Dolls, Feramors, Esmeralda, A Night in Egypt, Mlada'.

——498.1.1143, 'On the Placement of the State Student *Lev Ivanov* in the School'.

Shiryaev, A[leksandr] V[iktorovich], *Peterburgskii Balet. Iz vospominanii artista Mariinskogo teatra* [The Petersburg Ballet. From the Recollections of an Artist of the Maryinsky Theatre], ed. Yu. O. Slonimskii (Leningrad: All-Russian Theatre Society, 1941). NB. This volume was typeset, but the only surviving copy in this

form seems to be a photocopy preserved in the St Petersburg Public Library, Is70
G-3/21. [*Shiryaev*]

Solyannikov, N[ikolai] A[leksandrovich], 'Recollections', ed. N. A. Shuvalov; literary working-out by Nonna Solyannikova [typescript]. St Petersburg, Library of the St Petersburg Branch of the All-Russian Theatrical Society, Inv. no. 35-R2. [*Solyannikov*]

III Newspapers

Birzhevye vedomosti [Commercial News], St Petersburg, 1861–79, 1880–1917.

Golos [The Voice], St Petersburg, 1863–84.

Journal de Saint-Pétersbourg, St Petersburg, 1812–1914.

Moskovskie vedomosti [Moscow News], Moscow, 1756–1916.

Moskovskii listok [Moscow Leaflet], Moscow, 1881–1918.

Muzykal'nyi i teatral'nyi vestnik [Musical and Theatrical Messenger]; sometimes published under the title *Teatral'nyi i muzykal'nyi vestnik* [Theatrical and Musical Messenger], St Petersburg, 1856–60.

Novoe vremya [The New Time], St Petersburg/Petrograd, 1868–1917.

Novosti i birzhevaya gazeta [News and Commercial Gazette], St Petersburg, 1883–1906.

Peterburgskaya gazeta [The Petersburg Gazette], St Petersburg/Petrograd, 1867–1914.

Peterburgskii listok [The Petersburg Leaflet], St Petersburg, 1864–1914.

Rech' [Discourse], St Petersburg/ Petrograd, 1906–16.

Russkie vedomosti [The Russian News], Moscow, 1863–1916.

Sanktpeterburgskie vedomosti [The Saint Petersburg News], St Petersburg, 1728–1914.

Severnaya pchela [The Northern Bee], St Petersburg, 1825–64.

Suflyor [Souffleur], St Petersburg, 1878–86.

Syn otechestva [Son of the Fatherland], St Petersburg, 1862–1900, 1904–5.

Teatr i zhizn' [Theatre and Life], Moscow, 1884–93.

Vsemirnaya illyustratsiya [World Illustration], St Petersburg, 1869–98.

Index